OCR Ancient History

AS AND A LEVEL

COMPONENT 1

ALSO AVAILABLE FROM BLOOMSBURY

OCR Classical Civilisation GCSE Route 1: Myth and Religion,
Ben Greenley, Dan Menashe and James Renshaw

OCR Classical Civilisation GCSE Route 2: Women in the Ancient World,
Robert Hancock-Jones, Dan Menashe and James Renshaw

OCR Classical Civilisation AS and A Level Component 11: The World of the Hero,
Sally Knights

OCR Classical Civilisation AS and A Level Components 21 and 22: Greek Theatre and Imperial Image,
Robert Hancock-Jones, James Renshaw and Laura Swift

OCR Classical Civilisation A Level Components 23 and 24: Invention of the Barbarian and Greek Art,
Athina Mitropoulos, Laura Snook and Alastair Thorley

OCR Classical Civilisation A Level Components 31 and 34: Greek Religion and Democracy and the Athenians,
Athina Mitropoulos, Tim Morrison, James Renshaw and Julietta Steinhauer

OCR Classical Civilisation A Level Components 32 and 33:
Love and Relationships and Politics of the Late Republic,
Matthew Barr, Lucy Cresswell and Alastair Thorley

OCR Ancient History GCSE Component 1: Greece and Persia,
Sam Baddeley, Paul Fowler, Lucy Nicholas and James Renshaw

OCR Ancient History GCSE Component 2: Rome,
Paul Fowler, Christopher Grocock and James Melville

OCR Ancient History AS and A Level Component 2: Rome,
Robert Cromarty, James Harrison and Steve Matthews

Books published for the OCR specifications in GCSE and AS / A Level Latin and Classical Greek are
also available, including editions of every set text for A Level. Please see our website
www.bloomsbury.com/uk/education/secondary/classics

OCR Ancient History

AS AND A LEVEL

COMPONENT 1:
Greece

CHARLIE COTTAM
DAVID L. S. HODGKINSON
STEVE MATTHEWS
LUCY NICHOLAS
JAMES RENSHAW

GENERAL EDITOR:
JAMES RENSHAW

Bloomsbury Academic
An imprint of Bloomsbury Publishing Plc

BLOOMSBURY
LONDON · OXFORD · NEW YORK · NEW DELHI · SYDNEY

Bloomsbury Academic

An imprint of Bloomsbury Publishing Plc

50 Bedford Square	1385 Broadway
London	New York
WC1B 3DP	NY 10018
UK	USA

www.bloomsbury.com

BLOOMSBURY and the Diana logo are trademarks of Bloomsbury Publishing Plc

First published 2017

© Charlie Cottam, David L. S. Hodgkinson, Steve Matthews, Lucy Nicholas, James Renshaw, 2017

British Library Cataloguing-in-Publication Data
A catalogue record for this book is available from the British Library.

ISBN:	PB:	978-1-3500-1523-4
	ePDF:	978-1-3500-1525-8
	ePub:	978-1-3500-1524-1

Library of Congress Cataloging-in-Publication Data
A catalog record for this book is available from the Library of Congress.

Cover design by Terry Woodley and Olivia D'Cruz
Cover image © Getty/Scott E Barbour

Typeset by RefineCatch Limited, Bungay, Suffolk
Printed and bound in Great Britain

To find out more about our authors and books visit www.bloomsbury.com. Here you will find extracts, author interviews, details of forthcoming events and the option to sign up for our newsletters.

ACKNOWLEDGEMENTS

The authors divided the text between them as follows:

- Chapter 1: Relations between Greek States and between Greek and Non-Greek States by Steve Matthews and James Renshaw
- Chapter 2: The Politics and Society of Sparta by Charlie Cottam
- Chapter 3: The Politics and Culture of Athens by David L. S. Hodgkinson and James Renshaw
- Chapter 4: The Rise of Macedon by Lucy Nicholas

The authors would like to thank the many anonymous reviewers at universities, schools and OCR who read and commented on drafts of this text. All errors remain their own.

CONTENTS

Introduction | vii

How to Use this Book | viii

PART 1   **PERIOD STUDY: RELATIONS BETWEEN GREEK STATES AND BETWEEN GREEK AND NON-GREEK STATES, 492–404 BC | 1**

Introduction to Relations between Greek States and between Greek and Non-Greek States, 492–404 BC | 2

  1.1   The Challenge of the Persian Empire, 492–479 BC | 4

  1.2   Greece in Conflict, 479–446 BC | 21

  1.3   Peace and Conflict, 446–431 BC | 34

  1.4   The Archidamian War, 431–420 BC | 46

  1.5   The End of the Peloponnesian War and its Aftermath, 419–404 BC | 59

PART 2   **DEPTH STUDIES | 71**

Introduction to the Depth Study Options | 72

DEPTH STUDY 1: THE POLITICS AND SOCIETY OF SPARTA, 478–404 BC | 73

Introduction to the Politics and Society of Sparta, 478–404 BC | 74

  2.1   Education and Values in Sparta | 75

  2.2   The Social Structure of Sparta | 90

  2.3   The Political Structure of Sparta | 106

  2.4   The Spartan Military Culture and its Importance in the Society and Politics of Sparta | 121

  2.5   Other States' Views of Sparta and the Effect of the Spartan System on its Policy | 131

DEPTH STUDY 2: THE POLITICS AND CULTURE OF ATHENS, c. 460–399 BC | 143

Introduction to the Politics and Culture of Athens, c. 460–399 BC | 144

  3.1   Athenian Political and Social Culture | 145

  3.2   The Influence of New Thinking and Ideas on Athenian Society | 167

  3.3   Art and Architecture and their Significance in the Culture of Athens | 178

3.4   Drama and Dramatic Festivals and their Significance in the Culture of Athens | 189

3.5   Religion and its Significance in the Culture of Athens | 199

DEPTH STUDY 3: THE RISE OF MACEDON, 359–323 BC | 209

Introduction to the Rise of Macedon, 359–323 BC | 210

4.1   The Growth in Macedonian Power and the Role of Philip in that Process | 211

4.2   The Major Events of Alexander's Career and their Significance | 229

4.3   Change and Continuity in the Aims of Philip and Alexander | 248

4.4   The Character and Beliefs of Philip and Alexander | 257

4.5   The Relationships between the Monarchs and Others, including the Army and
Greek and Conquered States | 265

What to Expect in the AS Level Exam for the Greek Period Study | 276

What to Expect in the A Level Exam | 281

Glossary | 293

Sources of Illustrations | 296

Sources of Quotations | 297

Index | 302

INTRODUCTION

Welcome to your textbook for OCR AS and A Level Ancient History.

This book has been created to support the Greek half of the OCR AS and A Level specifications for first teaching from September 2017. It contains the compulsory Period Study 'Relations between Greek States and between Greek and non-Greek States, 492–404 BC' as well as the three Depth Study options, one of which you will study: 'The Politics and Society of Sparta, 478–404 BC', 'The Politics and Culture of Athens, *c.* 460–399 BC' and 'The Rise of Macedon, 359–323 BC'.

Through your reading of this textbook and your wider study in class, you will be able to gain a broad understanding of military, political, religious, social and cultural aspects of the history of the ancient world. You will read and analyse ancient source material, and study certain debates by modern scholars related to this material. This will enable you to develop the skills to formulate coherent arguments about key issues and concepts.

The specification requires you to respond to the prescribed source material and assess its content through analysis and evaluation. The box features (see p. viii) are designed to build up your skills and knowledge, while exam tips, practice questions, and chapters on assessment will prepare you for taking your final examinations.

A Companion Website, available at www.bloomsbury.com/anc-hist-as-a-level, supports this textbook with further information, resources and updates. If you have any suggestions for improvement and additional resources please get in touch by writing to contact@bloomsbury.com.

HOW TO USE THIS BOOK

The layout design and box features of this book are designed to aid your learning.

ICONS

The Prescribed Source icon **PS** flags a quotation or image that is a source prescribed in the specification.

The Stretch and Challenge icon **S&C** indicates that an exercise extends beyond the core content of the specification.

The Companion Website icon **CW** highlights where extra material can be found on the Bloomsbury Companion Website www.bloomsbury.com/anc-hist-as-a-level.

BOX FEATURES

In the margins you will find feature boxes giving short factfiles of key events, individuals and places.

Other features either **recommend** teaching material or highlight **prescribed** content and **assessment** tips and information.

Recommended teaching material is found in the following box features:

Activities
Debates
Explore Further
Further Reading
Modern Parallels
Study Questions
Topic Reviews

Prescribed content and assessment-focused tips and information are found in the following box features:

Exam Overviews
Exam Tips
Practice Questions
Prescribed Debates
Prescribed Sources

Material that extends beyond the specification is found in the Stretch and Challenge box features. Remember that the specification requires students to study extra sources and material not listed in the specification, so S&C information and exercises will provide a good place for you to start.

A NOTE ON QUESTIONS

Discussion prompts found in Topic Review boxes and Study Question boxes are not worded in the form you will find on the exam papers. They are intended to encourage investigation and revision of the material, but do not reflect the questions you will answer in the exam. Practice Questions at the end of each topic, and the questions found in the 'What to Expect in the Exam' chapters do mirror the format and wording you will encounter in the exam.

GLOSSARY

At the back of the book you will find a full glossary of key words. These words are also defined on pages in margin features.

Spellings of names and texts are formatted in line with the OCR specification.

On the Companion Website you will find a colour-coded glossary that highlights which components the words come from.

IMAGES

Images of the prescribed visual/material sources are flagged with the PS icon, but other images illustrate other relevant aspects of the ancient world. Often what survives from the ancient world does not provide us with ways to illustrate what we study. Thus, art, drawings and reconstructions from later periods and the modern day may be used to illustrate this book. Don't forget that these are not sources like your prescribed texts and visual material – they are later interpretations of aspects of antiquity and do not represent evidence for analysis.

COMPANION WEBSITE

Resources will include

- further information about Prescribed Sources
- annotated further reading
- links to websites that give useful contextual material for study
- quizzes on key topics and themes
- worksheets to supplement Activity box features in the book

DON'T FORGET

Look out for cross references to other pages in the book – this is where you will find further information and be able to link concepts or themes.

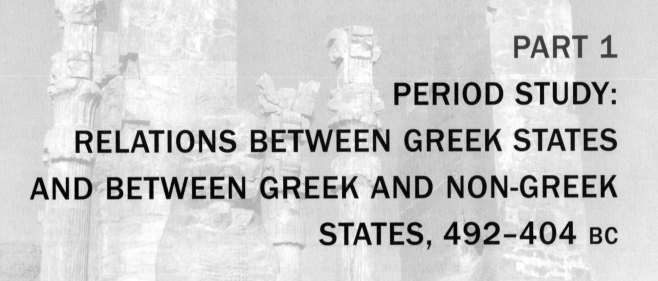

PART 1
PERIOD STUDY:
RELATIONS BETWEEN GREEK STATES
AND BETWEEN GREEK AND NON-GREEK
STATES, 492–404 BC

Introduction to Relations between Greek States and between Greek and Non-Greek States, 492–404 BC

Half of your AS and a quarter of your A level in Ancient History involves a Greek Period Study. This component covers the years 492 to 404, and focuses specifically on the nature of two sets of relations: the relations between different Greek cities, and the relations between Greek cities and the Persian Empire and its peoples. The period study is divided into five timespans: 492–479; 479–446; 446–431; 431–420; and 420–404. The fifth century is the first period in Greek history that modern historians have a wide variety of source material to work from. You will be able to examine evidence from both the Greek and the Persian side, and from inscriptional and narrative accounts of events and peoples.

The fifth century BC was a time of extraordinary change and dynamism in the Greek world. During this era, some of the greatest writers and thinkers of the ancient world emerged, including Herodotus, Thucydides, Aeschylus, Sophocles, Euripides, Protagoras and Socrates. It was also a period which saw great achievements of art and sculpture, most notably in the building programme which the Athenians commissioned for their Acropolis. To understand such cultural excellence fully, it is essential to explore the history intertwined with it.

The history itself is fascinating. The period begins with the conflict between Greeks and Persians, when a relatively small number of Greek cities managed to see off two Persian invasions against great odds. Later Greeks liked to remember this as a defining moment of Greek history. However, as Athenian power grew the century was then defined by a different clash, between Athens and its allies and Sparta and its allies. This was initially a 'cold war', but full hostilities broke out in 431 and lasted until 404. The conflict has remained a focus for study and debate ever since, and modern politicians and scholars still use it to inform them on the modern world. This is one reason that it is a compelling and important period to study.

EXAM OVERVIEW: AS LEVEL   H007/01

Your assessment for the Period Study option will be

        50% of the AS Level   1 hr 30 mins   60 marks

15 marks will test AO1: demonstrate knowledge and understanding of the key features and characteristics of the historical periods studied

15 marks will test AO2: analyse and evaluate historical events and historical periods to arrive at substantiated judgements

30 marks will test AO3: use, analyse and evaluate a range of ancient source material within its historical context to:

- reach conclusions about historical events and historical periods studied
- make judgements about how the portrayal of events by ancient writers/sources relates to the social, political, religious and cultural contexts in which they were written/produced

EXAM OVERVIEW: A LEVEL   H407/11, H407/12, H407/13

Your assessment for the Period Study option will be found in Section A of your exam paper. It comprises

25% of the A Level	1 hr 20 mins	50 marks
	out of 2 hrs 30 mins	out of 98 marks
	for the whole paper	for the whole paper

10 marks will test AO1: demonstrate knowledge and understanding of the key features and characteristics of the historical periods studied

10 marks will test AO2: analyse and evaluate historical events and historical periods to arrive at substantiated judgements

15 marks will test AO3: use, analyse and evaluate a range of ancient source material within its historical context to:

- reach conclusions about historical events and historical periods studied
- make judgements about how the portrayal of events by ancient writers/sources relates to the social, political, religious and cultural contexts in which they were written/produced

15 marks will test AO4: analyse and evaluate, in context, modern historians' interpretations of the historical events and topics studied.

1.1 The Challenge of the Persian Empire, 492–479

TIMESPAN OVERVIEW

- Mardonius' expedition of 492 BC
- Persian approaches to the Greek states
- the Battle of Marathon
- Greek and Persian strategy
- the threat of Greek medising
- Sparta's response
- Persian aims and intentions in 480s: Darius' and Xerxes' policies towards the Greek states
- Greek and Persian preparations in 480s
- differences in responses to the Persians among the Greek states, including medising
- the formation of the Hellenic League and its leadership
- the states involved in the Hellenic League
- the involvement of Greek states in the events of 480–479, including examples of medising, co-operation and conflict, debates and differences of opinion before Salamis and Plataea on strategy

The prescribed sources for this timespan are:

- Herodotus, *Histories*
  - 6: 42–49; 94–117, 120–124
  - 7: 1; 5–10h; 49–50; 102; 131–133; 138–139; 141–145; 151–152; 174–175; 207, 219–222; 228.2
  - 8: 1–3; 49–50; 56–63; 74; 94; 100–103; 143–144
  - 9: 1–3; 6–8; 16–18; 40; 62–64; 71; 98–99; 105–106

- The Serpent Column
- Naqs-e Rustam inscription No.1 and 2
- Xerxes' inscription

This timespan will examine the series of events surrounding the conflict between the Persians and the Greeks who opposed them between 492 and 479. It will begin by looking at the build-up to and events of Darius' invasion of 490, and then focus on the events of the 480s, which culminate in Xerxes' great invasion of 480–479. It is important to remember the focus of this period study is on the nature of the relations between different Greek states and between Greek states and the Persian Empire.

It is important to be aware from the outset that ancient Greece did not become a unified political entity until the late fourth century BC. In our period, the Greek world consisted of hundreds of individual political entities, many of them very small. A further important point is that Greeks had moved well beyond the Greek mainland and the Aegean Sea – Greeks had established settlements in many areas around the Mediterranean Sea and Black Sea.

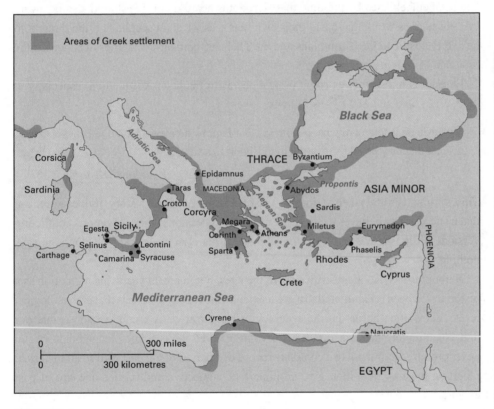

FIGURE 1.1
Areas of Greek settlement in *c.* 500.

PRESCRIBED SOURCE

Title: *Histories*

Author: Herodotus (*c.* 484–*c.* 425)

Date: written during the third quarter of the fifth century; probably published in full in the early 420s

Genre: history

Significance: the first recorded work of Greek history, covering the causes and course of the wars between the Greeks and the Persians *c.* 546–479

Prescribed sections: see Timespan Overview opposite

Read it here: Herodotus, *The Histories*, translated by Aubrey de Sélincourt (Penguin 1996)

THE SOURCES

Herodotus

Without Herodotus, we would know very little about the conflicts between the Greeks and the Persians, or indeed about many aspects of the Greek world of the sixth and early fifth centuries BC. However, we know only a little about his life. According to tradition, he was born, probably in the 480s, in Halicarnassus in Asia Minor, a Greek city which was at that time under Persian control, as were all the Greek cities of Asia Minor. He researched and wrote his work, today known as the *Histories*, in the third quarter of the fifth century, several decades after the events he wrote about. He seems to have lived in Athens for part of his life, perhaps in the early 440s and then again in the late 430s.

Herodotus uses a variety of research methods and made use of sources literary, epigraphic, archaeological and oral. However, scholars agree that it is the oral sources which are predominant – the Greek world was still largely an oral, memory-based society, and the bulk of Herodotus' research seems to have consisted of conversations with those who were present at the events or, far more commonly, their descendants or those who knew them. It is important to reflect on how much such stories will already have changed and been embellished by the time that Herodotus heard them. We should also be aware that his sources would have had their own bias – as we shall see, he is often thought to be overly hostile to the Corinthians and the Thebans, both bitter enemies of Athens at the time that Herodotus was writing.

Herodotus himself gives some indications as to his historical method, especially at 2.99, 2.123, and at 7.152 **(PS)** as follows:

> My business is to record what people say, but I am by no means bound to believe it – and that may be taken to apply to this book as a whole.
>
> Herodotus, *Histories* 7.152

This warning is to be taken seriously – just because he reports a story, it does not mean that he necessarily believes it. There are also many occasions where he reports conflicting versions of the same event – at times he states his own preference, at others he says nothing.

EXPLORE FURTHER

To learn more about Herodotus and his work, read John Marincola's introduction to the Penguin Classics translation by Aubrey de Sélincourt (see Further Reading, p. 19).

Herodotus has had many critics down the ages, but in recent years, his reputation as a historian has been rehabilitated to a great extent. One reason for this is that archaeological research has often borne out the accuracy of his narrative. A second reason is that our understanding of what constitutes history has evolved – it is acknowledged that we can never produce anything like a complete record of a period of the past, and so all historical reporting must by definition give an imperfect, subjective and limited account of past events.

DARIUS' POLICY TOWARDS THE GREEKS

KEY INDIVIDUAL

Darius I
Dates: reigned 522–486
King of Persia

Our period begins in 492, but this was far from the first engagement between the Greeks and the Persians. In fact, the Greek cities of Asia Minor had been under Persian rule since *c*. 546 and the Greek cities of Cyprus since *c*. 525. Darius came to power in 522, and over the following ten years or so he also incorporated a number of eastern Aegean islands and cities of the northern Aegean coastline into the vast Persian Empire, which stretched as far east as the Indus Valley. In 499, the Persians made an unsuccessful attempt to invade Naxos, the largest of the Cyclades Islands, and the events surrounding this failure caused many cities under Persian control in Asia Minor and Cyprus to revolt soon afterwards. This is known as the Ionian Revolt, since it began in the region of Ionia on the eastern Aegean coastline. It took the Persians a number of years to quash the rebellion, but they did so in 494 with a sea battle at Lade in the eastern Aegean and a brutal suppression of Miletus, the large Ionian city which had played a central role in leading the revolt.

This is the context in which our time period begins, and the events of the years 492–491 are covered at 6.42–49 **PS**. At 6.42 **PS**, Herodotus lists two important reforms which Artaphernes, the Persian **satrap** (the Persian name for a provincial governor), puts in place in Ionia after the revolt to try to stabilise the region. Furthermore, the following year Mardonius, the newly appointed Persian commander of forces in the Aegean, introduced a further reform (6.43 **PS**).

Each reform seems measured and reflects well on the Persian policy of trying to work with local peoples to make the Empire function effectively. In 492, Mardonius led a campaign in northern Greece. Herodotus says initially that attacking and punishing Eretria and Athens was the main objective of the expedition. Eretria was a city on the island of Euboea, which together with Athens had sent a number of ships to assist the Ionian Revolt in its earliest days – both cities were therefore obvious targets for a Persian revenge mission. However, both were situated much further south than this invasion, and Herodotus goes on to comment:

> At any rate, these two places were the professed object of the expedition, though in fact the Persians intended to subjugate as many Greek towns as they could.
>
> Herodotus, *Histories* 6.44

Herodotus presents the expedition as a failure, after the fleet was wrecked off Mount Athos. None the less, it should be observed that the Persians captured the wealthy island of Thasos.

In 491 we are told that Darius sent out heralds to all the Greek states to demand **earth and water** for the king, as well as ordering the Greek cities already under Persian control to contribute to a Persian invasion force. Giving 'earth and water' was the symbolic way, according to Herodotus, in which states indicated their acceptance of Persian rule. It is unlikely that the moment of giving earth and water meant that a state automatically became a full member of the Empire, but that it was accepting the necessity to do so when the Persians required it. Those Greeks who refused to submit came to look down on those who did, and coined the word **medise** to describe the act of submitting to the Persians (the Greeks often referred to the Persians as the 'Medes', who were in fact a Persian subject people).

Herodotus goes on to say that many cities on the Greek mainland and all the islands gave earth and water in 491. He specifically mentions Aegina, a powerful trading island in the Saronic Gulf (see Figure 1.6 on page 16) which was at that time at war with Athens. However, he does not at this point report the response of Athens or Sparta. It is only later that he reveals this, while recording a similar demand for earth and water by Darius' successor Xerxes in 481:

(see Figure 1.6 on page 16)

KEY EVENT

Ionian Revolt
Dates: 499 and 494

A revolt between many Asiatic Greek cities against Persian rule

---

satrap a Persian provincial governor

KEY INDIVIDUAL

Mardonius
Date: d. 479

Commander of the Persian taskforce in 492, and a significant advisor to Xerxes for the 480 invasion

---

earth and water the symbolic tokens offered to the Persians by foreign states submitting to their rule.

---

medise the act of a Greek state submitting to the Persians

S & C

To find out more about the relationship between the Persians and the Greeks before 492, read chapters 2, 3 and 4 of *The Greek Wars* by George Cawkwell (see Further Reading, p. 19).

To Athens and Sparta Xerxes sent no demand for submission because of what happened to the messengers whom Darius had sent on a previous occasion: at Athens they were thrown into the pit like criminals, at Sparta they were pushed into a well.

Herodotus, *Histories* 7.133

This was an extraordinary statement of defiance by both cities, since heralds were normally given sacred protection on diplomatic missions. Athens had a strong motive for resisting the Persians. In 510, the city had expelled its tyrant, Hippias, and established a democratic system instead. Hippias had gone over to the Persians soon afterwards, and was urging a Persian attack on his homeland, no doubt so that he could be reinstalled as a Persian-backed ruler. Moreover, members of Hippias' aristocratic clan, the Pisistratids, were still living in Athens. Many Athenians no doubt felt nervous about a return to tyranny and this must have influenced their decision to back the Ionian Revolt. The motivation of Sparta is less clear, although it is likely that the city simply saw itself as the leader of the Peloponnese and did not wish this status to be challenged.

A possible insight into Persian policy can be found at Naqs-e Rustam, about 6 km north of Persepolis, the great royal city built by Darius. It is the burial site of four Persian

FIGURE 1.2
A map of the Aegean Greek world in the early fifth century.

kings, including Darius and Xerxes. In the iconography of the tomb of Darius, the king is presented on a throne in front of a fire altar and an incense-burner. Carrying him on the throne are human figures, each one representing the lands of the empire. It is thought that Darius had this tomb built during the final years of his reign.

The inscriptions at Naqs-e Rustam are just one of a number of Persian royal inscriptions, in which Persian kings set out their ideology. It should be said that there were no historians in the Persian Empire, and so we are very limited in our access to sources on the Persian side. The royal inscriptions are in fact our most detailed written documents from the Persian perspective. No royal inscription makes any mention of a military campaign in the Greek world – the only mention of Greeks is simply as one of the subject peoples of the empire.

Nevertheless, the inscriptions give us a fascinating insight into how Darius wished to portray himself as king. They also provide a useful source of contrast and comparison to Herodotus. One key point is that in both sections he sees himself as divinely appointed by the Persian great god, Ahura Mazda, to carry out his wishes and bring order to a world in commotion. Darius presents himself as a just king, and one who wishes to protect the weak from the strong:

FIGURE 1.3
The tomb of Darius
at Naqs-e Rustam.

> I reward the man who seeks to contribute according to his efforts; I punish him who does harm, according to the harm done; I do not wish that a man should do harm; nor do I wish that, if he should do harm, he should not be punished. What a man says against a man, does not convince me, until I hear the testimony of both.

> DNb, LACTOR 16, 103

Darius then goes on to identify himself as the ideal Persian warrior – he is skilled on horseback and with the bow, all thanks to Ahura Mazda.

PRESCRIBED SOURCE

Naqs-e Rustam inscription No.1 and 2 (No. 48 and 103)

Genre: a Persian Royal tomb and Inscription

Location: Naqs-e Rustam, about 6km north of the royal capital of Persepolis

Significance: a statement of Darius' ideology as Persian King

Read it here: LACTOR 16: *The Persian Empire from Cyrus II to Artaxerxes* (KCL, 2000) 48 and 103

Study questions

1 How useful might the inscriptions at Naqs-e Rustam be as historical evidence?
2 To what extent does the way in which Darius portrays his rule correspond to Herodotus' account of Persian policy in *Histories* 6.42–49; 6.94–117, 6. 120–124; and 7.1 **PS**?

ACTIVITY

Create a copy of the art on Darius' tomb. What statements of power and policy do you think are made through this artwork?

S & C

The Persians were well
known for working with
local religious leaders
and respecting local
religious traditions, as
long as the local peoples
were prepared to work
with them in return.
Read the following
sources. What picture of
Persian policy can we
form from them?

The Cyrus Cylinder
(LACTOR 16, No. 12)

Darius' letter to
Gadatas (LACTOR 16,
No. 198)

The Book of Ezra, 6

Study questions

1 How reliable do you
   think the speech
   of Miltiades is at
   6.109 **PS** as a source
   for the reasons for
   fighting at Marathon?
2 What sources do you
   think that Herodotus
   might have used for
   his account of the
   battle?

THE BATTLE OF MARATHON

In 490 the invasion came. According to Herodotus (6.94–101 **PS**), the double motivation of revenge and imperial expansion was driving Darius, and he appointed new commanders, Datis and Artaphrenes, to replace Mardonius and lead an invasion force of 600 ships. Naxos was the first key target, which the Persians soon sacked. Herodotus then relates the respectful Persian approach to the holy island of Delos – believed to be the birthplace of both Apollo and Artemis. The Persians next moved on Eretria, which was ultimately betrayed by two of its own citizens. It is notable that at both Naxos and Eretria the Persians burnt the temples in revenge for the Greek burning of an important temple at Sardis during the Ionian Revolt. This stands in great contrast to their treatment of the shrine at Delos, an island with which they had no quarrel.

Herodotus' account of the battle of Marathon (6.102–117 **PS**) gives important information about the inter-relationships between the Greeks and Persians in 490. On the Greek side, the Athenians were aided by soldiers from Plataea, a city in the region of Boeotia to the north of Attica (the region controlled by Athens, which is shown in Figure 3.1 on page 148). The largest city in Boeotia was Thebes, and many cities in the region were joined in an alliance under Theban leadership. However, the Plataeans were bitter enemies of the Thebans, and so were allied to Athens. They had originally asked for an alliance with Sparta, but the scheming Spartan king, Cleomenes, had directed them to ally with Athens instead, thereby hoping to set Thebes and Athens against one another. Cleomenes' plan was successful (6.108 **PS**).

The Persian strategy was to invade Attica at Marathon, following the advice of Hippias. After the battle, the Persian fleet sailed round the tip of Attica to attack Athens directly from the west, but the Persians gave up when they saw that the Athenians had already returned. The Persians clearly hoped that medising Greeks would help them in the campaign. During Miltiades' speech to the other generals at 6.109 **PS**, the reason he gives for wanting to engage in battle is political not military:

> If we refuse to fight, I have little doubt that the result will be bitter dissension; our purpose will be shaken and we shall submit to Persia.
>
> Herodotus, *Histories* 6.109

Such fears about treachery amongst the Greeks seem to be validated by Herodotus' tale of the 'shield signal' given to the Persians after the battle (6.121–124 **PS**).

The battle saw a remarkable victory for the Greek allies, who were significantly outnumbered. Marathon held a vital place in the Athenian consciousness for the rest of the fifth century, and the following lines surely reflect how Athenians understood the significance of the battle and its consequences for the second Persian invasion:

> The Athenians . . . were the first Greeks, so far as we know, to charge at a run, and the first who dared to look without flinching at Persian dress and the men who wore it; for until that time, no Greek could hear even the word Persian without terror.
>
> Herodotus, *Histories* 6.112

The Spartans only arrived after the battle (6.120 **PS**). They were held back by the timing of the Karneia, a major religious event when no military action could be taken. When they did arrive at Marathon, their inspection of Persian arms and armour on the battlefield may have given them important intelligence for future battles.

PERSIAN PREPARATIONS FOR THE 480 INVASION

Book 7 of Herodotus' *Histories* begins with Darius' response to the defeat at Marathon (7.1 **PS**) – he is set upon revenge by launching an invasion on a far grander scale. However, this revenge mission was doubly delayed in the year 486 – by a rebellion in Egypt and then by the death of Darius himself. Darius' son and chosen heir, Xerxes, now succeeded him.

Herodotus presents discussions taking place in the Persian court about whether or not to invade Greece (7.5–10h **PS**) soon after this. Although no one believes that Herodotus had a source who could accurately recall speeches from the Persian court decades before, there were Greeks at the Persian court, including Hippias and Demaratus (see p. 14). We also learn at 9.16 **PS** that one senior Persian was able to speak Greek. However, the debate presented in 7.8–10 **PS** seems to be very Greek in its character, and some have compared it to a set of speeches in a Greek law court. Moreover, the leading opponent of the invasion, Artabanus, Xerxes' uncle, is presented as a wise advisor with great foresight, and yet one who is not listened to – a character type readily identifiable with Athenian tragedy.

The leading proponent of an invasion was Mardonius. He had not been involved in the events of 490 after leading the 492 campaign, but as Xerxes' cousin and brother-in-law he was influential in the new king's court. At 7.5 **PS** we learn that he is constantly urging Xerxes to invade Greece. He argues that Xerxes can win great renown by taking revenge on Athens, and that the land of Europe was well worth conquering for its fertility. Herodotus also adds the detail that Mardonius' case was supported by two aristocratic Greek families who stood to benefit from the invasion – the Pisistratids in Athens and the Aleuads in the region of Thessaly.

The presentation of Artabanus as a 'wise advisor' re-emerges at 7.49 **PS**, where he warns Xerxes that he is at risk of getting into trouble through poor supply lines and lack of resources the further he goes into Greece. In his turn, at 7.50 **PS** Xerxes presents himself as a well-prepared risk taker in the tradition of his predecessors as kings. Indeed, there is evidence of significant Persian preparations, including the building of a canal through the Mount Athos promontory and the bridging of the Hellespont.

In the Greek sources, Xerxes is often portrayed as arrogant, impetuous and immature. Unsurprisingly, there is no sense of this in the royal inscriptions which have survived in his name. Rather, there is a clear attempt to portray him in the same light as his father and as the continuer of his legacy.

One example of this comes in a royal inscription discovered on the inner walls of the Gate of All Lands on the terrace of the royal palace at Persepolis. Xerxes commissioned

FIGURE 1.4
The remains of the **PS**
Gate of All Lands today.

Study questions

1 List the arguments outlined for and against the invasion at 7.5 to 7.10 **PS**.
2 Read the two prescribed Persian royal inscriptions. To what extent do they correspond to the Persian objectives presented by Herodotus at 7.5 to 7.10 **PS**?

KEY INDIVIDUAL

Themistocles
Dates: *c.* 524–459

Athenian general who convinced the Athenians to develop their navy and led the Greek forces to victory at Salamis

Hellenic League modern term for the alliance of Greek states who resisted the Persian invasion of 480–479

this magnificent gate as an extension to the royal palace built by Darius. In the inscription, Xerxes takes credit for this innovation, but also presents himself as continuing in the royal tradition. He is particularly keen to associate himself with his father:

> Xerxes the king says: 'By the favour of Ahura Mazda, I built this Gate of All Lands. Much other good (construction) was built within this (city of) Parsa, which I built and which my father built. Whatever good construction is seen, we built all that by the grace of Ahura Mazda.

XPa, LACTOR 16, 63

GREEK PREPARATIONS FOR THE 480 INVASION

At 7.131–133 **PS**, Herodotus tells of the Greek responses to the Persian heralds in 481, and at 7.132 **PS** he gives a list of those states in central Greece which had chosen to medise – those were the states who were feeling confident about the situation, in contrast to those who had chosen to stand and fight (7.138 **PS**). We have also seen at 7.6 **PS** that some Greeks were actively encouraging the Persians to invade.

At 7.141–144 **PS**, Herodotus gives a more detailed report of the reaction in Athens to the Persian advance. His tale of the 'wooden wall' oracle is famous, but the key strategic point is that it was the Athenian general Themistocles who persuaded the Athenians to put their trust in their navy. In 483/2, Themistocles had also persuaded the Athenian assembly to spend a windfall from the silver mines at Laurium on building many more ships to defend the city in their war against Aegina. Themistocles is therefore credited with the policy which did a great deal to help the Greeks win the Persian wars.

At 7.139 **PS**, Herodotus had explained that he believed that the Greeks owed their victory in the wars to the Athenian navy. It is also interesting that he has to qualify what he says as follows:

> At this point I find myself compelled to express an opinion which I know most people will object to; nevertheless, as I believe it to be true, I will not suppress it.

Herodotus, *Histories* 7.139

At the time that Herodotus was writing, Athens was very unpopular amongst many cities of the Greek world (see pp. 38–42). This quotation is therefore a reminder that Herodotus' history is much affected by the era in which he is writing.

As well as Athens, there were thirty or so other Greek states which decided to resist the Persians. At 7.145 **PS**, Herodotus describes the first formal meeting of states who formed the anti-Persian alliance. This alliance is known by modern scholars as the **Hellenic League**. At this first meeting, the following decisions were taken:

- to end all conflict between allied Greek states
- to send out spies to discover the nature of Persian activity
- to try to recruit more Greek states to the cause

In addition to these decisions, we can glean the following information about the terms of the alliance from other sources:

- There was an oath to resist the Persians and punish those who did not (Herodotus 7.132 **PS**; Thucydides 1.102 **PS**)
- there was a pledge not to secede (Herodotus 9.106 **PS**)
- there was an undertaking to provide mutual defence against attacks from all enemies, not just the Persians (Thucydides 1.102 **PS**)
- it was agreed that Sparta should provide the military leadership (Herodotus 8.2–3 **PS**). This made sense since the city was already the leader of a League of Peloponnesian allies, today known as the **Peloponnesian League** (described on p. 24)
- there was an agreement to make major decisions by congresses (e.g. Herodotus. 7.175 **PS**), but lesser decisions by councils of war (e.g. Herodotus 8.49 **PS**, 8.56–63 **PS**, 8.74 **PS**).

One piece of archaeological evidence about the cities which combined to fight the Persians is the Serpent Column **PS**. It was dedicated to Apollo at Delphi as a thanks offering for the Greek victory at Plataea in 479. The column was made in the shape of the bodies of three serpents whose bodies were intertwined and whose open jaws supported a golden tripod. The tripod was stolen in the fourth century BC, but the Serpent Column was preserved and centuries later brought to Constantinople, where it remains today.

Delphi was normally a place where Greek cities tried to outdo one another with ostentatious dedications, and so it was remarkable to see a common dedication of so many Greek cities – thirty-one are named in all, with the Spartans at the top, followed by the Athenians and then the Corinthians. It is notable that thirteen cities are from the Peloponnese, while two others – Aegina and Megara – were probably either members of the Peloponnesian League or at least under Spartan influence. Moreover, four other cities were colonies of Corinth (Ambracia, Anactorium, Leukas and Potidaea) and these may too have been in some sort of alliance with the Peloponnesian League.

However, it is likely that there was plenty of politics about whether some cities got onto the column in the aftermath of the war: five cities named by Herodotus as part of the Hellenic League are not named on the column.

> **Peloponnesian League** modern term for the alliance of Peloponnesian states led by Sparta which had existed in its fullest form since *c.* 504

EXPLORE FURTHER

Research the order in which the cities were listed on the Serpent Column. Can you find any significance in this?

FIGURE 1.5
Today the Serpent Column stands in Istanbul, Turkey.

PRESCRIBED SOURCE

The Serpent Column

Date: erected in 478

Location: originally at Delphi, moved to Constantinople in AD 330

Significance: a dedication of thanks to the gods by the states who combined to fight against the Persians at Plataea in 479

View it here: Figure 1.5

THE INVASION OF 480–479

Thermopylae

The prescribed sections relating to the battle of Thermopylae begin at 7.174–175 **PS**. Just before this, the Greeks had withdrawn their force of 10,000 men from Thessaly and the Thessalians had gone over to the Persians. This was a major blow to the Greeks, as the Thessalians were famed for the skill of their cavalry. There followed another congress of the Hellenic League at the isthmus (the narrow strip of land joining the Peloponnese to the rest of mainland Greece), where it was decided to meet the Persians at the narrow pass at Thermopylae in central Greece. At the same time, the Greek fleet would be stationed at Cape Artemisium at the north of the island of Euboea to prevent the Persian fleet from landing troops behind Greek lines at Thermopylae. There was a series of inconclusive naval engagements at Artemisium, in which the Greeks largely held their own.

One of the key figures in Herodotus' account of the battle is Demaratus. He was one of the two kings in Sparta until he was deposed in *c.* 491, after which he left the city and defected to the Persians. Herodotus records that Darius rewarded him with a great gift of land, and by the time of the 480 invasion, he was serving as an advisor to Xerxes. Herodotus therefore uses him as a mouthpiece for Greek pride – Demaratus will warn the Persian king about the courage of the Spartans, but he will not be believed. He puts forward the view that the Greeks will be hard to conquer because of their courage and their obedience to their laws (7.102 **PS**).

At 7.207 **PS**, Herodotus introduces a key theme – the differences in opinion within the Hellenic League about strategy. Those who live in the Peloponnese wish to withdraw there, believing that it is much easier to defend due to the fact that the isthmus at Corinth is just four miles wide at its narrowest point. Greeks living outside the Peloponnese are understandably opposed to this idea. The Locrians and Phocians of central Greece argue against it, knowing that it would mean that they would have to abandon their cities to enemy destruction.

The focus of 7.219–222 **PS** is on the final day of the battle at Thermopylae. Clearly, by the time that Herodotus came to research the battle it had become part of Spartan folklore. However, these sections do give us important information about inter-Greek relations at the battle. Herodotus reports some dispute as to why most of the Greek force

KEY EVENTS

Date: August 480
Battle of Thermopylae

A battle in which about 7,000 Greeks, led by 301 Spartans, tried heroically but unsuccessfully to block the Persian advance

Battle of Artemisium

A series of inconclusive naval engagements which took place off Cape Artemisium between the Greek and Persian fleets at the same time as the battle of Thermopylae

of 7,000 left the scene before the final day's fighting: in his opinion, Leonidas dismissed them because he could see that they were afraid, but by another view he did so because he could see that the situation was hopeless and so chose to save their lives: such a course of action was out of the question for a Spartan, who was duty bound to fight to the death.

However, soldiers from two Boeotian cities did remain to fight: 700 Thespians and 400 Thebans. The Thespians apparently fought bravely to the death, although their deeds were little remembered by the Spartans, for whom the battle soon won legendary status, as seen by the dedication left at Thermopylae mentioned by Herodotus at 7.228b **PS**. However, Herodotus' treatment of the Thebans at 7.222 **PS** has come in for much criticism. Against his claim that Leonidas kept them there to fight as hostages against their will, it can be pointed out that the Thebans were unlikely to fight bravely in such circumstances, and this decision does not fit with Leonidas' decision to send away the other Greek allies. Most probably, the story is evidence of anti-Theban bias in Herodotus' Athenian sources.

Salamis

Book 8 opens with a list of the Greek states' contributions to the combined naval force sent to Artemisium. The level of detail here suggests careful research on the part of Herodotus. The historian then goes on to introduce the Spartan commander of the Hellenic League fleet, Eurybiades, and to explain the reason for Spartan command – we can see here signs of his favouring of the Athenians and their supposedly magnanimous role in stepping aside from taking a leadership role (8.1–3 **PS**).

At 8.49–50 **PS**, the Greek ships are moored on the east coast of the island of Salamis, and the commanders hold the first of a series of councils of war. The key debate was whether to fight at Salamis, close to Athens, or to move back on the Peloponnese and plan a defence from there. Athens was now being burnt by the Persians, but the Athenians had evacuated most of their people. Their fighting men were all now at Salamis.

The debate continues at 8.56–63 **PS**. It is here that Themistocles emerges as the key player, arguing to fight at Salamis. Opposing him is Adeimantus, the Corinthian commander, who does not get a good press. At the time of Herodotus' writing, Athens and Corinth were bitter enemies, and this no doubt influenced his Athenian sources. Ultimately, Themistocles wins the argument by making one threat – if they do not agree to fight at Salamis, he will instruct the Athenian ships to leave for Siris in southern Italy, where the Athenians will set up a new city. Eurybiades knew that the Greek navy was helpless without the Athenian ships.

In his account of the battle, Herodotus reveals once again the anti-Corinthian nature of his Athenian sources, reporting an Athenian story at 8.94 **PS** that Adeimantus panicked at the start of the battle and led the Corinthian ships away. To his credit, Herodotus also records that the rest of the Greeks reported that this story was false, and that the Corinthians played a distinguished part in the battle.

In the aftermath of the battle (8.100–103 **PS**), Herodotus presents a discussion in the Persian high command about what to do next. Mardonius tries to minimise the defeat and suggests to Xerxes that he either launch an immediate attack on the Peloponnese, or else leave him behind with an army of 300,000 (a figure which must be a great exaggeration)

KEY INDIVIDUAL

Eurybiades

The Spartan who was commander of the Hellenic League forces in 480

KEY EVENT

Battle of Salamis
Date: September 480

A naval battle in which the Greeks defeated the Persians

FIGURE 1.6
A map of the Persian invasion, 480–479.

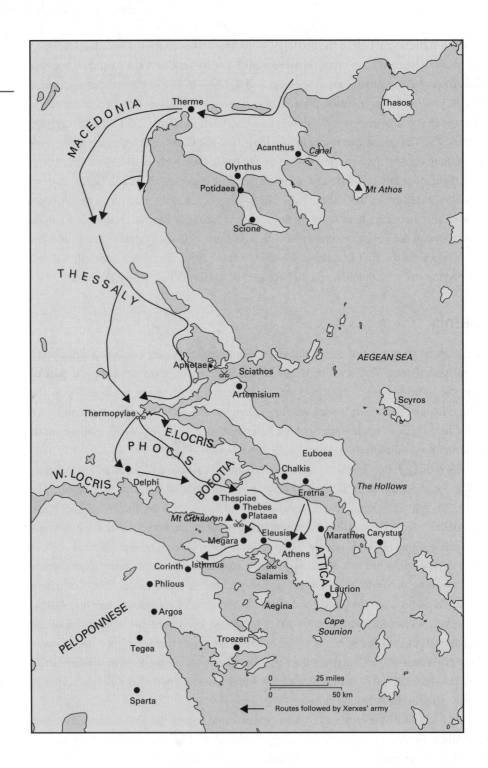

to finish the job. Xerxes turns to Artemisia for advice. She was the Greek queen of Halicarnassus, which was fighting on the Persian side. Artemisia's reply focuses on maintaining Xerxes' sense of prestige as the king of a great empire, although Herodotus presents him as frightened by events.

It was late September, and the campaigning season was almost done. The Persians withdrew to northern Greece. During that winter, the Persians once again made overtures to the Athenians, offering good terms – the Athenians could have their city back and any other territory they wished for, as long as they were prepared to accept Persian rule. The Persians sent the Macedonian king Alexander to offer these terms, and his visit caused alarm in Sparta, where there was fear that an Athenian submission would leave the Peloponnesians badly exposed. The Athenian reply to Alexander comes at 8.143 **PS**, and the Athenians remain defiant. At 8.144 **PS** comes their reply to the Spartans. In one of the most famous passages in Herodotus, the Athenians explain why they will never desert the Greek cause:

> There are many compelling reasons against our doing so, even if we wished: the first and greatest is the burning of our temples and images of our gods – now ashes and rubble. . . Again, there is the Greek nation – the community of blood and language, temples and ritual, and our common customs; if Athens were to betray all this, it would not be well done.'

> Herodotus, *Histories* 8.144

Despite these fine words, however, the Athenians make it clear that they expect the Spartans to lead the Peloponnesian troops out to meet the Persians in Boeotia, north of Attica. A successful battle there would allow the Athenians to hold onto their homeland.

Plataea

Book 9 opens with Mardonius marching south again towards Athens. The Thebans urged him to set up base in Boeotia and to try to buy off individual Greek leaders, but Mardonius was set on revenge over the Athenians. When he arrived in Athens, he found the city evacuated again, as it had been the previous summer (9.1–3 **PS**). 9.6–8 **PS** develops the story of the Athenian desertion – the Athenians had been waiting in the hope that the Spartans would lead the Peloponnesians out into Boeotia, but evacuated when they realised that this was not going to happen. In their turn, the Peloponnesians had been building a defensive wall across the isthmus. The Athenians once again appealed to the Spartans for help, this time asking them to come out and fight in Attica. Herodotus is scathing of Spartan motivation here – giving his opinion that the Spartans had simply been buying themselves time when they sent envoys to Athens in the winter, and that their real concern was to defend the Peloponnese alone.

As we have seen, 9.16 **PS** shows evidence of Persian officers being able to speak Greek. It also illustrates how closely the Persians and the Thebans were working together, a theme which re-emerges at 9.40 **PS** where Herodotus describes the Thebans as 'Persia's firm friends' who are brave in the Persian cause in battle. 9.16 **PS** also presents a Persian view that their mission is doomed but that the commanders will not accept it. Herodotus rarely names his sources, as he names Thersander here, so he must have wanted to convince his readers of the truth of the story.

Herodotus (9.17–18 **PS**) relates an episode which illustrates the contradictions and divisions in the relations between the Greek states. The Phocians had submitted to the Persians after the summer of 480 (they had been part of the Greek defence force at Thermopylae), and were now part of the Persian army preparing for battle. But there was still great distrust of them, and Herodotus' story suggests that the hatred between the

KEY EVENT

Battle of Plataea
Date: 479

The final battle of the Persian invasion, at which a combined force of Greeks defeated the Persians at Plataea in Boeotia

Thessalians and the Phocians was so deep that the Thessalians persuaded the Persians to turn their arms on the Phocians. The whole episode shows that relations between Greeks could be volatile, as they could be between medising Greeks and Persians.

The heart of the battle of Plataea is described at 9.62–64 **PS**. The key point is that the Spartans lead the attack on the Persians, and the reason for their victory is that the Persians were poorly armed against the Spartan hoplites. This goes against his view put forward elsewhere that the Greeks won simply because they were fighting for a higher ideal – that of freedom. Herodotus goes on to claim that the Spartan commander Pausanias deserved the credit for the victory, which he describes as the greatest ever known. At 9.71 **PS**, he goes on to confirm that the Spartans deserved the greatest credit for the victory at Plataea.

Mycale

The last battle of the Persian Wars took place at Cape Mycale in Ionia – Herodotus claims that it took place later on the same day as the battle of Plataea. The Greek fleet had been based at Delos during the winter of 480/79, but during the summer of 479 it was encouraged by Samian rebels to help the Ionians free themselves again. The Persians had been based at Samos, but now withdrew to Cape Mycale, where they beached their ships and built a stockade with them to defend themselves. According to Herodotus, when the Greeks neared the shore at Mycale the Spartan king commanding the Greek forces, Leotychides, loudly encouraged the Ionians to revolt during the coming battle (9.98 **PS**).

In the following section (9.99 **PS**), Herodotus makes it clear that the Persians didn't trust the Ionian troops in their army – they disarmed the Samians and posted the Milesians away from the battleground. During the battle the Ionians did indeed desert the Persian cause and the Greeks won a comprehensive victory, burning the Persian ships in the process. Herodotus gives the main credit for the victory to the Athenians, followed by the men from Corinth, Troezen and Sicyon, all cities of the Peloponnese (9.105 **PS**).

The victorious Greeks then withdrew to Samos and held a conference about the future of Ionia (9.106 **PS**). The Peloponnesians, led by Sparta, argued that it would be impossible to protect the Ionians from future Persian attacks, and so proposed resettling them on the Greek mainland by settling the Ionians on the land of those Greeks who had medised. However, the Athenians argued strongly against this proposal, and they won the argument. As a result, Aegean islands such as Chios, Samos and Lesbos were formally brought into the Hellenic League.

TIMESPAN REVIEW

- Outline the ways in which relations between the Greek states shift and change during this period.
- Compare the Persian ideology put forward in the royal inscriptions of Darius and Xerxes with the presentation of these kings in Herodotus.
- Explain the limitations to our understanding of the motivations of those states which medised.
- Assess how reliable you find Herodotus' account of this period.

Further Reading

Briant, P., *From Cyrus to Alexander* (Warsaw IN: Eisenbrauns, 2003).

Brunt, P., *The Hellenic League Against Persia*, Historia 2 (1953).

Cartledge, P., *Thermopylae: The Battle That Changed the World* (London: Vintage, 2007).

Cawkwell, G., *The Greek Wars* (Oxford: Oxford University Press, 2006).

Gould, John, *Herodotus* (London: Bloomsbury 1989).

Herodotus, *The Histories*, trans. Aubrey de Sélincourt (London: Penguin, 1996).

Holland, T., *Persian Fire* (London: Abacus 2006).

Krentz, Peter, *The Battle of Marathon* (New Haven: Yale University Press, 2011).

Kuhrt, A., *The Persian Empire* (Abingdon: Routledge, 2007).

Lazenby, G., *The Defence of Greece* (Liverpool: Aris & Phillips, 1993).

PRESCRIBED DEBATE: THE REASONS FOR THE VICTORY OVER THE PERSIANS IN 480–479 BC

There are a number of views as to why the Greeks managed to see off the Persian invasion of 480–479. Most scholars would agree that there were a number of contributory reasons, but would choose to emphasise one reason over another. Some would cite Athenian naval supremacy, while others would focus on the fact that the Greek hoplites were better armed and trained than their Persian opponents. A further reason proposed is that the Greek alliance managed to bring together a number of cities which were more committed to their freedom than the Persian forces were to conquest. Others might focus further on the Persian perspective, arguing either that they simply did not have the ready supply lines to pull off the conquest, or that they realised that their empire in the west had reached its natural extent. Many scholars would factor into these views the simple idea that there was also an element of luck involved.

Try to read as widely as possible about this issue. For a start, you might like to read from the following works by modern scholars:

Cartledge, P., *After Thermopylae* (Oxford: Oxford University Press, 2013).

Cawkwell, G., *The Greek Wars* (Oxford: Oxford University Press, 2006), chapter 5.

Lazenby, G., *The Defence of Greece* (Aris & Phillips, 1993), final chapter.

Green, Peter, *The Greco-Persian Wars* (University of California Press, 1998).

Shepherd, Wiliam, *Salamis 480: The naval campaign that saved Greece* (Osprey 2010)

Shepherd, Wiliam, *Plataea 479 BC: The most glorious victory ever seen* (Osprey 2012)

PRACTICE QUESTIONS

AS Level

1. How much did smaller Greek states contribute to the victories against the Persians in 480–479 BC? [10]

A Level

2. Read the following passage and answer the question below:

In immediate military terms, the value of Salamis was unambiguous. Had Xerxes won, then the Persians would have had the Peloponnese at the mercy of a naval assault; and, if it is still not quite a forgone conclusion that they would then inevitably have won overall, by land as well as sea, their task would have been eased immensely. Victory at Salamis did not, on the other hand, inevitably mean victory for the resistant coalition Greeks in the Graeco-Persian Wars overall. From that perspective, it was not Salamis but Plataea that was the decisive battle. 'It was at Plataea, not at Salamis, that the new satrapy was lost', as George Cawkwell has crisply put it. Xerxes may have retired to Asia after Salamis, but Great Kings did not necessarily lead all major campaigns in person, and he left behind, under the command of the more than competent Mardonius, sufficient forces to complete the job by land as well as by sea. But Mardonius was decisively defeated on land in the summer of 479 at Plataea in southern Boeotia in central Greece, by the largest land army ever mustered by Greeks to that date (some forty thousand in all). Herodotus – even Herodotus . . . was forced to concede that Plataea was essentially a Spartan victory.'

Thermopylae: The Battle That Changed the World, Paul Cartledge, p.166

How convincing do you find Cartledge's view that the Spartans deserve at least as much credit as the Athenians for the Greek victory over the Persians in 480–479 BC?

You must use your knowledge of the historical period and the ancient sources you have studied to analyse and evaluate Cartledge's interpretation. [20]

1.2 Greece in Conflict, 479–446 BC

TIMESPAN OVERVIEW

- the consequences of victory for the Greek states, especially relations between Sparta and Athens
- the growth of Athenian power in the Delian League
- Sparta's concerns
  the consequences for relations between Sparta and Athens and their respective allies of the earthquake and helot revolt 465–464 BC
- the events of the First Peloponnesian War 461–446 BC that involved changing relationships between Greek states: Megara's defection from the Peloponnesian League
- Corinth's relations with Megara, Sparta and Athens
- the Battle of Tanagra
- continued conflict with the Persians followed by the cessation of hostilities in 449 BC
- the Spartan invasion of Attica 446 BC

The prescribed sources for this timespan are:

- Aristotle, *Politics* 1284a38
- Diodorus, *Universal History* 11.46–47; 11.50; 12.2.1–2; 12 4.4–6; 12.38.2
- Harpokration s.v. *Attikois grammasin*
- Herodotus, *Histories*, 7.151
- Plutarch, *Aristeides* 23; 24.1–5
- Plutarch, *Cimon* 11–12.4; 13.4–5
- Plutarch, *Pericles* 23.1–2
- Thucydides, *The History of the Peloponnesian War* 1.89–118; 5.16

- Chalkis Decree

This timespan will examine how Greek politics developed in the aftermath of the Persian wars, focusing particularly on the growing enmity of Athens and Sparta, and the alliances that each state formed.

THE SOURCES

Unlike the opening decades of the fifth century, we have no detailed historical narrative for the events of the years between 479 and 446 in the Greek world. Herodotus himself occasionally refers to the period after 479, but we largely have to rely on the accounts of three very different writers: Thucydides, Diodorus Siculus and Plutarch. Thucydides lived from *c.* 460 to *c.* 400, and so he was writing about recent events. By contrast, Diodorus and Plutarch both lived centuries later. Their accounts depend partly on Thucydides but also on other earlier works now lost which differ from Thucydides.

Thucydides' history focused on the conflict between Athens and Sparta and their respective allies which began in 431. He is therefore introduced as a prescribed source in timespan 3 on pp. 35–7. For the purposes of this timespan, his brief description of events which came between 479 and 431 is important. This section of his work (1.89–118 **PS**) is today known as the **Pentecontaetia** (the fifty-year period – although technically it is not quite fifty years long). Thucydides claims (1.97 **PS**) that he has given this account to improve on the meagre offering of another local historian, Hellanicus of Lesbos. However, scholars have been unable to provide dates with any certainty for many of the events which he describes, including the key battle of Eurymedon. It is important to be aware that at 1.89 **PS**, Thucydides says that he seeks only to explain how Athenian

Pentecontaetia modern term given to Thucydides' account of the events between 479 and 431 in Book 1 of his history (1.89–118 **PS**)

PRESCRIBED SOURCE

Title: *Universal History*

Author: Diodorus Siculus

Dates: first century BC

Origin: from Sicily, hence: Siculus, 'the Sicilian'

Work: *Universal History*, fifteen of the original forty books survive

Genre: history

Significance: an attempt to write a history of the known world down to 60 BC

Prescribed sections: 11.46–47 (No. 19); 11.50 (No. 28); 12.2.1–2 (No. 52); 12 4.4–6; (No. 53); 12.38.2 (No. 113)

Read it here: LACTOR 1: *The Athenian Empire* (4th edn, KCL, 2000) 19, 28, 52, 53, 113

power grew after 479 to a point where the Spartans and their allies felt threatened enough to go to war in 431.

Diodorus was a Greek from Sicily who wrote his *Universal History* between 60 and 30 BC. His account of fifth century Greece largely follows that of Ephorus (*c.* 405–330), who had composed a universal history of Greece in thirty books, only a few fragments of which have survived. Although Ephorus was a native of Cyme on the coast of Asia Minor, he seems to have spent time at Athens at the rhetoric school of the leading speechwriter Isocrates. Ephorus' writing was therefore probably influenced by rhetoric, and the desire to frame events in a dramatic and exciting light.

One issue with Diodorus' use of Ephorus is that Ephorus organised his work by topic whereas Diodorus gave a year-by-year account. As a result, Diodorus sometimes merges the events of a number of years into one year. Few of Diodorus' sources have survived outside his work, so his reliability is a matter of great scholarly debate. Where he adds plausible information to an earlier source without contradicting it, it is generally felt acceptable to follow his account.

Plutarch was born some time before AD 50 in the town of Chaeronea in Boeotia, and he died soon after 120. He came from a wealthy background and was well-educated. Although he lived more than five centuries after the fifth century, he was a learned man who consulted and cites a wide variety of sources, some of which are early, and most of which are lost to us. Plutarch is most famous for his *Parallel Lives*, biographies which sought to compare a famous Greek with a famous Roman.

Plutarch makes clear at the start of his biography of Alexander that he is a biographer rather than a historian, and so he is more interested in character than in a detailed analysis

EXPLORE FURTHER

To find out more about the method and reliability of these two sources, read *Aspects of Greek History* by Terry Buckley (see reading list on p. 33), pp. 5–8 and pp. 14–18.

PRESCRIBED SOURCE

Title: *Lives of Aristeides, Cimon* and *Pericles*

Author: Plutarch

Dates: before AD 50 to after 120

Origin: from Chaeronea in central Greece

Work: *Parallel Lives*, comparative biographies of famous Greeks and Romans

Genre: biography

Significance: biographies of three of the key figures in Athenian politics of the period

Prescribed sections: *Aristeides* 23 (No. 10); 24.1–5 (No. 20); *Cimon* 11–12.4 (No. 33); 13.4–5 (No. 51); *Pericles* 23.1–2 (No. 71); 28.1–3 (No. 89); 30–31

Read it here: LACTOR 1: *The Athenian Empire* (4th edn, KCL, 2000) 10, 20, 33, 51, 71, 89; Plutarch, *The Rise and Fall of Athens*, translated by Ian Scott-Kilvert (Penguin 1960)

of events. At times, he seems to weigh up earlier sources well, but at others he is far less critical. As with Diodorus, he is most useful when he supplies us with information which is plausible and which doesn't contradict earlier sources.

THE CONSEQUENCES OF THE PERSIAN WARS

Thucydides' account of the Pentecontaetia begins exactly where Herodotus had finished his work, with the siege of Sestos in 479 (1.89 **PS**). After the battles of Plataea and Mycale in 479, the Peloponnesians headed home, but troops from Athens, Ionia and the Hellespont moved north to the Persian stronghold of Sestos on the European side of the Hellespont. They successfully besieged it under the leadership of the Athenian Xanthippus. Thucydides then goes on to outline the tensions between Athens and Sparta in the aftermath of the Persian Wars as the Athenians sought to rebuild their city (1.89–93 **PS**).

The Peloponnesian League

Sparta had long been the most powerful state in the Greek world, having exerted control of much of the Peloponnese since the middle of the sixth century through the **Peloponnesian League**. This was an alliance of city-states largely based in the Peloponnese peninsula, although some member states came from elsewhere, including the island of Aegina in the Saronic Gulf and the state of Megara which bordered Attica. The League probably originated in the 550s and reached its fullest form by c. 504. Its members were all independent allies of Sparta. They did not need to be allied to each other, although in practice many were. The key principles of the League were as follows:

- if any city of the League was attacked by a non-member, Sparta was duty-bound to come to its aid
- the League was bi-cameral (i.e. it had two voting blocks). One block was the Spartan assembly, and the other was a congress of all the other allied states, each with one vote. If the Spartan assembly voted for war or peace, then it needed a majority in the congress for the vote to be carried
- if the Peloponnesian League declared war, then Sparta levied the League army and provided its commander-in-chief

As we have seen, the Peloponnesian League states formed the bedrock of the Hellenic League. However, Athens had also played a critical role in the victory over the Persians, in particular through its supply of ships to the Greek navy. Thucydides cites growing Athenian power as a cause for concern for Sparta's Peloponnesian allies, while it seems that the Spartans too did not want a rival to emerge within the Greek world.

The story of Themistocles' trickery of the Spartans over the rebuilding of Athens' walls in 478 (1.90–91 **PS**) is borne out by archaeology, which indicates that city walls were indeed hastily built at that time. A further key point made by Thucydides is that Themistocles urged the Athenians to complete the building programme at Piraeus which

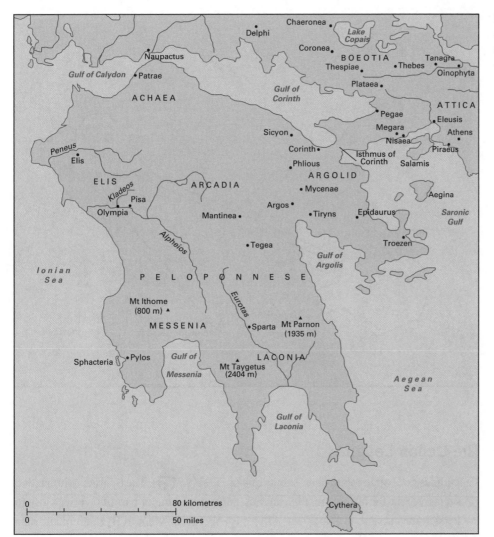

FIGURE 1.7
A map of the Peloponnese
and southern Greece.

he had first instigated during his year as eponymous **archōn** (493/2 – the eponymous archōn was the chief magistrate at Athens). One can see great foresight and planning here. The city of Athens lay about five miles from its harbour at Piraeus, and Themistocles saw that Piraeus itself needed to be fortified and protected so that the Athenians could always retain access to the sea. Thucydides later tells us (1.107) that in about 458 the Athenians built the **Long Walls** down to both Piraeus and Phaleron, its old harbour. These defensive walls allowed the city of Athens to have guaranteed access to its ports, and therefore imports of food and other goods, even in times of war.

According to Thucydides, the seeds for the future conflict between Athens and Sparta were sown when the Spartans' learnt that the Athenians had rebuilt their walls:

> . . . the Spartans showed no open signs of displeasure towards Athens . . . All the same the Spartans had not got their own way and secretly they felt aggrieved because of it.

> Thucydides, *The History of the Peloponnesian War* 1.92

archōn a magistrate
responsible for a key area
of Athenian government
each year

Long Walls defensive
walls which joined Athens
to Piraeus and Phaleron

PS

FIGURE 1.8
The Long Walls which joined
Athens to both Piraeus and
Phaleron.

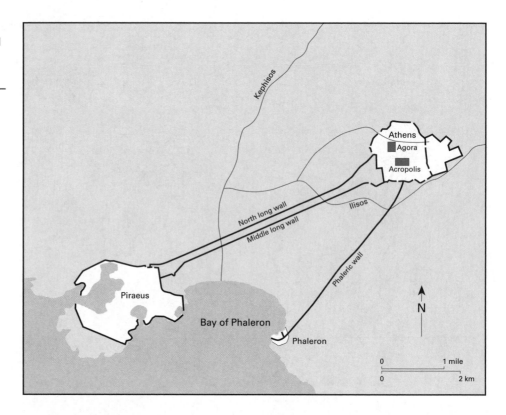

EXPLORE FURTHER

To find out more about
the downfall of
Pausanias, read
Thucydides 1.128–134.

KEY INDIVIDUALS

Aristeides
Dates: died *c.* 460

Aristocratic Athenian
famous for his fairness
who organised the
amount of tribute each
city paid to the Delian
League

Cimon
Dates: *c.* 510–450

Aristocratic Athenian, the
son of Miltiades, who
was the military
commander of the Delian
League in its early years

The Delian League

Thucydides goes on to relate other events of 478 (1.94–95 **PS**). The Spartan commander,
Pausanias, regent for his cousin, Pleistarchus, subdued the major part of Cyprus, close to
the Persian naval bases in Phoenicia. After this success, he went to Byzantium and also
completed a victory. However, the Ionians resented the arrogant way in which he was
treating them and so asked the Athenians to take the command. A number of sources
speak of Pausanias' arrogance and treachery at this time, and it is clear at least that he
was unpalatable to the other Greeks. However, given Thucydides' comments about the
Spartan annoyance with Athens mentioned above, it is mysterious that the Spartans were
apparently so content to allow the Athenians to take over the leadership of the anti-
Persian alliance.

Plutarch gives more details about how the Greek allies fell out with Pausanias (*Life of
Aristeides* 23 **PS**). Here, two Athenians come to the fore. One is Aristeides, the subject
of the biography, and the other Cimon. Both were aristocratic Athenians with conservative
views. Aristeides was famous for his fairness, and would become a key figure in the
establishment of the new alliance. Cimon had great pedigree as the son of Miltiades, the
hero of Marathon in 490. He would emerge as the military commander of the new
alliance in its early years. It is also worth commenting that Chios, Lesbos and Samos are
named as key instigators of the plot to rid Pausanias of the command. These islands of
the eastern Aegean had significant navies and would continue to provide ships to the
alliance for many decades.

The formation of the **Delian League** itself is described by Thucydides at 1.96–97 **PS**. It should be noted that the term 'Delian League' is a name given to the alliance by modern historians. In the ancient sources, there does not seem to have been a particular name given to it. The League first met in the spring of 477 at Delos, the small island sacred as the birthplace of the gods Apollo and Artemis. It was the major sanctuary of the Cyclades and had a long history of receiving valuable dedications from Greek states. It also had the advantage of being relatively central to the southern Aegean, around which the allied states were situated.

Delian League the modern name for the naval alliance established by the Athenians and their allies in 477

The initial task was to assess which cities would provide ships and which would provide money for the upkeep of the navy, something which was very expensive (such money is usually referred to as 'tribute'). Thucydides claims that the stated purpose of the formation of the League was as follows:

> . . . to compensate themselves for their losses by ravaging the territory of the King of Persia.

Thucydides, *The History of the Peloponnesian War* 1.96

There is much debate about the true motives of the Athenians in forming the alliance. One interpretation is that while the Athenians declared that their intention was to take revenge on the Persians, the hidden agenda was to build a naval empire. Another interpretation suggests that the original intention really was to take revenge on the Persians, but that this intention changed as time went on and the Athenians grew more powerful.

Thucydides gives some information about the structure of the League. The treasury was set at Delos but the Athenians elected representatives from their own citizen body to manage it. The figure of 460 talents has long been controversial, since this is more than Athens is known to have been collecting in the late 450s, when there were more members of the alliance. Also unclear is the nature of the alliance at this point. The two most likely scenarios are either that each city had one vote each as had happened in the Hellenic League, or the Athenians formed one voting block and the allies another, following the example of the Peloponnesian League.

Diodorus (11.46–47 **PS**) and Plutarch (*Aristeides* 24.1–5 **PS**) both give more information about Aristeides' role. Diodorus' figure of 560 talents is an example of where his facts can be discounted when set against the earlier record of Thucydides. However, the account of Aristeides' fairness in both authors is borne out by inscriptional evidence: the tribute figures, which first appear from 453, show that cities did contribute according to their size and ability to pay.

Study question
Compare the accounts of Diodorus and Plutarch mentioned here. How plausible does Plutarch's description of Aristeides sound in comparison to that of Diodorus?

Diodorus (11.50 **PS**) has a story which suggests that the Spartans were soon alarmed about Athens' new status. Scholars are divided on the reliability of this source, which seems to contradict Thucydides' comment that the Spartans were content to leave the leadership of the alliance to Athens. However, there is a way of reading these sources so that they do not contradict. The Diodorus passage speaks of pro-peace and pro-war factions in Sparta, which certainly existed later in the century. If the pro-peace faction did indeed prevail as Diodorus suggests, then it may just be that Thucydides did not acknowledge the presence of dissenting views in Sparta at 1.95 **PS**.

Thucydides' narrative at 1.97–101 **PS** outlines the achievements of the League in its early years. It acted vigorously and successfully against Persia: all Persian garrisons but one were driven out of the northern Aegean; piracy was suppressed; and the Greeks extended their control down to the south-west of Asia Minor. The greatest triumph came in the early 460s with a remarkable victory at the mouth of the River Eurymedon in southern Asia Minor. Under the leadership of Cimon, the Greeks destroyed a Persian fleet and then routed the accompanying Persian army. After this, the Persians did not campaign again in the Aegean again for many decades. Xerxes died soon afterwards in 465 and his successor Artaxerxes seems to have changed policy towards the Greeks.

It would be interesting to know how influential the Battle of Eurymedon was for this change in Persian policy, but it remains a frustrating mystery. It gets only a brief mention in Thucydides, Diodorus' account of it has been shown to be very unreliable, while Plutarch's seems more reliable but is clearly too fulsome in its praise of Cimon. The lead in to Plutarch's account of Eurymedon is given in the *Life of Cimon* 12.1–4 **PS**, where Cimon is presented as the great foe and humbler of the Persian king. This portrayal seems unrealistically praising of Cimon, and we should therefore be cautious about believing that Cimon really was the only Athenian general who treated the allies well, as Plutarch claims at *Cimon* 11 **PS**.

What does seem true, however, is what is echoed from Thucydides 1.98 **PS** – that the rule of the Athenians in the Delian League became oppressive towards those who wished to leave the alliance. Thucydides' first statement about Athenian oppression relates to the treatment of Naxos after it had tried to secede from the League in about 470:

> This was the first case when the original constitution of the League was broken and an allied city lost its independence, and the process was continued in the cases of the other allies as various circumstances arose.
>
> Thucydides, *The History of the Peloponnesian War* 1.98

Both Thucydides and Plutarch ascribe some blame to the allied cities, suggesting that they were content to allow the Athenians to do their fighting for them. However, the first evidence of Athenian coercion had already come in 472, when the Euboean town of Carystus was forced to join the League.

Thucydides then goes on to mention the revolt of the wealthy island of Thasos in 465 following Athenian interference in its valuable trade markets and a mine it controlled in nearby Thrace. He claims that the Thasians appealed to the Spartans for help, and that they were about to give it when their attentions were diverted by a terrible earthquake at home. Thucydides obviously believed that the Spartans were indeed set upon attacking Athens, although we have no way of establishing if this was true. It has aroused scepticism among some scholars, who place it in the same category as the story of the Spartan debate mentioned by Diodorus: a possible later Spartan invention to explain their inaction against Athens.

Indeed, Sparta and Athens did not break their alliance until 461, and before that Sparta had even asked Athens for military assistance with its helot revolt. Moreover, Cimon was known to favour a policy of co-operation with Sparta, and of dividing the leadership of the Greek world between the two cities. However, it is also true that relations between

Athens and Sparta did break down just a few years after the Athenian interference at Thasos.

THE FIRST PELOPONNESIAN WAR

The first open quarrel between the two cities came as a result of a terrible earthquake which struck Sparta in about 465 and a helot revolt which followed it (you can read more about the role of the helots in Sparta on pp. 95–101). Thucydides describes it in some detail in 1.101–103 **PS**. The subsequent dismissal of the Athenian troops by the Spartans produced a dramatic response in Athens: anti-Spartan views now hardened and foreign policy changed dramatically. The Athenians denounced the treaty of alliance they had made with Sparta through the Hellenic League in 481, and instead formed an alliance with Sparta's great Peloponnesian rival, Argos, as well as with the region of Thessaly in the north of Greece, with which Sparta had been at war in the 470s. In about 461, the pro-Spartan Cimon was ostracised from Athens for ten years (see pp. 154–6 to read about ostracism).

At around the same time, two allies of Sparta, Corinth and Megara, entered into a border war (1.103 **PS**). When the Megarians were faced with defeat, they seceded from the Peloponnesian League and instead allied themselves with Athens, their eastern neighbour. This was a significant coup for the Athenians, since the location of Megara provided them with a buffer against an attack by Peloponnesian land forces. This new alliance meant that members of the two Leagues, Corinth and Megara, were at war with one another for the first time. Crucially, it also set Athens and Corinth against one another, as Thucydides observes:

> It was chiefly because of this that the Corinthians began to conceive such a bitter hatred for Athens.
>
> Thucydides, *The History of the Peloponnesian War* 1.103

The enmity between these two peoples would be central to the outbreak of the Peloponnesian War in 431. Over the next fifteen years or so a series of conflicts was played out between members on each side – these are sometimes referred to collectively as the First Peloponnesian War, described by Thucydides at 1.105–108 **PS**. Both Athens and Sparta were involved in the fighting at times. The Athenians were particularly harsh against their long-term rival Aegina, an important trading hub in the Saronic Gulf. Although the Athenians were generally successful against the Corinthians, the Athenians felt threatened enough to build the Long Walls in about 458.

In 457 Athens marched out with some allies to meet a Spartan-led force at Tanagra in Boeotia – this was the first battle of the war where the Athenians and Spartans fought directly against one another. Although the Spartan-led forces won, the success was short-lived. The Athenians soon returned to Boeotia and won a comprehensive victory over the local peoples at Oinophyta. As a result, for the next ten years or so, Athens controlled a wide area of central Greece: Phocis, Eastern Locris and the whole of Boeotia except for Thebes. In the same year, the Athenians forced the Aeginetans to join the Delian League. This was the greatest extent of land that the Athenians would ever control.

KEY EVENTS

First Peloponnesian War
Date: between 460 and 446

A set of conflicts between members of the Delian and Peloponnesian Leagues

Battle of Tanagra
Date: 457

A battle in Boeotia which was the first battle in the first Peloponnesian War in which Athenian and Spartan forces fought one another

ACTIVITY

Draw up a chart indicating the changing alliances in the Greek world between 478 and 450.

War on two fronts

In 460, just as the alliances in the Greek world were changing, the Delian League expanded its operations against the Persians by sending troops to Persian-controlled Egypt in support of a rebellion by Inaros, a Libyan prince (Thucydides 1.104 **PS**). It is easy to see why the Athenians had their eyes on a foothold in Egypt: potential trade links, the weakening of Persian power in the Mediterranean, and access to the rich grain supply of the Nile valley. The Athenian-led Greeks campaigned there for six years, initially with great success, but in 454 the Persians sent a task force to face the rebels and routed them (1.109–110 **PS**). The Athenians lost most of their fleet of 250 ships and withdrew their forces from the region.

This defeat was probably a major factor in the Athenian decision to relocate the treasury of the Delian League to Athens in 454/3 (Diodorus 12.38.2 **PS**). At this moment, all pretence of the Delian League being an alliance of equals was cast off. From this year onwards there appear **Tribute Quota Lists** in Athens – annual inscriptions on stone giving 1/60 of the tribute offered by each city to be dedicated to the treasury of Athena. Since the lists give a breakdown of what each city paid as tribute, they provide vital historical evidence. The first fifteen lists were recorded on all four sides of a huge stone pillar, 3.5 metres in height, known today as the **First Stēlē**. The next eight lists were recorded on another, smaller pillar, and after that lists seem to have been inscribed on separate blocks of stone.

Pericles had now emerged as a key military and political leader in the city. The Athenians continued to wage wars against Peloponnesian cities, but in 451 they made a five-year peace with the Peloponnesians (1.111–112 **PS**). This allowed them to launch a campaign on Cyprus under the leadership of Cimon, now back in Athens after his ostracism. Cimon died in the resulting conflict, but the Greeks managed to win on land and sea (1.112 **PS**). However, Thucydides gives scant details of this very significant campaign. Diodorus (12.2.1–2 **PS** and 12.4.4–6 **PS**) claims that these Athenian successes forced the Persians into proposing a peace treaty to the Athenians. He records that the Athenians sent a delegation under a man named Callias to negotiate the terms of

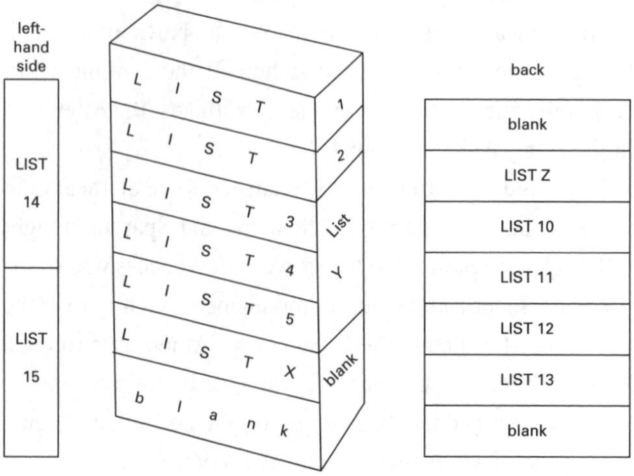

Tribute Quota Lists annual lists inscribed on stone giving 1/60 of the contributions of allied cities into the Delian League. Each 1/60 was offered as a dedication to Athena

---

First Stēlē the huge pillar on which the first fifteen Tribute Quota Lists were inscribed

---

KEY INDIVIDUAL

Pericles
Dates: *c.* 495–429

The dominant figure in Athenian politics from the 450s until his death in 429. He was elected general 15 years in a row between 443 and 429.

FIGURE 1.9
A drawing of the First Stēlē.

the peace in 450 or 449, and so it has become known as the Peace of Callias. According to Diodorus, the main terms of the peace were as follows:

- all the Greek cities were to live under laws of their own making
- the satraps of the Persians were not to come nearer to the sea than a three days' journey and no Persian warship was to sail inside of Phaselis (see Figure 1.1 on p. 5) or the Cyanean Rocks (near Byzantium at the entrance to the Black Sea)
- if these terms were observed by the Persian king and his generals, the Athenians were not to invade Persian territory

There is much scholarly debate about the authenticity of this treaty. Indeed, this debate began in the fourth century, when the peace was denounced as a forgery by the historian Theopompus of Chios (Harpokration, s.v. *Attikois grammasin* (PS)), who believed that it had been invented to exaggerate the achievements of the Athenians in the light of their reduced status at that time. Moreover, Plutarch (*Cimon* 13.4–5 (PS)) places the peace to the aftermath of the battle of Eurymedon in the early 460s.

PRESCRIBED SOURCE

Harpokration, s.v. *Attikois grammasin*

Author: Harpokration, a commentator working on the history of Theopompus

Dates: Theopompus: *c.* 380–315; Harpokration: second century AD

Genre: history

Relevance: a reference to a comment in a fourth century work of history denouncing the Peace of Callias as a forgery

Read it here: LACTOR 1: *The Athenian Empire* (4th edn, KCL, 2000) 54

Those who believe that Theopompus was correct point to the fact that Thucydides makes no mention of the peace. Yet such a peace would have been highly relevant to his account of the Pentecontaetia, since it would have caused the allied cities to believe that they had no need to continue to contribute to the Delian League. Moreover, there are no fifth-century sources which mention the Peace, although Herodotus does refer to Callias having discussions in Susa with the Persians in *c.* 461 (7.151 (PS)). Unless more evidence comes to light, it will be impossible to resolve the issue of the Peace of Callias. However, a central and uncontested point is that all hostilities with Persia came to an end at this time, whether formally or through a more informal understanding. It must therefore have been in the interests of both sides to come to an agreement of some sort.

The cessation of hostilities certainly did not see the break-up of the Delian League. By 450, only Chios, Samos and Lesbos were providing ships for the League's navy besides

KEY EVENT

Peace of Callias
Date: *c.* 449

A supposed peace treaty between the Delian League and the Persian Empire. Its authenticity has been debated since the fourth century

Title: *Politics* 1284a38

Author: Aristotle

Dates: 384–322

Genre: political theory

Relevance: a comment by Aristotle on Athens' harsh treatment of Chios, Samos and Lesbos during the years of its empire

Read it here: LACTOR 1: *The Athenian Empire* (4th edn, KCL, 2000) 84

Chalkis Decree

Date: most likely 446/5

Significance: a decree passed by the Athenian assembly which illustrates that the Athenians now required its allies to obey their commands

Read it here: LACTOR 1: *The Athenian Empire* (4th edn, KCL, 2000) 78

Athens. The fourth century philosopher Aristotle (*Politics* 1284a38 (PS)) reflects that the Athenians would go on to humble even these three island states. Evidence from the Tribute Quota Lists suggests that the Athenians did now see the League as their empire. Whereas in the early tribute lists, the League was described as 'the Athenian alliance', by the middle of the 440s the language had changed so that it is made clear that the cities owed their allegiance to Athens. The Chalkis Decree (PS), made between the Athenians and the people of Chalkis on the island of Euboea probably in about 446, is one such example:

> The Chalcidians are to swear an oath on the following terms: 'I will not revolt from the people of the Athenians by any means or device whatsoever, neither in word nor in deed. . . and I will obey the Athenian people.'
>
> IG, 1³ 40, LACTOR 1, 78

Elsewhere in this decree, there is a clause restricting the power of local courts – thereafter, important legal cases were transferred to Athens, something which happened in other cities too.

Thucydides continues with an account of the early years of the 440s (1.112–114 (PS)). Despite the supposed peace in the Greek world, conflict flared up in 448 over control of the sanctuary at Delphi. The following year, the Athenians sent troops to put down a revolt in Boeotia, but they were ultimately defeated at Coronea and the Boeotians regained their independence.

The year 446 was crucial in the development of relations. When Euboea revolted from Athens, Pericles took a force there, but he had to return to deal with a crisis closer to home. Megara too had rebelled against the Athenians, reversing their defection of 460 by inviting the Peloponnesians – including the Corinthians – to help them. A Spartan-led Peloponnesian force, under the command of the Spartan king Pleistoanax, invaded the western part of Attica but soon withdrew again. Later in Thucydides' work we learn that the king was exiled by the Spartans for having taken a bribe to withdraw his troops (5.16 (PS)), while Plutarch (*Pericles* 23.1–2 (PS)) reports a story suggesting that it was Pericles who paid this bribe. Once the Peloponnesians had retreated, Pericles returned to Euboea and regained control of the island for the Athenians.

TIMESPAN REVIEW

- Discuss whether Athens and Sparta were clearly set on a collision course after the Persian Wars.
- Explain the role played by Greek states other than Athens and Sparta in the development of relations between the Greeks during this period.
- Assess the level of threat the Persians presented to the Greeks between 478 and 449.
- Compare the strength and weaknesses of the sources for this period.

Further Reading

Buckley, T., *Aspects of Greek History* (2nd edn; Abingdon: Routledge, 2010).

Cawkwell, G., *The Greek Wars* (Oxford: Oxford University Press, 2006), chapter 6.

Hornblower, S., *The Greek World: 479–323* (Abingdon: Routledge, 2011, 4th ed.), chapters 2 and 3.

Kuhrt, A., *The Persian Empire* (Abingdon: Routledge, 2007).

Rhodes, P.J., *A History of the Classical Greek World: 478–323* (Oxford: Blackwell, 2006).

Powell, A., *Athens and Sparta: Constructing Greek Political and Social History* (3rd edn; (Abingdon: Routledge, 2016), chapters 1–4.

PRACTICE QUESTIONS

AS Level

1. Read Thucydides 1.91.1–1.91.4 and answer the following question:

   'Relations between Athens and Sparta were doomed from the moment that the Persians were defeated in 479'.

   On the basis of this passage, and the other sources you have studied, how far do you agree with this view? [20]

A Level

1. 'Relations between Athens and Sparta were doomed from the moment that the Persians were defeated in 479'.

   How far do you agree with this view? You must use and analyse the ancient sources you have studied as well as your own knowledge to support your answer. [30]

1.3 Peace and Conflict, 446–431 BC

TIMESPAN OVERVIEW

- the Peace of 446 BC; the balance of power outlined in the Peace of 446 BC and the relations between Athens and Sparta
- the role of Corinth and Sparta in the revolt of Samos
- the events leading up to, and the causes of, the outbreak of war in 431 BC

The prescribed sources for this timespan are:

- Aristophanes, *Acharnians* 524–539
- Plutarch, *Pericles* 23.1–2; 28.1–3; 30–31
- Thucydides, *History of the Peloponnesian War* 1.23; 1.33; 1.35; 1.40–1.41; 1.44, 1.55–1.58; 1.60–1.61; 1.66–1.69; 1.75–1.77; 1.86–88; 1.103; 1.115–1.118, 1.121–1.122; 1.139–1.140, 5.14; 7.18

- Chalkis Decree

This timespan will first examine the peace made between Athens and Sparta in 446. It will then focus on how conflict arose again within a few years, at Samos in 440, at Epidamnus-Corcyra in 435–433, and at Potidaea in 432. These conflicts led to the outbreak of the full-scale Peloponnesian War itself. The timespan will also examine the academic debate about the causes of this war.

THE PEACE OF 446 BC, THE BALANCE OF POWER OUTLINED IN THE PEACE OF 446 BC AND THE RELATIONS BETWEEN ATHENS AND SPARTA

In 446 Euboea and Megara both revolted from Athens. The Spartan king Pleistoanax also led an army into Attica, but he only just crossed the border before returning home. Megara was lost, but Pericles subdued the Euboean revolt. Soon after, the Athenians and Spartans made a 30 Year Peace. Thucydides (1.115 PS) describes these events in the Pentecontaetia and is characteristically brief. The terms of the peace, drawn from various references in Thucydides, were as follows:

1. It was to last 30 years (1.115 **PS**).
2. Athens was to give up Nisaea and Pegae, the harbours traditionally belonging to Megara (see Figure 1.7 on p. 25), together with Troezen and Achaea in the Peloponnese (1.115 **PS**).
3. Each side was to keep the allies it possessed at the conclusion of the treaty (1.140 **PS**).
4. If an ally revolted and joined the other alliance, the treaty was broken (1.35 **PS**).
5. A list of the allies on each side was annexed to the treaty (inferred from 1.40 **PS**).
6. Any neutral state not listed could ally itself with either side (1.35 **PS**, 1.40 **PS**).
7. Argos was specifically excluded from the treaty, but was permitted to be at peace with Athens. It was already at peace with Sparta because of the thirty-year truce established in 451–450 (5.14 **PS**).
8. Neither side was to make an armed attack on the other if either wished to go to arbitration (1.140 **PS**, 7.18 **PS**).
9. There may have been a clause pertaining to Aegina because of a later complaint that they were wronged by a treaty. However, it is unclear if this refers to the 30 Year Peace or another treaty with Athens (1.67 **PS**).

> **KEY EVENT**
>
> **The 30 Year Peace**
> **Date:** 446
>
> A peace agreement between Athens and Sparta in which rules were drawn up for relations between each League

This peace was comprehensive and well thought out. In view of subsequent conflict, it might be seen as overly ambitious, yet at the time it was conciliatory. It clearly defined areas of interest. Sparta acknowledged Athenian domination of the Aegean, its superior status as a naval power and its control of the trade routes. It also acknowledged the, by this time, imperial nature of Athens' **hegemony** over its allies. The clause that prevented states changing allegiance would prevent a defection such as Megara's in 460 that had started the First Peloponnesian War. The clause requiring arbitration in future disputes seemed genuinely to look for a way of avoiding further warfare. The treaty was a compromise, but an intelligent one. However, internal disagreements at Sparta and the calls of Peloponnesian allies, most frequently Corinth, brought pressure to bear on the peace and ultimately caused it to fail.

> **hegemon**, **hegemony** the Greek terms for leader and leadership, particularly in a political or military sense

The primary source for the conflict in the later fifth century is Thucydides' *History of the Peloponnesian War*. Thucydides lived through the whole war and served as an Athenian general in 424, and so his is a first-hand account. Thucydides was very influential on subsequent historical writing, not least because of his claim to truthfulness:

> And with regard to my factual reporting of events of the war I have made it a principle not to write down the first story that came my way, and not even to be guided by my own general impressions; either I was present myself at the events which I have described or else I heard of them from eye-witnesses whose reports I have checked with as much thoroughness as possible. Not that even so the truth was easy to discover: different eye-witnesses give different accounts of the same events, speaking out of partiality for one side or the other or else from imperfect memories.
>
> Thucydides, *The History of the Peloponnesian War* 1.22

PRESCRIBED SOURCE

Author: Thucydides

Title: *The History of the Peloponnesian War*

Produced: *c.* 430–400 BC

Genre: historical monograph

Relevance: a comprehensive history of the war that engulfed Thucydides' own generation. He calculated that the war lasted from 431 to 404, although his own narrative breaks off in 411

Prescribed sections: 1.23; 1.33; 1.35; 1.40–1.41; 1.44; 1.55–1.58; 1.60–1.61; 1.66–1.69; 1.75–1.77; 1.86–88; 1.89–1.118; 1.121–1.122; 1.139–1.140

2.8; 2.11; 2.13; 2.63; 2.65

4.19–4.20; 4.40–41; 4.50; 4.80–81; 4.108; 4.117

5.13–18; 5.25–26; 5.43

6.8; 6.12–13; 6.15; 6.24; 6.31; 6.82–83; 6.89–91

7.18; 7.27–28

8.2; 8.6; 8.9; 8.17–8.18; 8.29; 8.37; 8.52; 8.87

Read it here: Thucydides, *The History of the Peloponnesian War*, tran. Rex Warner (Penguin 1972)

Thucydides' claim to veracity set the standard that subsequent historians sought to emulate. According to the constraints of the day, he sought to investigate matters thoroughly before writing. Yet in 1.22 he also reports how he dealt with speeches: without accurate transcripts of the texts, and with fading memories, he tried to reproduce the gist of the speech if not the actual words. This would, of course, be unacceptable today. However, it is possible to see a dramatic truth behind the words recorded in the speeches.

Thucydides was writing within the spirit of **Greek rationalism** that sought to find scientific explanations for the way the world worked, and for man's place in it. He intended his work to be useful to future generations in understanding the role of human nature in conflict and society. The gods, superstition and oracles have no place in his history. His work is scientific and humane. He claims, not without some arrogance, that his was a 'work for all time'. Nevertheless, Thucydides is not without fault. In dwelling on certain events he is selective; for example, relations with Persia are brushed over in the Pentecontaetia. He rarely gives alternative views: the history that we receive is Thucydides' history.

Greek rationalism a modern term used to describe the movement in the sixth and fifth century Greek world which sought to find scientific explanations, based on reason, for the way the world worked

As we have seen, fighting between Peloponnesian and Athenian forces had lasted between *c.* 461 and 446, and it would continue during the so-called Corinthian War of 395–387. Because of this and because of a pause in hostilities between 421 and 413, the Peloponnesian War of 431–404 is seen by some as Thucydides' own invention. Moreover, he is clearly biased towards certain individuals: Pericles is depicted as Athens' greatest ever asset, while Nicias also receives praise despite his failings in Sicily. Both were, like Thucydides, aristocratic. On the other hand, the non-aristocratic Cleon is depicted as base and dishonourable. Therefore, Thucydides' work cannot be accepted without caution. Moreover, he died with it incomplete and parts were clearly left unedited.

Beyond Thucydides, Plutarch certainly followed his work, but does on occasion add greater detail. The comedies of Aristophanes and inscriptions can also illuminate the period further.

THE ROLE OF CORINTH AND SPARTA IN THE REVOLT OF SAMOS

Six years into the 30 Year Peace in 440, Athens' allies Samos and Miletus were at war. Samos was the more powerful state, being one of the three remaining ship-providing allies. Miletus sought Athenian intervention, which resulted in Athens replacing Samos' oligarchy with a democracy and leaving behind a garrison (see p. 159 to read more about the Athenian policy of promoting democracies in place of oligarchies). The Samian oligarchs turned to the Persian satrap of Lydia, Pissuthnes, and with his help ejected the Athenian garrison. There followed a naval encounter and two sieges. Nine months later the Samians surrendered, handed over their fleet and were instead required to pay tribute to Athens from then on (Thucydides 1.115–117 **PS**; Plutarch, *Pericles* 28.1–3 **PS**). This is the last event in Thucydides' Pentecontaetia.

That an Athenian ally had enlisted Persian help to revolt is not at all remarkable. This sort of thing had happened before among Athens' allies. Certainly, the Persian satraps had not gone away and were always willing to try and reassert their authority. Why this event is noteworthy arises elsewhere in Thucydides (1.40 **PS**). Here the Athenians debated forming an alliance with Corcyra, which was then a neutral state, and received a Corinthian delegation which sought to dissuade them from doing so. Part of the Corinthian argument hinged on the fact that when Samos had revolted from Athens in 440, the Peloponnesian League had debated going to the aid of Samos. Corinth had sided with those who said Athens had the right to control their own allies as they saw fit. This opinion won the argument and there was no Peloponnesian intervention.

Given the bi-cameral nature of the Peloponnesian League described on page 24, if Sparta's allies were debating whether to go to war, the Spartans must already have voted to do so. Therefore, in 440, just six years after the 30 Year Peace had been agreed, there was sufficient feeling at Sparta to renew hostilities with Athens. Yet, because of the bi-cameral voting system, the Peloponnesian League did not do so and the Athenians were free to deal with Samos as they saw fit.

EXPLORE FURTHER

To learn more about Thucydides' methodology and utility, read the following:

Buckley. T., *Aspects of Greek History* (Routledge), chapter 1, pp. 21–8.
Kagan. D., *Thucydides: The Reinvention of History* (Penguin), Introduction and chapter 1
Woodman. A.J., *Rhetoric in Classical Historiography* (Routledge), chapter 1.

S & C With reference to the modern writers who consider Thucydides' methodology, how far was Thucydides a revisionist?

Study question
With reference to the sources, how did Corinth's attitude to Athens change over time?

THE EVENTS LEADING UP TO, AND THE CAUSES OF, WAR IN 431 BC

> As to the reasons why they broke the truce, I propose first to give an account of the causes of complaint which they had against each other and of the specific instances where their interests clashed: . . . But the real reason for the war is, in my opinion, most likely to be disguised by such an argument. What made war inevitable was the growth of Athenian power and the fear which this caused in Sparta.

> Thucydides, *The History of the Peloponnesian War* 1.23

Thucydides was in no doubt as to the reason for war: Spartan fear of growing Athenian power. The idea is repeated in two further chapters that frame the Pentecontaetia (Thucydides 1.88 **PS**, 1.118 **PS**). After making this statement he goes on to explain two causes of complaint: the events at Epidamnus-Corcyra and those at Potidaea. He also alludes to two other complaints concerning Megara and Aegina. It is Thucydides' own certainty about the cause of the war and the distinction between the 'complaints' and the 'real reason' above, together with the relative space he gives over to each of the complaints, that has led to debate among modern historians as to the causes of the war.

A complaint attested: Epidamnus-Corcyra

colony A city founded by settlers from another city. Many colonies retained close links with their 'mother city'.

Epidamnus lay high on the north-western Adriatic coast of Greece (see Figure 1.10). It was a **colony** of Corcyra (in other words, it had originally been founded by Corcyraean settlers), an island further to the south (today known as Corfu), which itself was a colony of Corinth. In 435, a local conflict in Epidamnus led to the democratic party there asking for help first from Corcyra. When this was not forthcoming, a request was sent to Corinth. The Corinthians felt that Corcyra did not show them sufficient respect and were therefore happy to interfere. It is notable that Corinth was an oligarchic state, but was still prepared to aid a democratic party at Epidamnus.

There resulted a siege and a naval battle off Leucimme on Corcyra, where the Corcyraeans defeated the Corinthians. Undeterred, the Corinthians prepared for fresh attacks, and in 433 Corcyra appealed to Athens for help. Corcyra was an accomplished naval power, with 120 ships. Since it was a neutral state, it was free to ally with Athens according to the terms of the 30 Year Peace. The Corcyraeans argued that war between the Athenians and the Spartans was inevitable. They therefore suggested that, with their own large navy, they could be a powerful support to the Athenians in a forthcoming conflict. Equally, they pointed out that if they were defeated by Corinth, their ships would become part of the Peloponnesian navy.

The Corinthians also sent an embassy to deter the Athenians from making an alliance. It is at this point that the Corinthians claimed that they had argued against Peloponnesian interference with the revolt of Samos in 440. The Corinthians also argued that the clause in the 30 Year Peace concerning neutral states did not apply if the neutral state sought to

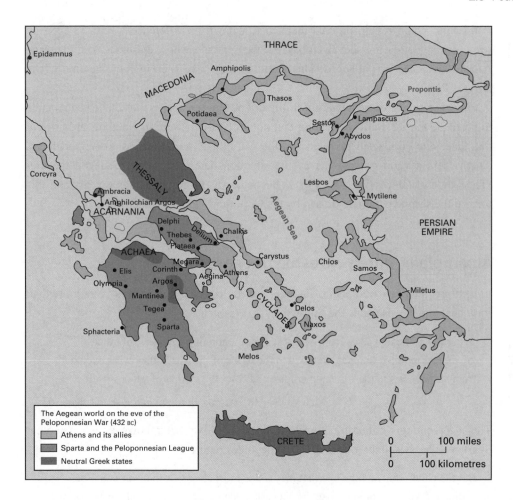

join one side simply to start hostilities (1.40–41 **PS**). Athens decided to ally with Corcyra, but only in a limited defensive manner: they would engage to stop the Corinthians landing on the island of Corcyra, but that was all. This was unusual and possibly aimed at avoiding war. It also meant that the Athenians could claim that the Corinthians had started hostilities if battle was joined (1.44 **PS**). In September 433, the Corinthians did attack the Corcyraeans in a naval encounter at Sybota off Corcyra. When the Corinthians looked to be gaining the upper hand and threatening Corcyra itself, the Athenian ships engaged and turned back the Corinthians. Corcyra was left unharmed, but this was the first complaint (1.55 **PS**).

A complaint attested: Potidaea

Potidaea sat on the isthmus of Pallene in Chalcidice, the three-pronged peninsula on the north coast of the Aegean (see Figure 1.10). It was a subject state of Athens, but also a Corinthian colony, from which it still received annual magistrates (1.56 **PS**). After the events at Epidamnus-Corcyra, Corinth was searching for a means of retaliation. The Corinthians now felt a deep hatred towards Athens that went back to the First Peloponnesian War (1.103 **PS**). As a result, by early 432, Athens, in expectation that the

ephor one of the five Spartan magistrates elected annually (see p. 113)

Potidaeans would revolt, ordered them to tear down their defences (1.56–58 **PS**). In response, the Potidaeans sent an embassy to the Spartans, whose **ephors** agreed to invade Attica if Potidaea was attacked. This would clearly have been in contravention of the 30 Year Peace.

However, the agreement was not fulfilled. The Spartan ephors must have been unable to persuade the assembly, indicating that not all Spartans were inclined towards war at this time. The Potidaeans revolted and the Corinthians sent an army to support them. Athens sent several contingents as the situation deteriorated and besieged the city (Thucydides 1.60–61 **PS**, 1.66 **PS**). The siege was to go on for three years and this formed the second complaint raised by the Corinthians against Athens.

A complaint barely attested: Megara

In contrast to the two complaints just mentioned, to which Thucydides gives more than forty chapters, he also adds the following single sentence:

> In particular the delegates from Megara, after mentioning a number of other grievances, pointed out that, contrary to the terms of the treaty, they were excluded from all the ports in the Athenian empire and from the market of Athens itself.
>
> Thucydides, *The History of the Peloponnesian War* 1.67

This is a seemingly minor issue in Thucydides' narrative. Later, however, when another Spartan embassy sought to avoid war, Thucydides reports:

> But the chief point and the one that they made most clear was that war could be avoided if Athens would revoke the Megarian decree which excluded the Megarians from all ports in the Athenian Empire and from the market in Attica itself.
>
> Thucydides, *The History of the Peloponnesian War* 1.139

The suggestion of revoking the Megarian decree was vigorously opposed by Pericles (Thucydides 1.140 **PS**). The importance of this decree has exercised scholars since antiquity. Plutarch repeats the idea that it was the greatest impediment to peace and, because of Pericles' intransigence, puts the blame for the war on him. He also reports that the formal reason for the decree was that the Megarians had profaned sacred land and had then killed an Athenian envoy sent to complain about this. A decree was therefore passed that the Athenians were to be irreconcilable with the Megarians (Plutarch, *Pericles* 30 **PS**). Plutarch then reiterates:

> It is not easy to discover what the original reason was for the proposal being accepted, but everyone blames Pericles for the fact that it was not overturned.
>
> Plutarch, *Pericles* 31

Having suggested a connection with Pericles' mistress, Aspasia, through Aristophanes' *Acharnians*, Plutarch also suggests that Pericles was seeking to divert attention from the trial of his friend, the sculptor Pheidias, for embezzlement, or from Aspasia and himself for impiety.

FIGURE 1.11
Pericles, shown wearing the helmet of a general.

Plutarch is following a section of Aristophanes' *Acharnians* (524–539 **PS**). This comic play was produced in 425 at the Lenaea drama festival, which was attended by thousands of Athenians. In these lines the main character, Dikaiopolis, jokes that the Peloponnesian War began after some loutish Athenians and Megarians stole prostitutes from each other's cities. The prostitutes stolen from Athens are said to have been pimped by Aspasia, the **metic** (non-Athenian) woman from Miletus who was Pericles' partner. Dikaiopolis claims that this led Pericles to ban the Megarians from the limits of the Athenian Empire. Clearly, it cannot have been the case that the war was started over the thefts of a small number of prostitutes, but it is interesting that Aristophanes links Pericles to the Megarian decree so firmly. Since Aristophanes was a satirist, his jokes could not have had much force if they did not have some basis in truth.

> **metic** a non-Athenian resident of Athens. Metics had no political rights, but were given some legal rights. They had to have an Athenian sponsor and pay a monthly tax

The Megarian decree was clearly an impediment to peace and so one ought to consider why it was established and to what purpose. To kill an envoy was a serious religious offence, and one that might cause complaint, but it was not enough to start a war. The decree may have been a punitive action because Megara changed sides at the end of the

PRESCRIBED SOURCE

Title: *Acharnians*

Author: Aristophanes

Date performed: 425 BC

Genre: comic play

Relevance: highlights
the tension at Athens
between those who
wanted to militarily
oppose the annual
invasion of Attica and
those that wanted
to make peace with
Sparta. The prescribed
sections deal with an
Athenian embassy
to Persia and the
Megarian decree as a
cause of war

Prescribed sections:
61–71; 524–539

Read it here: LACTOR 1:
The Athenian Empire
(4th edn, KCL, 2000)
58, 99

First Peloponnesian War, but this was probably too long after the event. However, eight Megarian ships had sailed with the Corinthian fleet at Leucimme, and twelve at Sybota. Therefore, it may have been a punishment for siding with Corinth, or a deterrent aimed at dissuading other states from aiding Corinth militarily. The motivation remains unclear, be it profaning sacred land, killing an envoy, or joining the Corinthian fleet.

The effect on Megara was probably economic. Although it was not now allied with Athens, Attica remained Megara's chief market. Moreover, the Megarians engaged in sea-borne trade and so were also dependent on the markets of the Athenian empire. Modern historians disagree as to Athens' intention regarding the decree. Was it a provocation to war, as some believe, by economically strangling a member of the Peloponnesian League? Or was it a punitive measure deliberately designed to stay within the terms of the peace of 446 and so to avoid war? This latter view may be supported by a report in Plutarch that Pericles' sent ten talents annually to Sparta, if not to buy peace, at least to prolong it (*Pericles* 23.1–2 **PS**). Another view holds that because a good deal of Megarian trade was in the hands of Megara's metics, then the decree would not have impacted seriously on Megara's citizens. According to this view it was the Spartan envoys that made a bigger deal of the decree than necessary when they stated that it was the chief point obstructing peace (Thucydides 1.139 **PS**).

This still does not answer why Pericles was so obstinate about the Megarian decree. Aristophanes' suggestions may at least reflect public opinion, that Pericles was deliberately diverting attention from attacks against him and his associates. Plutarch's assessment that this made Pericles the man most responsible for war in 431, even if he had earlier sought to avoid it, seems to hold good.

A complaint barely attested: Aegina

Without elaborating, Thucydides reports that the people of Aegina sided with Corinth when they brought their complaints to Sparta because they had been denied their independence in contravention to a treaty (1.67 **PS**). Aegina had been defeated in the First Peloponnesian War in 457 and was subject to Athens. However, the terms of any treaty between Athens and Aegina remain unknown. The importance of Aegina's complaint remains uncertain, but it is generally felt by modern historians to have been less significant than the two complaints Thucydides did report and the Megarian decree.

A complaint unattested: The Ambracian Gulf

ACTIVITY

With reference to the
sources, rate the relative
importance of the
reasons for war for each
state

There was a final irritation to the Corinthians that is not reported by Thucydides as a complaint, but appears later in his narrative at 2.68. Late in the 430s, on the Ambracian Gulf in the west of Greece, there was on a local conflict between three communities: Ambracia, which had Corinthian connections, and Amphilochian Argos together with the Acarnanians. How the dispute unfolded is unimportant; what is important is that the Amphilochians and Acarnanians appealed for, and received, Athenian military help. As with Corcyra, this was another example of Athens dabbling in Corinthian affairs.

The outbreak of war

Thucydides acknowledged that both sides had grievances, without apportioning blame (1.66 **PS**). In 432, the Corinthians urged the Peloponnesian allies who felt wronged by Athens to petition Sparta. Thucydides reproduces a speech made by the Corinthian delegation. Here, rather than dwell on Athens' actions, the Corinthians turned on Sparta as hegemon of the Peloponnesian League for ineffectually standing up to Athenian expansion (1.68–69 **PS**). This is known as the **Corinthian Complaint**:

> When one is deprived of one's liberty one is right in blaming not so much the man who puts the fetters on as the one who had the power to prevent him, but did not use it – especially when such a one rejoices in the glorious reputation of having been the liberator of Hellas. **PS**
>
> Thucydides, *The History of the Peloponnesian War* 1.69

Corinthian Complaint
the speech reported by Thucydides which was made by Corinthian representatives at Sparta in 432 urging war against Athens

An Athenian delegation at Sparta was also allowed to speak. Rather than defend their actions with regard to the complaints, Thucydides gives them a speech that is the first of several defences of imperialism through his work (1.75–77 **PS**). After listening to all parties, the Spartans debated the matter between themselves. King Archidamus II, who would be responsible for prosecuting the war, cautioned against hasty action. His argument rested on Sparta's inability to defeat Athens: they had no navy and no money with which to pay one; neither did they have the resources of empire that Athens possessed. He advised seeking new alliances – Persia was inferred, but also the Athenian allies. If Thucydides is to be believed, he had identified the three things necessary to defeat Athens that would only come about twenty years later: Athens' allies had to be in revolt, the Spartans would need a navy to equal the Athenian navy, and they would need Persian support – if only financially to pay for the navy.

KEY INDIVIDUALS

Archidamus II
Dates: reigned *c.* 476–*c.* 427
King of Sparta who cautioned against war

Sthenelaidas
An ephor in Sparta in 432 who argued strongly in favour of war

Archidamus was opposed by one of the ephors for that year, Sthenelaidas. In a short, sharp nationalistic rant that failed to answer any of Archidamus' valid concerns, he advocated immediate action. His view prevailed and the Spartans voted for war (1.86–88 **PS**). There was then of course a second assembly among the Peloponnesian allies to debate whether to endorse Sparta's vote for war. Here the Corinthians re-iterated their complaints and pointed to the ability of Athens to impact on the economic vitality of other Greek states, as the Megarian decree had done (1.121–122 **PS**). Further Spartan delegations came to Athens; the last delivered a final offer of peace if Athens gave the Greeks their freedom. This would have required the Athenians to renounce their empire from which they derived their wealth through trade, taxation and tribute. It would also have been at odds with the 30 Year Peace, which had acknowledged their right to rule the empire. The Athenians simply could not accept these terms. Pericles strongly opposed them, by this time convinced that Athens could win a war (1.139–140 **PS**).

EXPLORE FURTHER

Read Thucydides 1.75–77 **PS**.
How does the Athenian delegation at Sparta defend its imperialism?

PRESCRIBED DEBATE: THE CAUSES OF THE PELOPONNESIAN WAR IN 431 BC

The 30 Year Peace was a valiant attempt at reasonableness that recognised the relative spheres of influence of both parties. Yet, soon afterwards, both sides were discussing war again, which indicates that there were pro-war parties in both states. Thucydides was in no doubt that it was Spartan fear of Athenian expansion that caused the war. However, were the Spartans at fault for fearing Athens, or were the Athenians at fault for their imperialistic expansion? Here are some of the most common views:

- Some see Athens being at fault because of their expansionist moves into the west that impacted upon Corinth's interests, and also the Megarian decree and Pericles' intransigence at rescinding it. According to this view, these actions pushed Sparta to war to support their allies and preserve their hegemony of the Peloponnesian League.
- Others see Sparta at fault and as actively looking for an excuse to fight because of their fear of Athenian power. They had seemingly voted for war over Samos in 440, and the ephors had agreed to invade Attica if Potidaea revolted. Those who see Sparta at fault argue that they made more of the Megarian decree than was necessary. Moreover, at no point did Sparta submit to arbitration. Later in Thucydides' narrative (7.18 **PS**), the Spartans acknowledge this failure and view their subsequent defeats as things that they had brought upon themselves.

In addition, modern historians dispute the relative importance of the complaints attested as causes of the Peloponnesian War: Epidamnus-Corcyra, Potidaea, Megara, Aegina and the Ambracian Gulf. One particular area of disagreement is whether the Megarian decree was intended to provoke war or to avoid it. The events at Corcyra and the Ambracian Gulf may suggest a desire for westward expansion, but these were only really worrying to Corinth.

Buckley, T., *Aspects of Greek History 750–323* BC (2nd edn; Abingdon: Routledge 2010), chapter 17.
Cawkwell, G., *Thucydides and the Peloponnesian War* (London: Penguin 1997), chapter 2.
Kagan, D., *Thucydides: The Reinvention of History* (New York: Penguin, 2009), chapters 2, 3.
Powell, A., *Athens and Sparta* (Abingdon: Routledge 2016), pp. 113–28.
Tritle, L.A., *A New History of the Peloponnesian War* (Chichester: Wiley-Blackwell, 2010), chapters 1, 2.

TIMESPAN REVIEW

- Analyse the extent to which any party had just cause for war.
- Consider why the 30 Year Peace did not last.
- Assess how influential the Corinthians were in Spartan foreign affairs.
- Make an appraisal of Pericles' responsibility for the outbreak of the Peloponnesian War.

Further Reading

Buckley, T., *Aspects of Greek History 750–323* BC (2nd edn; Abingdon: Routledge 2010), chapters 1 and 17.
Cawkwell, G., *Thucydides and the Peloponnesian War* (London: Penguin, 1997), chapter 2.

Hanson, V.D., *A War Like No Other* (London: Methuen, 2005), chapter 1.

Hornblower, S., *Thucydides* (London: Bloomsbury Academic, 1994).

Hornblower, S., *The Greek World 479–323 BC* (Abingdon: Routledge, 2011), chapter 9.

Kagan, D., *Thucydides: The Reinvention of History* (New York: Penguin, 2009), Introduction, chapters 1–3.

Kagan, D., The Peloponnesian War (New York: Penguin, 2003), chapters 2–4.

Morrison, J.S., J.F. Coates and N.B. Rankov, The Athenian Trireme (Cambridge: Cambridge University Press, 2000), chapter 4.

Powell, A., *Athens and Sparta: Constructing Greek Political and Social History from 478 BC* (3rd edn; Abingdon: Routledge 2016), chapter 4.

de Ste.Croix, G.E.M., *The Origins of the Peloponnesian War* (London: Duckworth, 1972)

Rhodes, P.J., *A History of the Classical Greek World 478–323 BC* (Oxford: Blackwell, 2006), chapters 6 and 8.

Tritle, L.A., *A New History of the Peloponnesian War* (Chichester: Wiley-Blackwell, 2010), chapters 1 and 2.

Woodman, A.J. *Rhetoric in Classical Historiography* (Abingdon: Routledge, 1988), chapter 1.

PRACTICE QUESTIONS

AS Level

1. Read the following sections of prescribed sources: Thucydides, 1.68.1–1.69.1 **PS**; 1.86.1–2 **PS**.

On the basis of these passages and others you have studied, how far was Spartan inaction and conservatism responsible for the outbreak of war in 431? [20]

A Level

1. Read the following passage and answer the question below:

The Megarians, being well aware of Athenian sensitivities over the issue, may have been urged on by the Corinthians to cultivate the sacred land in order to provoke the Athenians into a hostile reaction, and thus give cause for complaint. For these reasons de Ste. Croix believes that the Athenians should be absolved from blame, but the Megarians (to a smaller extent) and the Spartans in particular should be blamed for exploiting the issue and making it a pretext to war.

T. Buckley, *Aspects of Greek History 750–323 BC*, p. 323

How convincing do you find the interpretation of de Ste. Croix (as reported by Buckley) that the Spartans and Megarians exploited the Megarian decree in order to go to war?

You must use your knowledge of the historical period and the ancient sources you have studied to analyse and evaluate the interpretation of de Ste. Croix. [20]

1.4 The Archidamian War, 431–420 BC

TIMESPAN OVERVIEW

- Athenian and Spartan strategies in the Archidamian War 431–421 BC
- the invasions of Attica and their effects on the states, including the plague in Athens
- the course of the Archidamian War: Pylos and Sphacteria and its effects on the Spartan war effort and reputation; Brasidas in Thrace
- differences within Athens and Sparta on the relations between the states and the move towards a peace settlement
- the Peace of Nicias – the main terms and the aftermath: the failures of the peace and the refusals of allies of both Athens and Sparta to support the Peace
- Spartan-Athenian alliance.

The prescribed sources for this timespan are:

- Aristophanes, *Peace* 619–622, 639–648
- Herodotus, *Histories* 6.108
- Thucydides, *History of the Peloponnesian War* 1.23; 1.96; 1.114; 1.139; 2.8; 2.11; 2.13; 2.63; 2.65; 4.19–4.20; 4.40–4.41; 4.80–4.81; 4.108; 4.117; 5.13–5.18; 5.25–26; 6.31; 7.18 and 7.28

- Thoudippos Decree

hoplite a heavily armoured infantry man, armed with breastplate, shield, helmet and spear. Hoplites fought in a phalanx – a dense formation of fighting men.

This timespan will examine the first decade of the Peloponnesian War, often known as the Archidamian War. It will explore how Athens tried to avoid a full **hoplite** battle with Sparta, fearful of Sparta's superiority on land, and relied on sea-power to preserve its empire. It will then focus on the push for peace in the late 420s, which only succeeded in bringing about a temporary pause in hostilities.

ATHENIAN AND SPARTAN STRATEGIES IN THE ARCHIDAMIAN WAR 431–421 BC

The Spartan embassy to Athens had presented an ultimatum that peace was possible if the Athens would free the Greeks. The Athenians, if Thucydides is to be believed, following Pericles' lead, were having none of it. Empire was good for Athens and a war was, in Pericles' view, winnable (Thucydides 1.139 **PS**). As a result, in 431 Archidamus had no option but to commence operations against Athens with a stated policy of liberating the Greeks (2.8 **PS**). The Spartan strategy was predictably simple, to invade Attica and provoke a fight, so there were annual invasions in 431, 430, 428, 427 and 425 (the strategy is discussed at 5.14 **PS** and 7.28 **PS**). The plague and earthquakes prevented invasions in 429 and 426. The conflict between 431 and 421 is often referred to as the Archidamian War, after the king who directed Spartan policy.

Traditional hoplite warfare rested on the assumption that most Greeks (but not the Spartans), were farmers and so if men from a neighbouring state attacked and damaged the crops of a community, then that community would respond by marching out to defend its livelihood (e.g. 2.11 **PS**). In pitched battles, hoplites fought hand-to-hand with shield and spear, and tried hard to maintain a dense but orderly formation. Also present were light infantry, who used missiles and operated in more mobile and fluid groups, which was regarded as a less daring style of fighting. Who the hoplites were, how exactly they fought, and how much more important and effective they really were than light infantry, are questions that continue to be debated (see S&C box below). However, it is clear that by the time of the Peloponnesian War, cavalry and various kinds of light-armed specialists played crucial roles alongside the hoplites. The number of fatalities in a hoplite battle was relatively low, and all the casualties were adult males. It was therefore a very limited form of warfare.

> **S & C**
> One of the most keenly debated issues in ancient Greek history is how a hoplite battle was fought. Ancient texts sometimes speak of a 'push' as the decisive moment. Some take this literally, meaning that the two sides physically threw their weight against each other and tried to shove the enemy back until he broke rank and ran away. Others find this hard to imagine and suggest instead that 'push' is meant figuratively as the moment when one side got the upper hand in hand-to-hand fighting and caused the enemy to run. A related question is just how dense a hoplite 'phalanx' was: did the men stand so close together that their shields touched or even overlapped, or was there space between them to wield their weapons and for rear ranks to come forward when soldiers in the front ranks fell? For these and other problems relating to hoplite warfare, see the contrasting views in Victor Hanson, *The Western Way of War* (1989), Hans van Wees, *Greek Warfare: myths and realities* (2004), Louis Rawlings, *The Ancient Greeks at War* (2007), and the debates in D. Kagan and G. Viggiano, *Men of Bronze* (2013).

Athens' power resided in its navy. Archidamus had apparently recognised this much when the Spartans debated going to war. Thucydides reports that Pericles advocated that Athens treat themselves as an island and trust in the resources of empire, controlling the empire through their navy. The nub of Periclean policy was to avoid hoplite battle with the Spartan army because the Spartans could not be beaten (e.g. 2.65 **PS**). As far as Attica was concerned, Pericles directed the rural population to abandon

KEY EVENT

Archidamian War
Date: 431–421

The modern name for the first decade of the Peloponnesian War, after the Spartan King Archidamus II

their fields, move inside the city for the duration of the invasion, and resist the temptation to defend their land (2.13 **PS**). This policy was not uniformly accepted, and Pericles was forced to defend his policy and Athenian imperialism in general (2.63 **PS**, 2.65 **PS**), and there was certainly unrest at the sight of crops being destroyed.

However, the Spartan army never stayed very long during their incursions. It has been shown that to destroy crops is far from easy, even cereals could only be fired just before harvest. Moreover, Attica was mainly turned over to the cash crops of olives and vines, both of which are almost impossible to destroy. Therefore, any destruction on the part of the Peloponnesian army was probably only done in order to feed themselves. The longest invasion in 430 only lasted forty days, because, apart from the Spartans themselves, the Peloponnesian allies were all farmers who had to return in time to harvest their own crops. Additionally, Pericles insisted that Athens ought not to increase the size of its empire while it waged war (2.65 **PS**). The Periclean strategy was not to defeat the Spartans in battles, but rather to survive the war, to overcome, or to win through. By this policy, avoiding a defeat at the hands of the Spartan army could be considered a victory.

However, Pericles did not advocate inaction. Athens had 13,000 hoplites, a large number for any Greek state, as well as a further 16,000 men in garrisons around the empire and at Athens itself (2.13 **PS**). At its greatest size the Athenian fleet numbered 250 ships. Since triremes are thought to have had crews of 200, this would have meant 50,000 sailors. This was considerably more than the Peloponnesian forces. The Athenians were to make limited responses: guard duties and cavalry action against the invaders, together with naval raids against the Peloponnese; but most of their efforts were focussed on securing the resources of empire in the Aegean. The Spartans only had the Corinthian fleet: despite Archidamus' advice to build a navy, this did not happen until much later. The Peloponnesian War pitted two antithetical states against each other, a land power versus a naval power. Pericles' policy almost worked, except for one unforeseen event: the plague at Athens.

THE COURSE OF THE ARCHIDAMIAN WAR

The first event of the war involved neither Sparta nor, initially, Athens. Thebes, a Peloponnesian ally, knowing that war with Athens was coming and looking to expand its influence in Boeotia, attacked Plataea, an Athenian ally. This was in direct contravention of the 30 Year Peace, something that Sparta reportedly later admitted (Thucydides 7.18 **PS**). Thebes' enmity towards Plataea stretched back to 519, when, rather than join the Boeotian confederacy the Plataeans had aligned with Athens (Herodotus, *Histories* 6.108 **PS** – see page 10). The Thebans succeeded in taking Plataea but were later overpowered and used as human shields. The Athenians helped to garrison the city and a three-year siege followed. Finally the city fell to the Spartans who killed all those who had opposed them. The bulk of the Plataean population had been evacuated by the Athenians and resided for the rest of the war at Athens.

THE INVASIONS OF ATTICA AND THEIR EFFECTS ON THE STATES, INCLUDING THE PLAGUE IN ATHENS

The first annual invasion of Attica by the Spartans had achieved little. Soon after the second invasion in 430, the plague hit Athens. It carried on for two years with a brief resurgence in 426. What the contagion was remains unknown. Thucydides, who suffered from and survived the plague himself, gives an extensive description of its effects at 2.47–55. Whatever it was, it was limited to Attica and Athenian troops elsewhere, and the Peloponnese was unaffected. The effects were worsened by the evacuation of the Attic countryside, since up to 200,000 people were crammed into Athens during the annual Peloponnesian incursions. The heat of summer combined with a lack of water, shelter and sanitation, caused the disease(s) to spread rapidly. However, immunity also spread rapidly through the survivors so that without a steady influx of new victims the plague burnt itself out in a few years.

Even before beginning his narrative, Thucydides had told the reader that the plague did more damage than any other single factor (1.23 **PS**). In total 4,400 out of 13,000 hoplites died. Thucydides claimed that it was impossible to determine how many more of the civilian population died. Estimates of the size of the Attic population vary from 250,000 to 350,000 before the war. If the plague had a 30 per cent mortality rate (as it did with the hoplite soldiers), then the population would have been reduced by about 100,000. These losses must have been a significant setback to Athens.

In 430, the Peloponnesians sent out an embassy to Persia, although its envoys were detained by the prince of Thrace and executed. This suggests that the Peloponnesians were following Archidamus' advice in trying to gain new allies in the Persians. In the second year of the war, Potidaea fell to Athens. The Athenians also operated in western Greece: their general Phormio was hoping to capitalise on the successes in Ambracia and gain allies to the north of the Peloponnese. Phormio blocked the Gulf of Corinth (see Figure 1.7 on p. 25), which led to naval battles at Naupactus where the Peloponnesian fleet, mostly made up of Corinthian ships, was resoundingly defeated. The Athenians had clearly shown their dominance on water which prevented further significant naval encounters for the period of the Archidamian War. Operations in Ambracia continued until a fair peace between the local inhabitants, independent of Athenian or Peloponnesian involvement, was agreed in the winter of 426–425.

In 428, Athens suffered a serious revolt on the part of their allies at Mytilene on the island of Lesbos, who were received into the Peloponnesian League. Mytilene was an important ally and one of only two remaining ship-providing allies (Chios being the other). The Athenians were incensed by the revolt and decided to vote for a motion of Cleon, who is presented as the leading **demagogue** of his day, that the entire population of Mytilene should be put to death. On the day after the vote, there was a change of mood and a second debate, where the decision was rescinded. The speeches in this debate as reproduced by Thucydides are indicative of differing opinions at Athens towards their allies (see p. 160 for more on this debate).

Athens' attitude towards its allies was changing in other ways too because after five years money was running out. The Cleonymos Decree of 426 and the Thoudippos Decree **PS**

Study questions
Consider Thucydides 2.59–65 (2.63 **PS**, 2.65 **PS**).

1 In Thucydides' presentation, how does Pericles defend his policy?
2 How does Thucydides portray Pericles' attitude to empire?
3 What is Thucydides' attitude towards Pericles?
4 What is Thucydides' attitude to those politicians that came after Pericles?

demagogue a politician who encourages and exploits the support of the common man through populist language and measures

ACTIVITY CW

Consider
Thucydides
2.13 PS, 3.17, 6.31 PS.

- How much money did Athens need to wage the war?
- How did Athens survive the first few years of the war?
- Would the increase in tribute in 425 meet the cost?

of 425, each insisted on the tightening up of tribute collections and placed penalties on officials who failed in their duties to exact the tribute. According to the list appended to the Thoudippos Decree, tribute from the allies was increased across the board – the total rising from the 460 talents first levied by Aristeides (Thucydides 1.96 PS) and the 600 talents reported at the start of the war (2.13 PS) to 1460 talents at this time. This figure was aspirational: 400 states are listed here, but there is no indication how many actually paid up. However, the large amount of tribute collected is corroborated by statements in Plutarch's *Aristeides* that tribute was increased to 1,300 talents and Aristophanes' *Wasps* that revenue (i.e. tribute and income) at that time was 2,000 talents. To continue the war, it seems that Athens' allies now paid more.

PRESCRIBED SOURCE

Title: Thoudippos Decree

Date: 425–424

Proposer: Thoudippos

Relevance: an inscription delegating the responsibilities for assessing the size of the allies' tribute onto particular courts and officials at Athens. It further requires an increase in the tribute levied. A list of the assessments made on the allies was attached, totalling 1,460 talents

Read it here: LACTOR 1: *The Athenian Empire* (4th edn, KCL, 2000) 138

Pylos and Sphacteria, and its effects on Spartan war effort and reputation

In 425, the sixth and final invasion of Attica occurred. At the same time, the Athenian general, Demosthenes, fortified a position on the promontory of Pylos in the south-western coast of the Peloponnese (see Figure 1.7). This tactic of building a fort in enemy territory is known as **epiteichismos**. Demosthenes was hoping to incite fresh revolts among the helots living there. The immediate result was that the Spartans withdrew from their annual invasion of Attica after the shortest stay of all of only fifteen days.

Demosthenes was the first to pursue a more aggressive offensive strategy than that proposed by Pericles. Rather than survival he was in favour of taking the war to the enemy, something which did run the risk of battle between Athenian and Spartan hoplites. At Pylos, the Spartans immediately counter-attacked by land and sea. They occupied the island of Sphacteria to the south, hoping to control the entrance to the harbour below the promontory, so that the Athenians would have nowhere safe to shelter. The Athenians had to repel attacks until an Athenian fleet arrived. It secured the harbour and thus isolated the Spartan hoplites on the island.

epiteichismos the action of building a fort on the territory of the enemy. This was successfully employed by the Athenians at Pylos in 425 and by the Spartans at Decelea in 413

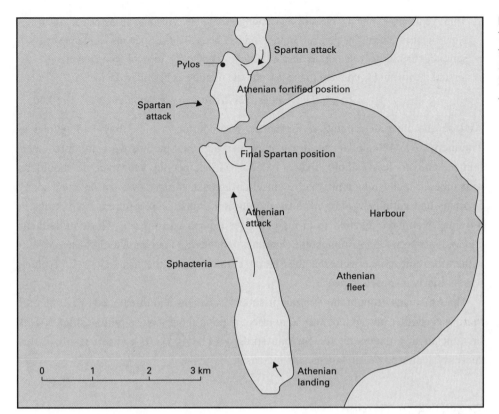

FIGURE 1.12
The engagement between the Athenians and the Spartans at Pylos and Sphacteria in 425.

The Spartans were so concerned by this outcome that they arranged an armistice before sending an embassy to Athens to call for peace (Thucydides 4.19–20 **PS**). At Athens, Cleon incited the assembly to ask for better terms. All the sources treat Cleon as an opportunistic rabble-rouser. However, his mustering of popular support and his belligerent nature would naturally have offended the aristocratic Thucydides and Aristophanes, from whom later sources also derive. Despite their hostile presentation of Cleon, he was evidently popular with the people. He called for a return of those places Athens had given up as part of the terms of the 30 Year Peace: Nisaea, Pegae, Troezen and Achaea. The Spartan embassy could not accommodate such demands and returned empty handed.

Later that year there was a realisation at Athens that they would not be able to continue the blockade through the winter. The Athenians regretted that they had not taken the peace offer. This led to challenges and disagreement between Cleon and the general Nicias. Nicias offered to relinquish his command if Cleon thought that he could do a better job. As a result Cleon claimed that he would take the island within twenty days. This showed no little arrogance given that he had no military experience. The Athenians landed 800 hoplites on the island together with the crews of seventy ships and another 1,600 archers and javelin throwers. The Spartans fell back under sheer weight of numbers to the north end of the island and dug in. Cleon and Demosthenes offered to cease the attack if the Spartans surrendered. This they did, to the great surprise of the rest of the Greeks:

KEY INDIVIDUAL

Cleon
Dates: d. 422
An Athenian politician and general who is presented in the sources as a rabble-rousing demagogue

This event caused much more surprise among the Hellenes than anything else that had happened in the war. The general impression had been that the Spartans would never surrender their arms whether because of hunger or any other form of compulsion; instead they would keep them to the last and die fighting as best they could.

Thucydides, *The History of the Peloponnesian War* 4.40

And so the Spartan reputation for never surrendering, which they had gained at Thermopylae in 480, collapsed. It was now seen that the Spartans were no more super-human, and no less fallible, than any other Greek people. However, it should be remembered that Archidamus had counselled against going to war in 432 and many Spartans had initially voted with him. In addition, Pleistoanax's retreat from Attica in 446 may well have resulted from his being well disposed to peace. These individuals cannot have been alone amongst the Spartans in believing that war should be avoided. It is therefore quite conceivable that the Spartan commander on the ground in 425, Styphon, was similarly disposed to peace.

> **Study question**
> With reference to the sources, why did the annual Peloponnesian invasions of Attica fail to defeat Athens?

The Athenians brought the Spartan prisoners to Athens and threatened to kill them if there was another invasion of Attica, in effect making the prisoners human shields. This brought about a change to the Spartan strategy (4.41 **PS**). As a direct result of this success Cleon's power at Athens was increased.

Brasidas in Thrace

> **KEY INDIVIDUAL**
>
> **Brasidas**
> **Dates:** d. 422
>
> An enterprising Spartan general who led a Spartan campaign to the Thrace-ward region in 424 You can read more about his career on pp. 115–16.

The Athenians continued to look to hem the Spartans into the Peloponnese. Nicias next took the island of Cythera off the south of the Peloponnese (see Figure 1.7). This caused much consternation amongst the Spartans, who accepted that annual invasions of Attica and hoplite phalanxes were not working for them. They felt that they needed a new theatre of war, and a new type of leader. The man they chose was Brasidas, who is described by Thucydides as follows:

> Brasidas . . . was a man who in Sparta itself had a great reputation for energy in every direction and who on his foreign service had shown himself to be so valuable to his country.

Thucydides, *The History of the Peloponnesian War* 4.81

> **helots** the enslaved populations of Lakonia and Messenia
>
> **neodamōdeis** helots who had been set free because of good service

In 424, Brasidas took a force of freed **helots**, known as **neodamōdeis**, and mercenaries to open up a new theatre of war in the Thrace-ward region on the northern Aegean coastline.

> The Spartans were also glad to have a good excuse for sending some of their helots out of the country, since in the present state of affairs, with Pylos in enemy hands, they feared a revolution.

Thucydides, *The History of the Peloponnesian War* 4.80

Athens had many tributary allies in the area, which was rich in both minerals and timber. The latter was, of course, vital for Athenian ship-building. Yet these Athenian allies were now ripe for revolt (Aristophanes, *Peace* 619–622 **PS**). Brasidas first approached the city of Acanthus. Different factions within the city were unsure as to whether to receive him. However, he was allowed to address the people and although he spoke fine words about freeing the Greeks, the threats that accompanied these words gave the inhabitants little option than to receive him.

PRESCRIBED SOURCE

Title: *Peace*

Author: Aristophanes

Date: performed in 421

Genre: comic play

Relevance: reflects a desire for peace in some quarters at Athens. One prescribed section reports how Athens' allies had been in revolt. The other is critical of Cleon for perpetuating the war at the expense of the allies

Lines: 619–622, 639–648

Read it here: LACTOR 1: *The Athenian Empire* (4th edn, KCL, 2000) 110, 202

EXPLORE FURTHER

Read Brasidas' speech to the Acanthians at Thucydides 4.85–87. What are the options that Brasidas presents to the people of Acanthus? Is Brasidas' claim to be freeing the Greeks a sham?

At the same time, in central Greece, the Athenian generals Demosthenes and Hippocrates tried to turn several Boeotian cities in an attempt to re-establish the land empire they had held during the First Peloponnesian War. In this they were opposed by members of the Boeotian confederacy led by Thebes. This resulted in the first major hoplite battle of the

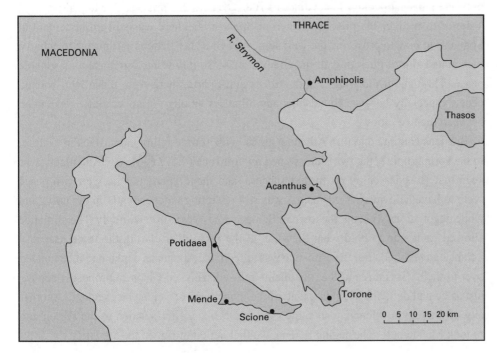

FIGURE 1.13
The main cities of the Chalcidice peninsula.

war at Delium in Boeotia. Again, it was Demosthenes who pushed for expeditionary warfare contrary to Pericles' policy, and it was here that Athens suffered its first major defeat.

In the winter of 424, Brasidas turned his attention to Amphipolis, a recently-founded Athenian settlement on the river Strymon. He took the bridge across the Strymon which was strategically important since it controlled access towards the Hellespont to the east. The historian Thucydides was a general at the time and he sailed from Thasos in support of the town. Fearful that with Thucydides' arrival the town would resist him, Brasidas was compelled to offer moderate terms to the inhabitants. He knew that there were few actual Athenians among the settlers, and that most were allies. With a little persuasion the inhabitants opened the town to Brasidas before Thucydides arrived, as Thucydides himself explains:

> The Athenians also feared that their allies would revolt, since Brasidas was behaving with great moderation and was constantly declaring wherever he went that his mission was the liberation of Hellas. The cities subject to Athens, when they heard of the capture of Amphipolis, of the terms being offered, and of the considerate behaviour of Brasidas himself, eagerly embraced the idea of a change.
>
> Thucydides, *The History of the Peloponnesian War* 4.108

DIFFERENCES WITHIN ATHENS AND SPARTA ON THE RELATIONS BETWEEN THE STATES AND THE MOVE TOWARDS A PEACE SETTLEMENT

Following his successes, Brasidas sought additional troops. However, rivalries at Sparta prevented this happening. Thucydides (4.108 **PS**) says that this was due to jealousy and a desire to recover the prisoners taken at Sphacteria. There was still disagreement at Sparta as to how to prosecute the war: some saw Brasidas' actions as a means to achieve their stated aim of liberating all the Greeks, others simply wanted to make a reasonable peace. Throughout the war, at both Athens and Sparta, there were those who wanted peace, especially because friendships and alliances among the upper classes extended between the two cities.

Brasidas continued to turn Athenian allies, with Torone falling next. Back in Greece, in the spring of 423, the two sides signed an armistice (4.117 **PS**). The Athenians were keen that Brasidas enjoy no further success, and those Spartans who were pro-peace seem to have held sway. Yet Brasidas was still operating independently in the north and while negotiations went on, the town of Scione came over to him willingly. The armistice allowed each side to hold what they had at the point of declaring the truce. Because Scione had revolted after the armistice was agreed, the Athenians demanded it be handed over to them. Brasidas and the inhabitants refused. This led Cleon to propose a decree, just as he had done for Mytilene, that all the inhabitants of Scione be executed. Another city of the region, Mende, also came over to Brasidas. Nicias sailed to the region and re-took Mende before besieging Scione. Neither action infringed the armistice.

Study question
With reference to the sources, how similar or different were Pericles and Cleon?

The Spartan peace party had hoped that the Athenians would become accustomed to peace. However at Athens, Cleon was agitating for the losses in the north to be turned around. The assembly was not inclined to continue the armistice after a year. As a result, in 422, Cleon sailed north. He re-took Torone and then turned on Amphipolis. Here Cleon and Brasidas fought a battle. In Thucydides' narrative, Cleon died ingloriously: after turning tail he was killed by a javelin in the back. Brasidas was also wounded and died later.

> **S&C** Read *The Old Oligarch* 1.14–2.14. How did Athens maintain control of her allies during the Archidamian War?

THE PEACE OF NICIAS – THE MAIN TERMS AND THE AFTERMATH

Cleon and Brasidas were dead – the two people who on each side had been most opposed to peace, Brasidas because of his success and honour which had come to him through war, Cleon because he thought that in time of peace and quiet people would be more likely to notice his evil doings and less likely to believe his slanders of others.

Thucydides, *The History of the Peloponnesian War* 5.16

While Thucydides is full of admiration of Brasidas, he is equally full of disdain for Cleon. Thucydides' undoubted bias comes from his own aristocratic upbringing. Cleon was considered vulgar, but he was not as low born as his detractors, especially Aristophanes (*Peace* 639–648 **PS**), might have claimed. His father owned a tannery but he was a businessman who did not partake in the particularly dirty task of tanning. For Cleon, political success rested in being able to appease the common man in the assembly who stood to benefit from imperialism and a continuation of the war. By contrast, the aristocracy was much more closely allied to the Spartans and so much more disposed towards peace.

With these two men dead, peace made sense. The Athenians had suffered two recent defeats at Delium and Amphipolis. Their confidence was damaged and many must have questioned the wisdom of expeditionary warfare in contrast to Pericles' original cautious strategy (Thucydides 5.14 **PS**). Moreover, they must have feared that more allies would revolt. Although the Spartans wanted to regain the men captured at Sphacteria, they also had other problems (5.13–15 **PS**). They had lost their reputation and confidence militarily, Athens had established fortified positions through the practice of epiteichismos at Pylos and Cythera, and the helots were deserting.

An additional factor was that Sparta's thirty year truce with Argos was due to end. Argos and Sparta had been on bad terms since they had contended for leadership of the Peloponnese during the sixth century. However, the prospect of having to fight another foe in addition to Athens was too daunting for the Spartans. Negotiations with Athens were led by King Pleistoanax, who had only recently been restored to Sparta, but who was still facing criticism. He therefore hoped for a political success and a period of calm (5.16–17 **PS**). His banishment arose over claims that he had taken a bribe to retreat from Attica in 446 (1.114 **PS**). However, Pleistoanax was a moderate and the retreat from

Attica in 446 may well have been an attempt to avoid further conflict then. This was certainly his intention in 422–421. On the Athenian side, Nicias was well regarded by many and Plutarch has this to say about him:

> People were ready to believe, in fact, that Nicias was the man responsible for the peace as Pericles had been for the war.
>
> Plutarch, *Nicias* 9

A peace agreement was signed in 421. Today it is referred to as the Peace of Nicias. Thucydides (5.18 **PS**) lists the terms of the peace as follows:

1. Everyone had the right to go to pan-Hellenic temples.
2. The treaty was to last fifty years.
3. Neither Athens and its allies, nor Sparta and its allies, were to attack each other.
4. The Spartans were to give back the cities they had taken in the Thrace-ward region.
5. The Spartans were to relinquish Panactum, a strategically important fort on the border between Attica and Boeotia.
6. The Athenians were to give back Cythera and other islands off the Peloponnese.
7. The Athenians were to give back the prisoners taken at Sphacteria.
8. The allies were to swear to the agreement.
9. The Athenians and the Spartans were entitled to adjust conditions if they agreed.

The cities that Sparta was to give back were divided into two categories. The Athenians could treat as they saw fit those that had firmly resisted Athenian authority – Amphipolis, Scione and Torone. For the people of Scione, this meant death in accordance with Cleon's edict. But most of the other cities that had simply followed suit were allowed to hold onto their newly-won independence as long as they continued to pay the original tribute set by Aristeides in 478, rather than the increased tribute recorded on the Thoudippos Decree of 425 **PS**. This saved the Spartans some face because they had of course persuaded the allies to rebel in the name of freedom.

The refusals of allies of both Athens and Sparta to support the peace

This peace suffered problems from the beginning. It was very much a peace between Athens and Sparta, rather than between Athens and the Peloponnesian League. A number of Sparta's allies did not accept the terms: the Boeotians, Corinthians, Eleans and Megarians (Thucydides 5.17 **PS**, 5.25 **PS**). Moreover, the inhabitants of Amphipolis did not return to Athens, and the Spartan commander on the ground was unwilling to compel them to do so. Nor did Argos renew its treaty with Sparta. All these issues left Sparta concerned that the peace would not hold. As a result, the Spartans went further and brokered a defensive alliance with the Athenians for fifty years whereby the two peoples agreed to defend each other's territory, and to make peace and war together. Sparta was clearly still concerned about its position, particularly in regard to Argos.

S
&
C
Refer to Thucydides 1.1, 1.21, 5.25–26 **PS** and the following further reading:

D. Kagan, *Thucydides: The Reinvention of History* (2009), chapter 1.

A.J. Woodman, *Rhetoric in Classical Historiography* (1988), chapter 1.

Given what you know about the Persian Wars and the First Peloponnesian War, do you think that Thucydides was right to claim that the Peloponnesian War was the greatest war?

TIMESPAN REVIEW

- Explain why the events at Pylos and Sphacteria were a turning point in the Archidamian war.
- Assess why the Archidamian War was inconclusive.
- Outline how Athens' relations with its allies changed during the Archidamian War.
- Analyse the extent to which the Spartans did not deserve to win the Archidamian War.

Further Reading

Buckley, T., *Aspects of Greek History 750–323 BC* (2nd edn; Abingdon: Routledge, 2010), chapter 19.

Delbruck, H., *History of the Art of War: Within the framework of political history*, Vol.1 (Westport: Greenwood Press, 1975), book II, chapter 1.

Hanson, V.D., *The Western Way of War* (London: Hodder & Stoughton, 1989).

Hanson, V.D., *Warfare and Agriculture in Classical Greece* (Berkeley: University of California Press, 1998).

Hanson, V.D., *A War Like No Other* (New York: Random House, 2005), chapters 2–6.

Hornblower, S., *The Greek World 479–323 BC* (Abingdon: Routledge, 2011), chapters 11–13.

Kagan, D., *The Peloponnesian War* (New York: Penguin, 2003), chapters 5–15.

Kagan, D., and G.F. Viggiano (eds), *Men of Bronze, Hoplite Warfare in Ancient Greece* (Princeton: Princeton University Press, 2013), chapters 1 and 12.

Kagan, D., *Thucydides: The Reinvention of History* (New York: Penguin, 2009), chapters 4, 6 and 7.

Osborne, R., *The Old Oligarch* (Lactor: Kingston, 2004).

Powell, A., *Athens and Sparta: Constructing Greek Political and Social History from 478 BC* (3rd edn; Abingdon: Routledge, 2016), chapter 5.

Rawlings, L., *The Ancient Greeks at War* (Manchester: Manchester University Press, 2007)

Rhodes, P.J., *A History of the Classical Greek World 478–323 BC* (Chichester: Wiley-Blackwell, 2006), chapters 9–11

van Wees, H., *Greek Warfare: Myths and Realities* (London: Bloomsbury, 2004).

Woodman. A.J., *Rhetoric in Classical Historiography* (Abingdon: Routledge, 1988), chapter 1.

PRACTICE QUESTIONS

AS Level

1. How far did the plague affect the Athenian war effort? [10]

A Level

1. 'Leadership was lacking at both Athens and Sparta during the Archidamian War.' How far do you agree with this view?

You must use and analyse the ancient sources you have studied as well as your own knowledge to support your answer. [30]

1.5 The End of the Peloponnesian War and its Aftermath, 419–404 BC

TIMESPAN OVERVIEW

- the breakdown of relations: the alliance of Athens, Argos, Mantinea and Elis
- the effect of the battle of Mantinea 418 BC
- the consequences of the Sicilian Expedition 415–413 BC for Athens and Sparta
- occupation of Decelea
- Sparta and Athens: relations with Persia in the final years of the war, and Persia's aims and impact on the course of the war

The prescribed sources for this timespan are:

- Andocides 3.29
- Aristophanes, *Acharnians* 61–71
- Thucydides, *History of the Peloponnesian War* 2.65; 4.50; 5.43; 6.8; 6.12–6.13; 6.15; 6.24; 6.31; 6.82–6.83; 6.89–6.91; 7.18; 7.27–7.28; 8.2; 8.6; 8.9; 8.17–8.18; 8.29; 8.37; 8.52; 8.87
- Xenophon, *History of My Times* 1.4.1–7; 1.5.1–3; 1.6.6–11; 2.1.7–14; 2.1.20–32

This timespan will explore how the breakdown of the Peace of Nicias led to the Battle of Mantinea in 418 and how thereafter renewed imperialism led to a disastrous Athenian expedition to Sicily between 415 and 413. It will then move on to examine how between 413 and 404 four factors wore down Athens to the point of defeat: the establishment of a Spartan stronghold in Attica; revolts by allies; the development of a Peloponnesian navy; and Persian financing of the Peloponnesian war effort.

THE BREAKDOWN OF RELATIONS: THE ALLIANCE OF ATHENS, ARGOS, MANTINEA AND ELIS

The Peloponnesian allies were unhappy about the peace of Nicias. During the series of negotiations that followed, each party changed allegiance several times. Eventually they all finished up back where they had started.

Corinth and the other Peloponnesian allies were upset by the clause that allowed Sparta and Athens to adjust the treaty by mutual consent, but without the allies' agreement. Seeking to turn other Peloponnesian allies against Sparta, the Corinthians went to Argos, who agreed to try to arrange a new alliance in secret. The Argives felt that a war with Sparta was inevitable and, after Sphacteria, believed that they could now gain the leadership of the Peloponnese. Mantinea and Elis allied with them. The former had taken much of Arcadia in recent years and feared Spartan reprisals. The Boeotians and Megarians, although unhappy with Sparta, did not join because they did not trust the democratic government of Argos. At the same time, Sparta was still unable to compel Amphipolis to return to Athens. Because of this they did not give up Pylos, even though the Athenians did return the Spartan prisoners.

New ephors at Sparta brought a change of attitude. They entered negotiations with Boeotian envoys, trying to get Boeotia first to ally with Argos and then to bring Argos back into alliance with Sparta. The matter was poorly steered through the Boeotian council and faltered. The Spartans then asked the Boeotians for control of Panactum, a small fort on the border with Attica which they hoped to exchange for Pylos. The Boeotians agreed to this if Sparta made a fresh alliance with them. Although this was at variance with Sparta's alliance with Athens, the Spartans agreed. The Boeotians dismantled the fort at Panactum. When the Athenians discovered this and learnt of the alliance between Sparta and Boeotia, they were incensed. The chief agitator was Alcibiades, who had taken over as the favourite of the people after Cleon was killed. He sought to make a new alliance with the Argives (Thucydides 5.43 **PS**).

The Spartans immediately sent envoys to renew relations with Athens. Although they persuaded the Athenian council of their good intentions, Alcibiades tricked them into not revealing all their powers to the assembly, and so he was able to turn popular support away from the peace of Nicias and towards the Argives. Alcibiades now sponsored a four-way alliance between Athens, Argos, Mantinea and Elis. This move was inspired. Beyond ringing the Peloponnese through the policy of **epiteichismos** at Pylos and Cythera, it was now proposed to hem Sparta in with three hostile states to the north.

THE EFFECT OF THE BATTLE OF MANTINEA 418 BC

Despite these moves there was no formal renouncement of the treaty between Athens and Sparta. Alcibiades enticed Patrae in the northern Peloponnese to come over to Athens. Meanwhile Argos attacked Epidaurus which lay to the south of Corinth. Both moves would have isolated Corinth from the Peloponnese. Sparta came to the help of Epidaurus first in 419. The next year, fearful that more cities within the Peloponnese would fall, Sparta sent a large army, including allies from Boeotia and Megara, under King Agis into the northern Peloponnese. An Argive army marched against them, joined by 1,000 Athenian hoplites and a Mantinean force. Collectively they hoped to win over the city Tegea, which was located to the south of Mantinea. In alliance, Mantinea and Tegea could then control the route into and out of Laconia. This prospect led to the Battle of Mantinea, where the Spartans won a resounding victory (see pp. 122–3, 125–6).

In this battle, the Spartans answered all the criticisms levelled against them after Sphacteria: they showed themselves to be overwhelmingly militarily superior. Within a few months an oligarchic faction at Argos seized control of the city and concluded a fresh fifty-year peace with Sparta. Without Argos, Mantinea could not remain allied to Athens and so made a new agreement with Sparta. As a result, by 417 Sparta had reaffirmed its alliance with all its previous allies and Argos remained neutral.

Study question
With reference to the sources, why did the Peace of Nicias not last?

THE CONSEQUENCES OF THE SICILIAN EXPEDITION, 415–413 BC, FOR ATHENS AND SPARTA

Thucydides devotes two whole books of his history to the Sicilian expedition. He saw it as the central event and Athens' greatest disaster. Early in Book Two when extolling the virtues of Pericles' wisdom in not seeking to expand the empire, Thucydides is critical of those who succeeded him and sought to expand. Specifically, he reports the Sicilian expedition as a mistake (2.65 **PS**).

In 415, the Sicilian community of Egesta called for Athenian support in a conflict with its neighbour Selinus, which was aided by the major power on the island, Syracuse. Egesta offered to pay the Athenians for their support. The Athenian assembly initially voted to send sixty ships to Sicily, under a tripartite general-ship of Alcibiades, Nicias and Lamachus (Thucydides 6.8 **PS**). The mission statement was rather vague: to help the Egestaeans, to re-establish Leontini on the other side of the island which had also been attacked by Syracuse, and to do what they saw fit according to Athenian interests.

What were Athenian interests in Sicily? Twice Thucydides claims that Athens wanted to conquer Sicily. Yet the number of ships was insufficient to guarantee success, suggesting mixed views at Athens. A difference of opinion existed between two of the generals, Nicias and Alcibiades. The former spoke at length against the expedition when they had so many difficulties at home (6.12–13 **PS**). He attacked Alcibiades as a reckless adventurer who was advocating the expedition for his own personal aggrandisement. Thucydides goes on to explain that Alcibiades was an extravagant aristocrat who had been brought up in Pericles' house and played the people as Pericles had done (6.15 **PS**).

Alcibiades answered these criticisms and claimed that Sicily would easily fall to their superior naval power. Nicias now changed tack and asked for far greater forces in the hope that the enormity of the undertaking would dissuade the Athenian assembly. The assembly was undeterred and agreed to send many more men (6.24 **PS**). As a result, Nicias was largely responsible for turning what might have been a significant setback in the loss of sixty ships, to an un-mitigated disaster with the loss of two fleets: the first of 100 ships and 5,000 hoplites, the second of sixty ships and 1,200 hoplites. Ultimately, when the crews are counted, 45,000–50,000 Athenians and allies perished. When the fleet sailed, there was a huge display of nationalistic pride (6.31 **PS**). Just before the departure of the first fleet, many of the hermae – the statues of Hermes that were positioned about the city – were desecrated. This was taken as a bad omen because Hermes was the patron god of

KEY EVENT

The Sicilian Expedition
Date: between 415 and 413

A large expedition of Athenian forces to campaign in Sicily. It ended in defeat and disastrous losses

FIGURE 1.14
A modern reconstruction of
an Athenian trireme.

EXPLORE FURTHER

In the winter of 415–414,
the Athenians attempted
to gain the support of the
Sicilian city Camarina.
Read Thucydides 6.82–
83 **PS**, how do the
Athenians justify their
presence in Sicily?

travellers. In the subsequent investigations, Alcibiades was implicated in other acts of religious impropriety. This was almost certainly an attempt to smear him. Nevertheless, he departed for Sicily with an impending prosecution hanging over him.

The Sicilian expedition saw a catalogue of Athenian failures. Egesta did not have the money that it had promised to fund the expedition. The generals could not agree as to the best course of action. Alcibiades and Nicias were not going to back down from their own views, so to break the deadlock Lamachus agreed to a plan of Alcibiades that failed. Then, just as operations got underway, Alcibiades was summoned home to face the charges of impropriety. Nicias was now the senior commander, but he prosecuted the war half-heartedly.

Over the winter of 415/414, Syracuse requested Peloponnesian help. Corinth was keen to help, while Sparta was influenced by Alcibiades, who had now gone there in exile. He advised sending out a Spartan commander (6.89–91 **PS**). According to Thucydides, Alcibiades made his own view of democracy very clear:

As for democracy, those of us with any sense at all knew what that meant, and I just as much as any. Indeed, I am well equipped to make an attack on it; but nothing new can be said of a system which is generally recognized as absurd.

Thucydides, *The History of the Peloponnesian War*, 6.89

He went onto inflame the Peloponnesians by claiming that the Athenian intention had been to capture Sicily, Italy, and then Carthage, before using the resources of these conquests against the Peloponnese (6.90–91 **PS**).

The following spring Nicias seized the heights of Epipolae above the city of Syracuse and then began to build fortifications around the city to prepare for a siege (see Figure 2.9

on p. 128). The Syracusans contemplated surrender. However, perhaps because he was receiving overtures of peace, Nicias now reduced his efforts. He preferred to make the southern section a double wall, rather than to press on with the northern wall and the isolation of the city. Then early in 414, the Spartan commander Gylippus landed with only a skeleton force. With Gylippus' arrival Nicias now turned his attention to the sea and allowed the siege walls to be taken. Nicias sent a letter home requesting more forces, or to be allowed to retreat. A belligerent Athens sent Demosthenes with sixty more ships and 1,200 hoplites. By this stage, two years into the adventure, Athens had committed 45,000–50,000 men and more than 200 ships, representing possibly half the assets of the empire.

Before Demosthenes arrived, Gylippus had defeated the Athenian fleet in the harbour. Demosthenes decided upon immediate action as soon as he arrived. However, his choice of a night attack on the heights of Epipolae was inappropriate for hoplites and a disastrous defeat followed. Seeing sickness in the Athenian camp, he decided that the Athenians should escape. However, Nicias did not want to depart, since he was still in contact with a dissident party in Syracuse and he feared the Athenian assembly. Belatedly, after they had lost two more naval engagements, 40,000 Athenians departed Syracuse on foot. Harassed on the march, the Athenians finally reached the river Assinarus. Here the men were slaughtered by Syracusan troops as they fought each other to drink from the river already dirty with their colleagues' blood. Nicias surrendered to Gylippus: 7,000 prisoners were put in the quarries, while Nicias and Demosthenes were executed (you can read more about the campaign in Sicily on pp. 127–9).

The initial reaction to news of Sicily at Athens in 413 was shock. The people turned against those who had advocated the expedition, but they also vowed to keep control of their allies and to fight on. Two years later there was briefly an oligarchic coup, with a new government of only 400. Many aristocrats had shunned politics through the fifth century when the democracy had such power, although they could still do well out of Athenian imperialism. After Sicily it was the aristocrats who bore the brunt of re-equipping a fleet and prosecuting the war. As a result, dissent arose first among the Athenian ship captains at Samos, whose representative brought about change at home. Yet this oligarchy was short lived. There was infighting between the radical and moderate oligarchs. This and a naval defeat off Euboea soon brought an adjustment to a broader oligarchy of 5,000. Then, when further unexpected naval victories occurred, full democracy was restored.

OCCUPATION OF DECELEA

Finally, at the end of 414, Sparta decided that peace with Athens was impossible and decided to act decisively. Alcibiades had advised the Spartans to fortify a strategic position in Attica to reproduce the tactic of epiteichismos on Athenian soil. He suggested Decelea (see Figure 3.1 on p. 148), which sat on the main road from the port at Oropus, where Euboean produce was landed, to Athens itself (Thucydides 6.91 **PS**, 7.18 **PS**). The Spartans followed his advice. The impact of this was considerable, although only a few chapters of Thucydides are given over to it because once the fort was established the effects were on-going and so required no further comment.

> **KEY INDIVIDUAL**
>
> **Gylippus**
>
> The Spartan commander sent to help the Syracusans in 414. You can read more about his career on pp. 127–9.

> **KEY EVENT**
>
> **The Occupation of Decelea**
>
> The Spartan occupation of a position north of Athens to blockade a key Athenian supply route and prevent the Athenians accessing many fields

ACTIVITY

At a time when a Spartan King was setting up camp thirteen miles outside the city walls at Decelea, the Athenians dispatched their second fleet under Demosthenes to Sicily. Was this madness or boldness? Discuss.

KEY EVENT

Ionian War
Date: between 413 and 404

The final section of the Peloponnesian War

KEY INDIVIDUALS

Tissaphernes
Dates: late fifth century

The Persian satrap of Caria in Asia Minor

Pharnabazus
Dates: late fifth century

The Persian satrap of the Hellespont

Darius II
Dates: reigned 423–*c.* 404

King of Persia

KEY PLACE

Bosporan kingdom: A non-Greek kingdom on the northern shores of the Black Sea.

Thucydides (7.27–28 PS) reports that Decelea was one of the chief reasons for Athens losing the war. Rather than the flawed annual invasions of the Archidamian War that denied the Athenians their fields for four to six weeks, now they were deprived of these for the whole year. The Athenians had to continually guard the city walls and send cavalry against the Peloponnesians. As a result, their horses soon became lame. Additionally, 20,000 slaves deserted. Most critically, the main supply route from Euboea was interrupted, so that ships had to travel around the Sounion peninsula to deliver food. Yet still the Athenians continued with the operations in Sicily.

SPARTA AND ATHENS: RELATIONS WITH PERSIA IN THE FINAL YEARS OF THE WAR AND PERSIA'S AIMS

The final years of the Peloponnesian War are often referred to as the Ionian War, since its battles were largely played out in the eastern Aegean.

Before the oligarchic coup happened at Athens, the news from Sicily encouraged parties among Athens' allies to rebel (Thucydides 8.2 PS). King Agis, by this time at Decelea, received representatives from Euboea and from Lesbos, while representatives from Chios travelled to Sparta; all were looking for support if they were to revolt. Accompanying the Chians was a representative of Tissaphernes, the Persian satrap of Caria in Asia Minor. Other Asiatic Greeks were accompanied by an embassy from Pharnabazus, the satrap of the Hellespont (8.6 PS). The satraps would have followed the Peloponnesian War closely in the hope of re-asserting their authority in Ionia and recovering taxes from the Asiatic Greeks. At the start of the war, Archidamus had suggested to the Spartans that an alliance with Persia would be necessary to achieve success. In 425, a Persian message to Sparta had been intercepted and read at Athens; the contents implied that the Spartans were asking for Persian support (4.50 PS).

Soon after, there may have been a renewed Athenian treaty with Persia, possibly termed the peace of Epilycus. This is suggested in a speech by Andocides (3.29 PS) and an inscribed decree. Moreover, in Aristophanes' *Acharnians* of 425 (61–71 PS), an embassy had just returned to Athens from Persia. A treaty in 424–423 would make sense because, with Brasidas' capture of Amphipolis, the Athenians would have been concerned that they might lose control of the Hellespont and the supply of grain from the Black Sea region. This was becoming increasingly important because of friendly relations with the recently established, but confusingly named, Spartocid dynasty in the Bosporan kingdom. At the same time the Persian king, Darius II, had only just come to the throne and was threatened by many other sons of Artaxerxes. A peace with Athens would avoid distractions in the Aegean.

By 413, Darius II was secure and had charged his satraps with recovering the tribute of the Asiatic Greeks. That meant needing to defeat Athens in the Aegean. The Chians were the last remaining ship-providing ally of Athens, and without them Athens would find it hard to rebuild their fleet. Therefore, the Spartans decided to act in Chios', and so Tissaphernes', interests (Thucydides 8.6 PS). This did not initially go well, because the people at Chios were unaware of their oligarchs' embassy to Sparta (8.9 PS). Alcibiades convinced the Spartans to sail quickly, and through some persuasive speech at Chios, he brought about the revolts of first Chios and then Miletus (8.17 **PS**). Now the Spartan commander Chalcideus made a formal alliance with the king of Persia through Tissaphernes. The terms were (8.18 **PS**):

1. All the territories previously belonging to the king and his ancestors shall be his.
2. All money paid by subjects previously to Athens was to go to the Persian king.
3. The war will be carried on jointly.
4. Any people who revolt from Persia shall be enemies of Sparta.
5. Any who revolt from Sparta shall be enemies of Persia.

There were two further versions of this agreement. The issue with the first two treaties was the clause laying claim to former possessions of the kings' ancestors. This effectively conceded not only the Asiatic Greeks but Thessaly, Locris and Boeotia, all states which had allied with Persia during the Persian Wars (8.37 **PS**, 8.52 **PS**). Finally, a third treaty with Sparta was agreed, whereby the king was only to have control and the taxes of the Asiatic Greeks, but Tissaphernes was to pay for the Peloponnesian fleet until a Persian fleet arrived.

It is very unlikely that three consecutive agreements were made in so short a space of time. The third version given in Thucydides is probably the final version, the others being drafts that were discussed by both parties. The key factor here was the involvement of the Persian money to pay for the rowers. However, Tissaphernes' attitude throughout was seemingly to weaken the Greeks as they fought amongst themselves. He was influenced by Alcibiades, who had fallen out of favour with the Spartans and was now resident at Tissaphernes' court. As a result, Tissaphernes was tardy in paying up for the rowers of the Peloponnesian fleet (8.29 **PS**). Then after mustering a Phoenician fleet to

PRESCRIBED SOURCE

Andocides 3.29

Author: Andocides

Date: *c.* 392 BC

Genre: speech

Relevance: the prescribed section records a peace made by Andocides' uncle Epilycus between the Athenians and the Persians.

Read it here: LACTOR 1: *The Athenian Empire* (4th edn, KCL, 2000) 61

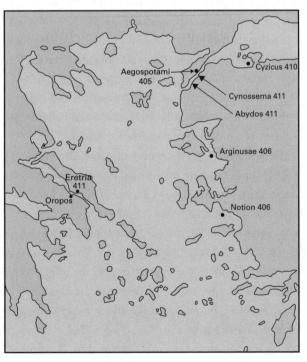

FIGURE 1.15
The locations of the key battles of the Ionian War.

aid the Peloponnesians, he failed to bring it fully into the Aegean, and so, according to Thucydides, prolonged the naval war (8.87 **PS**).

Spurred on by the example of Chios and Miletus, the Athenian allies continued to revolt. Yet in 411, a democratic revolution at Samos gave the Athenian fleet space to remain democratic when the fleet's own captains had sponsored the oligarchic coup back at Athens. Alcibiades was now recalled by the Athenian democrats at Samos. He spoke persuasively against immediately sailing against the regime of the oligarchic 400 at Athens. This was very wise; to have done so would have abandoned the Aegean completely to a Peloponnesian and Persian alliance, in effect giving up the empire.

The Peloponnesians sent another fleet to Oropos opposite Eretria in Euboea, which had long been ripe for revolt. Euboea was Athens' chief source of food because of its cleruchies – estates owned by often absentee Athenian landlords. The Athenians had moved their flocks and herds there from Attica at the beginning of the war. Its loss would be serious and so the Athenians manned a fleet with inexperienced rowers to intercept the Peloponnesians. Arriving at Eretria, a city covertly opposed to Athenian rule, the rowers were poorly supplied and forced into a battle which they lost. Worse still, when the Athenian fleet retreated to Eretria, thinking it friendly, they were murdered by the locals. This defeat triggered such consternation at Athens that it caused the oligarchy of the 400 to be deposed in favour of the more moderate oligarchy of 5,000, to include all who could provide a hoplite's arms.

PERSIA'S IMPACT ON THE COURSE OF THE WAR

Eventually, Tissaphernes' miserliness in paying the crews, borne out of his desire to weaken the Greeks on both sides, backfired on him. In response to the supportive calls from Pharnabazus, the Spartans, under the command of Mindarus, moved their main operations to the Hellespont. Control of the Hellespont was potentially far more damaging to Athens as intercepting the grain convoys from the Spartocid Bosporan kingdom would now become doubly important in the face of revolt in Euboea. This resulted in the first major sea battle between the Athenians and Spartans at Cynossema, a resounding Athenian victory which brought a renewed belief in their maritime prowess. Soon after, Athens won another naval victory at Abydos.

By March 410, the Spartans had clearly decided on a war of attrition. Mindarus saw the possibilities of cutting off Athens' remaining supply chain. Three Athenian commanders, Alcibiades, Thrasybulus and Theramenes, now forced him into battle at Cyzicus, where the Spartans were outmanoeuvred by the Athenian fleet. The Spartan losses were considerable: sixty ships lost and perhaps 10,000 dead including Mindarus. Pharnabazus offered help to the crews. At this point the full democracy was restored at Athens. Diodorus reports that the Spartans sued for peace at this time, but the offer was rebuffed by the leading demagogue Cleophon, who persuaded the people that to continue the war was to their advantage.

Thucydides' narrative breaks off with operations against Abydos in 411. After this the main prescribed source is Xenophon's *History of my Times* (also known as *Hellenica*). Xenophon was never regarded as equal to Thucydides in terms of depth of analysis or

---

PRESCRIBED SOURCE

Author: Xenophon

Title: *History of My Times*

Date: first quarter of fourth century

Genre: history

Relevance: continues the account of the Greek wars from the point where Thucydides breaks off

Prescribed sections: 1.4.1–7; 1.5.1–3; 1.6.6–11; 2.1.7–14; 2.1.20–32

Read it here: Xenophon, *History of My Times*, translated by Rex Warner (Penguin 1979)

EXPLORE FURTHER

To learn more about Xenophon's credibility, read the following:

Buckley, T., *Aspects of Greek History* (Routledge, 2010), pp. 28–34.

Rhodes, P.J., *A History of the Classical Greek World 478–323 BC* (Wiley-Blackwell, 2006) pp. 146–7.

style. Yet he did, until the mid-twentieth century, represent a continuous history of the period that was near contemporary and therefore preferable to the much later Diodorus Siculus. However, the discovery of fragments of the work known as the Oxyrhynchus Historian has caused a re-appraisal of Xenophon's credibility. The Oxyrhynchus Historian can be seen to have been near contemporary to the events and objective. He can also be seen to have been the source for Ephorus who was in turn the source for Diodorus with regard to the Ionian War. Therefore, Diodorus becomes as credible a witness to events in this period as Xenophon. Where the two differ, then scholarly opinion is divided.

Pharnabazus paid for the rebuilding of the Peloponnesian fleet after the defeats of Cynossema, Abydos and Cyzicus, but this required a three year pause in hostilities. In 407, a Spartan embassy returned from the court of Darius II, to announce that the king had decided to act in the Spartan's interests (*Hellenica* 1.4.1–3 **PS**). An Athenian embassy, seeking to negotiate with Persia directly was, according to Xenophon, detained to prevent news of Persian support for Sparta reaching Athens (*Hellenica* 1.4.4–7 **PS**). There was possibly a new treaty at this time between Persia and Sparta, known as the Treaty of Boeotius, although this is not universally accepted by all scholars.

Irrespective of whether there was a treaty or not, Darius' sponsorship was the turning point of the war. His son, Cyrus, was to have charge of affairs and now the Spartans would at last be fully funded. Also at this point, Lysander was appointed to the command of the Spartan forces. He was a tough and innovative soldier in the model of Brasidas and Gylippus. Lysander met with Cyrus and there was mutual admiration from their first meeting. The pay for the ships' crews was immediately increased in an attempt to entice rowers away from the Athenian fleet (*Hellenica* 1.5.1–3 **PS**).

In the interim, Alcibiades had returned to Athens and was warmly received. The assembly voted him huge resources but expected instant results. While absent on a mission, he had delegated the command of the fleet to a certain Antiochus with specific instructions to avoid any battle. Antiochus disobeyed the order and sailed to Notion close to the harbour of Ephesus which was home to the Peloponnesian fleet. Here Lysander enjoyed an early success; Antiochus was killed and fifteen Athenian ships were lost. Alcibiades was once again banished by the Athenian assembly. As a result, Athens lost its most determined and innovative commander at the critical point when Sparta had an equally outstanding commander in Lysander.

Spartan law only allowed Lysander a single year of command and he was replaced by Callicratidas in 406. The two did not get on and the transfer was difficult. It appears that there were still divisions of policy among the Spartans, Lysander representing the party in favour of dealing with Persia in order to defeat Athens, Callicratidas being supportive of appeasement with Athens and non-engagement with Persia. Callicratidas was not well received by Cyrus (*Hellenica* 1.6.6–11 **PS**). However, he gained initial naval success and managed to blockade the Athenian naval commander Conon at Mytilene. In response, the Athenians sent a new fleet which met with the Spartans at Arginusae. Here Athens was victorious in a massive battle, seventy-seven Peloponnesian ships were destroyed and Callicratidas was killed. The Athenians lost just twenty-five ships. However, in the aftermath of the battle the Athenians did not recover the bodies of many of their dead sailors from the water. This caused fury back in Athens, and the assembly put the successful generals on

S & C Investigate the arguments for and against there being a Peace of Epilycus and a Peace of Boeotius; then consider what these tell us about Persian attitudes to the Greeks?

KEY INDIVIDUAL

Lysander
Dates: d. 395

Appointed a Spartan admiral in 407, he played a key role in securing Sparta's victory in the Peloponnesian War

EXPLORE FURTHER

Read Thucydides 5.43 **PS**–5.46 and Plutarch *Nicias* 9. Compare the information here with what you know of Alcibiades' career. Is Alcibiades fairly represented in these sources?

Study questions
With reference to the sources:

1 Why was Athens able to come back from defeat so many times?
2 How important was Persian involvement in the Peloponnesian War?

trial and condemned them to death. The Spartans may have asked for peace again at this juncture but again Cleophon opposed the offer in an act of imperialistic fervour.

In the spring of 405 a conference of the Asiatic Greeks was held at Ephesus, where they demanded that Lysander be re-established as naval commander. The Spartans made him vice-admiral to another, but made it clear the decision making was to rest with him (*Hellenica* 2.1.7 🅿🅢). At the same time, Cyrus was recalled by his father but before he departed he gave over as much tribute as he could muster to Lysander (*Hellenica* 2.1.8–14 🅿🅢). Now Lysander turned his attentions once again to the Hellespont. The Spartans held Abydos and Lampsacus on the Asian side of the Hellespont, the Athenians held Sestos on the Chersonese. The Athenians positioned themselves at Aegospotami, opposite Lampsacus, two miles across the strait.

After four days of posturing, Lysander attacked the Athenian fleet which was complacent and mostly beached, with crews absent gathering supplies. One hundred and seventy ships were taken, and the Athenian sailors were executed (*Hellenica* 2.1.20–32 🅿🅢). Although Plutarch reports that Lysander had within a single hour put an end to twenty-seven years of war, it was not the scale of this particular victory which brought an end to the war, rather it was the cumulative effect. The Ionian war had been a war of attrition and the Athenians had no resources left. Ultimately the Peloponnesian fleet, equipped with Persian money, had won.

KEY EVENT

The Battle of Aegospotami

Date: 405

The final battle of the Peloponnesian War, at which the Spartan fleet defeated in Athenian fleet in the Hellespont

---

PRESCRIBED DEBATE: THE REASONS FOR ATHENIAN FAILURE IN THE PELOPONNESIAN WAR

A combination of factors brought about Athens' defeat, and scholars put more or less emphasis on particular factors:

- not keeping to Pericles' strategy in the Archidamian War may have been a mistake
- a loss of a third of the population to the plague would have reduced their military effectiveness
- the defeat in Sicily was down to the poor leadership and the failure to support the expedition at home and cost a huge number of ships and men
- after Sicily, the rebellion of allies denuded Athens of tribute and trade and required them to exhaust resources trying to regain control of the allies
- the Spartan decision to engage in a naval war especially after Pharnabazus lent his support was the only way that Athens could be effectively challenged
- Sparta also had a dynamic leader in Lysander, while the democracy at Athens banished their best hope in Alcibiades
- even then, it required Cyrus to bring the financial support with which to pay the rowers, for the Peloponnesian fleet really to become effective
- at the same time and for over a decade Peloponnesian forces garrisoned Decelea to prevent Athens gaining easy access to Euboea and requiring them to retain significant forces in Attica

Cawkwell, G., *Thucydides and the Peloponnesian War* (London: Penguin, 1997), chapter 6.
Buckley. T., *Aspects of Greek History 750–323 BC* (2nd edn; Abingdon: Routledge, 1996), chapter 20.
Hanson. V.D., *A War Like No Other* (London: Methuen: 2005), chapters 7–10.
Meiggs, R., *The Athenian Empire* (Oxford: Oxford University Press, 2002), chapter 20.
Tritle, L.A., *A New History of the Peloponnesian War* (Chichester: Wiley-Blackwell, 2010), chapters 8–11.

- Examine the reasons why the Peace of Nicias was not upheld.
- Analyse the extent to which naval power was more important than hoplite infantry power in the Peloponnesian War.
- Assess the impact of Alcibiades upon Athens from 421.
- Discuss whether the sources play down the significance of Persian intervention in the Peloponnesian war.

Further Reading

Buckley, T., *Aspects of Greek History 750–323 BC* (2nd edn; Abingdon: Routledge, 1996), chapters 20–2.

Cawkwell, G., *Thucydides and the Peloponnesian War* (London: Penguin, 1997), chapter 6.

Hanson, V.D., *A War Like No Other* (London: Methuen, 2005), chapters 7–10.

Hornblower, S., *The Greek World 479–323 BC* (Abingdon: Routledge, 2011), chapters 11–14.

Kagan, D., *The Peloponnesian War* (New York: Penguin, 2003), chapters 16–37.

Kagan, D., *Thucydides: The Reinvention of History* (New York: Penguin, 2009), chapters 8–9.

Meiggs, R., *The Athenian Empire* (Oxford: Oxford University Press, 2002), chapter 20.

Morrison, J.S., J.F. Coates, N.B. Rankov, The Athenian Trireme (Cambridge: Cambridge University Press, 2000), chapters 5 and 6.

Powell, A., *Athens and Sparta: Constructing Greek Political and Social History from 478 BC* (3rd edn; Abingdon: Routledge, 2016), chapter 5.

Rhodes, P.J., *A History of the Classical Greek World 478–323 BC* (Malden: Wiley-Blackwell, 2008), chapters 12–15.

Rhodes, P.J., *Alcibiades Athenian Playboy General and Traitor* (Barnsley: Pen & Sword, 2011).

Tritle, L.A., *A New History of the Peloponnesian War* (Malden: Wiley-Blackwell, 2010), chapters 9–11.

AS level

1. 'Treaties stood no hope of succeeding in keeping the peace in the fifth century'. How far do you agree with this view?

   You must use and analyse the ancient sources you have studied as well as your own knowledge to support your answer. [30]

A Level

1. Read the following passage and answer the question below:

Deprived of Alcibiades' services as a result of Notion and of the victors of Arginusae by the subsequent trial, the Athenians, who between 410 and 406 had looked like winning the war after all, could now hardly fail to lose it. Just before the final defeat, which was at Aegospotami on the Hellespont in 405, we glimpse Alcibiades for the last time, warning the Athenian generals against recklessly beaching their ships where they would be exposed to attack by Lysander . . . His help was rebuffed; the battle was won and the Athenians now faced starvation.

S. Hornblower, *The Greek World 479–323 BC* (2011), p. 189

How convincing do you find Hornblower's interpretation that it was the loss of competent leadership that lost Athens the Peloponnesian War?

You must use your knowledge of the historical period and the ancient sources you have studied to analyse and evaluate Hornblower's interpretation.   [20]

PART 2
DEPTH STUDIES

Introduction to the Depth Study Options

One quarter of your A Level in Ancient History involves the study of a substantial and coherent short time span.

OCR offers the choice between three options:

The Politics and Society of Sparta, 478–404 BC	H407/11
The Politics and Culture of Athens, *c.* 460–399 BC	H407/12
The Rise of Macedon, 359–323 BC	H407/13

The following pages of this textbook guide you through the content of all three of these options, but you will only study one. Translations are cited for the prescribed sources and further guidance on these is given online. **(CW)**

All three Depth Studies develop what you have learned in the Period Study about the Greek world. The material studied in the Politics and Society of Sparta overlaps with that of the Period Study and allows you to study the politics and institutions which lie behind her decisions and relationships with other Greek and non-Greek states. In the Politics and Culture of Athens, you will study similar material from the Athenian point of view. In the Rise of Macedon you have the chance to learn how, during a later period of Greek history, inter-state relations were no less important as the long-standing dominance of Athens and Sparta gave way to a new power from the north.

EXAM OVERVIEW   **H407/11, H407/12, H407/13**

Your assessment for the Depth Study option will be found in Section B of your exam paper. It comprises

25% of the A Level	1 hr 10 mins out of 2 hrs 30 mins for the whole paper	48 marks out of 98 marks for the whole paper

12 marks will test AO1: demonstrate knowledge and understanding of the key features and characteristics of the historical periods studied

12 marks will test AO2: analyse and evaluate historical events and historical periods to arrive at substantiated judgements

24 marks will test AO3: use, analyse and evaluate a range of ancient source material within its historical context to:

- reach conclusions about historical events and historical periods studied
- make judgements about how the portrayal of events by ancient writers/sources relates to the social, political, religious and cultural contexts in which they were written/produced

DEPTH STUDY 1
The Politics and Society of Sparta, 478–404 BC

Introduction to the Politics and Society of Sparta, 478–404 BC

This component studies the social, political and military aspects of Spartan society, 478–404 BC, and how these aspects affected each other. Students study Spartan society during this period through particular events and individuals as mentioned in the prescribed source material.

The Politics and Society of Sparta in this period were heavily influenced by the events studied in the Period Study, and indeed those events were also influenced by the institutions and society of Sparta. The events of the Persian Wars and immediately afterwards had a huge effect on the Spartans. They had always previously been the natural leaders of Greece, but that leadership was now being challenged by the success of Athens in the Persian Wars and, from 478, by Athenian leadership of the Delian League. This was a serious challenge for Sparta, as its leadership in the Greek world was a result of its position as leader of the Peloponnesian League. However, any challenge to its overall leadership could also lead to the loss of its position in the Peloponnese with the ever-present threat of helot revolt. Sparta was compelled to maintain its position, in Sparta itself, the Peloponnese, and the wider Greek world.

To understand this period of Spartan history properly, it is important to appreciate the different pressures which were coming to bear on the Spartans. Internal politics and external relationships both had an effect on the institutions of Spartan society, and we should not be surprised to see them changing through the period. In studying this fascinating period, we should also be aware that we are doing so largely through the eyes of non-Spartans. This in turn can give us an insight into how other Greek cities viewed the extraordinary society which was ancient Sparta.

EXAM OVERVIEW   H407/11 SECTION B

Your examination for Sparta, in Section B of your paper, will require you to show knowledge and understanding of the material you have studied. This component is worth 48 marks – 12 based on AO1 skills, 12 on AO2, and 24 on AO3.

In this section, you will answer two questions:

- a 12-mark stimulus question focusing on an issue relating to a historical event or situation, where you will need to assess the source's utility;
- one of two essay questions, each worth 36 marks. The questions will require you to use, analyse, and evaluate source material to address issues in the question. The essays will target one or more of the themes listed.

2.1 Education and Values in Sparta

TOPIC OVERVIEW

- the education of boys and men, including details of the organisation and content of the agōgē
- the education of girls
- the values the agōgē was intended to develop in the Spartans
- the decline of the values in Sparta and effects of oliganthrōpia

The prescribed sources for this topic are:

- Alcman fragments 1–3
- Aristophanes, *Lysistrata* 78–84; 1241–1321
- Herodotus, *Histories* 7.104.4
- Kritias, *Governance of the Spartans*, fr. 6
- Pausanias, *Description of Greece* 3.14.9–10
- Plato, *Protagoras* 342d
- Plato, *Laws* 633b–c
- Plutarch, *Agesilaos* 1
- Plutarch, *Lycurgus* 14; 16–18; 21–22; 25; 27–28
- Plutarch, *Sayings of the Spartans, Agis*, 2–4 and 6; *Gorgo*, 2
- Thucydides, *History of the Peloponnesian War* 4.80
- Tyrtaeus fragments 10–12
- Xenophon, *Constitution of the Spartans* 1–4; 9

- Bronze figurine of a woman, BM 1876,0510.1

The Spartan education system is fundamental to understanding Spartan society. It prepared young Spartans, both male and female, for everything which was to follow, and instilled in them the values which formed the very basis of Spartan society.

Before we study the evidence, we need to consider the nature of the sources and their reliability.

Xenophon was an Athenian, born *c.* 430. However, having fought as a mercenary in Asia Minor he later found himself with a Spartan force, and even fought against Athens in 394 with the Spartan king, Agesilaus, for which he was exiled from Athens. The Spartans gave him land near Olympia, and some sources suggest that his

KEY INDIVIDUALS

Brasidas
Dates: d. 422

A Spartan commander during the Peloponnesian war. There is a more detailed discussion of Brasidas in topic 4 of this chapter.

Lycurgus
Dates: unknown, but likely seventh century

The legendary founder of the Spartan system, social, educational and political. He is mentioned as such by both Plutarch and Xenophon. Modern scholarship rather sees the system as having evolved over time.

EXAM TIP

You may find names have different spellings in your prescribed texts. In this book any alternative spelling used in LACTOR 21 is given in brackets at first mention e.g. Lycurgus (Lykourgos) here.

sons went through the Spartan education system. He thus had a good knowledge of the Spartan constitution and system, and especially of military matters, as they existed in his time. Although he ascribes most of the Spartan institutions to Lycurgus (Lykourgos), and was clearly a great admirer of the whole system, the details of what he says are probably accurate.

Plutarch was from Chaeronea in Boeotia, and lived in the first and second centuries AD. He was a priest at Delphi so had access to many sources now lost to us, including a *Spartan Constitution* written by Aristotle or a member of his school, many of which he quotes. Some of these are very useful, but because of the large gap in time, many of his sources were themselves written well after the period of Sparta with which we are concerned. However, he also clearly used Xenophon as a source, and where the two agree we can be fairly confident of the picture they present. As well as lives of the Spartan Kings Agesilaus II, Agis IV and Cleomenes III (all after our period), he also wrote lives

FIGURE 2.1
There are very few remains at the ancient site of Sparta and we rely heavily on ancient writers for our source material.

of Lycurgus and Lysander, as well as recording many sayings by Spartans and Spartan women from other authors. (For more discussion of Plutarch, see pp. 22–3.)

Aristophanes was an Athenian playwright of the late fifth and early fourth centuries; the play which has sections as a prescribed source, *Lysistrata*, was performed in 411. All his plays are comedies, and are therefore designed to make people laugh, so what he says might be a comic version of actual events. However, he can be useful in showing what he thought the Athenians would find funny about the Spartans, and what an average Athenian knew, or thought he knew, about the Spartans.

As we have seen in the period study, Thucydides was an Athenian historian who wrote a history of the Peloponnesian War, although his account ends in 411. He was exiled from Athens in 423 for failing to prevent the Spartan general, Brasidas, from capturing Amphipolis; he returned to Athens, probably after the end of the war in 404. It may, therefore, be thought that he would be biased, as an Athenian, but he is generally thought to be impartial and accurate, especially for the period before his exile when he was in the thick of political life in Athens. An exception to this is his negative account of the Spartan regent, Pausanias, in Book 1. He seems rather to have reserved his bitterness for those individual Athenians he saw as responsible for his exile, and those whom he saw as

Lysander
Dates: d. 395

A Spartan naval commander during the final years of the Peloponnesian war. There is a more detailed discussion of Lysander in topic 4 of this chapter.

PRESCRIBED SOURCE

Title: *Lives of Agesilaus, Aristeides, Lycurgus, Lysander; Moralia* (contains the *Sayings of the Spartans*)

Author: Plutarch

Date: *c.* AD 50–*c.* AD 120

Genre: biography and moral philosophy

Significance: Plutarch had access to works now lost to us and was a careful researcher; he mentions several different sources in his *Lycurgus* alone. However, he was writing well after the decline of Sparta, so we need to be careful with him unless he actually mentions an earlier, classical source.

Prescribed sections: *Agesilaus* 1; *Lycurgus* 5.6, 6–10, 12–22, 24–28, 29.6, 30; *Lysander* 3–11, 16, 17.1–2 and 17.4–5; *Moralia* 219D, 241F, 215 D–E (= *Agis* 2–6), 240E (*Gorgo* 2), *Gorgo* 6

Read it here: LACTOR 21: *Sparta* (KCL, 2017) E82; D14, D48, D17, D57, D58, D63, D63, D49, D70, D71, D73, D76, D78, D80, D97, D90, D93, D94, D95, D15, B35b, D44, F6, E76, D82, E120, E124, E75; F33, F35, F32; F30

Translations for *Aristeides* 23; *Lycurgus* 19–21, 24–25; *Lysander* 3, 6–11, 16; *Gorgo* 6 are available on the Companion Website.

PRESCRIBED SOURCE

Title: *Constitution of the Spartans; Hellenica (Hellenika)*

Author: Xenophon

Date: *c.* 430–*c.* 350

Genre: political philosophy and history

Significance: he fought for the Spartan king, Ageslaos II, was exiled from Athens and settled by Agesilaos near Olympia. He has first-hand knowledge of Sparta and the Spartans, and before their defeat at Leuctra in 371 and the subsequent reforms. However, he admired Sparta and had reasons to be grateful to the Spartans, so his works do tend to set out to defend their system against contemporary criticisms.

Prescribed sections: *Constitution of the Spartans*

Read it here: LACTOR 21: *Sparta* (KCL, 2017) D68, D74, D77, D79, D61, D50, D32, D53, D19, D96, D12, D51, F1, D88, D89, D7, E70, D9. Translations for 1.1–1.2 are available on the Companion Website.

Prescribed sections: *Hellenica* 2.1.6–7, 2.1.13–14, 2.1.23–24, 2.1.27–28, 2.2.19–20

Read it here: LACTOR 21: *Sparta* (KCL, 2017) E125, E126, E127, E128, E144

Study questions

There is a general lack of agreement about the life of Lykourgos, the lawgiver, both in its broad perspective and its particulars, since accounts vary about his origins, travels, and death. Above all, the record of his legal and constitutional reforms is inconsistent, the history of the times in which he lived being, perhaps, the most widely disputed subject of all.

Plutarch, *Lycurgus* 1.1 (LACTOR 21, F2)

Well, having considered once how Sparta, although it was one of the most sparsely populated cities, appeared to be both the most powerful and most well known city-state in Greece, I was amazed how this ever came about; however, when I had thought about the institutions of the Spartiates I was no longer amazed. Indeed Lycurgus, who established laws for them, which they obeyed and so prospered, I both admire and believe him to be most exceedingly wise.

Xenophon, *Constitution of the Spartans* 1.1–2

1 What do these two short quotations tell us about the attitudes of the two authors to Lycurgus?
2 Which do you think might be more reliable?
3 Which do you think provides a more accurate representation of the Spartans' own beliefs about Lycurgus?

responsible for Athens' defeat. He was from an upper-class family and resented the radical democracy. (For more discussion of Thucydides, see pp. 22–3.)

THE AGŌGĒ: EDUCATION OF BOYS

The purpose of the **agōgē** was to produce young men who would be loyal and brave warriors, and, as modern scholars have recently argued (see Explore Further box, right), who would have the full range of qualities and virtues needed to fulfil their lives as citizens.

The agōgē was carefully organised and supervised by the government. The system began as soon as a child was born. The baby would be inspected for any defects and those who did not come up to the mark were left to die (Plutarch *Lycurgus* 16.1; LACTOR 21, D73 **PS**). Until the age of seven boys stayed at home. Then they were put into groupings within communal barracks where they had to sleep every night until they were thirty (even if they got married).

When boys reached the age of fourteen life became even harsher. There were restrictions about what they were allowed to wear (see Plutarch *Lycurgus* 16.6; LACTOR 21, D76 **PS**). They exercised naked, were kept short of food, and encouraged to steal (although they were whipped if they were caught). Xenophon gives us further details about how the young men were expected to behave:

> So when they were out on the streets he required them to keep their hands firmly under their cloaks, to walk in silence, not to look around but to keep their eyes firmly fixed on the ground. **PS**
>
> Xenophon, *Constitution of the Spartans* 3.4 (LACTOR 21, D77)

The content of this later education, which lasted until they were nineteen, was simple. It consisted of elementary reading and writing, and physical exercise in various forms. They had some musical training, probably the flute and lyre, and also learnt dance and poetry (Plutarch *Lycurgus* 21 **CW** **PS**).

Most of these activities were organised within teams or communally, rather than encouraging individuality. This was true even in some of the more physical games; Pausanias (*c.* AD 110–180) records one such game:

> Lykourgos set in place laws regarding the constitution but also for the fighting of the ephebes . . . on the following day, a little before midday, they enter the aforementioned place by bridges. Lots drawn during the night predetermine the route by which each side enters. They fight with fists, kick with their feet, bite, and gouge opponents' eyes. I have just described the way they fight man to man: but they also charge at each other violently in a group and push each other into the water.
>
> Pausanias, *Description of Greece* 3.14.8–10 (LACTOR 21, D81)

It should perhaps be noted that neither Xenophon nor Plutarch mention this competition. However, they do both mention the ordeal the young men had to face at the sanctuary of Artemis Orthia. This sanctuary was on the eastern boundary of the city of Sparta; Artemis seems to have been a goddess of boundaries, certainly between the wild and the tamed,

agōgē a traditional term for the Spartan education and training system for boys and young men, although not used by any source in the classical period

EXPLORE FURTHER

The following two articles are recent discussions of the role of the agōgē in Spartan society, from slightly different points of view.

Ducat, J., *Spartan Education* (Classical Press of Wales, 2006), chapter 5 'The Social function of education'.
Hodkinson, S., 'Was classical Sparta a military society?' in S. Hodkinson and A. Powell (eds), *Sparta and War* (Classical Press of Wales, 2006), pp. 111–62

FIGURE 2.2
The remains of the temple of Artemis Orthia.

PRESCRIBED SOURCE

Title: *Description of Greece*

Author: Pausanias

Date: AD 110–180

Genre: geography

Significance: a Greek traveller who wrote his description of Greece from his own observations

Prescribed sections: 3.14.9–10

Read it here: LACTOR 21: *Sparta* (KCL 2017) D81

but also between youth and adulthood (Cartledge, *Spartan Reflections* (Duckworth, 2001) p. 86). She may even have been regarded almost as a patron deity of the agōgē.

The skills the boys needed to display during the ordeal were speed and agility, but also cunning, as the original purpose was for them to steal as many cheeses from the altar as they could.

Study questions

He made it a special competition to steal cheeses from the altar of Artemis Orthia, while giving others the task of whipping the would-be thieves, thus seeking to demonstrate that a little pain means a long term gain in fame and delight. In this there was a supplementary lesson also: that where speed is of the essence, idleness brings the least reward and the greatest supply of troubles.

Xenophon, *Constitution of the Spartans* 2.9 (LACTOR 21, D74)

1 According to Xenophon what is the object of this exercise, and what quality did the boys need in order to be successful?

. . . when we think of what happens to present day young adults (*ephebes*), many of whom I have seen being flogged to death at the altar of Artemis Orthia.

Plutarch, *Lycurgus* 18.1 (LACTOR 21, D80)

2 What is missing in Plutarch's description? What does this omission imply is happening in his description?

Pausanias also seems to imply that the boys were simply beaten in his time, with no mention of the cheeses (3.16.10–11, LACTOR 21, C93); this probably means that a rather more gruesome ordeal had been substituted by the time of Plutarch and Pausanias, in place of the original trial of speed. Others might argue that Xenophon plays down the gruesome aspects because he admired Sparta, but in that case why mention it at all? The context in which he mentions it also implies that it was intended as a test of speed and cunning, ultimately in preparation for deploying these skills on the battlefield. It is certain that the agōgē was a harsh upbringing, as Plutarch admits.

> Agesilaos seemed likely to pass his life as a private citizen, and was put through
> the so-called 'agoge' at Lakedaimon. This was a harsh and painful way of life
> but one which taught the young boys to be obedient. It was this, they say, that led to
> Sparta being dubbed 'man-breaking' by Simonides as having customs which made
> her citizens especially obedient to her laws and submissive, just like horses which are
> broken in from the very start.
>
> Plutarch, *Agesilaos* 1.2 (LACTOR 21, E82)

The dance and music was probably also intended to assist military manoeuvres.

> . . . so that the whole effect on their enemies was one of shock and awe, as the
> army advanced in step with the rhythm of the pipes, in close order with no gaps
> in the line, with no hint of hesitation, and with their battle hymn ringing in their ears
> as they marched into deadly danger with courage high and hearts aglow. When
> soldiers are fired up in this way, they are unlikely to feel fear or uncontrolled
> aggression, so much as fixity of purpose combined with high hopes and total
> confidence that God is on their side.
>
> Plutarch, *Lycurgus* 22.3 (LACTOR 21, D93)

The Athenians certainly seem to have been aware of, and admired, Spartan dancing:

> LAKONIAN: Here, kind sir, you take the bagpipes,
> So that I can dance the two-step and sing a fine song
> In honour of the Athenians and also ourselves.
> ATHENIAN 2: I beg you by the gods do take the blowers, 1245
> For I enjoy seeing you all dance.
>
> Aristophanes *Lysistrata* 1241–1246 (LACTOR 21, G7)

The most famous Spartan dancing festival was the **gymnopaidia** in which teams of men competed in a dancing competition. It took place in the middle of summer, so must also have been another feat of endurance. Aristophanes expects his audience to be aware that the Spartans were known for their dancing. We know that foreigners went to Sparta to witness this festival.

> **gymnopaidia** a festival of dancing for teams of men who competed against each other

> Lichas used to entertain foreign guests who were on a visit to Lakedaimon at the
> Gymnopaedia.
>
> Xenophon, *Memorabilia* 1.2.61 (LACTOR 21, C76)

PRESCRIBED SOURCE

Title: *Lysistrata*

Author: Aristophanes (*c.* 446–*c.* 386)

Date: 411

Genre: comedy

Significance: written for an Athenian audience, but containing two Spartan characters, Lampito (a woman) and a herald.

Prescribed sections: lines 78–84; 1241–1321

Read it here: LACTOR 21: *Sparta* (KCL 2017) D66; G7

Study questions

> Reading and writing lessons were restricted to the minimum necessary. All the rest of their education was directed towards the habit of instant obedience, endurance of pain, and military success.
>
> Plutarch, *Lycurgus* 16.6 (LACTOR 21, D76)

Read the rest of Plutarch *Lycurgus* 16–18 (LACTOR 21, D73, D76, D78, D80) and Xenophon *Constitution of the Spartans* 2–3 (LACTOR 21, D74, D77)

1 To what extent do the details given by Plutarch and Xenophon support Plutarch's comment above?
2 Are there any differences between their two accounts?
3 Can you think of any reason(s) for this? **S&C**

> **eirēn (pl. eirenes)** a young man in charge of the troops of younger boys and able to punish them, aged at least twenty
>
> **paidonomos** the official in charge of the agōgē
>
> **hippagretai** the three men appointed to choose the 300 hippeis, each picking 100

When they were twenty, boys might be chosen as **eirenes** whose role was to enforce discipline over the younger boys and who carried whips. In charge of the whole system was an official called the **paidonomos**, who could inflict punishments on the boys at any time, as could any Spartan (Xenophon *Constitution of the Spartans* 2.10, LACTOR 21, D74). **PS**

The military training continued after the age of twenty; once the young men were twenty they were regarded as adult, and could be required to fight.

Xenophon also records another means by which young men were encouraged to maintain their fitness and compete with each other:

> [3] The ephors start by selecting the three outstanding members of the year group, who are designated *hippagretai*, (guard commanders). Each of these selects a hundred others, openly stating the reasons for choosing this one and rejecting that. [4] As a result, those who fail to win the honour of selection become enemies of those who rejected them and bitter rivals of those who were chosen in their stead. So they all keep an eye on each other to see if any of them offends the established code of honour . . . [6] This arrangement ensures that everyone takes pains to remain

physically fit, because wherever they meet each other fist fights break out. Anyone who happens to be present has the legal right to separate the warring parties; if they refuse to obey him, then the *paidonomos* marches them in front of the ephors, who impose a heavy fine in order to make it clear that one must never allow a fit of hot temper to override the duty of obedience to the laws.

Xenophon, *Constitution of the Spartans* 4.3–4 and 6 (LACTOR 21, D79, D50)

The **Three Hundred** chosen were probably the elite army unit elsewhere referred to as the **hippeis**. Plutarch records a different reaction, from a man who was not chosen:

For when Paidaretus was not chosen for the Three Hundred, he went away beaming greatly as though he was glad that the city had three hundred men better than he.

Plutarch, *Lycurgus* 25.4

This would seem to represent the 'ideal' reaction, whereas Xenophon's account might represent the reality!

Another part of the young Spartans' training was the **krypteia** (literally meaning 'secret or hidden service'). There is much disagreement about this, and it may well not have been a formal part of the agōgē for all Spartans (J. Ducat, 2006), although Paul Cartledge puts forward a case that it was (*Spartan Reflections* (Duckworth, 2001) p. 88).

We shall discuss this matter further in the section on the Social Structure of Sparta (pp. 98–100). For the moment we shall merely note how Plutarch describes it.

THE EDUCATION OF GIRLS

In these states it is not only the men who think highly of education, but also the women.

Plato, *Protagoras* 342d (LACTOR 21, D72)

The states Plato is describing here are Crete and Sparta. Unlike in most other Greek city-states, the women were expected to exercise, but for a very special reason, according to Plutarch (*Lycurgus* 14, LACTOR C69).

ACTIVITY

Read Plutarch *Lycurgus* 28 (LACTOR 21, D44) and Thucydides 4.80 (LACTOR 21, E68).

- Make notes of the main points of the krypteia as described by Plutarch, and the details of the incident recorded by Thucydides.
- Do you think Plutarch thought that the krypteia was part of the agōgē as set up by Lycurgus? Give your reasons.

Lycurgus thought that women with strong bodies would produce strong, healthy babies. He therefore had them wrestle and throw the javelin and discus. Xenophon says much the same, and here he may well be the source Plutarch used. The girls also had their own choral dancing competitions.

Three Hundred the elite unit of the Spartan army, otherwise known as the hippeis

hippeis the elite unit of the Spartan army, sometimes also called after their number: Three Hundred. The word means cavalrymen literally, so this may have been their original function. They were chosen from young men aged between twenty to twenty-nine and acted as the king's bodyguard

krypteia the secret institution in which a select group of young Spartans were sent out equipped only with daggers; one of their roles was to kill potentially troublesome helots

EXPLORE FURTHER

These two books give slightly different views of the krypteia, whether it was a formal part of the agoge, or a more marginalised activity on occasion for a select few.

Cartledge, P., *Spartan Reflections* (Duckworth, 2001).
Ducat, J., *Spartan Education* (Classical press of Wales, 2006), chapter 9.

PS
1

So we may sing of Sparta,
Which cares about dancing for the gods   1305
  And stamping feet,
And like ponies the young girls
  Beside the Eurotas
Busily prance, their feet raising
  Clouds of dust.   1310

Aristophanes, *Lysistrata* 1304–1310 (LACTOR 21, G7)

PRESCRIBED SOURCE

Title: *History of the Peloponnesian War*

Author: Thucydides

Date: *c.* 455–400

Genre: history

Significance: certainly wrote from an Athenian perspective, and tends to characterise Sparta as the opposite to Athens.

Prescribed sections: 1.6, 1.10, 1.68–71, 1.79–87, 1.101–103, 1.119.1, 1.128–135

Read it here: LACTOR 21: *Sparta* (KCL 2017) G2, E141, E29, E30, E31, E142, E62b, E26, B6

Translations for sources not covered in LACTOR 21 are available on the Companion Website.

Prescribed sections: 2.9.2, 2.25, 2.91–2

Read it here: LACTOR 21: *Sparta* (KCL 2017) D100, E34

Translations for sources not covered in LACTOR 21 are available on the Companion Website.

Prescribed sections: 3.31, 3.79, 4.8, 4.15–16, 4.23, 4.26, 4.33–35, 4.38, 4.80–81, 4.117

Read it here: LACTOR 21: *Sparta* (KCL 2017) E68, E90, E91, E93, E94, E68, E35, H40

Translations for sources not covered in LACTOR 21 are available on the Companion Website.

Prescribed sections: 5.16–17, 5.23, 5.34, 5.57, 5.63–74

Read it here: LACTOR 21: *Sparta* (KCL 2017) E39, H33, D4, E143, B18, E52, E98, E99, E100, E101, E102, E103, E104

Translations for sources not covered in LACTOR 21 are available on the Companion Website.

Prescribed sections: 6.93, 7.11–12, 8.3.2, 8.5

Read it here: LACTOR 21: *Sparta* (KCL 2017) E118, E41, E150

Translations for sources not covered in LACTOR 21 are available on the Companion Website.

PRESCRIBED SOURCE

Title: *Alcibiades*, *Laws* and *Protagoras*

Author: Plato

Date: *c.* 429–347

Genre: philosophy

Significance: a contemporary of the latter part of our period so many of his writings do refer to Sparta. Amongst his associates and family members were both supporters and opponents of Sparta.

Prescribed sections: *Alcibiades* 1.122d–123b; *Laws* 633b–c; *Protagoras* 342d

Read it here: LACTOR 21: *Sparta* (KCL 2017) E72; C74, C85, D42; D72

PRESCRIBED SOURCE

Author: Alcman

Date: seventh century BC

Genre: songs composed to be sung by competing teams of girls at festivals

Significance: early, but one of our very few sources written in Sparta

Prescribed sections: Fragments 1–3

Read it here: LACTOR 21: *Sparta* (KCL 2017) A14–A16

Study questions

As far as Lykourgos was concerned, there were enough female slaves to produce clothing, whereas the most important task for freeborn women was producing children. So as a first priority he laid it down that physical fitness was as important for women as for men. So he established women's competitions in both running and wrestling, in the belief that the offspring of two strong parents would be all the more robust.

> Xenophon, *Constitution of the Spartans* 1.4 (LACTOR 21, D68)

1 How far do the accounts of Plutarch in *Lycurgus* 14 (LACTOR 21, D70) and the passage from Xenophon above agree?

2 Does either include any additional detail, and if so what?

He had no time for the idea of a sheltered upbringing for girls any more than boys, and eliminated all forms of feeble effeminacy, even to the extent of compelling them to take part in processions naked and to dance and sing at certain festivals in the presence of young men as spectators.

> Plutarch, *Lycurgus* 14.2 (LACTOR 21, D70)

Read Alcman 1–3 (LACTOR 21, A14–16)

1 What is there in what Alcman writes which might support what Plutarch says in the passage above?

Read Aristophanes *Lysistrata* 78–87 (LACTOR 21, D66)

2 What does this suggest the Athenians knew about Spartan education for girls?

FIGURE 2.3
Statuette of a running
Spartan girl, now in
the British Museum.

PRESCRIBED SOURCE

Title: Bronze figurine of
a woman or girl (BM
1876,0510.1)

Date: 520–500

Genre: statuette

Significance: a girl or
woman dancing or
running; she seems
to be hitching up her
skirt, which would
reveal her thigh

View it here: LACTOR
21: *Sparta* (KCL 2017)
D64 and Figure 2.3

We perhaps should note that neither Xenophon nor Plutarch say that the girls exercised naked, though this may have been the case. However, the term 'thigh-flashers' used first by a sixth century poet, Ibycus, to describe Spartan girls would suggest that they wore a type of slit gym-slip. This would be supported by a series of sixth century bronze statuettes of girls running in some sort of garment. The great fifth century tragic playwright Euripides makes Peleus say that Spartan boys and girls exercised together naked, but this should probably be discounted as literary invention (*Andromache* 597–60).

Girls even had a role in the education of the boys:

Sometimes they in turn would poke fun and hurl good-natured abuse at a young man who got out of line; and by contrast they would also write hymns of praise and deliver them in honour of those who deserved it, thus encouraging competitiveness and an eagerness to excel in the young men themselves.

Plutarch, *Lycurgus* 14.3 (LACTOR 21, D70)

The boys were constantly being watched and judged by someone so they were always trying to ensure they gave of their best in order to impress those watching, and to avoid criticism.

THE VALUES THE AGŌGĒ WAS INTENDED TO DEVELOP

The main value that the agōgē was devised to instil was that individuals always put the state above themselves. The ultimate sacrifice was to give one's life for the state, as is shown by these comments from Plutarch and Xenophon:

Those burying the body were not allowed to inscribe the name, unless the man had fallen in battle or the woman was a priestess.

Plutarch, *Lycurgus* 27.2 (LACTOR 21, B35b)

Another admirable feature of Lykourgan policy was to create a culture in the state where a noble death was seen as preferable by far to a disgraceful life.

Xenophon, *Constitution of the Spartans* 9.1 (LACTOR 21, D96)

It should be noted that the interpretation of the Plutarch passage is disputed as the reading 'a priestess' has until relatively recently been read as 'in childbirth'. Modern scholarship prefers the reading given here.

PRESCRIBED SOURCE

Author: Tyrtaeus

Date: *c.* middle of the seventh century BC

Genre: patriotic poetry

Significance: his poetry survives in fragments, mostly in quotations in other authors. Much of it is written to instil courage and patriotic feelings in the Spartans in their war against the Messenian helots

Prescribed sections: 6, 10–12

Read it here: LACTOR 21: *Sparta* (KCL 2017) A6–9

S & C

Explore Further

These two articles discuss the reasons why modern scholars prefer the reading 'priestess' in Plutarch and the implications of this.

Brulé, P. and L. Piolot, 'Women's way of death: fatal childbirth or hierai? Commemorative stones at Sparta' and Plutarch *Lycurgus* 27.3, in T.J. Figueira (ed.), *Spartan Society* (Classical Press of Wales, 2004), pp. 151–78.

OR

Dillon, M., 'Were Women Who Died in Childbirth Honoured with Grave Insciptions?' in *Hermes* 135 (2007), pp. 149–65, available in JSTOR: http://www.jstor.org/stable/40379113

S & C

Activity

Read Plutarch *Sayings of Spartan Women*.

- Find and note down **five** examples of sayings which reflect the values just outlined.

Now read Tyrtaeus 10–12 (LACTOR 21 A7–9)

- Find and note down **five** quotations from these poems which support these same values.

Read Plutarch *Sayings of the Spartans, Agis*, 2–4 and 6 (LACTOR 21, F32)

- How do these sayings reflect Spartan values?

Tyrtaeus (Tyrtaios) was probably writing *c.* 650, and was trying to instil patriotic valour in the Spartans in their war against the Messenians, but the values he stood for were certainly admired in later Sparta and young men in the agōgē would have learnt them. Plutarch records that Leonidas, when asked what he thought of Tyrtaeus as a poet, replied,

> good for firing-up the spirit of the young.

> Plutarch, *Cleomenes* 2.3

The other values which Lycurgus apparently tried to instil in the Spartans were that they were all equal, had the same land allotment and turned their backs on luxury and extravagance, and always tried to develop virtue in all areas (see Xenophon *Constitution of the Spartans* 10, LACTOR 21, D12, D51, F1). We shall consider the extent to which these were actually true in the final topic, in particular the equal land allotments. The chief areas of virtue were obedience to authority both political, military and social (Herodotus 7.104.4, LACTOR 21, D46 **PS**), respect, and self-restraint (Xenophon *Constitution of the Spartans*, 2.14, LACTOR 21, D74). Kritias also refers to this self-restraint in terms of the Spartans' drinking.

PRESCRIBED SOURCE

Title: *Histories*

Author: Herodotus

Date: fifth century BC

Genre: history

Significance: he lived in Athens, but does claim to have used Spartan sources. He admired Sparta and their courage at Thermopylae (Thermopylai)

Prescribed sections: 5.75, 6.56–60, 7.3, 7.104.4, 7.228, 7.234.2, 8.3, 9.28

Read it here: LACTOR 21: *Sparta* (KCL 2017) E14, D5, D8, D10, D24, D3, D46, B4, E27, E84; translations for sources not covered in LACTOR 21 are available on the Companion Website.

oliganthrōpia the shortage of, and decline in, manpower in Sparta

At Sparta it is custom and established practice   1
To drink from the same wine-cup
And not to name people to drink their health . . .

For as a result of such drinking, tongues are loosened   9
To shameful stories; bodies grow weak;
Cloudy weakness sits on the eye,
Forgetfulness of mind wastes memory away:
The mind is deceived: household slaves become
Undisciplined; ruinous expense descends on the house.
Lakedaimonian boys drink just enough to bring   15
The minds of all to cheerful optimism,
Their tongues to friendliness and restrained laughter . . .

Kritias, *Governance of the Spartans*, fr. 6, quoted in Athenaios *Sophists at Dinner*, 432d and f, (LACTOR 21, D60) **PS**

Gorgo worried that more wine would make Spartans less good (Plutarch *Sayings of Spartan Women, Gorgo*, 2, LACTOR 21, F30). **PS**

The idea of equality was supported by all Spartans having to go through the same education, although it is interesting that within the agōgē there were elements which encouraged competition and to a certain extent rewarded it. They also had to live in the barracks and eat the same food. As we shall see in the next topic, they all had to contribute the same to communal meals.

The meagre rations and rules about what the boys could wear and where they slept were all designed so they did not become used to more luxurious life-styles. The physical training and tests of endurance were designed to develop fitness and obedience.

We shall consider these again in later topics, as well as whether Sparta actually lived up to these values. As we shall see, one of the problems which she faced was **oliganthrōpia**, which means a shortage of manpower. This became steadily worse through the fifth century.

PRESCRIBED SOURCE

Author: Kritias

Date: *c.* 460–403

Genre: drama, philosophy and on Sparta

Significance: a contemporary of our period, but Athenian and admired Sparta; only preserved in quotations in other authors

Prescribed sections: 81B37; fr6 (81B6 = Athenaios *Scholars at* Dinner, 11.41)

Read it here: LACTOR 21: *Sparta* (KCL 2017) D40, D60; C61

- Explain the details of the various stages of the agōgē. Support your answer with references to the sources (noting that Xenophon is the only reliable source for our period).
- Explain the role of the eirenes.
- Describe the training of Spartan women with references to the sources, and explain the reasons given for this training in the sources.
- Give references to the sources to illustrate Spartan values and the treatment of cowards.

Further Reading

Cartledge, P.A., *Spartan Reflections* (London: Duckworth, 2001), pp. 79–90.

Cartledge, P.A., *The Spartans, an Epic History* (London: Pan Books, 2003) pp. 153–66

Ducat, J., *Education: Youth and Society in the Classical Period* (Swansea: Classical Press of Wales, 2006).

Hodkinson, S., 'Social Order and the Conflict of Values in Classical Sparta', in *Sparta*, ed. M. Whitby (Edinburgh: Edinburgh University Press, 2002), pp. 108–15.

de Ste. Croix, G.E.M., *The Origins of the Peloponnesian War* (London: Duckworth, 1972) App. XVI, pp. 331–2.

The first question in the exam will be a passage selected from the prescribed sources with one question assessing its usefulness as a source.

The question below is of the same style, but is a longer passage than is prescribed from this work of Plato. Even so, it is also slightly shorter than those which would normally be set in the exam.

> . . . the endurance of pain – which is very much a feature of our society, in fighting by hand with each other, and in the 'raids' with many whippings resulting each time. In addition there is the so-called *krypteia* which is amazingly physically demanding as regards endurance: in winter they go without shoes or blankets; they look after themselves without servants, and spend night and day wandering about the countryside. In addition, at the Gymnopaidia, they have to show endurance, competing in the full heat of the summer.

Plato, *Laws* 633b (LACTOR 21, C74, C85, D42)

1. How useful is this passage for our understanding of the education of Spartan boys in the agōgē? [12]

2.2 The Social Structure of Sparta

TOPIC OVERVIEW

- the different status, roles and contributions of Spartiates, perioikoi and helots
- the effects the helots had on Spartan policy
- helot revolts
- the krypteia
- the status and role of women in Sparta.

The prescribed sources for this topic are:

- Aristotle, *Politics* 1269
- Aristotelian *Spartan Constitution*: Herakleides Lembos 373.10
- Diodorus Siculus, *Library of History* 11.63.1–4
- Herodotus, *Histories* 9.28
- Myron of Priene FGrH 106 F2
- Plato *Laws* 633b–c
- Plutarch, *Lycurgus* 8–10, 12, 14–15, 24, 28
- Plutarch *Sayings of Spartan Women, Gorgo* 6
- Strabo, *Geography* 8.5.4
- Thucydides, *The History of the Peloponnesian War* 1.68–71, 79–84, 101–103, 4.8, 4.80, 5.23, 5.34, 5.64, 5.67–68
- Tyrtaeus 6 and 10
- Xenophon, *Constitution of the Spartans* 1, 5, 7, 9, 15

Lakonia the area of the south-eastern Peloponnese controlled by Sparta

perioikos (pl. perioikoi) literally 'dwellers-around', free inhabitants of settlements around Lakonia and Messenia

By about 1,000 BC, groups of Greeks from further north had moved down into the Peloponnese. These Greeks were Dorians, as opposed to the original inhabitants, who were Achaean. The Dorian newcomers quickly became dominant throughout the Peloponnese.

In the south-eastern Peloponnese, referred to as **Lakonia**, Sparta, a settlement in the fertile valley of the river Eurotas, became the leading settlement and by *c*. 650 had gained control of all of Lakonia. The inhabitants were enslaved, becoming **helots**. The other settlements were left free and their inhabitants became **perioikoi**.

FIGURE 2.4
The isthmus between the Peloponnese and mainland Greece is a remarkably thin strip of land, as seen here.

About the same time, Sparta began to need more land, so crossed the Taygetos mountains to the west of the city and conquered the south-western Peloponnese, **Messenia**. The inhabitants of Messenia were enslaved and became helots.

Sparta then began to look northwards, but was defeated by Argos *c*. 669. About 650, the Messenian helots revolted and Sparta had to fight another war across the Taygetos mountains. This was the period when **Tyrtaeus** wrote his patriotic poems, and many scholars also see it as a possible date for the so-called Lycurgan political reforms.

Sparta recovered and went from strength to strength. By the middle of the sixth century it had defeated both Tegea in Arcadia (Arkadia) and Argos to the north, but instead of occupying their territory, it made treaties. Sparta continued this policy with other states in the Peloponnese, and thus it formed and became head of the Peloponnesian League (though Argos consistently refused to join). This was Sparta's position when the threat from Persia arose at the start of the fifth century.

> **Messenia** the south-western Peloponnese, conquered by the Spartans in the Archaic Period

SPARTIATES

Agesilaus . . . ordered the allies to sit down with each other all mixed-up, and the Spartans on their own by themselves. Then he told the potters to stand up . . . then the blacksmiths . . . carpenters, builders, and each of the other crafts. And so all the allies stood up except a few, but none of the Spartans, for they were not allowed to work in or learn a manual trade.

Plutarch, *Agesilaus* 26.5

The passage records an incident which occurred a little after the end of the period for this depth study (478–404), as Agesilaus became king in 400. However, it is useful as the

Spartiate adult male Spartan citizen (they are sometimes also called 'Equals', or 'homoioi' in books)

syssition (pl. syssitia) Spartan dining-mess, consisting of about fifteen Spartiates

point which Agesilaus was making was that the small number of Spartans he had led on the campaign did not have to work for a living as opposed to the allies who did. This was due to the helots providing for the **Spartiates'** material needs. Xenophon *Constitution of the Spartans* 7 (LACTOR 21, D53) also makes this point.

To be a Spartiate, both parents had to be Spartan and the young man had to have gone through the agōgē as described in the previous section. He also then had to be accepted into a **syssition** by its existing members (probably when he was about twenty).

The Spartiates would also have to continue their physical and military training (see Xenophon *Constitution of the Spartans* 5.8 (LACTOR 21, D61) and Plutarch *Lycurgus* 24.1), and not display cowardice in battle.

As we have seen, Spartiates did not have jobs as citizens of other Greek states might have done. Plutarch repeats this idea in our prescribed sources:

> He (Lycurgus) did not allow them (the Spartans) to engage in any manual trade at all, and there was no need whatever for them to gather wealth with its associated trouble and hard work on account of the fact that wealth was just not envied or thought highly of.
>
> Plutarch, *Lycurgus* 24

Study questions
Read the extract from Plutarch *Lycurgus* below:

> each mess member would contribute every month a bushel of barley-meal, eight gallons of wine, five pounds of cheese, and five half-pounds of figs, plus a very small sum of money for "extras". One particular custom was that anyone who had made a sacrifice of first-fruits or had enjoyed a successful hunt would send a share of it to the mess. The reason was that it was permitted for anyone who had been kept late by sacrificing or hunting to dine at home; but everyone else was required to be present at the mess dinner.
>
> Plutarch, *Lycurgus* 12.2, (LACTOR 21, D63) PS

1 What information does this passage give us about the syssitia?
Read the rest of Plutarch *Lycurgus* 12 (LACTOR 21, D63 PS), and Xenophon *Constitution of the Spartans* 5 (LACTOR 21, C62)

2 How do you think the syssitia contributed to the comradeship of the Spartans?

ACTIVITY
Herodotus tells us that a coward was known as a 'trembler' (7.231)

Read Xenophon *Constitution of the Spartans* 9.4–6 (LACTOR 21, D96 PS), Thucydides 5.34, Tyrtaeus 10 (LACTOR 21, A7) and Plutarch *Lycurgus* 15.1–3 (LACTOR 21, D71).

- Make a list of the various ways in which a coward was treated in Sparta, noting the source which gives us each piece of information.

We also need to consider the way of life the Spartiates led.

Xenophon (*Constitution of the Spartans* 7, LACTOR 21, D53 **PS**) gives a number of ways in which Lycurgus tried to curb wealth and greed. These are:

- Spartans were banned from the pursuit of wealth
- making money was not necessary as provisions were all contributed on an equal basis
- someone who helped his fellows by physical labour was more well-thought of than one who spent money
- the currency Lycurgus introduced was very bulky, needing a waggon to move a relatively small amount
- searches were made for gold and silver and anyone found with it was fined

Plutarch (*Lycurgus* 9 & 10, LACTOR 21, D58, D63 **CW** **PS**) seems to have based his account on that of Xenophon, even including some of the same details and language. It is therefore likely that Plutarch, being a later writer, based his account on that of Xenophon.

Plutarch says that Lycurgus banned gold and silver coinage. This cannot be true as, if Lycurgus did actually exist, he would have done so before the Greeks introduced coinage. However, archaeology shows that the Spartans did not issue coins as other states later did. Plutarch also adds that the ban on coined money led to a decline in trade and luxury goods, and the archaeological record can also support this.

ACTIVITY **PS**

Read Xenophon *Constitution of the Spartans* 7 (LACTOR 21, D53) and Plutarch *Lycurgus* 9–10 (LACTOR 21, D58, D63).

- Find **two** details in Plutarch which are also in Xenophon's account.

EXPLORE FURTHER **S&C**

The following two articles give recent discussions of the overall nature of Spartan society and their treatment of the so-called 'tremblers'

Ducat, J., 'The Spartan Tremblers', in S. Hodkinson and A. Powell (eds), *Sparta and War* (Classical Press of Wales, 2006), pp. 1–55.

Hodkinson, S., 'Was Sparta a Military Society?', in S. Hodkinson & A. Powell (eds), *Sparta and War* (Classical Press of Wales, 2006), pp. 111–62.

PERIOIKOI

. . . specified tracts of high quality land in many of the territories of the *perioikoi* shall belong to him, sufficient to sustain the royal household adequately but without excessive wealth.

> Xenophon, *Constitution of the Spartans* 15.3 (LACTOR 21, D9)

. . . but they were interrupted by an earthquake, which occurred at about the same time and led to a revolt by the helots. (The majority of the helots were descendants of the original indigenous population of Messenia, who had been enslaved by the Lakedaimonians. Thus they were all known as Messenians). Together with the neighbouring *perioikoi* of Thouria and Aithaia, they seceded to Mount Ithome.

> Thucydides, *The History of the Peloponnesian War* 1.101.2 (LACTOR 21, D38)

After the Peloponnesians pulled back from Attika, the Spartiates themselves and the *perioikoi* who lived closest went immediately to help at Pylos.

> Thucydides, *The History of the Peloponnesian War* 4.8.1 (LACTOR D104)

Apart from a few more military contexts, the three passages above are the only references to the perioikoi in any of the prescribed sources to the perioikoi; this does not tell us a great deal, so much of what we will say about them is based on assumptions.

FIGURE 2.5
Map of the Peloponnese
showing regional
boundaries.

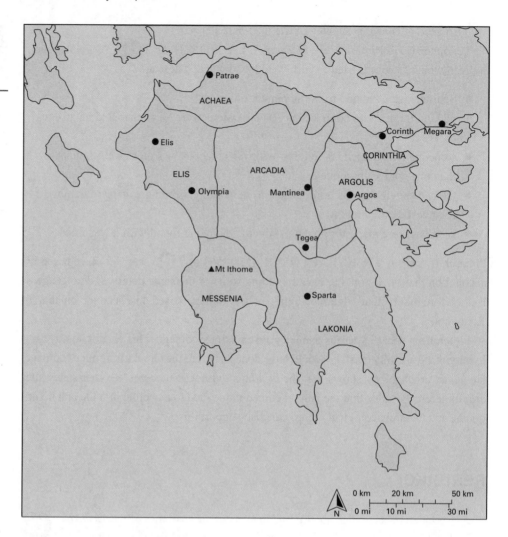

The perioikoi were mostly inhabitants of the towns and villages of Lakonia and Messenia. It seems as though the towns were able to govern themselves, but could not have an independent foreign policy and served in the Spartan army alongside the Spartiates, though they did not go through the agōgē. We will discuss their military obligations later (p. 95).

We have seen that the Spartiates were not allowed to take part in manufacture or trade, but they will have needed weapons, cooking and eating pots and utensils, shoes and other leather goods and, not least, items to be used as offerings at sanctuaries. It is normally therefore assumed that these were made by the perioikoi. Some of those who lived in coastal settlements no doubt were fishermen, and some may have even engaged in trade with other states, but there is very little evidence for any of this. Many must have been farmers and some could also have been wealthy. (Xenophon refers to some kaloi kagathoi from amongst the perioikoi volunteering to join an expedition in 381 (*Hellenica* 5.3.9, LACTOR 21, E57). The term 'kaloi kagathoi' is normally used by Greek authors to refer to the leisured upper-class in Greek society.

Cartledge (*Sparta and Lakonia: A Regional History 1300–362 BC* (Routledge, 2002) p. 159) identifies a list of about eighty perioikic settlements referred to in the sources, a little fewer than Androtion, an early fourth century orator, who states there were about 100. It is also worth noting that the distance of the furthest of these from Sparta by road was considerably greater than that of say Sounion from Athens, or even of Corinth from Athens. The more recent project of the Copenhagen Polis Centre attests fifty-four settlements for the Archaic and Classical periods.

The perioikoi certainly also were required to fight, as we can see from the third passage on page 93 and it is clear from Herodotus (9.28, LACTOR 21, E84 (PS)) that as many perioikoi fought at the battle of Plataea as Spartiates. Apart from that, they do not get many other specific mentions in the sources, apart from at the battle of Mantinea (418):

> On this occasion the left wing was held by the *skiritai*, who always have this privilege (unique in the Lakedaimonian army) of operating on their own as a unit.
>
> Thucydides, *The History of the Peloponnesian War* 5.67.1 (LACTOR 21, E101)

The question of the inclusion of the perioikoi in the Spartan regiments will be discussed in Topic Four (pp. 122–4).

So why did the perioikoi not revolt during our period, apart from the two communities mentioned in the Thucydides extract at the start of this section? There are many possible answers, and again not much evidence.

HELOTS

The helots were the enslaved populations of Lakonia and Messenia. We will consider their position in three parts, first what they did, secondly how they were treated, and thirdly how their existence affected Spartan policy.

Consider these statements from the prescribed sources:

> The helots farmed the land for them, handing over the due tribute I spoke of
>
> Plutarch, *Lycurgus* 24.3

The 'tribute' Plutarch says he spoke of earlier is in chapter 8:

> Each man's allocation was sufficient to produce an annual crop of 70 measures of barley, 12 measures for his wife, and an appropriate amount of other fresh produce.
>
> Plutarch, *Lycurgus* 8.4 (LACTOR 21, D57)

The first of these two passages is one of only two references in the prescribed sources as to what the **helots** actually did, apart from military references. The other, Xenophon *Constitution of the Spartans* 1.4, (PS) LACTOR 21, D68, refers to female slaves making clothes. The Spartans certainly did have household slaves, and there is probably sufficient evidence from elsewhere to support the idea that helots acted in this capacity.

The idea that the helots contributed a fixed amount as stated by Plutarch is now no longer widely accepted. Stephen Hodkinson argues that their contribution was a 50/50 share of what they produced (*Property and Wealth in Classical Sparta* (Duckworth/The Classical Press of Wales, 2000), pp. 125–31). This is supported by Tyrtaeus (fragment 6, LACTOR 21, A6 (PS)) who states that the helots contributed half of what they produced.

KEY PLACES

Lakedaimonioi used by Thucydides to refer to any Spartan force, whatever its composition

Skiritai perioikoi from northern Lakonia

Study question

Read Shipley's article 'Perioecic Society' in M. Whitby (ed), *Sparta* (Edinburgh, 2002), pp. 177–89.

- What reasons does this chapter suggest for the continuing loyalty of the perioikoi?

> **S & C**
>
> Most of the evidence for helots serving as household slaves is gathered together in J. Ducat, 'The Obligations of Helots' in M. Whitby (ed.), *Sparta* (Edinburgh, 2002), pp. 195–9.
>
> This includes a reference to Plato when he is describing the **krypteia** (for which see below, pp. 98–9):
>
>
>
> > In addition there is the so-called *krypteia* which is amazingly physically demanding as regards endurance: in winter they go without shoes or blankets; they look after themselves without servants.
> >
> > Plato, *Laws* 633c (LACTOR 21, C74, C85, D42)
>
> Ducat argues that this implies that the young men did have attendants the rest of the time when they were not involved with the krypteia.

So, some helots were farming the Spartiates' estates and handing over a set proportion of produce, a set amount of which in turn the Spartiate had to contribute to his syssition. It is normally assumed that the helot was allowed to keep any surplus above what he had to hand over. Others worked as household slaves, and attended on the young Spartiates as they went through the agōgē. Those who worked on the land at least probably lived a family life on the farm with a wife and children as in the hinterland of Mt Parnon immediately east of Sparta. However, there is archaeological evidence from Messenia which suggests that in that region they lived in settlements rather than scattered around on individual farms (N. Kennell, *Spartans: A New History* (Wiley-Blackwell, 2010) p. 81). This is supported by Strabo who also implies that they lived in settlements.

> For the Lakedaimonians held them as state-slaves in a particular way, assigning certain settlements for them and particular duties.
>
> Strabo, *Geography* 8.5.4 (LACTOR 21, D35, H3)

PRESCRIBED SOURCE

Title: *Geography*

Author: Strabo

Date: 64/63 BC–*c.* AD 24

Genre: geography – a description of the Greco-Roman world

Significance: the period he is writing about is not always clear, nor are his sources. He also includes historical as well as geographical information

Prescribed sections: 8.5.4

Read it here: LACTOR 21: *Sparta* (KCL 2017) H3, D35

So, different regions seem to show different patterns of helot settlement.

Helots also acted as servants for Spartiates when they went to war. We shall now consider the nature of this military service, and how it might have changed through our period.

Just before the start of our period, at Thermopylae in 480, there is the famous story in Herodotus (7.229, LACTOR 21, F21) of the Spartan Eurytus ordering 'his helot' to lead him back into the battle. So it was normal for a Spartiate to have at least one helot attendant with him.

The following year, at Plateia (479):

> Ten thousand Lakedaimonians held the right wing: of them, five thousand were Spartiates who were guarded by thirty-five thousand light-armed helots – seven serving each man.
>
> Herodotus, *Histories* 9.28.1 (LACTOR 21, E84)

It is not entirely clear what Herodotus means by this. He implies that 7 helots guarded each Spartan. The helots do not feature at all in his actual description of the battle, and it is almost certain that the ninety-one Spartan casualties he records do not include any helots.

> By the time we get to the battle of Mantineia, we find a slightly different situation: This finally spurred them into action, and they mustered all their forces, Lakedaimonians and helots alike, to go to their aid with the largest army they had ever raised.
>
> Thucydides, *The History of the Peloponnesian War* 5.64.2 (LACTOR 21, E99)

When he describes how the Spartan army was drawn-up for the battle, Thucydides says that the Skiritai were set on the left wing and next to them were the 'Brasidian' soldiers from Thrace and with them the **neodamōdeis** (5.67.1, LACTOR 21, E101 **PS**).

So, at Mantinea we have freed helots fighting as **hoplites**. To understand the reason why, we must consider what had happened between 479 and 418.

Why did Brasidas take helots with him in 424? In 425, the Athenians had captured and fortified Pylos on the coast of Messenia; this was helot country. The Spartans badly wanted to recover Pylos, but needed something with which to bargain, so in 424 they sent the general Brasidas to Thrace to try to capture some of the cities there that were Athenian allies.

> **hoplite** heavily armoured infantry man, armed with breastplate, shield, helmet and spear. They functioned as a phalanx – a body of men, who took part of their protection from the shield of the man on their right

> They also welcomed an opportunity to send some of their helot population out of the country, in case the current situation and the capture of Pylos might encourage them to plot revolution. **PS**
>
> Thucydides, *The History of the Peloponnesian War* 4.80.2 (LACTOR 21, E68)

> On this occasion too they were willing enough to send out about 700 of them as hoplites with Brasidas, though the rest of the army were mercenaries recruited from the Peloponnese. **PS**
>
> Thucydides, *The History of the Peloponnesian War* 4.80.5 (LACTOR 21, E68)

How the helots were treated and the krypteia

It is clear that the Spartans treated the helots badly. A third century BC source, Myron of Priene, says,

they impose on the helots every arrogant task leading to their complete humiliation. For example, they insisted that they must all wear a dog-skin cap; be dressed in animal skins; receive a set number of beatings each year irrespective of any wrongdoing, so that they would never forget that they were slaves.

> Myron of Priene, *Messenian History*, FGrH 106 F2,
> quoted in Athenaios (14.74) (LACTOR 21, D41)

Their owners also had to punish them if they got too fat! Tyrtaeus described the conquered Messenian **helots** as

> Like mules distressed by great burdens,
> Bringing to their masters from grievous necessity
> Half of all the produce the ploughland bears.

Tyrtaeus frg 6, in Pausanias 4.14.5 (LACTOR 21, A6)

So, from fairly early on, the helots' situation was recognised as being pretty unpleasant. We have already considered what Thucydides has to say about the relationship between the Spartiates and the helots. The problem for us is that the other sources do not have much to say on this, apart from Plutarch, who is relatively late. However, let us look at what he does say.

Plutarch clearly does not want to ascribe the krypteia to Lycurgus, but, as we have already said, the idea of one single person coming up with the whole Spartan system and constitution at one time is probably not something we need to consider. However, he does prefer to date it to after the revolt of 464. On the other hand, the earlier Aristotelian *Spartan Constitution* ascribes it to Lycurgus, although he does say 'it is said that' (Herakleides Lembos 373.10, LACTOR 21, D43).

Study questions
Read Plutarch *Lycurgus* 28 again (LACTOR 21, D44)

Look back at the summary of this section you made in Topic 2.1.

1 Does Plutarch's description of the krypteia suggest that it was something that happened every year for all young Spartiates at a certain stage in the agōgē?

2 Do you think Plutarch approved of the krypteia? Give your reason(s).

PRESCRIBED SOURCE

Title: *Spartan Constitution*

Author: School of Aristotle

Date: fourth century BC

Genre: political philosophy

Significance: one of 158 constitutions written by Aristotle's students, which only survives as quoted in later authors. Plutarch probably used this as a major source for his writings on Sparta

Prescribed sections: as quoted in Herakleides Mebos 373.10

Read it here: LACTOR 21: *Sparta* (KCL 2017) D43

S & C

Talbert's note 87 on this chapter is useful (Plutarch *On Sparta* (Penguin, 2005), pp. 230–1).

Cartledge also has a good discussion of the incident recorded by Thucydides and referred to by Plutarch (*Spartan Reflections* (Duckworth, 2001), pp. 128–30). He argues that we should not take this as an isolated example, but that Thucydides intends us to see this incident as an example of the type of treatment the **helots** habitually suffered. See the pair of articles in the Figueira *Spartan Society* book referenced in the Explore Further box at the end of this section.

For an alternative argument, see P. Cartledge, *Spartan Reflections* (Duckworth, 2001), p. 88.

Study question

PS

. . . just as the helots seem continually to be lying in wait for disasters to befall the Lakedaimonians. . . . For if they are given any lassitude they become insolent and claim equal treatment to their masters; but if they suffer brutality in their lives they hate and plot against them. So it is clear that the people in these cases have not found the best way to deal with the helot-system.

Aristotle, *Politics* 1269a.38–1269b.12 with omission (LACTOR 21, D27)

On the basis of the evidence from the sources you have studied, why was the Spartan system established as it was?

Consider whether it was the existence of the helots which made the system possible, or because of the helots, to guard against the possibility of a revolt?

Consider Thucydides 4.80.3–5 (LACTOR 21, E68), Xenophon *Constitution of the Spartans* 1.3–4 (LACTOR 21, D68) and Plutarch *Lycurgus* 28 (LACTOR 21, D44) and 24.3.

CW PS

You might feel that one argument is stronger, or that actually both are true and support each other.

Study question

 PS

Read Thucydides 1.101–103 (LACTOR 21, E62)

What reason does Thucydides give for the Spartans sending away the Athenians (1.102)?

CW

THE EFFECTS THE HELOTS HAD ON SPARTAN POLICY AND HELOT REVOLTS

Sparta suffered from an increasingly serious shortage of manpower through our period. This is called **oliganthropia**. We will consider this and its causes and effects in the final topic of this chapter (p. 140). For the moment we are concerned with the effect it had on the relationship between the Spartiates and the helots. In 464 a major earthquake hit Sparta. The account is given by Thucydides (1.101–3, LACTOR 21, E62 PS).

This was clearly very serious for the Spartans:

When Phaion was archon in Athens, at Rome Lucius Furius Mediolanus and Marcus Manilius Vaso received the consulship. This year a great and incredible disaster befell the Lakedaimonians. There were great earthquakes in Sparta resulting in houses falling down completely and more than twenty thousand Lakedaimonians died.

Diodorus, *Library of History* 11.63.1 (LACTOR 21, E63)

Diodorus goes on to say:

The helots and Messenians who were hostile to the Lakedaimonians had kept quiet up until then, in fear of the superior power of Sparta: but when they saw that the majority of them had been killed in the earthquake, they felt contempt for the survivors who were few in number.

Diodorus, *Library of History* 11.63.4 (LACTOR 21, E63)

The result was that the helots revolted.

PRESCRIBED SOURCE

Title: *Library of History*

Author: Diodorus Siculus

Date: first century BC

Genre: history

Significance: preserves accounts recorded in earlier historians now lost to us

Prescribed sections: 11.50; 11.63.1–4

Read it here: LACTOR 21: *Sparta* (KCL 2017) E28, E63

This fear of a helot revolt is a recurring theme in Thucydides, although the only example we have of one happening in our period is after the earthquake in 464. It may, however, be why the Spartans only sent 5,000 of their then population of 8,000 to Plataea in 479, and also why they sent so many helots (Herodotus 9.28, LACTOR 21, E84): to keep an eye on them. It is certainly interesting that after Athens and Sparta made peace with each other in 421 (the Peace of Nicias (Nikias)) they then also made an alliance. After the normal first two clauses in which each city agrees to come to the aid of the other if they are attacked by a foreign enemy there is a further clause:

> And if the slaves rise up in revolt, the Athenians must come to help the Spartans with all their strength as far as they can.
>
>
>
> Thucydides, *The History of the Peloponnesian War* 5.23, LACTOR 21, B18

This is a one-sided clause, in other words there is no requirement that the Spartans should come to help the Athenians if their slaves revolted!

It is not stated anywhere in the sources, but many people think that behind this apparent slowness to act was the Spartan fear of committing troops and so exposing themselves at home to a possible helot revolt. This would certainly be a factor in the years after 464, but also may have been a factor in their slowness to act during the Persian invasions in the years just before our period. However, Herodotus does give perfectly acceptable religious reasons, along with the situation in the Peloponnese where Argos was hostile and Elis and Mantinea shaky allies.

EXPLORE FURTHER **S&C**

The pages referred to below are the main study and summary of the evidence for the extent to which the helots influenced Spartan policy.

M. Whitby, 'Two shadows: Images of Spartans and helots' in A. Powell and S. Hodkinson (eds), *The Shadow of Sparta* (Routledge, 1994), pp. 87–126.

ACTIVITY

Read Thucydides 1.68–71 (LACTOR 21, E141) and 79–84 (LACTOR 21, E29)

- Sum up in one phrase what the Corinthians are accusing the Spartans of, and then find **five** quotations from their speech to illustrate it.
- Find **five** short quotations from Archidamus' speech in which he defends the way the Spartans react.

Study question
Read Kritias 81B37, LACTOR 21, D40

What additional measures does Kritias say the Spartans took as precautions against the helots?

SPARTAN WOMEN

We have already seen in the first section that Spartan girls and women undertook physical training (pp. 83–6). The reason was that Lycurgus thought that this would lead to them bearing strong and healthy babies and that this was their main role in Spartan society.

Let us now consider what else we are told about the life of women in Sparta. As often, it is useful to start with Xenophon, so read Xenophon *Constitution of the Spartans* 1 (LACTOR 21, D68 **PS**).

Study question

In addition the freedom given to women is harmful as regards both the purpose of the constitution and the prosperity of the state . . . This is what has happened there, since the law-maker wanted the whole state to be tough, and in respect of the men, he clearly did so, but neglected matters concerning the women. For they live wantonly in absolutely every way, and luxuriously.

Aristotle, *Politics* 1269b, LACTOR 21, D69 **PS**

Do you agree with Aristotle's description from what you have already learnt about the upbringing of girls and women? Give your reasons.

PRESCRIBED SOURCE

Title: *Politics*

Author: Aristotle

Date: 384–322

Genre: philosophy

Significance: Aristotle was born in the north of Greece but lived in Athens from 367, when he was seventeen. Having studied under Plato he then opened his own school, and, with his students, set about making accounts of the constitutional development of many Greek states. He then used many of these as the basis of his *Politics*. In Book II of this he sets out to analyse and explain the flaws in Spartan society in an effort to explain why, having been so powerful in the fifth century, it had gone into such rapid decline in the fourth when he was writing. He is therefore looking for weaknesses. His students researched the constitutions of 158 Greek city-states, which he himself used in *Politics*.

Prescribed sections: 1269a29–1271b19

Read it here: LACTOR 21: *Sparta* (KCL 2017) D47, D27, D69, D54, D28, D18, D13, D1, D62, D98, D84, D55

If we summarise what he says we learn that Spartan women

- did not work wool and make clothes
- exercised
- competed with each other

Xenophon then goes on to describe marriage customs in Sparta.

One of the things which Xenophon highlights in his account is the un-Greekness of Spartan life, especially for women. (Read chapter 1 again (LACTOR 21, D68 **PS**) and count how many times he compares Sparta with 'elsewhere' or 'other Greeks' or describes them as 'different'). We can summarise what Xenophon and Plutarch say about Spartan marriages as:

- a man should not be seen entering or leaving his wife's room
- a man could not marry when he wanted to
- an elderly husband of a young wife was required (Xenophon) to allow a younger man to have sex with his wife for the purpose of producing children
- an unmarried man could ask another man's permission to have sex with his wife to father children
- the woman would take control of both men's households
- Plutarch also gives the rather strange details of the 'wedding by capture'

Add to this the facts that the men were normally expected to dine in the syssitia, and to sleep in the barracks until the age of thirty, and that male children also went to barracks from the age of seven, we can see that family life was different from what we, or even other Greeks of the time, would recognise as normal. Everything was done for the sake of rearing strong and healthy children. However, Ducat notes 'There has been a general tendency to underestimate the part played in the Spartans' existence by their private life, which unfolded in the framework of the *oikos'*. The oikos was a private house.

However, there are some problems in the accounts of Xenophon and Plutarch. Xenophon says that a man who did not wish to marry might have sex with another man's wife (*Constitution of the Spartans* 1 **CW PS**), whilst earlier in the chapter he implies that Lycurgus obliged men to marry at a certain age. Plutarch says a 'respectable man' could have sex with another man's wife (*Lycurgus* 15, LACTOR 21, D71 **PS**). However, earlier in chapter 15 Plutarch makes it quite clear that an unmarried man was regarded as anything but 'respectable'.

We should perhaps go with Xenophon's account because he is closer in time to our period and also lived in Sparta, rather than Plutarch's later, more sensational account. However, of course, it may be that Xenophon is deliberately making little of some of these aspects due to his admiration for Sparta.

Aristotle seems to object to the freedom he feels Spartan women had, based on the 'un-Greek' aspects mentioned above. In the next section he goes on to discuss the ability of Spartan women to own property, also not normal in most Greek states. For Aristotle, according to Paul Cartledge, this was a 'world turned upside down'.

Study questions

Read what Xenophon says **PS** about married life, and then read Plutarch *Lycurgus* 15 (LACTOR 21, D71)

1 On what points do Xenophon and Plutarch agree?
2 What extra information does Plutarch give us?

ACTIVITY

Count how many further times in chapter 1 Xenophon emphasises that the purpose was to breed healthy children.

Study question

Read Plutarch **CW** *Sayings of the Spartans, Gorgo* 6. **PS**

Explain how this saying supports the picture given by Xenophon and Plutarch

Study question

PS

It seems that initially the freedom given to Lakonian women came about for good reasons. [1270a] This is because the men went abroad away from their homes for long periods on military campaigns, fighting the war against the Argives and then the one against the Arkadians and Messenians. But when they had gained leisure time they put themselves in the hands of a lawgiver and were prepared to obey him because of their military lifestyle (which has many virtuous elements). But as for the women, they say that Lykourgos tried to bring them under his laws, but gave it up when they resisted.

Aristotle, *Politics* 1269b, (LACTOR 21, D27, D69, D54, D28, D18, D13)

Aristotle is wrong when he suggests that in this he was trying to impose a proper discipline on women, but was forced to abandon the attempt because of their emancipated lifestyle and excessive powers derived from the fact that their menfolk were always away on military expeditions. The men had no choice but to leave the women in charge, and for this reason tended to mollycoddle them to an excessive degree.

PS

Plutarch, *Life of Lycurgus* 14.1 (LACTOR 21, D70)

From everything you have studied, do you agree with Plutarch that Aristotle was wrong to say that Lycurgus failed to control Spartan women?

We have to be a little careful here as the situation had changed by the time Aristotle was writing, for a number of reasons: the influx of wealth at the end of the war with Athens at the end of our period (404), the on-going oliganthropia, and, not least, the Spartans' defeat at Leuctra in 371 and the subsequent freeing of the Messenian helots.

TOPIC REVIEW

- Explain the meaning and different status of Spartiates, perioikoi and helots. Find two quotations from different prescribed sources about each.
- Explain the details of the syssitia with two quotations from different sources.
- Explain at least three ways in which the Spartans kept the helots subjected and humiliated, with reference to the sources.
- Give details of Spartan married life (e.g. marriage ages, treatment of new-born babies and bachelors) with support from the sources.
- Give references from the sources to illustrate Spartan values and the treatment of cowards.

Further Reading

Cartledge, P., 'Spartan Wives: Liberation or Licence?' in *Spartan Reflections* (London: Duckworth, 2001), pp. 106–26.

Cartledge, P., *The Spartans, An Epic History* (London: Pan Books, 2003), pp. 153–66.

Cartledge, P., 'Raising Hell? The Helot Mirage – a personal re-view', in N. Luraghi and S.E. Alcock (eds), *Helots and Their Masters in Laconia and Messenia* (Cambridge MA: Harvard University Press, 2003), pp. 12–30.

Ducat, J., 'The Obligations of Helots' (trans. Coombes), in M. Whitby (ed.), *Sparta* (Edinbirgh: Edinburgh University Press, 2002), pp. 190–5.

Figueira, P., 'Gynecocracy: how women policed masculine behaviour in archaic and classical Sparta' in A. Powell and S. Hodkinson (eds.), *Sparta: The Body* Politics (Swansea: The Classical Press of Wales, 2010), pp. 265–96.

Harvey, D., 'The clandestine massacre of the helots (Thucydides 4.80)', in T.J. Figueira (ed.) *Spartan Society* (Swansea: The Classical Press of Wales, 2004), pp. 199–217.

Hodkinson, S., 'Inheritance, Marriage and Demography: Perspectives upon the Success and Decline of Classical Sparta' in A. Powell (ed.), *Classical Sparta: Techniques behind her success* (Abingdon: Routledge, 1989), pp. 79–121.

Hodkinson, S., *Property and Wealth in Classical Sparta* (London and Swansea: Duckworth and The Classical Press of Wales, 2000), pp. 113–31 (an alternative view to that of Cartledge above).

Hodkinson S. 'Female property ownership and empowerment in classical and hellenistic Sparta, in T.J. Figueira (ed.), *Spartan Society* (Swansea: The Classical Press of Wales, 2004), pp. 103–36.

Kennell, N.M., *Spartans: A New History* (Malden: Wiley-Blackwell, 2010), pp. 76–88.

Lewis, D., *Greek Slave Systems and their Eastern Neighbours: A Comparative Study* (Oxford: Oxford University Press, 2017), chapter 6, 'Helotic Slavery at Sparta'.

Paradiso, A., 'The Logic of Terror: Thucydides, Spartan duplicity and an improbable massacre', in T.J. Figueira (ed.), *Spartan Society* (Swansea: The Classical Press of Wales, 2004), pp. 179–98.

de Ste Croix, G.E.M. 'The Helot Threat', in M. Whitby (ed.), *Sparta*, (Edinburgh: Edinburgh University Press, 2002), pp. 190–5.

Whitby, M. (ed), *Sparta*, with an introduction by M. Whitby (Edinburgh: Edinburgh University Press, 2002).

PRACTICE QUESTIONS

Read Plutarch *Lycurgus* 14 (LACTOR 21, D70 **PS**)

1. How useful is this passage for our understanding of the contribution women made to Spartan society?

[12]

2.3 The Political Structure of Sparta

Many ancients admired Sparta's constitution, partly because they thought it was very stable, and partly because it seemed to include elements from different types of constitution. It had kings, a small council who held office for life, and some officials elected annually by all adult male citizens.

We know the **ephors** were a slightly later addition to the Spartan constitution, and even during our period of seventy-four years we should not necessarily expect everything to remain static. The character and personality of individual kings could have a huge effect, as could individual ephors, although only for a year. At the start of our period the **gerousia** does seem very influential, but you could argue the ephors were more so by 432.

> **gerousia** the Spartan Council of 28 Elders plus the two kings

KEY INDIVIDUALS

Pausanias

Dates: died *c.* 470

The nephew of Leonidas and became **Agiad** regent after Leonidas was killed at Thermopylae in 480. He then commanded the Greek troops at the battle of Plataea (479) in which the Greeks defeated the Persians. He seems to have been seduced by Persian luxury and died in disgrace.

> **Agiad** one of the two dynasties of kings in Sparta

Hetoemaridas

A member of the gerousia who persuaded the Spartans not to declare war on Athens when they were beginning to fear the growing sea-power of Athens in the 470s.

Archidamus

Dates: reigned *c.* 469–*c.* 427

Eurypontid king. In the debate at Sparta about whether to declare war on Athens in 432 he urged caution, but was over-ruled. He then commanded the Spartan invasions of Attica for the first few years of the war before his death; the war from 431–421 is therefore sometimes called the Archidamian War. See also p.100. There is a discussion of the debate on p. 43.

> **Eurypontid** one of the two dynasties of kings in Sparta

Sthenelaidas

Dates: ephor in 432

In the debate, he persuaded the Spartans to declare war on Athens when the king, Archidamus (see above), urged caution. See also p. 113.

Brasidas

Dates: eponymous ephor in 431, d. 422

A Spartan general who gained a reputation during the Archidamian War (431–421). He is most famous for taking a force of mercenaries and helots to Thrace to attack Athenian allies there, where he was very successful. However, he was killed there in a battle outside Amphipolis. There is a detailed discussion of him on pp. 114–15.

> **eponymous ephor** the ephor by whose name the Spartans identified the year

Alcibiades

Dates: 450–404

An Athenian. He persuaded the Athenians to attack Syracuse in Sicily in 415 and was one of the generals in command of the expedition, but was recalled to stand trial for sacrilege. He escaped and went to Sparta where he gave the Spartans advice on how to defeat the Athenians. He then had to flee from Sparta, allegedly because he seduced the wife of King Agis II (see below). There is a detailed discussion of him on pp. 116–17 and see also pp. 61–8.

Agis II

Dates: reigned 427–400

The son of Archidamus and Eurypontid king. He is probably best known for winning the battle of Mantinea (418) and establishing a permanent Spartan fort in Athenian territory at Decelea (Dekeleia) (on the advice of Alcibiades).

THE ROLES, DUTIES AND RESPONSIBILITIES OF THE KINGS, GEROUSIA, EPHORS AND ASSEMBLY

Before we look at these four different aspects of the Spartan constitution we need to consider the sources. It is important to realise that each source describes each element as they were at the time they were writing. Therefore, if we find slightly different accounts,

FIGURE 2.6
The site of Sparta showing key buildings and areas.

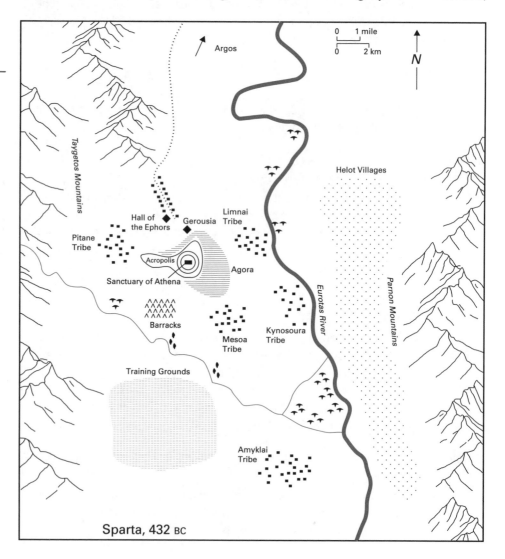

it may well be because the relative powers of the various elements changed over time, rather than that one of the sources has made a mistake. This is something to bear in mind throughout this section.

Kings

Sparta was unusual in having two royal families, and so two kings at any one time. Whatever the reason for this, it happened well before our period.

> When a (Spartan) king leaves the country he is commander in everything to do with the war; furthermore matters concerning the gods are also entrusted to the kings. So this kingship is like a permanent generalship of men with absolute power.
>
> Aristotle, *Politics* 1285a

> The fourth of these (types of kingship) is the Spartan which, so to speak, is simply a permanent hereditary generalship.
>
> Aristotle, *Politics* 1285b

Aristotle in these two passages describes his impression of the Spartan kingship. We will return to these later. First we will look at what other sources tell us about the kingship.

Plutarch does not say much about the kings in *Lycurgus*, but does give us one piece of information, that they were members of the gerousia (*Lycurgus* 6.1–3, LACTOR 21, D48). We can also add one other important power of the kings, that they could propose business to the Assembly, but maybe only through their membership of the gerousia. Plutarch also mentions one extra privilege in *Agesilaus* 1.2, LACTOR 21, E82 the next in line to the kingship did not have to go through the agōgē.

We are also told by Herodotus (5.75, LACTOR 21, D6) that before our period the Spartans changed the law so that only one king was away with an expedition. This was after a quarrel between Demaratus and Cleomenes led to the abandonment of an expedition against Athens.

So, we have a good picture of the roles and responsibilities of the kings. We will now look at some examples of kings in action.

PAUSANIAS (REGENT 480–c. 470)

Plutarch tells us that Lycurgus banned money from Sparta (*Lycurgus* 9, LACTOR 21, D58 **PS**), although at the time no Greek state had coined money. However archaeological evidence supports the fact that the Spartans did not mint coins. He also says that Lycurgus banned Spartans from leaving Sparta and expelled foreigners (*Lycurgus* 27 **CW** **PS**). Thucydides, from within our period in Pericles' Funeral Oration when he is comparing Athens with Sparta, suggests that these exclusions were actually occasional acts:

> . . . and there is no time when we exclude someone with an expulsion of foreigners
>
> Thucydides, *The History of the Peloponnesian War* 2.39

ACTIVITY

Read Herodotus 6.56–59 and 6.60 (LACTOR 21, D5, D8, D10, D24).

- Make a table of **PS** all the duties, responsibilities and privileges of the kings as recorded by Herodotus under the following headings:
  ○ religious
  ○ military
  ○ constitutional
  ○ judicial
  ○ other privileges

ACTIVITY

Read Xenophon *Constitution of the Spartans* 13 and 15, LACTOR 21, D7, D9. **PS**

Chapter 13 gives us further details about the kings on campaign. Compare what Xenophon says in chapter 15 with what Herodotus says; make a table under two headings:

- similarities
- differences or additions

Study questions

Read Plutarch
Aristeides 23

1 Why did the other Greeks not like Pausanias?

2 What was the Spartans' reaction and what does Plutarch say about this?

Read Thucydides 1.128–135, LACTOR 21, E62b, E26, B6 (chapters 130–34)

3 Summarise Pausanias' actions as outlined by Thucydides.

4 Who seem to have been the Spartan authorities who brought him to book?

It is often said that this meant that Spartans did not have much contact with the outside world, and certainly not with the Greek world outside the Peloponnese. It may have been true that many leading Spartans had little contact with ordinary citizens from other cities outside the Peloponnese. Hodkinson lists the evidence for Spartiates' foreign connections (*Property and Wealth in Classical Sparta* (Duckworth/The Classical Press of Wales, 2000), pp. 338–40). However, some Spartan commanders and governors found it difficult to deal with ordinary troops from other states and civilian populations which were used to less authoritarian ways of running their armies and city-states.

Pausanias is a good example. When Leonidas was killed at Thermopylae in 480 his only son was still a child, so his nephew, Pausanias, served as regent. He commanded the Spartans, and the Greek alliance, at the battle of Plataea in 479. The following year he was again commander of the Greek forces in the Aegean.

According to Plutarch and Thucydides, the Spartans were happy to give up the command of the Greeks in order to preserve their customs. Clearly Pausanias was not so ready to lose the power he had held. After continuing to plot against Sparta he was eventually punished.

However, neither were all the Spartans so ready to allow Athens to step into their shoes, as Diodorus records in the 470s:

> . . . In the same year, the Lakedaimonians were angry at having thrown away their hegemony at sea. And so they blamed the Greeks who had switched from their side and threatened appropriate action against them. [2] A meeting of the *gerousia* was held at which they discussed war against the Athenians over the hegemony at sea.
>
> Diodorus, *Library of History* 11.50.1–2 (LACTOR 21, E28)

ARCHIDAMUS (469–427)

ACTIVITY

Read Thucydides 1.79–87, LACTOR D21, E29, E30, E31

Thucydides tells us that the Spartans dismissed all outsiders, so he cannot have known from the Athenians what was actually said. However, it is very likely that he would have known that there was a debate, and who spoke on each side. He maybe even knew the unusual way the debate ended. He therefore has given Archidamus the arguments he thinks someone in his position would have made.

We first hear about him at the time of the earthquake and helot revolt in 464 (see p. 100). According to Diodorus (11.63.5–6; LACTOR 21, E63) it was Archidamus who reacted quickly and then led the resistance to the helots. Indeed, he may have been behind the request sent to Athens for help, as Thucydides tells us that he was a guest-friend of Pericles (2.13 CW). This would explain why at the debate about war with Athens in 432, aged about seventy, he advised caution.

Although he may actually have made the better arguments, Archidamus was outmanoeuvred by the ephor Sthenelaidas. However, he did then command the Peloponnesian forces which invaded Attica in the first few years of the war, even if initially somewhat reluctantly. Indeed the part of the war from 431–421 is often known as the Archidamian War.

AGIS II (427–400)

Agis was the son of Archidamus. He took over his father's mantle of leading the annual invasion of Attica in 426, but the Spartans turned back at the Isthmus of Corinth because of earthquakes (Thucydides 2.89).

As we would expect, as king he was one of the Spartan signatories to the Peace of Nicias with Athens in 421 (Thuc. 5.19 **CW** and see pp. 55–6).

Fighting broke out again in 419 in the Peloponnese with Argos looking to expand and attack Spartan allies. This was under the influence of the Athenian Alcibiades. It was Agis who led the Spartan forces in response.

The following year he was in a position from which he might have defeated the Argive army and captured the city. However, two of the Argive generals persuaded him to make a truce for four months and Agis withdrew. This allowed the Argive allied army to capture Orchomenos. The Spartans were angry with Agis:

> But when they heard the news that Orchomenos had been captured, their sense of
> outrage was intensified, and in an uncharacteristic frenzy of anger they voted to tear
> down his house and to fine him 10,000 drachmas. [3] He begged them not to do so,
> promising to redeem his disgrace by heroic action when he next took the field, and after
> that they could do whatever they wished. [4] So they suspended the fine and the
> destruction of his house, but passed a temporary measure, of a kind hitherto unheard of
> there, by which ten senior Spartiate officials would be appointed as his advisers, and that
> he would not be allowed to lead an army out of the city without their official sanction.
>
> Thucydides, *The History of the Peloponnesian War* 5.63.2–4 (LACTOR 21, E98)

PS

These campaigns led to the Battle of Mantinea in 418, which is regarded as one of the finest battles fought by the Spartans, and also one of the most important. If they had lost, their position in the Peloponnese would have been under real threat.

We next come across Agis in 413 when he led an invasion of Attica and set up a fort in Athenian territory at Decelea. He seems to have remained at Decelea for most of the rest of the war, until the Athenian surrender in 404. This was important as it meant he was at war, and this meant he had much greater power than if he had been back in Sparta.

> He did all this independently of the Lakedaimonian state. For Agis, as long as he was
> at Dekeleia with his own army, had full powers to dispatch an expedition wherever he
> wished, to levy an army, and to raise money.
>
> Thucydides, *The History of the Peloponnesian War* 8.5 (LACTOR 21, E41, E150 and **CW**)

PS

This passage shows the power a Spartan king had when on campaign, even as late as the end of the fifth century.

In theory, having two kings should have meant that they balanced each other's power. However, in reality, they sometimes followed different policies which could lead to disunity and weaker government. Indeed, we have seen that they sometimes quarrelled.

There was an additional problem. Although in theory the two kings could act as a balance to each other, sometimes when a new king came to the throne, the other king had been on the throne for some time. This meant generally that he was older and had commanded the Spartiates on campaign, so often he might become the dominant king.

Herodotus (7.3, LACTOR 21, D3 **PS**) claims that only the son of a king born after he had become king could succeed to the kingship. This would mean that an elder brother would not become king, which could cause problems. However, it should be noted that

Study question
Read Thucydides
5.63–74, LACTOR 21,
E98, E99, E100, E101,
E102, E103, E104

What part does Agis play
in this battle according to
Thucydides?

Study question

From what you have learnt about Spartan kingship, how far do you agree with Aristotle's assessments of it as given at the start of this section?

EXPLORE FURTHER

The first of these references is a good summary of the Spartan kingship; the second gives two brief biographies, of the regent Pausanias and of King Archidamus.

Cartledge, P., *The Spartans an Epic History* (London: Pan Books, 2003), pp. 120–7 and 145–52.

Cartledge, P., *Spartan Reflections* (London: Duckworth, 2009), pp. 55–64.

Study questions PS

Read Plutarch *Lycurgus* 26, LACTOR 21, D15

1 What additional details does Plutarch give here about the gerousia and their election?

2 What does this chapter tell us about how the Spartans felt about the members of the gerousia?

Read Aristotle *Politics* 1270b–1271a, LACTOR 21, D28, D18, D13, D1, D62, D98, D84

3 What are Aristotle's criticisms of the gerousia?

we do not know of any actual examples of this. There were often disputes about the succession and rivalries between the kings could make these worse. This is probably best illustrated by looking at the kings during our period.

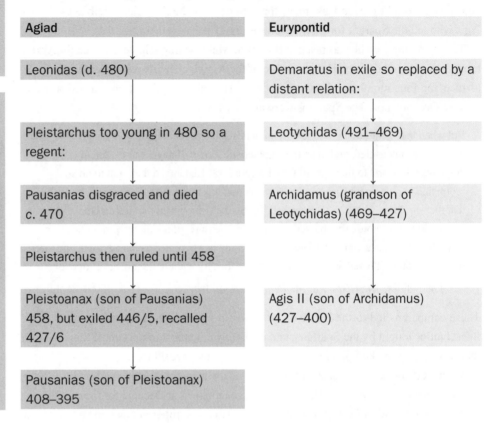

Agiad	Eurypontid
Leonidas (d. 480)	Demaratus in exile so replaced by a distant relation:
Pleistarchus too young in 480 so a regent:	Leotychidas (491–469)
Pausanias disgraced and died c. 470	Archidamus (grandson of Leotychidas) (469–427)
Pleistarchus then ruled until 458	
Pleistoanax (son of Pausanias) 458, but exiled 446/5, recalled 427/6	Agis II (son of Archidamus) (427–400)
Pausanias (son of Pleistoanax) 408–395	

So we can see that during our period there was only one occasion in each royal household when there was a normal, direct succession of a son from his father. The kingship was especially weak during the 470s with all the problems surrounding Pausanias, and also as the 'true' Eurypontid king Demaratus was in exile. The exile of Pleistoanax from 446/5 for allegedly accepting bribes not to attack Athens (Thucydides 5.16, LACTOR 21, E39, H33, D4 and CW PS) probably allowed Archidamus to become dominant.

THE GEROUSIA

We have already seen in Plutarch *Lycurgus* 6 that the kings were part of the gerousia, along with twenty-eight other men, and that they alone could make proposals to the assembly. Later on he adds another detail, that the gerousia and kings could veto a 'crooked proposal' (*Lycurgus* 6, LACTOR 21, D48 PS). As only they could make proposals to the assembly, this is normally interpreted as meaning that attempts to change or amend these proposals could be vetoed.

Finally, Xenophon adds a further duty, that they were judges (*Constitution of the Spartans* 10.2, LACTOR 21, D12 PS).

We can see the gerousia in action in Diodorus 11.50, LACTOR 21, E28 PS.

HETOEMARIDAS

Here we see Hetoemaridas, a member of the gerousia, persuading the assembly not to declare war on Athens. Presumably he had been unable to persuade the gerousia as the matter came before the assembly. Diodorus puts this debate in 475, but, as we noted earlier, his chronology is not always reliable and it may be that it should be placed in 477.

The power and influence of the gerousia lay in **probouleusis** (Plutarch *Agis* 11.1 **CW**). It debated matters first and then brought matters to the Assembly for it to vote on. Plutarch (*Lycurgus* 5.6–7, LACTOR 21, D14 **PS**) says that the gerousia was a source of stability, mentioning Plato as a source, and that it normally supported the kings and was a balance to the common people.

> **probouleusis** the power to debate matters first and to form proposals which were then put to the assembly

EPHORS

Plutarch does not tell us much about the ephors. In *Lycurgus* 7 (LACTOR 21, D17 **PS**) he discusses the origins of the ephors, quoting Plato, and describes their authority as a curb on the rest of the constitution – presumably the kings and gerousia. He also tells us that they were introduced by king Theopompus (late eighth–early seventh century), so were well established by the start of our period.

The only other detail Plutarch gives us is:

> Aristotle most certainly says that the ephors, whenever they first enter office, declare war on the helots so that doing away with them was free from pollution.
>
> Plutarch, *Lycurgus* 28.4 (LACTOR D44)

However, Xenophon, a contemporary source does give us some additional information.

There were five ephors elected every year from any full Spartiate (i.e. over thirty years old). As well as the duties mentioned in the sources above, they also received foreign envoys. Xenophon records an occasion in 405 when the ephors prevented Athenian envoys entering Sparta (*Hellenica* 2.2.13). They probably also called the meetings of at least the assembly, and maybe the gerousia as well.

We have already seen that Plutarch says it was only the kings and gerousia who could put proposals to the Assembly.

Study questions
Read Thucydides 1.87 again,
LACTOR 21, E31 **PS**

1 What does this imply about the ephors' control over the Assembly?

Read Plutarch *Lycurgus* 29.6, LACTOR 21, F6

2 To what extent do you agree with Plutarch's assessment of the office of ephor?

EXPLORE FURTHER

These two references catalogue what we know about the activities of individual non-royal Spartans during the Peloponnesian War.

Hodkinson, S., 'Warfare, Wealth and the crisis of Spartan Society', in J. Rich Jand G. Shipley (eds), *War and Society in the Greek World* (Abingdon: Routledge, 1993), pp. 146–76, especially table on p. 154.

Westlake, H.D., *Individuals in Thucydides* (Cambridge: Cambridge University Press, 1968).

STHENELAIDAS

Sthenelaidas only occurs once in our sources, and that is in the debate at Sparta over whether to declare war on Athens in 432. The content of what he says does not concern us here, and is covered in the Period Study (see p. 43). Our interest here is in the information Thucydides' account gives us about the process of decision-making in Sparta. We should be aware that Thucydides himself would not have been present, but there were Athenians at the meeting, although they were dismissed from the Assembly before the Spartans debated their final decision.

THE ASSEMBLY

The assembly consisted of all male Spartiates over the age of twenty. From the sources we have looked at already about the kings, gerousia and ephors we have seen the assembly in action. From this we can see a number of points:

- The assembly decided on whether to go to war in 432, despite Herodotus' statement that the kings could make this decision (6.56, LACTOR 21, D5 **PS**). Pierre Carlier (*La Royauté en Grèce avant Alexandre* (Strasbourg, 1984)) argues that Herodotus may well have seen an original Spartan document which used a deliberately ambiguous phrase meaning either 'to declare war' or 'to lead [the army] out to war'.
- Although it could be argued that both the gerousia and the ephors held a lot of power, they were both elected by the assembly. We do not know the process for the election of the ephors, but Aristotle describes it as childish (*Politics* 1270b27, LACTOR 21, D18 **PS**); this is the same way in which he describes the election of the gerousia (*Politics* 1271a9, LACTOR 21, D13 **PS**), a process described for us by Plutarch (*Lycurgus* 26, LACTOR 21, D15 **PS**). It is normally assumed that the ephors were elected in the same way.
- Changes in the law also had to be approved by the assembly.
- However, we have also seen that the assembly could not put forward its own proposals, these had to come from the gerousia. It is thought that the ephors could also make proposals. Neither Plutarch nor Xenophon mention this, but Sthenelaidas seems to do this in 432 (Thucydides 1.87, LACTOR 21, E31 **PS**).
- It may be that the Assembly could not debate the proposal, but listened to the opinions of the kings, gerousia and ephors. Certainly in the two debates in our sources in 475 (Diodorus 11.50, LACTOR 21, E28 **PS**) and in 432 (Thucydides 1.79–87, LACTOR 21, E29, E30, E31 **PS**) this is what happens.

We know of very few individual Spartans in the sources from our period before the Peloponnesian War. However, we know of many non-royal Spartan commanders outside the Peloponnese during the war.

We need to study two of these non-royal Spartan commanders in greater detail, Brasidas and Lysander, as well as the Athenian Alcibiades who falls roughly between them chronologically.

BRASIDAS

(See also the discussion of Brasidas in the Period Study, pp. 52–5).

431   Saved the southern perioikic town of Methone from an Athenian attack (Thuc. 2.25, LACTOR 21, E34 and **CW PS**)

431/0   The popularity he gained from this action may be what resulted in him being elected **eponymous ephor** (Xenophon *Hellenica* 2.3.10), though note that Cartledge has these two years reversed (*The Spartans, An Epic History* (Pan Books, 2003), p.172).

429   The Athenian admiral Phormio was operating with a fleet in the Corinthian Gulf. The Spartans sent a fleet under Cnemus to oppose him, which had been operating against Athenian possessions in the western Greek islands. The Spartan fleet was defeated, partly because Cnemus arrived late, so:

> The Spartans sent Timocrates, Brasidas and Lycophron as advisers to Cnemus concerning the fleet, ordering them to prepare better for a second sea-battle and not to be kept off the sea by so few ships. For especially as this was the first time they had experienced a sea-battle, it seemed to them to be very unexpected, and they didn't think it was so much that their fleet was weaker, but that there was a softness; they did not balance the great experience of the Athenians with their own brief training. Therefore they sent out the advisers in anger.

Thucydides, *The History of the Peloponnesian War* 2.85 **CW**

At the end of the year, still as advisor to Cnemus, Brasidas was involved in a daring raid which was intended to attack the Athenian port at Piraeus, but did not make it that far, laying waste the island of Salamis instead (Thuc. 2.93–4 **CW**).

427   Brasidas is again an advisor to the commander of a Spartan fleet, Alcidas. Their target was Corcyra (Kerkyra) which was an Athenian ally but where there was civil war (Thuc. 3.76). Brasidas was in favour of an immediate attack on Corcyra, but was over-ruled by Alcidas (Thuc. 3.79 **CW PS**).

425   Brasidas distinguished himself in the Spartan attack on the Athenian fortification at Pylos (Thuc. 4.11–12, LACTOR 21, E88).

424   He was at Corinth putting together the army to take to Thrace when the Athenians attacked Megara. Brasidas hurried to the rescue and eventually the Athenians retreated (Thuc. 4.70–74). Eventually Brasidas set off for Thrace with his force of mercenaries and helots (Thuc. 4.81, LACTOR 21, E35 **CW PS**).

Brasidas moved quickly and daringly and had a great deal of success in winning over the cities of Thrace from Athens. His success did not go down well with some back in Sparta who initially refused to send reinforcements (Thuc. 4.108.7 **CW**), although they were sent later (Thuc. 5.12–13 **CW**).

423   A truce was made between Athens and Sparta so that negotiations for a more lasting peace could take place (Thuc. 4.117, LACTOR 21, H40 **PS**).

Study question S&C CW PS
Read Thucydides' evaluation of Brasidas (4.81, LACTOR 21, E35) and that recorded by Plutarch (*Sayings of Spartan Women, Archileonis* 1, LACTOR 21, F33); Archileonis was Brasidas' mother.

How does this evaluation differ from what you have learnt about the behaviour of other Spartan commanders when they came into contact with non-Spartans?

EXPLORE FURTHER S&C CW

All of these references give longer and more detailed accounts of Brasidas' activities.

Buckley, T., *Apsects of Greek History, 750–323 BC*, 2nd edn (Abingdon: Routledge, 2010), chapter 19.

Cartledge, P., *The Spartans An Epic History* (London: Pan Books, 2003), pp. 171–6.

Westlake, H.D., *Individuals in Thucydides* (Cambridge: Cambridge University Press, 1968), chapter 10.

Two days after the truce, the city of Scione (Skione) went over to the Spartans and Brasidas refused to give it back, and then Mende also came over.

422 The truce ended and the Athenians sent Cleon (Kleon) to try to recover the cities, especially Amphipolis. The Spartans were successful in defending the city, mainly because of a charge led personally by Brasidas from the city (Thuc. 5.10 **CW**), but he was killed in the action.

ALCIBIADES

Although he was an Athenian, Alcibiades had a large influence on the events of the war even in Sparta. His connection with Sparta started early as Plutarch tells us that his wet-nurse was Spartan (*Alcibiades* 1). It is normally assumed that she was not a Spartan citizen woman. His name was also Spartan in origin. Alcibiades had a guest-friend relationship with a Spartan, Endios, and Thucydides suggests that this was a long-standing relationship between their two families (Thuc. 8.6, LACTOR 21, E42, E55 and **CW**), probably going back at least to the sixth century. See also the Period Study section on 419–401 (pp. 60–7).

420 Alcibiades took advantage of bad relations between Athens and Sparta in the aftermath of the Peace of Nicias. Having tricked some Spartan negotiators, actually including Endios, who were in Athens, he denounced them in the Athenian assembly (Thucydides 5.45), paving the way for an alliance between Athens and Argos. Alcibiades hoped to attract Elis and Mantinea into an anti-Spartan Peloponnesian alliance. All these three states were still democracies, despite Sparta's normal preference for its allies to be oligarchies (Thucydides 1.19).

419 Alcibiades persuaded the Athenians to inscribe on the pillar recording the Peace of Nicias 'The Spartans have not kept their oaths' (Thucydides 5.56).

418 The Spartans decided to act and marched against Argos (Thucydides 5.57 **CW** **PS**). Eventually this led to the Battle of Mantinea, a resounding victory for Sparta, which put an end to the anti-Sparta coalition in the Peloponnese Alcibiades had hoped for (Thucydides 5.63–74, LACTOR 21, E98, E99, E100, E101, E102, E103, E104 **PS**). The Spartans made a fifty-year peace treaty and alliance with Argos (Thucydides 5.79, LACTOR 21, B20).

415 Alcibiades persuaded the Athenians to send a large expedition to Sicily. The expressed purpose was to aid their (non-Greek) allies, Egesta, against Syracuse, but Alcibiades clearly had hopes to conquer the whole island. He was appointed as one of the generals. However, just as the expedition was about to sail some sacred statues outside Athenian homes were vandalised. Alcibiades was accused of being involved. He was allowed to depart with the expedition, but was then recalled to stand trial.

414 Having escaped he was invited to go to Sparta (Thucydides 6.89); in a speech to the Spartan assembly he persuaded the Spartans to

- send a Spartan officer to take over the command of the Syracusan resistance to the Athenians

- establish a permanent garrison in Athenian territory about 18 km from the city at Decelea.

413 The Spartans took his advice and sent Gylippus (Gylippos) to Sicily and decided to fortify Decelea (Thucydides 6.93; 7.11–12) under the command of King Agis (Thucydides 8.3, 5, LACTOR 21, E118, E41, E150 and).

411 Alcibiades persuaded the Spartans to intervene in the Aegean and promised that he would persuade Ionian cities to revolt from Athens (Thucydides 8.12). The Spartans made their first alliance with Persia (Thucydides 8.18, LACTOR 21, B21). It is perhaps significant that his friend, Endios, was one of the ephors for this year (Thuc. 8.6, LACTOR 21, E42, E55 and CW).

At some stage, while Agis was away, Alcibiades had seduced his wife (Plutarch *Alcibiades* 23 CW), though exactly when this happened is not clear. Thucydides says that Agis was a personal enemy of Alcibiades by 411 (8.45), saying that the Spartans now wanted his death. The seduction is normally assumed to have been in 414/13. Alcibiades started acting against the Spartans' interests with the Persian governor Tissaphernes, hoping for his recall to Athens. He managed to ingratiate himself with the Athenian army on Samos and they elected him general.

407 Alcibiades finally arrived back in Athens (Xenophon *Hellenica* 1.4.10–20 CW) and was elected general.

406 Alcibiades left the fleet in the command of his helmsman while he went off to obtain supplies and funds, who foolishly allowed himself to be drawn into battle at Notium by Lysander who won a victory. The Athenian people reacted by depriving Alcibiades of his command and he retreated to a castle he owned on the Hellespont (Plutarch *Lysander* 5, LACTOR 21, E124 PS).

405 In the run-up to the final battle of the war at Aegospotami (Aigospotamoi), Alcibiades warned the Athenian generals of the weakness of their position, but was dismissed (Xenophon *Hellenica* 2.1.25–26).

> **EXPLORE FURTHER** S&C
>
> These references both give more detailed accounts of Alcibiades' activities during the Peloponnesian War.
>
> Buckley, T., *Apsects of Greek History, 750–323 BC,* 2nd ed (Abingdon: Routledge, 2010), chapter 20.
>
> Westlake, H.D., *Individuals in Thucydides* (Cambridge: Cambridge University Press, 1968), chapter 12.

LYSANDER

Lysander was a **mothax**, a Spartan brought up not in his father's household. There were two kinds of mothax, the son of a Spartan father and a helot mother who was then sponsored by another Spartan, or the son of a Spartan who was too poor to pay the syssitia dues and so had lost full citizen status. It is normally thought that Lysander fell into the latter category based on Plutarch *Lysander* 2.1, and Phylarchos, FGrH 81 F43 (LACTOR 21, D30 PS CW) tells us that he was a mothax.

Some scholars think that it is only the latter who were mothakes. Xenophon uses another term for the sons of helot mothers, nothoi (Xen. *Hell.* 5.3.9, LACTOR 21, E57). See also Period Study pp. 67–8.

> **mothax (pl. mothakes)** a Spartan brought up not in his father's household.

407 Lysander was appointed **nauarchos**, commander of the Spartan navy, in the Aegean and befriended Cyrus, the commander of the Persian forces

> **nauarchos** a Spartan naval commander

PRESCRIBED SOURCE

Title: *Histories*

Author: Phylarchos

Date: *c.* 272–188

Genre: history

Significance: his work is lost and only preserved in fragments in other authors, and was used by both Polybius and Plutarch, though they were critical of him for being too pro-Spartan

Prescribed section: FGrH 81 F43 = Athenaios *Scholars at* Dinner, 6.102

Read it here: LACTOR 21: *Sparta* (KCL 2017) D30

(Plutarch *Lysander* 3–4 **PS** **CW**). Cyrus provided the funding needed for the navy.

406 The Battle of Notion (see Figure 1.15 on p. 65, and also p. 117). Lysander then set about trying to win over leading citizens in the cities of Ionia. (Plutarch *Lysander* 5, LACTOR 21, E124). **PS**

Spartan law did not allow an admiral to command for more than a year, so after the battle Lysander was succeeded by Callicratidas (Kallikratidas). Lysander somewhat undermined Callicratidas by returning the balance of the funds he had received from Cyrus, so Callicratidas had no means to pay his rowers. (Plutarch *Lysander* 6 **CW** **PS**). (See also Period Study p. 67.)

However, Callicratidas did have some success, blockading the Athenian fleet at Mytilene. The Athenians put together a completely new fleet and won a victory at Arginusae (see map on p. 65), where Callicratidas was killed (Plutarch *Lysander* 7).**CW** **PS**

405 Sparta's allies, and Cyrus, were eager for Lysander to be re-appointed, but this was not allowed in Spartan law. They therefore appointed Aracus, with Lysander as his deputy. Cyrus resumed his payments (Plutarch *Lysander* 8–9; Xenophon *Hellenica* 2.1.6–7; 13–14, LACTOR 21, E125, E126).**CW** **PS**

Lysander headed for the Hellespont. The Athenians had to follow him as they could not afford to lose control of the route their grain-supply ships took from the Black Sea. He won a decisive victory over the Athenians at Aegospotami (see map on p. 65) by clever strategy (Plutarch *Lysander* 9–11; Xenophon *Hellenica* 2.1.23–24; 27–28, LACTOR 21, E127, E128).**CW** **PS**

404 The Athenians could not recover from this as their food supply was cut off and they soon surrendered.

EXPLORE FURTHER **S&C**

These references give more detailed accounts of Lysander.

Buckley, T., *Aspects of Greek History, 750–323* BC, 2nd ed. (Abingdon: Routledge, 2010), chapter 22.

Cartledge, P., *The Spartans An Epic History* (London: Pan Books, 2003), pp. 182–5 and 188–90.

Pritchard, D.M., 'Sparta becomes Athens: The Peloponnesian War's Last 10 Years' in *Agora: The Journal of the History Teachers' Association of Victoria (Australia)*, 51.4. (This is downloadable from Pritchard's academia. edu page)

Lysander had become immensely powerful. A Spartan nauarchos had a huge amount of power:

> This is because on top of the kings who are permanent generals, the naval command has been established as virtually another kingship.
>
> Aristotle, *Politics* 1271a 39–40 (LACTOR 21, D98)

What Aristotle probably means by this is that the nauarchos had the same power as the kings, including that of life and death. It was probably for this reason that a nauarchos was not allowed to hold the position for longer than a year, or to hold it more than once, as Xenophon tells us. Lysander made himself virtually indispensable by his personal friendship with Cyrus, whose goodwill was crucial to the funding needed to support the navy. The friendships he made with citizens in the Greek cities formed the basis of the councils of ten through which Sparta governed the cities after defeating Athens. This gave Lysander a huge amount of power and influence in the Greek world, not just in Sparta.

CONCLUSION

> For four hundred years and more, until the end of the Peloponnesian War, the Lakedaimonians have had the same constitution, through which they have been able to bring about change in other states.
>
> Thucydides, *The History of the Peloponnesian War* 1.18 (LACTOR 21, F4)

We see this idea, that Sparta's solid government is what allowed it to be dominant in Greece, is quite common amongst the ancient sources. Many also were fascinated by the balanced mixture in the constitution. There was a hereditary kingship, two in fact; there was oligarchy, a council of only twenty-eight who held office for life; there was democracy as most ancient societies would have understood it, as all adult male citizens made important decisions and elected both the gerousia and the ephors; the latter were also a democratic element, elected but only in office for one year and with a role to oversee the kings and counter-balance the gerousia.

Aristotle discusses this in *Politics* 1294b, adding the equal education system, syssitia and lack of distinction between rich and poor as further democratic elements.

Plato discusses the checks each of the political bodies had on each other in *Laws* 691–692. **CW**

As we have seen, other individual Spartans increasingly came to the fore, especially in times of war when Sparta found itself pulled beyond its traditional theatre in the Peloponnese.

TOPIC REVIEW

- Explain the duties, selection process and qualifications for the kings, gerousia, ephors and assembly. Support your answer with at least two references to the sources for each.
- Give two actual examples when there was a problem with the succession of kings.
- Give three examples from the sources of the privileges of kings.
- Give at least two examples from the sources of limits on the kings' powers.
- Give examples supported from the sources of occasions when the assembly made important decisions, and the process involved.

Further Reading

Andrewes, A., 'The Government of Classical Sparta' in M. Whitby (ed.), *Sparta* (Edinbrugh: Edinburgh University Press, 2002), pp. 49–68.

Cartledge, P., 'Spartan Government and Society', Appendix E in R.B. Strassler (ed.), *The Landmark Xenophon's Hellenica* (New York: Pantheon Books, 2009), pp. 347–58.

Hodkinson, D. and A. Powell (ed.), *Sparta: The Body Politic* (Swansea: Classical Press of Wales, 2010).

de Ste Croix G.E.M., 'How Spartan foreign policy was determined', in *The Origins of the Peloponnesian War* (London: Duckworth, 1972), pp. 124–51.

PRACTICE QUESTIONS

1. Explain the extent to which the kings were able to control decision-making in Sparta during this period.

   Use and analyse the ancient sources you have studied as well as your own knowledge to support your answer.

   [36]

2.4 The Spartan Military Culture and its Importance in the Society and Politics of Sparta

TOPIC OVERVIEW

- the contributions of the different social groups to the Spartan military
- the organisation of the army
- reasons for the Spartan successes and failures in military action: the helot revolt (465–464 BC), Pylos (425 BC), Brasidas in Thrace (424–423 BC), Mantinea (418–417 BC)
- the organisation of the Spartan navy and its successes and failures during the latter part of the Peloponnesian War
- the importance and influence of individual military figures: Brasidas, Gylippus, Lysander

The prescribed sources for this topic are:

- Aelian, *Miscellaneous History* 12.43
- Plutarch, *Lycurgus* 30
- Plutarch, *Lysander* 16
- Thucydides, *The History of the Peloponnesian War* 1.80, 1.101–103; 2.91–92; 3.31; 4.8, 4.15–16, 4.23, 4.26, 4.38, 4.80, 4.117; 5.16, 5.34, 5.63–74; 6.93; 7.11–12
- Xenophon, *Constitution of the Spartans* 11
- Xenophon, *Hellenica* 2.1.1–7, 14, 23–24, 27–28

- Spartan epitaph (*IG* 5.1.1124)

Ancient Sparta is probably most well-known in popular imagination for its military achievements and the bravery of its warriors. We will need to consider whether this reputation is deserved for our period, and whether it was solely the Spartiates who earned it. We will also consider how the Spartan military machine was organised and how it adapted to changing circumstances.

THE CONTRIBUTIONS OF THE DIFFERENT SOCIAL GROUPS TO THE SPARTAN MILITARY

We have looked at the contributions the various social groups in Sparta made to the military when we discussed their general roles and contributions in the second section of this chapter (see pp. 95 & 97).

FIGURE 2.7
A lead figurine of a warrior found in the temple of Artemis Orthia (see p. 80).

(see p. 80)

ACTIVITY

Read the second topic of this component again, 'The Social Structure of Sparta'.

● Draw up a table with rows for each of the social groups in Sparta: Spartiates, perioikoi, helots. Your table should have columns for the military contribution of each group, specific examples and the relevant sources.

THE ORGANISATION OF THE ARMY

There are many descriptions of the organisation of the Spartan army in our sources, but they are to a certain extent contradictory. The main reason for this is that these sources came from different periods, so we will concentrate on those for our period, 478–404. At the start of the period the army was divided into five **lochoi** or regiments. Presumably each of these was made up of 1,000 men at the Battle of Plataea (479), but that was not the whole army. Demaratus tells Xerxes in 480 that there were 8,000 Spartans Herodotus 7.234.

ACTIVITY

Read Thucydides 5.67–68 (LACTOR 21, E101) about the organisation of the Spartan army at the Battle of Mantinea (418).

lochos (pl. lochoi) the groups or regiments of the Spartan army

Brasidians helots armed as hoplites whom the general Brasidas had taken with him to Thrace in 424; they were freed on their return to Sparta in 421 (Thucydides 5.34.1)

pentēkostus (pl. pentēkostues) a company of men in the Spartan army

enōmotia (pl. enōmotiai) the equivalent of a platoon in the Spartan army

The first thing to note is the mention of the Skiritai. We have already seen that this was a unit of periokoi from northern Lakonia. We then have the **Brasidians** and neodamōdeis. Thucydides then mentions seven regiments (**lochoi**), not counting the Skiritai which would imply that the Brasidians and neodamōdeis had their own regiments, which leaves five lochoi of Spartiates.

He then tells us that each lochos consisted of four **pentēkostues** (companies), and each **pentēkostus** of four **enōmotiai** (platoons); the two key pieces of information are that each **enōmotia** was eight men deep and that the whole front line, excluding the Skiritai, was 448 men. Some calculations can therefore give us the following:

Total size of army:	3,584
Spartiates excluding Brasidians and neodamōdeis:	2,560
Men in a lochos:	512
Men in a pentēkostus:	128
Men in an enōmotia:	32

We should be wary of thinking that 2,560 represented the total number of adult Spartiates at the time:

When this battle was still in the future, Pleistonoanax, the other king, brought an army of reinforcements, consisting of older and younger soldiers, to support his army.

Thucydides, *The History of the Peloponnesian War* 5.75.1 (LACTOR 21, E104)

FIGURE 2.8
Drawing of the
tombstone of Eualkes.

PRESCRIBED SOURCE

Title: Tombstone of
Eualkes (Spartan
epitaph; IG 5.1.1124)

Date: 418

Genre: tombstone
inscription from
Geronthrai

Significance: Geronthrai
was a peroikic
settlement, so this is
evidence of perioikoi
fighting alongside the
Spartans at the battle
of Mantinea

Original inscription:
EUALKES || EN
POLEMOI || EN
MANTINEAI

Translation: Eualkes || in
the war || in Mantinea

Read it here: LACTOR 21:
Sparta (KCL 2017) B43

Some scholars think that Thucydides has halved the actual number of Spartiates and perioikoi at Mantinea because he was unaware of the way the Spartan army was organised in 418 (C. Hawkins, 'Spartans and Perioikoi . . .' in *Greek, Roman and Byzantine Studies*, 51 (2001), pp. 401–34). The extract above suggests there were reserve troops, and there were probably also others on garrison and guard duty. Countering this is the question of whether there were any perioikoi in the army at Mantinea. This is proved by a tombstone of a perioikos from the perioikic settlement of Geronthrai, who died in war (IG 5.1.1124, LACTOR 21, B43 **PS**). They must have been included in the lochoi with the Spartiates.

Scott Rusch (*Sparta at War*, Frontline Books, 2014, p. 111) argues that there were seven lochoi as this gives a total of 4,200 (actually 4,184) when the 600 Skiritai are added to the seven lochoi numbers at Mantinea. This is ten times the number of troops sent to Sphacteria in 425 (Thucydides 4.38 **PS**), so Rusch argues that the Spartans sent a tithe of their forces (note that the Penguin translation gives the number as 440, but the original Greek is 420). He then uses this to argue that the Brasidians and neodamōdeis were not included in the seven lochoi because they did not exist in 425. The problem is that, although he cites Thucydides 5.75.4 in regard to the Argive numbers at the battle, he ignores 5.75.1 quoted above which shows that the numbers in Thucydides were not the full Spartan levy, so the calculation of 420 as being a tenth of the total Spartan levy is flawed. It is safer to take Thucydides at face value. The 448 in the front line included the Brasidians and neodamōdeis in separate lochoi.

There is the further problem that we know that the Spartan force of 420 in 425 included non-Spartiates. Thucydides tells us that of the 292 captured on Sphacteria, 120 were Spartiates (4.38 **PS**), so 172 were not.

By the end of our period there had probably been a further reorganisation with the introduction of a new division, the **mora**. Xenophon first mentions this (*Hellenica* 2.4.31) for 403, so it probably had happened towards the end of our period. The new organisation is given in *Constitution of the Spartans* 11.4:

> Thus equipped, he divided them into six regiments (*morai*) of cavalry and
> infantry. Each infantry regiment of hoplites had a *polemarchos* (war leader),
> four *lochagoi* (unit commanders), eight *pentēkonterai* (commander of 50 men),
> and sixteen *enōmotarchai* (section leaders). All these units at the word of command
> form up into sections, [two], three, or six abreast.

PS

> Xenophon, *Constitution of the Spartans* 11.4 (LACTOR 21, D88)

mora (pl. morai) a division
of the Spartan army

polemarchos a Spartan
officer

**lochagos (pl.
lochagoi)** commander
of a lochos

**pentēkontēr (pl.
pentēkonterai)**
commander of a
pentēkostus

**enōmotarchēs (pl.
enōmotarchai)**
commander of an
enōmotia

ACTIVITY CW PS

Read
Xenophon *Constitution of the Spartans* 11, LACTOR 21, D88

• Summarise in your own words the command structure of the Spartan army described by Xenophon.

In his description of the battle of Leuktra in 371 Xenophon adds that an enōmotia consisted of thirty-six men (in that battle they were arranged three abreast and twelve deep, *Hellenica* 6.4.12, LACTOR 21, E109). Thus we can make a further calculation:

16 enōmotiai @ 36 men each = 576 men in each mora
6 morai @ 576 men = a total of 3,456 men making up the hoplite army

As this is greater than the number in 418/17 it must have now included perioikoi. In addition, each mora also had 100 cavalry attached to it.

SPARTAN MILITARY SUCCESSES AND FAILURES

We will now look at some specific examples of Spartan military action.

Study questions
Read Thucydides 1.101–103 (LACTOR 21, E62) and Diodorus 11.63.1–4 (LACTOR 21, E63)

1 What reason does Thucydides give for the Spartans asking for Athenian help?
2 Would you classify this campaign as a success or failure for Sparta? (Look especially at chapter 103.)

Helot Revolt, c. 464

So, the Spartans themselves acknowledged that they had little skill in or knowledge of siege warfare in 464. By 425 they seem to have a little more confidence in this type of warfare.

Pylos and Sphacteria

In 425, an Athenian fleet was sailing round the Peloponnese to Corcyra and then intended to sail on to Sicily. However, bad weather forced them to put in to Pylos (see Figure 1.12, p. 51). For a detailed account of the events see pp. 50–52.

The result meant that 420 Spartan hoplites were cut off on the island with the Athenians in control of the sea.

A Spartan campfire then got out of control and set fire to and destroyed most of the scrub cover on the island, exposing the Spartans' numbers and positions. The Athenians took the opportunity to attack.

ACTIVITY PS

Read Thucydides 4.8, LACTOR 21, E87

ACTIVITY CW PS

Read
Thucydides 4.15–16 (LACTOR 21, E90 4.14), 23 (LACTOR 21, E91) and 26 (LACTOR 21, E92)

ACTIVITY PS

Read Thucydides
4.33–35 and 38, LACTOR 21, E93, E94

• From everything you have read, why would you say the Spartans were defeated at Pylos and Sphacteria? Support your answer by reference to Thucydides.

Brasidas in Thrace (424–423)

On his arrival in Chalcidice (see Figure 1.13, p. 54 and Figure 1.12, p. 51) in 424 with his army of helots and mercenaries (Thucydides 4.80 **PS**) many cities immediately revolted and joined him. He then addressed the citizens of Acanthus (Akanthos), which gave Thucydides the opportunity to comment,

> . . . and he was not without ability as a speaker, for a Spartan.
>
> Thucydides, *The History of the Peloponnesian War* 4.84

His speech was successful. Acanthus revolted from Athens and joined Brasidas.

See pp. 52–5 and p. 115 for Brasidas' campaigns in Thrace.

Brasidas hoped that his successes would lead the Spartans to send further forces, but he had mis-read the situation at home. Thucydides tells us that some Spartans were jealous of his success, and what they really wanted was to recover the prisoners the Athenians had captured on Sphacteria. They now had what they needed – something with which to bargain for their return.

Brasidas then had further success in 423, capturing Torone and Lekythos.

As we have seen (p. 115), the campaign resulted in the deaths of both Cleon and Brasidas.

The Battle of Mantinea 418

This is often seen as a classic example of a hoplite battle, though not everything went the Spartans' way throughout. It was important as it ended the Athenians' attempts (described on pp. 59–61 and p. 116) to disrupt the Peloponnesian League and re-established Spartan control.

The battle was important for the reasons mentioned above, but it also re-established the Spartans' military reputation which had suffered so much after the surrender on Sphacteria.

ACTIVITY **PS**

Read Thucydides 5.63–74, LACTOR 21, E98, E99, E100, E101, E102, E103, E104

From this account we can learn much about the Spartans in battle:

- They advanced to the sound of pipe-players to keep them in step (70).
- Hoplite armies tended to move to the right as they advanced (71).
- Agis was aware of this and ordered his left wing (Skiritai, Brasidians and neodamōdeis) to move left and two of the regiments from the right wing to move to fill the gap this would leave (71).
- The commanders of these two regiments did not obey, so Agis told the Skiritai to fill the gap, but this had not happened before the two armies came together (72).
- The Mantineans and elite Argive troops stormed through the gap, surrounded the Spartans and drove some back (72).
- But the Spartans' main charge defeated the main body of the opposing army (72).
- They then went to assist their left wing and put the Mantineans to flight (73).
- The Spartans did not normally pursue a defeated enemy (73).
- 1,100 of the enemy were killed, but only about 300 Spartans (74).

ACTIVITY **PS**

Read Thucydides 4.117, LACTOR 21, H40 for the reasons why the Spartans sent Brasidas to Thrace.

Study question **S&C**

Use the index of a translation of Thucydides to look up Brasidas.

Write a short character sketch of Brasidas, giving references to Thucydides for the points you make.

THE SPARTAN NAVY

> . . . Our navy? We are outnumbered, and it will take time to build up its numbers and train the crews.

Thucydides, *The History of the Peloponnesian War*
1.80.4 (LACTOR 21, E29)

So, according to Thucydides, Archidamus in his address to the Spartans in 432 admits that they are not strong at naval warfare. They also made mistakes which sometimes meant that successes became failures and their commanders did not always appear committed to naval warfare.

The Spartans lost control of the sea at Pylos and Sphacteria almost too easily. So how did they manage to defeat the Athenians in what eventually turned out to be a naval war?

The answer lies in the treaty made between Sparta and the Persian prince Cyrus. However, a more permanent fleet required a more permanent command structure. Previously a naval commander (nauarchos) was appointed as and when necessary. In 408, it became an annual position and the nauarchos had as much power as a king on campaign. It was against the law to be re-appointed, but there were ways round this, as we have seen in the case of Lysander (see p. 118).

This led to Spartan success, but not immediately, and not without a few reverses as well.

411   The very first chapter of Xenophon's *Hellenica* records a Spartan victory over Athens, but not where this occurred.

410   Alcibiades defeats the Spartan fleet at Cyzicus; the Spartan admiral Mindaros is killed

407   Lysander is appointed nauarchos

406   Lysander defeats the Athenians at Notion (Xenophon *Hellenica* 1.5.11–14, LACTOR 21, E122)

Callicratidas replaces Lysander as nauarchos; at first Cyrus refuses to give him any money but does so after he defeats the Athenian fleet at Mytilene on the island of Lesbos.

Although outnumbered and advised to retreat by his helmsman, Callicratidas engages the Athenian fleet at the Arginusae Islands and is defeated. He falls into the sea and is not seen again.

The Chians and others demand that the Spartans re-appoint Lysander who is sent out as **epistoleus** to the nauarchos Arakos but Lysander was given the actual command (Xen. *Hell.* 2.1.6–7, LACTOR 21, E125) **PS**

405   Cyrus tells Lysander to avoid battle until he has more ships (Xen. *Hell.* 2.1.14, LACTOR 21, E126) **PS**

The final battle is at Aegospotami

The specification mentions three specific individual Spartans in the topic, but we have already discussed Brasidas (pp. 114–115) and Lysander (pp. 117–119) in the previous topic.

Study question **CW** **PS**

Read Thucydides 2.91–92 (429/8), 3.31 (428/7) and 4.8 (LACTOR 21, E87), 15 (LACTOR 21, E90), 16, 23 (LACTOR 21, E91) and 26 (LACTOR 21, E92) (425)

What weaknesses or failures in naval tactics or command do these passages illustrate?

Study question **PS**

Read Xenophon *Hellenica* 2.1.23–24 and 27–28, LACTOR 21, E127, E128

Explain how Lysander achieved this final victory.

---

epistoleus the second-in-command to the nauarchos

Gylippus

Aelian tells us that Gylippus was a mothax (12.43, LACTOR 21, D31)

In the winter of 415–414 Alcibiades advised the Spartans to send a Spartan officer to Sicily to take over command of the Syracusans' defence against the Athenians (see pp. 61–63).

> And so they [the Spartans] turned their minds to sending some assistance at once to the Sicilians. They appointed Gylippus, the son of Kleandridas, as a commander for the Syracusans and ordered him to consult with them and with the Corinthians and to arrange whatever was the best and quickest means in the present situation by which assistance would reach the people there.
>
> Thucydides, *The History of the Peloponnesian War* 6.93

Gylippus took an army of Peloponnesians.

The Athenians were trying to cut Syracuse off with a wall. The Syracusans had already tried to prevent this by constructing two counter-walls. Having arrived outside Syracuse in 414 (partly due to Athenian negligence), he quickly realised the danger the Syracusans were in as the Athenians were well advanced with their wall.

The next day he captured a fort on the heights of Epipolae called Labdalon.

The Syracusans then started a third counter-wall and Gylippus launched an unsuccessful night attack on a weak section of the Athenian wall.

Gylippus' arrival had such an effect on the Athenian commander, Nicias, that he decided to fortify a headland opposite the city (Plemmyrium) with three forts rather than continuing to concentrate on the wall on Epipolae. This was a bad move as it meant the Athenian men stationed there had no easy access to water and were vulnerable to attack when they ventured out.

KEY INDIVIDUAL

Gylippus

A mothax (Aelian *Miscellaneous History* 12.43, LACTOR 21, D31, see p. 000). There was a slight cloud hanging over his family as his father had been an associate of King Pleistoanax who was exiled in 446 for accepting a bribe from the Athenians (Thucydides 5.16, LACTOR 21, E39, H33, D4). However, he seems to have found a patron and went through the agōgē and became a member of a syssition.

PRESCRIBED SOURCE

Title: *Miscellaneous History*

Author: Aelian

Date: AD 175–235

Genre: a collection of historical anecdotes, notes about natural phenomena, customs and quotations from earlier authors among which is information that Gylippus was a mothax

Significance: preserves snippets of other authors among which is information that Gylippus was a mothax

Prescribed section: 12.43

Read it here: LACTOR 21: *Sparta* (KCL 2017) D31

ACTIVITY CW PS

Read
Nicias' letter
(Thucydides 7.11–12)

**Study
questions** CW PS

Read Thucydides'
account of the Athenian
expedition against
Syracuse from the arrival
of Gylippus. (7.1–17;
21–26; 31–87)

1 What did Gylippus
   contribute to the
   defeat of the
   Athenians?
2 What other factors
   were there?

Meanwhile, Gylippus continued with the counter-wall, using the stones the Athenians had laid out for their own wall! He also attacked the Athenians but was defeated; he took the blame for this defeat himself, gave an encouraging talk to his men and led a second attack. Gylippus drew his army up better and won a victory and that night the Syracusans managed to complete their cross-wall beyond the end of the Athenian wall. The Athenians could not complete a landward siege of the city. This caused Nicias to send a letter to Athens.

In the spring of 413, Gylippus persuaded the Syracusans to man their fleet and go to fight the Athenians on the sea. There was a battle during which the Athenians stationed on Plemmyrion had gone down to the shore to watch. Gylippus seized his opportunity, and the three forts. This was a huge success for the Syracusans, although they lost the sea-battle. The Athenians lost supplies and equipment which were in the forts and the Syracusans now controlled both headlands either side of the entrance to the harbour.

The Syracusans also heard that Athenian reinforcements were on their way so decided to attack the Athenians again before they arrived. They made alterations to their triremes to suit the battle they were about to fight. At the same time as, or just before, they launched their naval attack, Gylippus led men out to attack the Athenian wall. The battles were indecisive.

Two days later they attacked again, and after a ploy which was almost a pre-cursor of the one Lysander was to use at Aegospotami eight years later, the Syracusans were victorious.

FIGURE 2.9
A plan of Syracuse and Epipolae with the Athenian walls and Syracusan counter-walls.

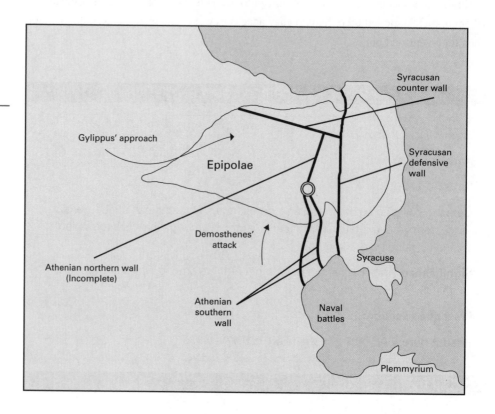

However, just when the Syracusans thought they were going to win, the Athenian general Demosthenes arrived with a large Athenian relief force. He quickly sized up the situation that Nicias had allowed to develop after the arrival of Gylippus. He used his fresh troops to inspire terror and then launched a night attack on Epipolae to try to recover control of it. After initial success, the Athenians were defeated in the confusion of the darkness

This renewed the Syracusans' confidence and Gylippus went off to raise further forces in Sicily. Demosthenes immediately felt the Athenians should retreat, but he could not persuade Nicias. Gylippus returned with reinforcements. Demosthenes now persuaded Nicias to retreat, but, according to Thucydides, there was an eclipse of the moon which the Athenians took as a bad omen and persuaded Nicias to delay for twenty-seven days as advised by the soothsayers with the army.

The Syracusans launched another double attack. They were victorious by sea, but the Athenians just managed to prevent Gylippus gaining control of the shore as well. However, the battle gave back to the Syracusans control of their harbour and they subsequently began to block up the mouth of the harbour. Just as the Spartans at Pylos had set out to besiege the Athenians and ended up being themselves cut off on Sphacteria, now the Athenians who had come to besiege Syracuse were trapped.

The Athenians decided to try to break through the blockade and the Syracusans sailed out to stop them. Thucydides' description of the battle is a superb piece of writing, what we might almost call 'war-reporting', although of course he was not there (see especially Thucydides 7.71 **CW**).

The Athenians were defeated and now had no other choice than to try to escape by land. They set off in two divisions. The first under the command of Demosthenes was routed eventually by the Syracusans and he surrendered. The one under Nicias managed to get a little further, still under constant attack, and he too surrendered when his division was attacked at a river-crossing. His men were so thirsty that they ignored their safety and were easily picked off by the Syracusans. He surrendered to Gylippus who tried to save the lives of the two Athenian generals so he could lead them back to Sparta, but he could not persuade the Syracusans.

However, Gylippus eventually fell into disgrace. Lysander entrusted to him what remained of Athens' public treasury after capturing the city in 404. Gylippus embezzled some of this from each sack and his dishonesty was discovered by the ephors. He left Sparta in disgrace (Plutarch *Lysander* 16). **PS** **CW**

> **Study question** **PS**
>
> Greeks made a habit of asking not for ships or money or even hoplites from them, but a single Spartiate commander. And when they got him, they would treat him with honour and respect, as for example the Sicilians with Gylippos, the Chalkidians with Brasidas, and all the Greeks of Asia with Lysander, Kallikratidas and Agesilaos.
>
> Plutarch, *Lycurgus* 30.5 (LACTOR 21, D82)
>
> From what you have read how far do you think that Gylippus, Brasidas and Lysander deserved to be treated in this way?

TOPIC REVIEW

- Explain the organisation of the Spartan army both before and after the late fifth century reforms.
- Give dates for major battles involving Sparta and its dealings with its Peloponnesian allies.

Further Reading

Cartledge, P., 'The Spartan Army (and the battle of Leuctra)', Appendix F in R.B. Strassler (ed.) *The Landmark Xenophon's Hellenica* (New York: Pantheon Books, 2009), pp. 359–64.

Hodkinson, D., and A. Powell (eds.), *Sparta and War* (Swansea: Classical Press of Wales, 2006).

Rusch, S.M., *Sparta at War: Strategy, Tactics and Campaigns, 550–362* BC (Barnsley: Frontline Books, 2014), especially pp. 69–147.

Sekunda, N., *The Spartan Army* (Oxford: Osprey Publishing, 2008).

Shepherd, W., *Pylos and Sphacteria 425* BC (Oxford: Osprey Publishing, 2013).

PRACTICE QUESTIONS

Read Thucydides 1.80–81, LACTOR 21, E29 **PS**

1. How useful is this passage for our understanding of the strengths and weaknesses of Sparta? [12]

2.5 Other States' Views of Sparta and the Effect of the Spartan System on its Policy

TOPIC OVERVIEW

- what other states say about the Spartans in the prescribed sources, especially the Corinthians and Athenians
- the Peloponnesian League and its importance for Sparta
- examples of when Spartan action was constrained by its system: lack of leadership in the 470s, helot revolts, fear of foreigners, slowness to act, use of commanders other than kings, reluctance to commit Spartiate troops, shortage of manpower
- the 'Spartan mirage', including the reputation gained from Thermopylae and the nature of the evidence

The prescribed sources for this topic are:

- Aristophanes, *Lysistrata* 79–84, 1254–1259
- Aristotle, *Politics* 1269b12–1270b5, 1271a26–1271b19
- Diodorus, *Library of History* 11.50, 11.63.1–4
- Herodotus, *Histories* 7.104.4, 228, 234.2; 8.3
- Plato, *Alcibiades* 1.122d–123b
- Plutarch, *Lycurgus* 9–10, 29.6, 30
- Plutarch, *Lysander* 17.1, 17.2, 17.4–5
- Plutarch, Moralia 219D (Brasidas 4) = 190B (Brasidas 3) = 240C (Argileonis 1)
- Plutarch, *Sayings of the Spartans* 215d = *Agis* 5
- Plutarch, *Sayings of Spartan Women* 16 = *Moralia* 241F
- Thucydides, *The History of the Peloponnesian War* 1.6, 10, 68–71, 87, 102, 103, 119.1; 2.9.2; 5.17, 68, 72
- Xenophon, *Constitution of the Spartans* 5, 7, 14
- Xenophon, *Hellenica* 2.2.19–20

We have seen that some commonly held ideas about Sparta should perhaps be questioned. Part of our problem is that we generally are not seeing Sparta through Spartan eyes, but through our sources, most of which were not Spartan. What other contemporary Greeks thought or knew about the Spartans is therefore important.

We have also seen that the Spartan system and the Spartans' reputation was perhaps not always reflected in reality. We have to consider some occasions when they did not live up to the legend.

All of these aspects of the legend and the Spartans' reputation have collectively been called the 'Spartan mirage' by the French scholar, François Ollier.

WHAT OTHER STATES SAY ABOUT THE SPARTANS IN THE PRESCRIBED SOURCES

ACTIVITY **CW**

Read Thucydides 1.68–71, LACTOR 21, E141, again **PS** and look back at the list you made from this passage in Topic 2 concentrating on those aspects which show what the Corinthians thought of the Spartans.

We have already seen in previous topics that the Athenians at least were aware that Spartan women trained (Aristophanes *Lysistrata* 79–84, LACTOR 21, D66 **PS**) and that they were aware of Spartan religious festivals, including some at which women and girls danced (1241–1321, LACTOR 21, G7). They were clearly also aware of the nature of the city of Sparta, presumably from reports of embassies sent there from time to time:

> For example, if the city of the Lakedaimonians were to be destroyed and abandoned, and all that was left were its temples and the foundations of its buildings, I suspect that future generations would find it impossible to believe historians' accounts of its present power. Yet today they occupy two fifths of the Peloponnese, control the whole of it, and are the leaders of an extensive alliance outside its boundaries as well. Yet to the uninformed observer its physical remains would seem to fall far short of the reality, because it lacks the conventional layout of a modern city, has no temples or extravagant public buildings, and is simply a collection of villages typical of ancient Greek society. **PS**
>
> Thucydides, *The History of the Peloponnesian War* 1.10 (LACTOR G2)

We should not be surprised that other Greeks knew what Sparta *looked* like. What we need to consider is what they thought of Spartan attitudes.

Thucydides was probably not present for this speech in Sparta, but he does tell us that some Athenians were, and that they heard the speech. It is therefore not too much to assume that he spoke to these Athenians and recorded the main points of what was said. It therefore gives us an outsider's view of the Spartans from people who were their allies!

We have already seen from Thucydides' account of the helot revolt in 464 that the Spartans were suspicious of outsiders, on this occasion the Athenians (Thucydides 1.102 **PS**). Maybe they had good reason to worry about what the Athenians might do as the Spartans had just made a promise to help one of Athens' allies which was in revolt, Thasos. They were probably doubly worried what the Athenians would do if they found out about this.

However, we find this fear of foreigners recorded elsewhere as well.

> Someone enquired how many Lakedaimonians there were. He replied, "Enough to keep wrong-doers away."
>
> Plutarch, *Sayings of the Spartans* 215d = *Agis* 5 (LACTOR 21, F32)

Thucydides also has Pericles make a more specific reference to this in the speech he made to persuade the Athenians to reject the Spartans' final ultimatum in 432–431:

> . . . if the Spartans excuse both ourselves and our allies from their expulsions of foreigners.

Thucydides, The History of the Peloponnesian War 1.144.2

We could take this as just point-scoring by an Athenian politician in a speech recorded by an Athenian writer, but Xenophon would seem to support it (Xenophon *Constitution of the Spartans* 14.4, LACTOR 21, E70 **PS**). Some sources ascribe the demise of the Spartans to the relaxation of this rule.

The Corinthians accused the Spartans of being slow to act. It may be that this reputation was earned from their perceived slowness to act at the time of the Persians invasions, just before our period. They arrived too late for the Battle of Marathon in 490, only sent Leonidas and 300 men to Thermopylae in 480 and did not want to advance beyond the Isthmus of Corinth afterwards. They also were slow to act in 479, although when they did march to Plataea, they did so in considerable force.

Thucydides repeats this point in his own narrative:

> . . . The Spartans . . . were of old not swift to go to war, unless compelled to . . .

Thucydides, The History of the Peloponnesian War 1.118

There was also the feeling that they allowed Athens to take over the Greek alliance in 478, which they perhaps regretted, although they decided not to do anything about it in the debate recorded by Diodorus (11.50, LACTOR 21, E28 **PS**) in the 470s. We need now to consider the reasons for these apparent policies, but first we need to look at Sparta's position in the Peloponnese.

THE PELOPONNESIAN LEAGUE: FORMATION AND EARLY HISTORY

Thucydides also gives us the extent of the Spartan alliance at 2.9.2 (LACTOR 21, D100 **PS**). Although it is earlier than our period, we need briefly to describe the early history of the Peloponnesian League. This is actually a modern term, the sources normally refer to 'The Spartans and their allies'.

After finally conquering Messenia in the seventh century, Sparta was keen that nothing should threaten its position. In the first half of the sixth century, Pisa and Elis were contesting control of Olympia, and the Olympic Games. Sparta intervened on the side of, and made an alliance with, Elis, possibly because Pisa was further south and close to the northern border of Messenia.

The main threat to Sparta came from Tegea, immediately to the north of Sparta's territory, and Argos. The Tegeans had assisted the Messenians in their revolt from Sparta in the mid seventh century. About 550, the Spartans finally defeated Tegea, after a number of reverses. Perhaps realising that they would be very dangerous as helots (though that

FIGURE 2.10
Map of the Peloponnese.

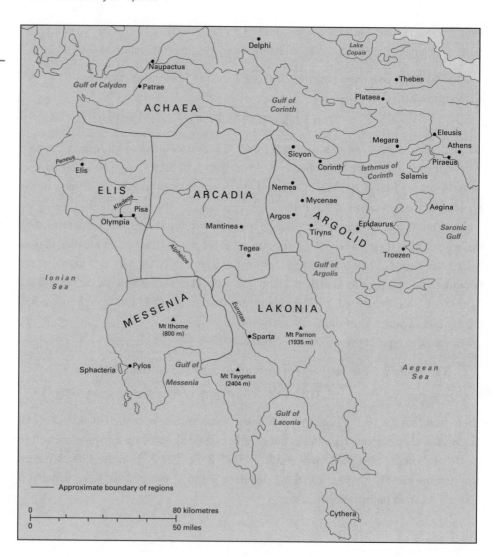

might well have been their original intention), they instead made a military alliance, with Sparta as the senior partner. This, alongside the alliance with Elis, was the basis of what was to become the Peloponnesian League, a series of individual alliances with separate states.

Sparta then turned its attention to Argos, and won a costly victory *c.* 544. This led to other Peloponnesian states making alliances with Sparta, including the northern states of Corinth and Sikyon. This meant that by 500 Sparta was certainly the most powerful state in Greece, which is why it was natural for the Ionians to ask for its help in revolting from Persia before they turned to Athens, and also why they were the natural choice to be leaders of the Greek forces against the Persian invasion in 480. Argos was always a threat as, although it had been defeated in 544, it does not seem to have joined the League. Argos's hostility to Sparta is to be seen in its refusal to join the Greek coalition against Persia because it was under Spartan leadership.

The key to these alliances may lie in the treaty Sparta made with Tegea:

. . . There was written on it among other things that (the Tegeans) were to expel the Messenians from the country and were not permitted to make them 'good'

> C.W. Fornara, *Translated Documents of Greece and Rome:*
> *Archaic times to the end of the Peloponnesian War*
> No. 27

Fornara interprets 'make them 'good' 'as meaning 'to make them citizens'. In other words, the Tegeans were not to harbour Messenians – i.e. helots.

Gradually other states were added in a series of alliances until Sparta had control of most of the Peloponnese. This gave them great security in case of a helot revolt.

THE PELOPONNESIAN LEAGUE (478–404)

> They then recalled their allies to the assembly and told them that the decision had been taken that the Athenians were the aggressors, but that they wanted to put the decision to the vote in the presence of their whole alliance, so that the decision for war, if such it proved to be, would be unanimous. **PS**
>
> Thucydides, *The History of the Peloponnesian War* 1.87.4 (LACTOR 21, E31)

This was in 432. By this time, the Spartans seem to have been careful to have the allies vote for war after they had themselves decided on the matter. Thucydides' phrasing here could be taken to mean that this was unusual. It does seem that Sparta was being careful as the usual terms of alliance were that the allies would have the same friends and enemies as Sparta – i.e they had to follow Sparta's lead.

> Even so, the Lakedaimonians summoned their allies to yet another assembly, wishing to take a vote on whether war was an unavoidable necessity. **PS**
>
> Thucydides, *The History of the Peloponnesian War* 1.119.1
> (LACTOR 21, E142)

Technically, Sparta could declare war and expect the allies to follow. In this instance, it was a foregone conclusion as it was the allies, principally but not solely Corinth, who were pressing the Spartans to act. It was, however, wise, as some twenty-eight years before our period starts it had been over-ruled by its allies when Cleomenes was wanting to attack Athens in 506. However, in 432 Sparta retained some degree of control as it was at its invitation that the allies came to Sparta to vote.

This made the Peloponnesian League rather different from others; the purpose was to neutralise opposition in the Peloponnese as no single state could take on the whole League, but also to have a powerful series of alliances on which Sparta could call in the event of a helot revolt. We have seen in Topic 2 (pp. 100–101) that the sources frequently mention this as an underlying reason for Spartan foreign policy.

However, Sparta had to balance this selfish reason for the alliances with the wishes of its allies.

The result of this was that in 421, Corinth made an alliance with Argos, Sparta's traditional enemy in the Peloponnese, and was joined by Mantinea and Elis. The Spartan

Study questions **S&C**
Read the Corinthians' speech in Sparta in 432 again (Thucydides 1.68–71, LACTOR 21, E141) **PS**

1 What is the threat the Corinthians make in 71 and why might this be a problem for the Spartans?

Read Thucydides 5.17 (LACTOR 21, E143) and 5.25, 421 **CW** **PS**

2 Who are the parties to the peace treaty? Is Corinth included?

3 Why might this have upset Corinth? (Clue – look again at 1.68–71, LACTOR 21, E141.)

victory at the Battle of Mantinea in 418 was vital in re-establishing Spartan control within the Peloponnese.

A similar problem recurred after the eventual defeat of Athens in 404 as the allies' wishes were again ignored (Xenophon *Hellenica* 2.2.19–20, LACTOR 21, E127 **PS**). What annoyed the allies on both occasions was that, although Sparta needed the allies' agreement to declare war, or at least consulted them, it had made peace unilaterally. So, to a certain extent, Sparta was constrained to listen to its allies, and sometimes to give in to them if it wanted to maintain its position. This was therefore always somewhat precarious.

LACK OF SPARTAN LEADERSHIP AND RECOVERY

We have already seen that Herodotus says that the Athenians used the bad behaviour of Pausanias as an excuse to seize control of the Greek anti-Persian alliance (Herodotus 8.3 **PS**) and that there were at least some in Sparta who thought they should seize it back (Diodorus 11.50, LACTOR 21, E28 **PS**). However, this latter passage also shows that there were some who were happy for Athens to take over, perhaps realising the far-off naval commitment continued leadership would involve. This group won on this occasion which leads Thucydides to say,

> the Lakedaimonians no longer sent out anyone else, fearing that those who went out there became corrupted, as they saw had happened to Pausanias, wishing to disengage from war with Persia, and thinking that the Athenians were quite capable of leadership and well-disposed to them at the present time.
>
> Thucydides, *The History of the Peloponnesian War* 1.95.7 (LACTOR 21, E25)

Thus, there were two groups of opinion in Sparta: those who did not want to be involved outside the Peloponnese and did not mind seeing Athens increase its power, and those who wanted to do something about it. The former were most likely motivated by the reasons of internal security we have already discussed. The position of the latter was undermined by events.

We have already considered the disgrace of Pausanias in Topic 3. He had been regent for Leonidas' son who was too young to take the throne, and may not have been of age until the 460s.

The other king in 478 was Leotychidas who had led the Greek forces in the final victory over the Persians at Mycale in Asia Minor in 479. However, he too was convicted for bribery after leading an expedition against the Aleuads, a royal family in Thessaly in northern Greece who had sided with the Persians. He was disgraced and exiled in *c.* 476 and was succeeded by his grandson, Archidamus, who may not officially have become king until Leotychidas died in 469.

The Spartan royal families were therefore somewhat in tatters in the 470s. At the same time, the Athenian Themistocles was trying to form an anti-Spartan coalition in the Peloponnese, much as Alcibiades was to do some fifty-five years later. There had been rumblings of trouble already during the Persian Wars. Argos, never part of the Peloponnesian League, had refused to join the Greek alliance against Persia under Spartan leadership, and Elis and Mantinea had both been 'too late' for the Battle of Plataea (this despite the various manoeuvrings before the battle taking up to two weeks!). In the late 470s both states had then joined their outlying villages into larger states, a process which normally also went hand in hand with democracy. This was a real threat to Sparta, with Elis just to the north of Messenia, and Mantinea controlling the centre of the Peloponnese.

Herodotus records two battles fought by the Spartans between 479 and 465 against Tegea and Argos, and against the combined Arcadians (excluding Mantinea), and that they were victorious; this was Sparta's successful response to the threat, but these problems in the Peloponnese were enough to allow Athens' power to increase.

When Sparta was finally strong enough to take steps against Athens in 465, promising to help the island of Thasos revolt from Athens, it was immediately again crippled by the earthquake and helot revolt. This lasted until 455 (Thucydides 1.103, LACTOR 21, E62 (PS)), though many scholars think there is an error in our text of Thucydides and it did not last so long. However, we have already seen the terrible effect it had on Spartan manpower (Diodorus 11.63, LACTOR 21, E63 (PS)).

Sparta did send one foreign expedition in this period (i.e. outside the Peloponnese), in 458 or 457. This expedition was again commanded by a regent, Cleombrotus (Kleombrotos) as Leonidas' son, Pleistarchos, had died in 458 and the next in line was Pausanias' son, Pleistoanax, who was still too young (Thucydides 1.107, LACTOR 21, H23). The reason for this was that in central Greece the state of Doris, the supposed spiritual origin of the Dorian Greeks of the Peloponnese, was under attack from its neighbour. The Spartans could not be seen to do nothing about this. After re-instating Doris, the Spartans set out to return via Boeotia, hoping to counter Athens by setting up a strong alliance under the leadership of Thebes, and maybe also intending to march on Athens. The Athenians marched to meet them. The Spartans won a victory at Tanagra, but left Athens alone and returned to the Peloponnese.

In 451, the return from exile to Athens of Cimon (Kimon), a pro-Spartan, allowed a five-year truce to be made. Sparta used this immediately to make a thirty-year peace with Argos, its traditional enemy and Athens' ally in the Peloponnese. (The expiry of this truce in 421, along with its desire to recover the prisoners from Sphacteria, was a major factor in Sparta wanting to make peace with Athens then.)

The truce with Athens expired in 446 and Megara and Euboea (Euboia) immediately revolted from Athens and King Pleistoanax led an expedition to invade Attica. However, he returned to Sparta without accomplishing anything and was charged with being bribed and went into exile. He returned in *c*. 427 and was later an important figure in bringing about the Peace of Nicias in 421.

Athens and Sparta made a thirty-year peace, which did not last as Athens' further imperialism in the 430s upset Sparta's allies, notably Corinth, leading to the declaration of war in 432.

Throughout all this period, certainly from 464, Sparta was also constrained by oliganthropia, a shortage of Spartiates, which was an increasing problem throughout the fifth century as we have seen.

So, we can see that Spartan foreign policy was influenced by a number of inter-related factors:

- the attitude of its allies in the Peloponnese, and Sparta's attitude towards their enemies
- the on-going threat of a helot revolt
- shortage of Spartiates
- the relative strength or weakness of the kingship
- the behaviour of Spartan kings or commanders when they did campaign outside the Peloponnese (see also Topics 3 and 4 on Pausanias, Gylippus and Lysander)

THE 'SPARTAN MIRAGE' AND THE REPUTATION GAINED AT THERMOPYLAE

The 'Spartan mirage' was a term first used by François Ollier, a French scholar, in the second quarter of the twentieth century. There are many aspects to it, but one of the most important was founded upon what happened at Thermopylae. Herodotus records the epitaph to the dead Spartans at Thermopylae:

Tell the Lakedaemonians, passer-by,
We followed orders, and here now we lie

Herodotus, *Histories* 7.228.2 (LACTOR 21, B4)

They do whatever it commands; and it always commands the same thing; not allowing them to run away, no matter what the number of men facing them in battle, but staying in the line of battle to conquer or die.

Herodotus, *Histories* 7.104.5

FIGURE 2.11
The memorial at
Thermopylae today.

The famous couplet on the previous page and Demaratus' comment to Xerxes the Persian king immediately established two parts of the mirage, or myth as we might otherwise call it. First, the Spartans obeyed orders (as they were trained to do through the agōgē), and secondly, they did not leave their post, retreat or surrender. This is reinforced by the famous anecdote in Plutarch's *Sayings of Spartan Women* (16 = *Moralia* 241F, LACTOR 21, F35 **PS**) when a mother was giving her son his shield and said 'with it or on it'.

There is no doubt that Herodotus' account helped to build the Spartan reputation amongst other Greeks, but we need to consider who his sources were. J.T. Hooker goes as far as to suggest that some of this reputation actually arose from propaganda from the Spartans themselves ('Spartan Propaganda' in *Classical Sparta: Techniques Behind her Success*, A. Powell (ed.) (Routledge, 1989), pp. 122–41).

The idea that Spartans blindly stayed in their post was emphasised the following year at the battle of Plataea where Herodotus tells us that a Spartan officer called Amompharetus initially refused to leave his post (although he was ordered to do so) (Herodotus 9.53, LACTOR 21, E85). We have already seen a similar problem occurred at Mantinea in 418 (Thucydides 5.72, LACTOR 21, E103 **PS**). The Spartans seemed to believe their own propaganda!

The events at Sphacteria give the lie to the idea that Spartans never surrendered, although Thucydides does note the amazement in the Greek world that their surrender on that occasion caused:

This was for the Greeks the most extraordinary thing to have happened in the war. For they thought the Lakedaimonians would not surrender their weapons through starvation or any other force, but would keep them, fight as long as they were able and die fighting

Thucydides, *The History of the Peloponnesian War* 4.40.1 (LACTOR 21, E95)

So there is ample evidence to show that the rest of the Greeks had bought into this aspect of the Spartan myth, and the Spartans continued actively to promote this idea to other

Greeks if we are to believe the anecdote about Brasidas' mother (Plutarch Moralia 219D, LACTOR 21, F33 PS).

We have already seen that another aspect of the myth was the role of Lycurgus. As we saw in the passage quoted in Topic 1, even Plutarch himself begins his *Lycurgus* with a *caveat* about the details of Lycurgus' life. However, again, the idea that Sparta had had a solid, unchanged constitution for centuries is to be found in Thucydides (1.18, LACTOR 21, F4 and CW) and Plutarch (*Lycurgus* 29, LACTOR 21, F6 and CW, see Topic 3 PS). His statement would date the Spartan constitution back to before 800, which we know is not true.

Part of the 'Lycurgus myth' is that Lycurgus removed wealth and extravagance, the so-called Spartan austerity.

Although Xenophon does ascribe these measures to Lycurgus, we can probably accept that they were in use when he was in Sparta. Archaeological evidence shows that there was a thriving Spartan material culture down to the second half of the sixth century (L.F. Fitzhardinge, *The Spartans* (Thames & Hudson, 1980)). It is true that there is far less of this material culture by our period in the fifth century, but to consider the reasons for this is beyond the scope of the specification.

The final aspect of the myth is that all Spartans were equal. There were many things which contributed to this. They ate common meals (Plutarch *Lycurgus* 10, LACTOR 21, D12, D51, F1 PS); they all went through the same state-run education; they were all given the same sized allotment of land and made the same contribution to the syssitia.

But it is impossible that all the allotments were of land of equal worth. Although Spartans were given the same allotment of state land, that does not mean that some families did not own additional land elsewhere. There was wealth, Spartans could be fined and from the earliest time in our period individual Spartans acquired wealth through bribery or foreign conquest, as we have seen. Even Thucydides implies that some Spartans were wealthier than others:

> The Spartans first adopted simple dress . . . and in other ways the wealthy did their best to establish a way of life the same as the people.
>
> Thucydides, *The History of the Peloponnesian War* 1.6.4, LACTOR 21, D52

Towards the end of our period, or just after it, the sources suggest that there was considerable wealth in Sparta (Plato *Alcibiades* 1.122d–123b, LACTOR 21, E72 PS) and that many of the values were being undermined.

We can see the effects of oliganthrōpia by looking carefully at the number of Spartiates at various battles throughout the period, although we have to be careful as we cannot guarantee in all cases that the numbers represent the full amount of Spartiates (see pp. 122–124).

By the battle of Leuctra in 371 this had fallen to just 1,500. As well as the reasons outlined above, the disastrous earthquake in 464 also had an effect, and, as we also saw on pp. 122–124, Sparta was relying increasingly on perioikoi and helots in battle.

S & C

There has been much debate about the nature of land ownership in Sparta, the older view being that the state gave each Spartiate an allotment of land and he could not sell this or give it away. More recent thought is that land was able to be bequeathed to children. This contributed to the oliganthrōpia from which Sparta suffered in two ways:

- If a Spartan had lots of children the amount of land inherited would become smaller; if this continued over a few generations it would be insufficient to supply the necessary contributions to the syssitia leading to loss of citizen rights.
- Spartans therefore produced fewer children.

The arguments and supporting evidence for both sides of this debate are well summarised by Terry Buckley (*Aspects of Greek History, 750–323* BC, 2nd ed. (Routledge, 2010), pp. 72–7).

ACTIVITY **S&C**

Read P. Cartledge, *Thermopylae, The Battle that Changed the World* (London: Pan Books, 2007), pp. 155–67

- What arguments does Cartledge use to support the idea that much of the Spartan mirage was due to the deliberate propaganda and actions of the Spartans themselves?

Study questions **PS**

Read Xenophon *Constitution of the Spartans* 14, Plutarch *Lycurgus* 30 and *Lysander 17* LACTOR 21, E70, E76, D82, E75 and .

1 What do these authors say were the reasons for the downfall of the Spartan way of life? Make sure that you note what each author says.

Read Aristotle *Politics* 1269b1–1270b5 and 1271a26–1271b19, LACTOR 21, D27, D69, D54, D28 and D62, D98, D84, D55

2 What criticisms of the Spartan system does Aristotle put forward as reasons for its downfall?

TOPIC REVIEW

- Give examples of occasions when the Peloponnesian allies caused problems for Sparta after 479.
- Give an example of when Corinth prevented Sparta from attacking Athens and support your answer with a reference from the sources.
- Give the details of how Corinth managed to get its way when it did want to attack Athens.
- Give examples from the sources of Sparta's relationship with Argos.
- Give at least three examples from the prescribed sources which reflect the 'otherness' of Sparta.
- Give at least three examples from the prescribed sources of other states' views of Sparta.
- Explain what is meant by the 'Spartan mirage' and give examples supported by the sources to illustrate it.

Further Reading

Buckley, T., *Aspects of Greek History, 750–323*BC, 2nd ed. (Abingdon: Routledge, 2010), pp. 72–7.

Cartledge, P., *Spartan Reflections* (London: Duckworth, 2001), pp. 169–84.

Cartledge, P., *The Spartans, An Epic History* (London: Pan Books, 2003), pp.131–52.

Cartledge, P., *Thermopylae, The Battle that Changed the World* (London: Pan Books, 2007).

Fitzhardinge, L.F., *The Spartans* (London: Thames and Hudson, 1980).

Forrest, W.G., *History of Sparta*, 3rd ed. (London: Bristol Classical Press, 1995).

Hooker, J.T., *The Ancient Spartans* (London: Dent, 1980).

Hooker J.T., 'Spartan Propaganda' in A. Powell (ed.), *Classical Sparta: Techniques Behind her Success* (Abingdon: Routledge, 1989), pp. 122–41.

de Ste Croix, G.E.M., *The Origins of the Peloponnesian War* (London: Duckworth, 1972), App. XVII, pp. 333–9.

de Ste Croix, G.E.M., 'Sparta's Foreign Policy', in M. Whitby (ed.), *Sparta* (Edinburgh: Edinburgh University Press, 2002), pp. 218–22

PRACTICE QUESTIONS

1. Explain the extent to which the sources help us to understand the Spartans' relationship with Corinth and Argos.

   Use and analyse the ancient sources you have studied as well as your own knowledge to support your answer. [36]

DEPTH STUDY 2
The Politics and Culture of Athens, c. 460–399 BC

Introduction to The Politics and Culture of Athens, c. 460–399 BC

The Politics and Culture of Athens in this period were heavily influenced by the events studied in the Period Study. The Persian Wars resulted in two key developments for the Athenians: they aspired to be leaders in the Greek world, and they gained the wealth and personal freedom to allow their city to become a cultural centre. Their leadership was not only political, but cultural. Leading thinkers from around the Greek world flocked to Athens to teach, while the playwrights of Athens were to produce masterpieces which reflected on key questions of human conduct in their tragedies, and made fun of the events of the day in their comedies. Such a freedom of thought was doubtless encouraged by, if not the product of, the Athenian democratic system, which fostered in the citizens of Athens the need to think about political questions, and to make decisions about those questions.

To understand this period effectively, it is important to appreciate the different elements which led the men and women of Athens to live as they did. Politics, religion and contemporary thought all come together in the great works of art and architecture created during this period. Indeed, perhaps the most enthralling aspect of this option is the way in which the seemingly separate elements come together to make one, interconnected narrative. It also offers the opportunity to look not only at the works of historians, but also at literary, archaeological and artistic evidence, and to use these to help reconstruct the lives and thought of those who lived at this fascinating time.

EXAM OVERVIEW	H407/12 SECTION B

Your examination for Athens, in Section B of your paper, will require you to show knowledge and understanding of the material you have studied. This component is worth 48 marks – 12 based on AO1 skills, 12 on AO2, and 24 on AO3.

In this section, you will answer two questions:

- a 12-mark stimulus question focusing on an issue relating to a historical event or situation, where you will need to assess the source's utility;
- one of two essay questions, each worth 36 marks. The questions will require you to use, analyse, and evaluate source material to address issues in the question. The essays will target one or more of the themes listed.

3.1 Athenian Political and Social Culture

TOPIC OVERVIEW

- the concepts of democracy and oligarchy
- the nature and level of participation in the democratic system by the population of Attica, including citizens, women, metics and slaves
- the workings of the ecclēsia (assembly), boulē (the council), the role and function of archōns (magistrates) and stratēgoi (generals)
- the use of ostracism
- the courts and their role in democracy
- critiques of this system
- the importance of rhetoric
- Athens as the leader of an empire, and her treatment of allied states
- the changing nature of leadership in the fifth century, including the actions and significance of Pericles, Cleon, Nicias and Alcibiades
- different elements of Athenian society, and their roles and duties: citizens, metics and slaves
- the position and roles of women, both citizen and non-citizen

The prescribed sources for this topic are:

- Aristophanes, *Thesmophoriazusae* 786–800, 830–842
- Aristophanes, *Wasps* 891–1008; *Knights* 147–395
- Aristotle, *The Athenian Constitution* 23–28
- Euripides, *Hippolytus*
- The Old Oligarch (Pseudo-Xenophon), *Constitution of the Athenians*
- Plato, *Apology*
- Plutarch, *Pericles* 11, 14–15, 30, 32, 36–37; *Nicias* 3.1–2, 11; *Alcibiades* 10, 16, 19, 20.2–4, 34
- Thucydides, *The History of the Peloponnesian War* 2.34–2.46; 3.36–3.50
- Xenophon, *Memorabilia* 2.2.2, 3.76
- Xenophon, *Poroi* 2.1–2, 5

This topic will examine the structure of the Athenian democratic state. It will look at the workings of the main organs of democracy, such as the assembly and the law courts. It will also focus on how far different groups in Athens could contribute to public life. A further consideration will be how the sources present the idea that the nature of the leadership of the state changed after the death of Pericles in 429.

It is in this context that the cultural and intellectual developments of this period must be seen, if they are to be understood fully.

OLIGARCHY, TYRANNY AND DEMOCRACY

> **oligarchy** rule of a state by a minority of its citizens
>
> **tyranny** a sole ruler takes power and rules unconstitutionally
>
> **democracy** all the citizens have the right to vote on political decisions

In the Greek world there were three political systems which had become common by the fifth century: **oligarchy**, **tyranny** and **democracy**.

Oligarchy was the term given by Greek political theorists to describe a state in which the minority of citizens – usually the wealthiest ones – held power (in Greek 'oligos' meant 'few' and 'archē' meant 'rule', so 'rule of the few'). The majority of cities started as aristocratic oligarchies, and this is how Athens was ruled until the middle of the sixth century. In the Greek world, the Spartans were particularly known for their policy of promoting oligarchies with whom they could do business. In contrast, they were usually strongly opposed to tyrannies.

Today, 'tyrant' is a byword for cruelty, but originally the Greeks used it simply to describe a sole ruler who had taken power unconstitutionally (it later came to have more negative connotations). A tyrant was typically a disillusioned member of the aristocratic class who had seized power by overthrowing an oligarchy with the support of a section of the common people. After taking control, he would usually seek to bolster his support by developing his city's economy, public works and arts. Therefore a tyrant could be an improvement on what had come before.

> **dēmos** the ancient Greek word to describe the people in a state

'Democracy' is formed of two Greek words – **dēmos** ('people') and kratos ('power') and so literally means 'people power'. The word dēmos originally meant 'township' or 'village' and it could refer to the people who lived in these settlements too. During the fifth century, the word also came to refer to the whole citizen body of Athens and writers such as Thucydides and Aristotle often use it when describing the decisions taken by the assembly. For some educated writers opposed to democracy, the word could also have a negative connotation, referring to what they saw as the ill-educated masses who controlled the state.

Many educated Athenians were in fact fundamentally opposed to democracy, believing it to be little more than the 'rule of the mob'. We should be very aware of this: the sort of Athenian who was likely to be in favour of the democratic system was not usually drawn from the educated classes, and so did not have the ability to set down his thoughts in writing. Indeed, most of the sources from the period show a hostility to democracy and a preference for oligarchy. One such individual is known today as the 'Old Oligarch' and he wrote a pamphlet about the state of Athens in his day, *The Constitution of the Athenians*. It is most likely to have been composed during the 420s.

PRESCRIBED SOURCE

Title: The Old Oligarch (Pseudo-Xenophon), *Constitution of the Athenians*

Author: Uncertain

Date: probably 420s

Origin: probably Athenian

Genre: political philosophy

Significance: one of the earliest examples of critical writing on Athenian democracy, which gives a detailed perspective on political and social life in Athens

Read it here: LACTOR 2: *The Old Oligarch* (2nd edn, KCL, 2004)

S & C
A passage in Herodotus (3.80–82) is often regarded as the first example of Greek political theory. It is set in Persia in 522, when three Persian nobles debate the relative merits of monarchy, oligarchy and democracy. Few scholars would accept that such a debate took place at that time in Persia, but it offers a fascinating insight into how the three systems may have been viewed in Athens at the time that Herodotus was writing in the third quarter of the fifth century. Read the passage. What arguments are made for and against each system?

Study questions
Read the Old Oligarch, 1.1–1.9 **PS** and 2.17–20 **PS**.

1 What points does the author make about the strengths and weaknesses of democracy as a system here?

2 List the areas of Athenian life that the Old Oligarch feels have been adversely affected by the involvement of the common people at 1.13 **PS** and 2.9–10 **PS**. Do these seem to be valid complaints, or simply snobbery?

The pamphlet was originally attributed to the historian Xenophon, but most modern scholars feel sure that it was not written by him. The author is therefore sometimes referred to as Pseudo-Xenophon, but he is more normally referred to as the Old Oligarch, because of his view that oligarchy works better than democracy. The 'Old' part of his name may or may not be accurate but it is a reflection more of his attitudes than his actual age: he seems to look back fondly on the old, pre-democratic days, when power was restricted to the wealthy few. Despite this bias, however, the text gives us valuable information about the workings of Athenian democracy in the later fifth century. Moreover, the author starts by grudgingly admitting that democracy benefits the mass of citizens of Athens, and that they deserve to run the state (1.2 **PS**).

CITIZENSHIP AND NON-CITIZENSHIP

What do we mean by the 'state of Athens'? Athens as a political entity entailed far more than the physical city of Athens. In fact, the city controlled the much larger region of

Attica the large region which formed the entire polis of Athens

polis a Greek word often translated as 'city-state', referring to a city and all the land it controlled as one political entity.

Attica, which consisted of about 1,000 square miles of territory in a triangular section of south-east Greece. The Greeks referred to all this territory as the **polis** of Athens – the Greek word polis referred not just to a physical city but to all the land it controlled. Polis is often therefore translated as 'city-state', although an alternative translation might be 'citizen-state', since a polis was defined by those who held citizenship. The polis of Athens was unusually large. In common with many parts of Greece, its landscape was a combination of mountain ranges and plains, and the region was fairly dry so that the soil was not especially fertile. Olive trees could grow in all regions, while grapes were also produced in abundance, but grain largely had to be imported from elsewhere.

Who was eligible to be a citizen in the polis of Athens? It is important to understand that the overwhelming majority of its inhabitants were denied citizenship. Until 451, an Athenian citizen was a free adult male over the age of eighteen who inherited his citizenship from a citizen father (as we shall see, after this date the law was tightened further to require a citizen to have two citizen parents). This meant that three other large groups of people were excluded from the political process: free Athenian women, slaves

FIGURE 3.1
Attica.

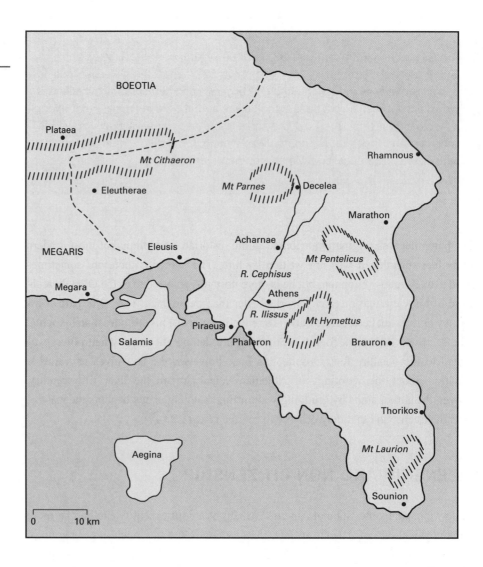

and immigrants. Immigrants living in Athens had a special status and were known as **metics**, while free Athenian women were regarded as minors in Athenian law; slaves had very few legal rights at all.

It is estimated that during the fifth century Athens had between 30,000 and 60,000 citizens from a population of up to 300,000. The proportion of the adult population of Attica who had citizenship was therefore somewhere between 10 per cent and 20 per cent. The roles and status of each of these four groups – citizens, free Athenian women, metics, and slaves – will be considered during the course of this chapter.

> a non-Athenian resident of Athens. **Metics** had no political rights, but were given some legal rights. They had to have an Athenian sponsor and pay a monthly tax

THE DEVELOPMENT OF THE DEMOCRATIC SYSTEM

The origins of democracy can be traced back to the early sixth century. Before this, the polis was ruled by an oligarchy of wealthy families. These leading families controlled the polis of Athens, and by 600 the lives of ordinary people had worsened so much that a popular revolution was brewing. In 594/3, the Athenians elected Solon as the eponymous **archōn**. An archōn was a magistrate: an archonship was held annually, and the archōns played a major role in the administration of the city. There were nine senior archōns in all, and the eponymous archōn was so-called as he gave his name to the civil year. In his year of archonship, Solon reformed the Athenian political system to encourage social mobility in the hope of preventing a revolution. He divided Athenian citizens into four classes according to wealth, which was measured by the amount of wet or dry goods each man could produce. These classes survived into the fifth century, and were as follows:

- **pentakosiomedimnoi** richest class
- **hippeis** second class of men
- **zeugitai** third class of men
- **thētes** lowest class

> **pentakosiomedimnoi** the wealthiest class of Athenian citizens
>
> **hippeis** the second class of Athenian citizens
>
> **zeugitai** the third class of Athenian citizens
>
> **thētes** the fourth and lowest class of Athenian citizens
>
> **ecclēsia (assembly)** a formal meeting of the people open to any citizen
>
> **Council of the Areopagus** the council of ex-archōns

Solon also gave all citizens the right to sit in a people's assembly (known in Greek as the **ecclēsia**), and the right to appeal to a jury for any conviction. All citizens could serve as jurors. This was a vital step as it gave all citizens a say in the rule of law. Solon is also credited with reforming the Athenian law code and publishing it for all to see.

Solon did not, however, introduce what might be considered a democracy. For example, although the thētes could now sit in a citizen's assembly and act as jurors, they were not allowed to hold any political position. Power still remained in the hands of the nine archōns, and an influential council of ex-archōns, the **Council of the Areopagus**.

Solon's reforms could not prevent an aristocrat, Peisistratus, from seizing control of Athens as tyrant in the middle of the sixth century. In fact, Peisistratus is reported to have ruled Athens relatively well, and to have left many of Solon's reforms in place. When he died in 527 he was succeeded by his son Hippias, who became so unpopular that he was driven out of Athens in 510 with the help of the Spartans. In the ensuing power vacuum various factions competed for power. One was led by the wealthy Cleisthenes. In 508/7 his faction took control of the city and introduced radical reforms which turned Athens into much more of a democracy.

tribe a group of citizens who were placed together for administrative purposes

deme a village or district of the town of Athens which formed a single political unit

boulē (council) an advisory body which prepared business for the assembly and oversaw the day to day running of the city

stratēgos (general) one of the ten Athenian generals who commanded troops in times of war

Cleisthenes divided the citizens of Athens into ten **tribes** (there had previously been four). He also ensured that each tribe drew members from across Attica by a sophisticated system based around the villages and city-districts of Attica, known as **demes**. Each tribe comprised a number of demes from across Attica. Cleisthenes also introduced a new council of 500 men, known as the **boulē**. Each year fifty men were selected by lot from each tribe to serve on the council, which prepared business for the assembly. The ten tribes also made up ten regiments of the Athenian army, and most citizens were expected to serve in times of war. Each year, ten generals were elected, one to lead each tribe. The Greek word for such a general was **stratēgos** (plural: stratēgoi). A general could be elected any number of years in a row.

The Greek victories in the Persian wars helped to strengthen the Athenian democratic system. When the Athenians won at Marathon in 490, it was their hoplite soldiers who were the key to the victory. These hoplites tended to be men who could afford their own weapons, but who were not necessarily very wealthy. After this, when the Athenians took the decision during the 480s to develop their naval power, their enlarged fleet required a great deal of rowing manpower, and the poorer men in the city therefore became essential to Athens' defence. With the growing importance of the navy after the formation of the Delian League, men of the lower classes came to hold greater influence in the Athenian democratic system, a point accepted by the Old Oligarch (1.2 **PS**).

Even after the reforms of Cleisthenes, Athens remained a society where the wealthy held much power, largely through the Council of the Areopagus. The reforms of Ephialtes and Pericles in the late 460s and 450s changed that, and gave ordinary people more power.

Our key source for these reforms is Aristotle in his *Athenian Constitution* (which will be shortened to *AC*). Aristotle (384–322) was not himself Athenian, but he moved to Athens to study under the great Athenian thinker Plato. He was a very careful researcher,

---

PRESCRIBED SOURCE

Title: *The Athenian Constitution*

Author: Aristotle (384–322), or one of his pupils

Date: 320s BC

Genre: political treatise

Significance: a detailed account of the Athenian democratic system as Aristotle understood it

Prescribed sections: 23–28

Read it here: Aristotle, *The Athenian Constitution*, translated by Peter John Rhodes (Penguin 1984)

who had a group of students to help him with his work. It is clear that he used records from fifth century Athens where he could. However, it is unlikely that the *Athenian Constitution* is a perfectly reliable account of the Athenian democratic system in the fifth century, since it describes Athenian democracy in the 320s.

In 487/6, the Athenians changed from electing the nine archōns to selecting them by lot from a list of 500 candidates. This meant that within a generation the Council of the Areopagus was no longer made up of the wealthiest citizens, but of ex-archōns who had been randomly selected. Aristotle suggests that during and after the Persian wars two rival factions had emerged in Athens. One was conservative and led by men such as Aristeides, the other was reformist and Themistocles was their early champion (Aristotle *AC* 23 **PS**). Aristotle (*AC* 25 **PS**) reports that by the late 460s an important leader of the reformist faction was Ephialtes. In 462/1, he introduced a major reform of the Council of the Areopagus to make Athens more democratic. According to Aristotle, Ephialtes' reform deprived the Areopagus of all its duties except for jurisdiction over murder and certain offences against the gods. All other powers, including responsibility for the Athenian law code and scrutiny of public officials, were transferred to the other bodies – the assembly, the law courts or the boulē.

Ephialtes was murdered soon afterwards, and at this point Pericles seems to have emerged as Athens' leading reformer. He went on to become the dominant political figure in Athens until his death in 429: from 443 he was elected general fifteen years in a row. Any man who wanted to make his mark would try to become elected as a general. Indeed, after the reform of the archonship in 487/6, the position of general had become the most powerful elected office in the Athenian state. None the less, the archonships retained important roles in the life of the city, including the organisation of important public festivals.

Aristotle relates that in 457/6 the zeugitai became eligible for the archonships. Pericles was likely involved in this change, and he was certainly behind a move to increase the political representation of poorer citizens by introducing payment for citizens who served as jurors (*AC* 27 **PS**). This allowed poorer citizens to play a greater role in the democracy since they were compensated for their time. Pericles' next reform (*AC* 26.3 **PS**; Plutarch, *Pericles* 37 **PS**) was to legislate that an Athenian citizen had to have an Athenian mother as well as an Athenian father. This prevented the citizen population from growing too much, and gave greater importance to citizen women. One reason for this law may have been that, with the growth of the Athenian empire, the city now had a large number metics who had moved from other cities to find work.

Plutarch, who wrote our only surviving biography of Pericles (see pp. 23–4 to revise Plutarch's usefulness as a source), relates that, near the end of his life, the law came back to bite Pericles: he lost many members of his family to the plague of 430, including his sister and both his legitimate sons. In these circumstances, he managed to convince the people to make an exception to his law so that his son by the metic Aspasia, who was also called Pericles, was allowed to be enrolled onto the list of citizens (*Pericles* 36–37 **PS**).

KEY INDIVIDUALS

Ephialtes
Date: unknown to *c.* 461
A popular leader who brought in a major reform of the Council of the Areopagus.

Pericles
Date: *c.* 495–429
The dominant figure in Athenian politics from the 450s until his death in 429. He was elected general fifteen years in a row between 443 and 429.

PRESCRIBED SOURCE

Title: *Life of Pericles*

Author: Plutarch (before AD 50 to after AD 120)

Genre: biography

Significance: our only surviving biography of Pericles

Prescribed sections: 4–6, 11–16, 30–32, 36–37

Read it here: Plutarch, *The Rise and Fall of Athens*, translated by Ian Scott-Kilvert (Penguin 1960)

THE WORKINGS OF THE DEMOCRATIC SYSTEM

The council (boulē)

sortition the principle of selection by lot

bouleutērion the council-house in the agora

agora the civic centre and main market-place of Athens

prytany one of ten administrative periods within the Athenian year, each lasting thirty-five or thirty-six days.

tholos the building in the agora in which the prytaneis were housed

prytaneis the fifty councillors of the tribe serving a prytany

epistatēs the president of the Council and the chairman of the assembly. He was drawn from the prytaneis and served for one day only

The council supported the government and advised the assembly. When each tribe selected its fifty councillors by lot annually, it ensured that every deme provided a fixed number of councillors, so making the body as representative as possible. Citizens could serve only twice on the council during their lifetime, to prevent any single individual from gaining too much power or influence. Selection by lot, known as **sortition**, was the usual way in which the Athenians selected public officials, since they believed that it was the fairest way to share out the powers and burdens of public office. There were only a few public officials who were elected, notably military positions such as the generals. In these cases, it was felt that it was important to have knowledgeable and experienced people in such roles.

The council met every day except public holidays in a council house, the **bouleutērion**, in the **agora**, the civic centre of Athens. Any citizen could observe its meetings. It prepared motions for the assembly, and oversaw the implementation of the assembly's decisions. Councillors were also responsible for meeting foreign ambassadors, and they supervised elections and ensured that all magistrates were scrutinised fully.

A key feature of the council was the **prytany** system. A prytany was a period of thirty-five or thirty-six days when the fifty councillors from one tribe were on-call all the time and lived at state expense in a designated building in the agora, the **tholos**. They were known as **prytaneis**. Their most important role was to prepare the agenda for the council meetings. At the end of a prytany, a new tribe was chosen by lot for the next prytany, with all the ten tribes serving once in the civil year. Every morning, one of their number was chosen by lot to be the chairman of the council for that day, and he also acted as chairman for the assembly if it was to be held on that day. He was known as the **epistatēs**.

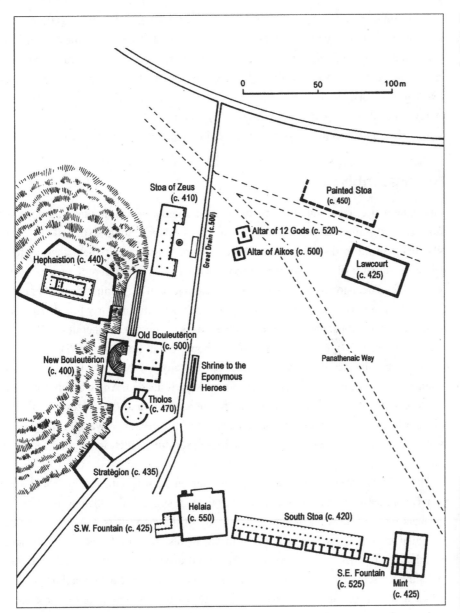

FIGURE 3.2
A plan of the agora in the fifth century.

EXPLORE FURTHER

Read the Old Oligarch 3.1–3.4 **PS**. What information does he give about the workings of the council here?

Magistrates

In addition to the 500 councillors, there were about 700 other magistrates serving in Attica each year (Aristotle, *AC* 24 **PS**). All these magistrates, also known as archōns, were selected by lot to serve on boards (usually of ten men) for one year. A citizen had to be thirty or over to be a magistrate, and could only hold a specific post once (although there were one or two exceptions, such as the post of general). Each board was responsible for a specific area of civic life, such as regulating the markets or keeping the streets clean. A particularly important board was the Eleven, which was in charge of administering legal punishments and managing the state prison.

dokimasia the scrutiny test given to a citizen before he could serve as a magistrate

euthunai the report in which a magistrate gave an account of his year in office

Magistrates were scrutinised before and after their year of service. Before a citizen was approved in a new role, he was examined for good character by the councillors in a test called the **dokimasia** ('scrutiny'). If a legitimate complaint was made against any magistrate during his year of office, he could be removed from office. At the end of his year's term, a magistrate had to give an account of his performance to the council; this report was called the **euthunai** ('accounts'). A magistrate could be taken to court for poor or dishonest conduct in office, and would receive a heavy fine if found guilty.

The assembly

quorum the minimum number of voters needed to make a decision valid

Pnyx the location of the Athenian assembly

principal assembly the main assembly of each prytany

rhetoric the ability to speak persuasively in public

Any Athenian citizen was allowed to attend the assembly, although of course it was much easier for men who lived in or near the city of Athens to do so than it was for those who lived in more distant parts of Attica. There was a requirement that some votes needed a **quorum** of at least 6,000 citizens (a quorum is the minimum number of voters required for a decision to be valid), so this gives an idea of the minimum number expected to attend an important assembly meeting. At such meetings, a fairly broad cross-section of the population must have been represented, as is suggested by Socrates in Xenophon's *Memorabilia* 3.7.6 **PS** (you can read more about Socrates on pp. 173–7).

The assembly met at dawn, four times per prytany, on the **Pnyx** hill. In addition, an assembly could be called for an emergency session if needed. An assembly began with a herald announcing the agenda drawn up by the council, and the citizens then voted on whether to proceed with this. Certain meetings of the prytany always dealt with certain issues. Each prytany would have a **principal assembly**, which would call for a vote of confidence in the magistrates.

Title: *Memorabilia*

Author: Xenophon (*c.* 430–354)

Date: *c.* 370–355

Genre: philosophical dialogue

Significance: Socrates reflects on the sort of people who make up the Athenian assembly

Prescribed sections: 3.7.6

Read it here: LACTOR 12: *The Culture of Athens* (KCL, 1978) 35

The right to speak in the assembly was fundamental to citizenship. There were no political parties in our modern sense, but the evidence suggests that there were some regular speakers with a following of supporters. Many of these speakers may have supported a particular general (however, it is likely that generals such as Pericles only attended the assembly on big occasions). The assembly could discuss all matters relating to the city, including laws, matters of foreign policy, tax, and the upkeep of public buildings. Once the debate was over, voting was normally by a show of hands, although for the most important topics, such as treason, secret ballots were held with black and white voting pebbles.

With the development of the citizen's assembly (and the law courts), **rhetoric** – the ability to speak persuasively in public – became of paramount importance. As we shall see on pp. 169–73, by the later years of the fifth century many sources reflect on a perceived culture of dishonest speakers who are able to manipulate the people with fine words.

OSTRACISM

ostracism an annual vote to banish one prominent citizen for a period of ten years

One notable feature of the democratic system was **ostracism**, which was first used in 487 as a safeguard against the return of tyranny. Under its rules, each year the assembly was allowed to banish one public figure for a period of ten years. A candidate for ostracism was thought to have become too powerful, and so to pose a threat to the state. However,

FIGURE 3.3
A view of the Pnyx today.

ostracism was merely a preventative measure and did not convict a citizen of any crime. Instead, the ostracised citizen was banished from Athens for a 'cooling-off period'. The man did not lose his property and his family was allowed to remain in Attica. When the ten years were up, he could return with the full rights of a citizen.

The process of ostracism could be triggered in December each year, when the assembly voted on whether to hold an ostracism in that year. If it voted to do so, then a further meeting of the assembly was scheduled for February or March. Plutarch relates what happened at such a meeting:

> Each voter took a piece of earthenware (ostrakon), wrote on it the name of the citizen he wished to be banished and carried it to a part of the agora which was cordoned off with a circular fence. Then the archōns first counted the total number of votes cast, for if there were fewer than 6,000 votes, the ostracism was invalid. After this they sorted the votes and the man who had the most votes recorded against his name was proclaimed to be exiled for ten years, with the right, however, to receive the income from his estate.

> Plutarch, *Life of Aristeides* 7.4–5

The term 'ostracism' was thus derived from the **ostrakon** (plural: ostraka), the broken piece of pottery with which a citizen cast his vote – an ostrakon might be considered to be the equivalent of a piece of scrap paper today. There is no doubt that ostracism was an important feature of the democracy, and the first man ostracised in 487 was Hipparchus, a prominent relative of Peisistratus. In the following decades, some of Athens' leading men were ostracised, including Aristeides, Themistocles and Cimon.

ostrakon a piece of broken pottery on which a citizen wrote the name of the person he wanted to see ostracised

PRESCRIBED SOURCE

Title: *Life of Nicias*

Author: Plutarch (before AD 50 to after AD 120)

Genre: biography

Significance: our only surviving biography of Nicias

Prescribed sections: 3.1–2, 11

Read it here: Plutarch, *The Rise and Fall of Athens*, translated by Ian Scott-Kilvert (Penguin 1960)

We can learn more about ostracism from Plutarch. He reports that Pericles managed to engineer the ostracism of his main rival in the assembly, Thucydides, the son of Melesias (he is not to be confused with Thucydides, the historian). At *Pericles* 11.1–4 **PS**, we are told that Thucydides had become the leader of the conservative faction in the assembly, and even organised it so that his supporters sat together in one grouping. At *Pericles* 14 **PS**, we read that Thucydides was the leading public figure to speak out against Pericles' building programme (see pp. 178–9). Pericles managed to win over the assembly and Plutarch reports that the ostracism of Thucydides in 443/2 effectively removed the major opposition to Pericles.

Plutarch also relates a story as to how the process of ostracism fell into disuse after 417. In his biography of the Athenian general Nicias (*Nicias* 11 **PS**), we read that in this year Nicias and Alcibiades set aside their bitter rivalry to ensure that their respective supporters combined to vote to ostracise a third politician whom they both detested, Hyperbolus.

THE LAW COURTS

The Athenians took great pride in their legal system, believing that it guaranteed justice and equality for all citizens. When a crime had been committed, it was up to a private citizen to bring a charge against a suspect. There were two different categories:

dikē a lawsuit filed by a citizen who claimed to be the victim of an offence committed by another.

graphē a lawsuit filed against a citizen claiming that an offence had been committed against a third party.

- **dikē** a lawsuit filed by one citizen, who claimed to be the victim of an offence committed by another
- **graphē** a lawsuit filed against a citizen claiming that an offence had been committed against a third party

Graphē cases could therefore include the misuse of public funds by a magistrate or poor tactics by a general on a military campaign. When a magistrate submitted his euthunai any citizen could bring a charge against him if he felt he had performed badly or dishonestly.

There was no professional judge, nor any prosecution or defence barristers. Accusers and defendants spoke for themselves, and were sometimes assisted by supporting speakers who could not be paid. The speeches were timed by a water-clock to ensure that both men spoke for the same length of time, and a case was heard and judged on just one day. One magistrate would act as the court chairman, but his role was simply to act as an administrator. **Dikasts**, citizens selected by lot, heard the case and acted as judge and jury, voting without discussion. If there was a guilty verdict, then they also voted between alternative penalties proposed by the prosecution and defence.

dikast a citizen who was both judge and juror in the Athenian court system

Any citizen of good character and over the age of thirty could serve as a dikast. There were 6,000 dikasts registered for a civil year, all of them selected by lot. The daily wage for dikasts was set at two obols by Pericles in 451, which meant that poorer citizens were encouraged to participate (the rate was increased to three obols by Cleon in the 420s). A dikast could choose which days he wanted to sit on by turning up early on the day. At dawn on a court day, an order of proceedings was published and those dikasts who had turned up were selected by the use of an allotment machine.

The size of juries varied depending on the importance of the case, but by our standards they were huge. Minor cases might involve a jury of 201 dikasts, while more serious cases could see numbers of 401, 501, going up to 1,501 for the most serious (the odd numbers of course ensured that there would not be a tie). Such large juries were one way to guard against bribery.

There are a number of interesting sources which shed light on the workings of the Athenian legal system, including the Old Oligarch (3.4–9 **PS**). Two others are particularly important for the critique they offer of the court system. The first is a comedy called *Wasps* presented at the Lenaea drama festival by Aristophanes in 422 (see pp. 189–97 to read more about drama festivals and Aristophanes). This play satirises the Athenian court system, presenting it as being at the mercy of conservative elderly dikasts, who are the only citizens with the time to serve as jurors.

The plot revolts around an elderly father, Philocleon (Cleon-lover), and his grown-up son, Bdelycleon (Cleon-hater). As their names suggest, one fervently supports the policies of Cleon (see p. 51) and the other strongly opposes them. Philocleon suffers from an addiction to jury-service, and so Bdelycleon locks him in the family home to prevent him going to court. To appease his father, he allows him to stage trials at home on domestic matters. In the prescribed lines (891–1008 **PS**), a dog, Labes ('Snatcher') is put on trial for stealing some cheese!

The second interesting source about the Athenian legal system is Plato's *Apology* **PS**. This is Plato's record of Socrates' defence speech after he was put on trial for corrupting the young and for atheism in 399. The life of Socrates and his trial is treated in much more detail on pp. 173–7, but the start and end of the speech are helpful for gaining a greater understanding of the proceedings of an Athenian court case. Plato wrote this account within a few years of the event, and so it must count as very reliable evidence of the Athenian court process of the day – of which Socrates seems to be critical.

PRESCRIBED SOURCE

Title: *Wasps*

Author: Aristophanes

Date: produced at the Lenaea in 422

Genre: comedy

Significance: a scene of the play which parodies the Athenian legal system

Prescribed Lines: 891–1008

Read it here: Aristophanes, *Frogs and Other Plays*, translated by David Barrett, revised by Shomit Dutta (Penguin 2007)

PRESCRIBED SOURCE

Title: *Apology*

Author: Plato (427–348)

Origin: Athenian

Genre: philosophical dialogue and defence speech

Significance: an account of Socrates' defence speech during his trial of 399

Read it here: Plato, *Apology, The Last Days of Socrates*, translated by Hugh Tredennick (Penguin 2003)

ACTIVITY

Using evidence from the Old Oligarch (3.4–9 **PS**), Aristophanes' *Wasps* (891–1008 **PS**) and Plato's *Apology* (17a–18e **PS** and 35e–38b **PS**), stage your own imaginary court case in an Athenian law court.

Study questions

1 Read *Wasps* 891–1008 **PS**. What might we learn about the Athenian court system from this passage? How reliable might a passage of satire such as this be as historical evidence?

2 Read Plato, *Apology*, 17a–18e **PS** and 35e–38b **PS**. What can we learn about proceedings of an Athenian trial from these sections?

PERICLES' FUNERAL ORATION

Perhaps the most famous statement of pride in Athens' democratic society comes in the speech attributed to Pericles by Thucydides (2.34–46 **PS**). The oration was made in memory of those men who had died in the first year of the Peloponnesian War. Such a speech was traditional in Athens, and it took place in the public cemetery of Athens located just outside the walls of the city in the kerameikos district. The speaker at such an event was expected to praise the city so as to explain why the fallen soldiers had not sacrificed their lives in vain. Pericles focuses on why Athens' democratic society was so superior to any other society in the Greek world. In particular, he draws a clear contrast between the lifestyle and values in Athens and in Sparta.

The speech is thematically divided into two halves, following a brief introduction referring to Athenian history. Between sections 2.37 **PS** and 2.41 **PS** Pericles talks about what makes Athens great. Between 2.42 **PS** and 2.46 **PS**, he focuses on the memory of the fallen and offers words of comfort to their surviving relatives. In terms of the reliability of the historian's account, remember what you have read on pp. 35–6 about

KEY PLACE

kerameikos the potters' district in Athens, near the agora, where many ostraka have been found

FIGURE 3.4
A map of fifth-century Athens.

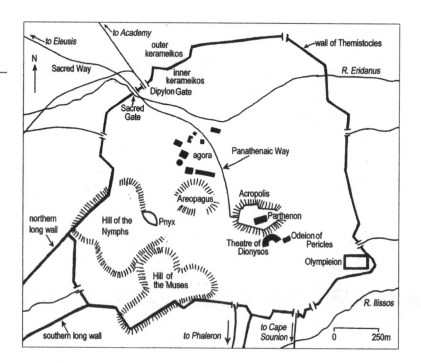

PRESCRIBED SOURCE

Title: *The History of the Peloponnesian War*

Author: Thucydides

Date: *c.* 400

Genre: history

Significance: a remarkable eulogy of democratic Athens delivered in 431

Prescribed sections: 2.34–2.46 (Pericles' funeral oration)

Read it here: Thucydides, *The History of the Peloponnesian War*, translated by Rex Warner (Penguin 1972)

Study questions
Read Pericles' Funeral Oration (Thucydides 2.34–2.46 **PS**).

1 What does Pericles say about the importance of citizens participating in the democratic process?
2 What features of the democratic system does he mention for praise?

Thucydides' own policy on reporting speeches. It is likely that he would have been present at this speech himself, and would also have been able to consult others who had heard it. Therefore, it is probably a fairly reliable account of what Pericles said.

ATHENS AS THE LEADER OF AN EMPIRE, AND HER TREATMENT OF ALLIED STATES

While Athens was a democracy at home, it was often accused of behaving like a tyrant to the allied states of its empire. Indeed, figures such as Pericles and Cleon are reported to have argued that this was unavoidable. What, then, can the sources tell us about Athens' relationship to the allied states of its empire?

The Athenians looked to promote democracies in their subject-allies, since they felt more likely to be sympathetic to democratic Athens, and two interesting passages reflecting on this practice can be found in the Old Oligarch (1.14–20 **PS** and 3.10–11 **PS**), where he claims that the Athenians look to undermine oligarchic elites. Since the Old Oligarch's sympathies naturally lie with such elites, we should not be surprised that he disapproves of this. He argues more generally that the Athenian people take a short-sighted and self-interested approach to running their empire, and that this leads to poor decision-making. For example, he claims that they charge too much tribute from allies and do not care if this ruins them as long as they get their money. He even suggests that they actively look to reduce their allies to poverty in order to reduce the likelihood that they will defect, although there is no other evidence to support this.

The Old Oligarch also complains about the practice of forcing members of allied states to come to Athens for trials. This certainly happened, since official public documents inscribed on stone refer to it. The Old Oligarch argues that the Athenians hold these trials from very narrow self-interest, for example since they can enjoy making money from rent and tax when these people come. What the author does not say is that by having such trials in Athens, the Athenians could ensure that their democratic friends and allies in other states were secure in their position, while oligarchs could be prosecuted. This allowed the Athenians to keep greater control over allied states.

A further interesting passage about the relationship between Athens and its allies comes in a section of Thucydides known as the Mytilene Debate (3.36–3.50 **PS**). This relates the debate in the Athenian assembly in 427 as to how the people should respond to the revolt of Mytilene, the main city on the island of Lesbos. Lesbos was one of the only remaining non-tributary states of the empire at this point. The island was made up of a confederacy of five cities, four of which were oligarchies (Mytilene, Antissa, Eresus and Pyrrha) and one a democracy (Methymna). It was unusual for allied states to be ruled by oligarchies, but the cities of Lesbos could afford more independence as they did not need to provide annual tribute. Mytilene had led the four oligarchies in a revolt, with the encouragement of the Peloponnesians, who sent an ambassador, Salaethus, to work with them. However, the Athenians sent a fleet led by Paches which successfully besieged Mytilene. Realising the hopelessness of their situation, the Mytileneans entered negotiations with the Athenians. They were allowed to send a delegation to Athens to plead for mercy.

Initially, the Athenian assembly decided to punish Mytilene with extraordinary severity: the entire adult male population was to be put to death, while the women and children were to be enslaved. The Athenians dispatched a ship to Lesbos to instruct Paches to carry out the order. The next day, however, it seems that many Athenians regretted the brutality of their decision, and another assembly was convened to debate the matter once more. In Thucydides' account, it is Cleon who speaks up strongly in favour of the decision, arguing that they should make an example of the Mytileneans as a show of strength (3.37–40 **PS**). Arguing for a more lenient approach is Diodotus (3.42–47 **PS**). He argues that it is in the Athenians' self-interest not to enact this measure.

Study questions

1 How objective and valid do you find the Old Oligarch's criticisms of Athens' treatment of its allies?

2 What arguments do Cleon and Diodotus make about how Athens should conduct its foreign policy? Why do you think that the arguments of Diodotus won the day?

3 What was the outcome of the Mytilene revolt (3.50 **PS**)? What can this tell us about the Athenian treatment of their allies?

PRESCRIBED SOURCE

Title: *History of the Peloponnesian War*

Author: Thucydides

Date: *c.* 430–400 BC

Genre: history

Relevance: the Mytilene Debate of 427 is a famous example of how the Athenian assembly could be easily swayed by powerful rhetoric, and gives an insight into democratic foreign policy

Prescribed Sections: 3.36–3.50 (Mytilene Debate)

Read it here: Thucydides, *The History of the Peloponnesian War*, translated by Rex Warner (Penguin 1972)

In the end, Diodotus' arguments won the day. A second ship was dispatched which only arrived at Lesbos in the nick of time.

The Mytilene Debate is a valuable source from a number of standpoints: it shows the democratic assembly in action, it illustrates the importance of rhetoric to it, and it gives an insight into democratic foreign policy.

THE CHANGING NATURE OF LEADERSHIP IN THE FIFTH CENTURY

The Mytilene Debate illustrates another theme of our sources for this period: that after the death of Pericles in 429, the quality of leadership in Athens declined dramatically. Thucydides himself promotes this view, and his most clear statement of this comes at 2.65, which has been covered in the period study as a prescribed source. While Thucydides' narrative often speaks very highly of Periclean Athens (e.g. 2.34–2.46 **PS**), it could be argued that the historian feels that democracy is fundamentally a bad idea, but one that can be made to work if a state is lucky enough to be led by an extraordinarily gifted man (the same argument is also advanced by Plutarch at *Pericles* 15 **PS**). Indeed, he famously says that Athens was not really a democracy because of the force of Pericles' personality:

> So, in what was nominally a democracy, power was really in the hands of the first citizen.
>
> Thucydides, *The History of the Peloponnesian War* 2.65

However, it should be remembered that Pericles had to retain the support of the people in order to be re-elected as a general each year. Moreover, Thucydides had reason to be hostile to the democratic system, which had exiled him in 423.

Thucydides' account presents the leaders who came after Pericles as self-serving demagogues, and this view is reflected by Aristotle (*AC* 28 **PS**). He comments that after 429 the aristocratic faction in the city was led by Nicias, while the common people took their lead from Cleon. Both Aristotle and Thucydides are scathing about Cleon: for example, the latter describes him as 'remarkable among the Athenians for this violence of his character' in his introduction to the Mytilene Debate (3.36 **PS**). Plutarch (*Nicias* 3.1–2 **PS**) follows the tradition of the earlier sources and is scathing about both Cleon and Nicias as successors to Pericles.

The comic playwright, Aristophanes, viciously satirized Cleon in some of his plays. In 424 he presented *Knights*, a brutal satire of Cleon's supposed immoral behaviour in manipulating the people in the assembly. This is the first example we have of a play entirely dedicated to attacking one politician – until that time, jokes had been made at politicians' expense, but we know of nothing like this before *Knights*. However, like Thucydides, Aristophanes is often seen as portraying the conservative elements of society more sympathetically. Moreover, we know that Cleon had prosecuted him for slandering the city in an earlier play of 426. We should also be careful when treating comedy as a source, since satire was of course meant to exaggerate things and to play for laughs.

PRESCRIBED SOURCE

Title: *Knights*

Author: Aristophanes

Date: produced at the Lenaea in 424

Genre: comedy

Significance: comically exaggerated criticism of how politicians such as Cleon try to appeal to the people, and the immoral use they make of their power

Prescribed lines: 147–395

Read it here: Aristophanes, *The Birds and Other Plays*, translated by Alan Sommerstein and David Barrett (Penguin, 2003)

KEY INDIVIDUALS

Cleon
Dates: d. 422
An Athenian politician and general presented in the sources as the demagogue who leads the Athenian common people during the 420s

Nicias
Dates: *c.* 470–413
A prominent aristocratic Athenian politician and general who led the aristocratic faction at Athens during the 420s

PRESCRIBED SOURCE

Title: *Life of Alcibiades*

Author: Plutarch (before AD 50 to after AD 120)

Genre: biography

Significance: our only surviving biography of Alcibiades

Prescribed sections: 10, 16, 19, 20.2–4, 34

Read it here: Plutarch, *The Rise and Fall of Athens*, translated by Ian Scott-Kilvert (Penguin 1960)

KEY INDIVIDUAL

Alcibiades
Dates: 451–403

An Athenian aristocrat who became a favoured leader of the common people after the death of Cleon

In the play, Aristophanes creates an allegorical situation in which the city of Athens is a household run by a bad-tempered and easily fooled master called 'Demos' (i.e. 'The People'). The master has been tricked by a new slave, the Paphlagonian, who is taking credit for other people's work. The Paphlagonian is clearly meant to be Cleon, who had recently claimed the credit for capturing the 300 Spartans at Pylos. The slaves decide that the only solution is to find someone who can 'out-demagogue' the demagogue. They try to find someone who has the ignorance and selfishness to do this.

In lines 147–395 (PS), the slave is explaining this to the Sausage-seller. The humour, and political point, come from the obvious reversal of expectations: the more stupid and unpleasant one is and the lower one's birth, the greater the chances of success in the assembly. There is no need to rule well, so the slave assures the Sausage-seller:

> Mix all the policies into a complete hash, butter the people up a bit, throw in a pinch of rhetoric as a sweetener, and there you are. (PS)

Aristophanes, *Knights* 214–216

After the death of Cleon, Alcibiades rose to prominence in Athens as the favourite of the common people, as we have seen in the period study. You can also read more about him on pp. 116–18. Once again, it is Plutarch who records our only biography of this important character, although he does of course feature prominently in Thucydides too. Alcibiades was born around 451 and brought up in the household of Pericles, who had become his guardian after the death of his father Cleinias. Plutarch records a number of stories to illustrate Alcibiades' influence over the Athenian people (*Alcibiades* 10, 16, 19, 20.2–4, 34 (PS)), and in particular *Alcibiades* 16 (PS) outlines the various ways in which he succeeded in winning them over. Elsewhere, Plutarch also claims that that Alcibiades and Nicias had a bitter hatred for each other (*Nicias* 11 (PS)).

Study questions
Read the following sources:

- Thucydides 2.65, 3.36–3.50 (PS)
- Aristophanes, *Knights* 147–395 (PS)
- Aristotle, *Athenian Constitution* 28 (PS)
- Plutarch: *Nicias*, 3.1–2, 11 (PS) *Alcibiades*, 10, 16, 19, 20.2–4, 34 (PS)

1 What does each source suggest about the nature of leadership at Athens after the death of Pericles?
2 How reliable and objective do you think each source is likely to be?

THE ROLES OF NON-CITIZENS AT ATHENS

Metics

Metics had no political rights in the city, but were given some legal rights in the courts. They had to have an Athenian sponsor and to pay a monthly tax: one drachma for a man, and half a drachma for a woman. They participated in various aspects of the cultural life of the city, and some played significant roles in religious festivals. A male metic was expected to fight for Athens in times of war: wealthier metics served as hoplites, but a larger number must have rowed in the fleet.

There is no doubt that the metics made a significant contribution: one estimate suggests there were as many as 20,000 living in Athens during the later fifth century. They could not own property in Attica, and so were generally found in non-farming industries such as crafts and commerce. Writing towards the end of his life, Xenophon (*Poroi* 2.1–2, 5 **PS**) emphasises the important economic role metics played in the Athenian state, and argues for them to be given more privileges in recognition of this. The Old Oligarch (1.12 **PS**) also acknowledges the economic contribution of metics, and additionally emphasises the importance of metics to the manning of the Athenian fleet.

A few metics became prominent members of Athenian society. For example, Plato's *Republic* is set in the house of Cephalus, a wealthy arms manufacturer, whose son Lysias went on to become an influential orator in Athens. Moreover, Pericles' mistress, Aspasia, was a metic. She was clearly an intelligent and influential woman, and Plutarch (*Pericles* 30, 32 **PS**) reports that the opponents of Pericles used slanders against her to attack the Athenian general.

Slaves

Slaves had no political rights whatsoever, but they did have some minimal legal rights: notably, a slave could seek refuge at a religious sanctuary if he felt his master was treating him unfairly. A state official would hear his complaints and could force the master to sell the slave or perhaps to swear an oath promising to treat the slave better in future. Moreover, slaves were allowed some rights of religious worship.

It seems that the institution of slavery was rarely, if ever, questioned. Xenophon (*Memorabilia* 2.2.2 **PS**) reports Socrates reflecting on the commonly held view that it was felt wrong to enslave ones friends but right to enslave one's enemies. Although Greeks generally felt more comfortable enslaving non-Greeks, there are a number of

---

PRESCRIBED SOURCE

Title: *Poroi* ('*Revenues*')

Author: Xenophon (*c.* 430–354)

Date: produced in *c.* 354

Genre: economic theory

Significance: a section explaining the importance of the metics to the Athenian economy

Prescribed sections: 2.1–2, 5

Read it here: LACTOR 12: *The Culture of Athens* (KCL, 1978) 44

PRESCRIBED SOURCE

Title: *Memorabilia*

Author: Xenophon (*c.* 430–354)

Date: *c.* 370–355

Genre: philosophical dialogue

Significance: Socrates reflects on the common view about the ethics of slavery

Prescribed sections: 2.2.2

Read it here: LACTOR 12: *The Culture of Athens* (KCL, 1978) 49

examples from the Peloponnesian war of Greeks enslaving Greeks, or intending to do so (e.g. Thucydides 3.36 **PS**).

Slaves provided the labour in areas like farming or mining that was necessary for Athenian citizens to lead a privileged life. In the home, there could be both male and female slaves who assisted with household duties. Some slaves could earn wages for their masters; for example, the Erechtheion (see pp. 184–5) was built by a combination of slaves, metics and citizens. There were also some state-owned slaves, who could hold important positions within the Athenian democratic system: the state executioner was a slave, as were the Scythian Archers, a form of police force.

It is difficult to generalise about the experience of slaves at Athens. No slave has left a record of his or her life, the nature of which would have depended heavily on the character of the master. The Old Oligarch (1.10–12 **PS**) claims that slaves in Athens are given far too much licence, but this might simply his reactionary view. Perhaps a more fruitful insight into the lives of slaves can be found in Athenian drama, where slaves are often characters in both tragedies and comedies. For example, in Euripides' tragedy *Hippolytus* **PS**, which is explored in more detail on pp. 165, 173, 194–5 and 202, one of the lead characters, Phaedra, confides in her nurse, who is most likely a slave. This suggests that close, trusting relationships could develop between slave and free. The play also shows us the important responsibilities that slaves held within a household; for example, caring for children.

Women

Women were regarded as minors in Athenian law, and they had no political rights and limited legal rights. Beyond this, however, it is important to remember that just as the men fell into groups of citizen, metic and slave, so did the women. Moreover, since women generally received little education and we have no textual writings by an Athenian woman of this time, the voices of this half of the population remain almost silent to us.

It seems that this is what many Athenian menfolk may have wanted. According to Thucydides (2.45 **PS**), at the end of his funeral speech Pericles reserved just a few words for women about their role in society, suggesting that their greatest glory was to be least talked about, for praise or for blame. However, it is likely that women's status at Athens rose after Pericles' citizenship law of 451, since Athenian citizen mothers now held greater importance.

How, then, can historians begin to build a picture of what life was like for Athenian women? We can assume that the need to produce enough children who survived into adulthood dictated the early age of marriage for them, and meant that they were expected to keep producing children throughout their lives. Moreover, the fact that the need for high fertility dominated a society's concerns was reflected in religious cult, and this is why women played an important part in the religious life of the city. One exceptional example of this is the **Thesmophoria**, an all-women festival in honour of Demeter and Persephone in which the women of Athens camped out for three days near the Pnyx, the symbolic heart of the democracy. Beyond this, archaeology can offer some help, particularly in the form of works of art depicting women and of epitaphs giving short descriptions of their lives and characters.

PRESCRIBED SOURCE

Title: *Hippolytus*

Author: Euripides (*c.* 480–406)

Date: 428

Genre: tragic play

Significance: a well-known tragedy from one of Athens' greatest playwrights

Read it here: Euripides, *Hippolytus*, in *Three Plays*, translated by Philip Vellacott (Penguin 1972)

Thesmophoria an all-women festival in honour of Demeter and Persephone in which the women of Athens camped out near the Pnyx for three days

Drama can also offer some insight into the relations between the sexes, and the anxieties felt about this in Athenian society. Athenian tragedy offers a number of powerful female characters and plots which focus on male/female relations. For example, *Hippolytus* **PS** revolves around the desire of the goddess, Aphrodite, to take vengeance on a young man, Hippolytus, who has declared himself to have no interest in her domain – sex and love.

Aphrodite cannot tolerate such a dishonour, and so decides to take matters into her own hands. She makes Phaedra, the wife of king Theseus, fall in love with her step-son Hippolytus. Phaedra tries to conceal her love but is tricked by her Nurse into revealing her secret. The Nurse betrays her by telling Hippolytus, who responds with fury and threatens to tell Theseus. In desperation, Phaedra commits suicide and leaves a note claiming that Hippolytus has raped her. Theseus curses Hippolytus, who is killed by a mighty bull sent by Poseidon. At the end of the play, the goddess Artemis reveals the truth of what has happened, and the dying Hippolytus forgives his father. Hippolytus' hatred of sex and marriage is a refusal to take on adult responsibilities, since providing heirs to continue the family line was an important duty for an Athenian man. The play also shows the overwhelming power of love, and how it can drive people to do terrible things.

Comedy also offers many examples of prominent female characters who pose questions about relations between men and women. In *Thesmophoriazusae*, Aristophanes sets his play among women at the Thesmophoria festival. The women are so angry at the way in which the tragic playwright Euripides portrays female characters in his plays that they devise a plan to punish him. In lines 786–800 **PS** and 830–842 **PS**, the women of the chorus step forward to complain about the treatment of women in Athenian society. It is worth noting that all the actors would have been men, and the play would have been performed to a largely or entirely male audience.

> **Study question**
> Read *Thesmophoriazusae* 786–800, 830–842 **PS**
> What complaints do the women make about their treatment in these lines? How reliable do you think this is as evidence for the lives of women in Athenian society?

PRESCRIBED SOURCE

Title: *Thesmophoriazusae*

Author: Aristophanes

Date: produced in 411, probably at the Great Dionysia

Genre: comedy

Significance: women of the chorus complain of the treatment of women in Athenian society

Prescribed Lines: 786–800, 830–842

Read it here: LACTOR 12: *The Culture of Athens* (KCL, 1978) 120

> **S & C**
> Research the plots of two other comedies by Aristophanes: *Lysistrata* and *Assembly-women*. How are male/female relations at the forefront of these plays?

TOPIC REVIEW

- Outline the arguments made in your sources for and against oligarchy and democracy.
- Discuss the ways in which an Athenian citizen contributed to the effective running of the state.
- Assess the influence non-citizens had on the running of the state.
- Compare the strengths and weaknesses of the sources on Athenian political and social culture.

Further Reading

Azoulay, V., *Pericles of Athens* (Princeton: Princeton University Press, 2010).

Benson, E.F., *The Life of Alcibiades: The Idol of Athens* (Createspace, 2010).

Buckley, T., *Aspects of Greek History* (2nd edn; Abingdon: Routledge, 2010), chapters 13 and 14.

Ehrenberg, Victor, *From Solon to Socrates* (Abingdon: Routledge, 2010), parts 4–7.

Harris, E.M., *Democracy and the Rule of Law in Classical Athens* (Cambridge: Cambridge University Press, 2006), chapter 2.

Ober, J., *The Athenian Revolution* (Princeton: Princeton University Press, 1996), chapter 4.

Ober, J., *Political Dissent in Democratic Athens* (Princeton: Princeton University Press 1998), chapters 1 and 4.

Renshaw, J., *In Search of the Greeks* (London: Bloomsbury, 2015), chapter 6.

Rhodes, P.J., *Athenian Democracy* (Edinburgh: Edinburgh University Press, 2004).

Samons, L.J. (ed.), *The Cambridge Companion to the Age of Pericles* (Cambridge: Cambridge University Press, 2007), chapters 1, 6, 10.

PRACTICE QUESTIONS

1. To what extent did life in the fifth century provide opportunities for all the inhabitants of Attica? [36]

3.2 The Influence of New Thinking and Ideas on Athenian Society

TOPIC OVERVIEW

- the sophists and the development of rhetoric
- the sophists and their views of Athenian society
- the teachings of the sophists
- Socrates: his philosophical method, its effects, his critique of democracy, and his trial and execution

The prescribed sources for this topic are:

- Aristophanes, *Clouds*, 92–118, 814–1302
- Aristotle, *Rhetoric* 1402a
- Euripides, *Hippolytus*
- Gorgias, *Encomium of Helen*
- Plato, *Apology*
- Plato, *Gorgias* 452d–e, 459b–c
- Plato, *Hippias Major* 282b–e
- Plato, *Protagoras* 316d–e
- Plato, *Republic* 6.488–4.489; 6.493
- Plutarch, *Pericles* 36
- Thucydides, *The History of the Peloponnesian War* 3.38
- Xenophon, *Memorabilia* 1.1.16; 1.6.13; 1.1.3; 1.2.62

This topic will examine the intellectual life at Athens during the fifth century, in particular the influence of the sophists and the challenge provided to the city by the radical thinker Socrates. Ultimately, Socrates' ideas were deemed so dangerous to the city that he was found guilty of corrupting the young and of atheism, for which he was executed in 399. He remains one of the defining figures of classical Athens, and indeed of the ancient Greek world.

AN INTELLECTUAL REVOLUTION

The Greek world had been undergoing an intellectual revolution since the early sixth century. Originally, this was centred on the Ionian cities of Asia Minor. Thinkers there posed questions on the nature of matter and the universe: for example, Thales of Miletus said that all life was born of water. Other thinkers debated why there was so much change in the world, and this led to Democritus developing his theory of the atom. People became more curious about the world around them, and an Ionian called Anaximander is said to have produced the first known world map. Other intellectuals started researching and writing about the behaviour, customs and beliefs of foreign peoples: these were the first works of anthropology and ethnography. Another discipline which developed along scientific lines was medicine, led by Hippocrates of the eastern Aegean island of Kos.

Such thinkers sought to challenge received wisdom and to find rational explanations for the world around them, and the key ideal uniting them was intellectual curiosity. Even beliefs about the gods were challenged. One Ionian thinker, Xenophanes, was unimpressed with the traditional view of them, claiming that people merely made them in their own image. From this he concluded that if horses or cows or lions had gods, they would look like horses or cows or lions. Xenophanes found this view of the gods unsatisfactory, and he also expressed frustration that great poets portrayed gods with human flaws:

> Homer and Hesiod have attributed to the gods everything that is blameworthy and disgraceful among humans – theft and adultery and mutual trickery.

> DK21 B11

Instead, Xenophanes believed that the gods should be understood to be perfect and blameless. This view would be shared by Socrates decades later.

THE SOPHISTS

By the middle of the fifth century, celebrated intellectuals and artists were attracted to move to the thriving city of Athens. The first to arrive was a man called Anaxagoras in about 460 (see p. 201), and others followed. Many of these thinkers tried to popularise the new learning and to 'bring it down to earth', since it had often been seen to be beyond the grasp of the ordinary citizen. These teachers were known as **sophists**, a word which originally meant 'wise men' in Greek; over the following decades they became influential but highly controversial figures in the city.

The sophists were professional teachers who made their money either by teaching privately or by giving public lectures for which there was often an admission fee. Most of them travelled widely, taking their knowledge to whoever would listen. They lectured on a wide variety of subjects, including grammar, linguistic theory, music, law, mathematics, literary criticism, ethics and religion. The most famous and influential sophist at Athens was Protagoras of Abdera, who specialised in law and government. He came to the city in the 430s and focused on how a citizen should interact with his city. He also put forward the view that each person should trust his own viewpoint and that there were no absolute truths, a position known as relativism. Another celebrated sophist was Hippias of Elis, a polymath who discussed fields as diverse as ethics, history, geography, literature, astronomy and geometry. A further notable sophist was Prodicus of Ceos, who was an expert in language.

KEY INDIVIDUALS

Protagoras
Dates: c. 490–420

A sophist from Abdera who specialised in law and government

Hippias
Dates: c. 460–400

A sophist from Elis who taught a huge variety of topics

The sophists and rhetoric

As we have seen, the study of rhetoric became very important in fifth century Athens, since speaking well was so vital to success in the democratic assembly and the law courts. In 427, Gorgias of Leontini in Sicily, who was regarded as the father of rhetoric, came to Athens on an embassy from his city. As well as delivering an address to the Athenian assembly, he gave other lectures which proved very popular.

We are fortunate that some of Georgias' work has survived. This includes the full text of the *Encomium of Helen* **PS**, a display speech in which he reflects on the overwhelming power of persuasive argument. Gorgias argues that Helen of Troy – who was often held responsible for the Trojan war after she left her husband, Menelaus, king of Sparta, and eloped with Paris, prince of Troy – could not be held responsible for her elopement or the war which followed. He asserts that she might have been persuaded to elope by one of four things: the gods, physical force, love, or speech. His key argument is that in all four cases, Helen was the weaker party and so could not have resisted. Therefore, just as she was unable to resist the gods, physical force, or love, so persuasive argument was irresistible to her:

> Speech is a powerful lord, who
> with the finest and most invisible body
> achieves the most divine works:
> it can stop fear and banish grief
> and create joy and nurture pity.
>
> Gorgias, *Encomium of Helen*, 8

Gorgias goes on to compare the effect of speech on the mind with the effect of drugs on the body, as though it is a type of witchcraft.

The *Encomium of Helen* is a rare surviving work of a sophist. In the main, we are dependent on other sources of information about them, and it is important to be aware

KEY INDIVIDUAL

Gorgias
Dates: *c.* 483–376

A sophist from Leontini in Sicily who specialised in rhetoric

---

PRESCRIBED SOURCE

Title: *Encomium of Helen*

Author: Gorgias (*c.* 483–376)

Date: unknown

Genre: rhetorical display speech

Significance: a display speech reflecting on the power of persuasion, in which Gorgias attempts to absolve Helen of guilt for the Trojan War

Read it here: Gorgias, *Encomium of Helen*, in *The Greek Sophists*, trans. John Dillon and Tania Gergel (Penguin 2003)

Study question

Read *Encomium of Helen* **PS**

What arguments does Gorgias present to absolve Helen of responsibility for the war? How effective do you find them?

PRESCRIBED SOURCE

Title: *Hippias Major*

Author: Plato (*c.* 427–348)

Origin: Athenian

Genre: philosophical dialogue

Significance: Hippias boasts to Socrates of the riches he makes from teaching

Prescribed sections: 282b–e

Read it here: LACTOR 12: *The Culture of Athens* (KCL, 1978) 214

PRESCRIBED SOURCE

Title: *Memorabilia*

Author: Xenophon (*c.* 430–354)

Date: *c.* 370–355

Genre: philosophical dialogue

Significance: Socrates dismisses the sophists' practice of selling their wisdom for money

Prescribed sections: 1.6.13

Read it here: LACTOR 12: *The Culture of Athens* (KCL, 1978) 216

that they appear to be strongly biased against them. Two of them, Plato and Xenophon, were followers of Socrates, who, as we shall see, wanted to distinguish their master strongly from the sophists. They present Socrates as being far more virtuous than the sophists since, while the sophists charged for their services, Socrates did not believe that it was right to charge to share one's wisdom. A passage of Plato (*Hippias Major* 282b–e **PS**) sees Hippias of Elis boasting of the vast riches he is able to make from his profession, while Xenophon (*Memorabilia* 1.6.13 **PS**) reports Socrates comparing the sophists to prostitutes in the way that they charge their students.

Both Xenophon and Plato wrote their recollections of Socrates after his execution in 399. It seems that both felt that the sophists were in part responsible for his death and this must have strongly affected their objectivity. However, Plutarch (*Pericles* 36 **PS**) reports that Pericles' son, Xanthippus, ridiculed his father for his engagement with the sophists. If this is so, then criticism of the sophists long predated the execution of Socrates. A further factor informing the bias of Plato and Xenophon may have been that both were from aristocratic backgrounds and may have resented the fact that the sophists offered to educate anyone who was able to pay their fees. Since the sophists' services were available to anyone, not just to the traditional aristocratic elite, these men were perhaps more in tune with the city's democratic spirit than men such as Xenophon and Plato were comfortable with.

Plato took particular issue with the sophists over their teaching of rhetoric. He clearly felt that, while they taught their pupils how to make their case well, they did not teach them to have any regard for the truth of what they were saying: what mattered was not producing arguments rooted in truth, but clever arguments to win victories at any cost (it is interesting to note that our word 'sophistry' today is derived from this understanding of the sophists' art). In two passages from Plato's *Gorgias* (452d–e, 459b–c **PS**), the sophist is seen to put his case that rhetoric is the most powerful skill of all, since a skilled orator can outdo an expert in his area of expertise if he is addressing an audience which doesn't know better:

Socrates: So the ignorant will be more persuasive than the expert before an ignorant audience, when you have the orator being more persuasive than the doctor?

Gorgias: In this instance, yes.

Plato, *Gorgias* 459b–c (LACTOR 12, 400)

The sophists are therefore portrayed as unscrupulous teachers, but it is hard to know how accurate or fair this is. In another dialogue, Plato describes Protagoras trying to defend the sophists' art by suggesting that what they do is really no different than what poets, prophets and music teachers had long done (*Protagoras* 316d–e). However, we have no original source which puts the sophists' case for them. Plato focuses narrowly on two things: the sophists' charging for their services, and their teaching of an unscrupulous form of rhetoric. The charges seem to have stuck, and Aristotle, a pupil of Plato writing a generation later, reflects the same view of the sophists' improper teaching of rhetoric (*Rhetoric* 1402a PS).

In fact, the sophists probably provided Athens with a much-needed form of higher education in a wide variety of fields. The traditional Athenian education system was based around three tenets, literature, music and sports, and it is likely that the sophists added greatly to the educational culture of the city, whatever faults some of them may have had.

PRESCRIBED SOURCE

Title: *Rhetoric*

Author: Aristotle (384–322)

Genre: philosophical treatise

Significance: Aristotle criticises the deceptive nature of the sophists' teaching

Prescribed Section: 1402a

Read it here: LACTOR 12: *The Culture of Athens* (KCL, 1978) 404

Study questions

Read *Hippias Major* 282b–e PS and *Apology* 19e–20c PS

1 What does Plato put forward here about the profession of the sophists and their difference from Socrates?

Read Thucydides 3.38 PS

2 What points does Cleon make about the influence of the sophists on the assembly?

PRESCRIBED SOURCE

Title: *Gorgias*

Author: Plato (*c.* 427–348)

Date: early fourth century

Genre: philosophical dialogue

Significance: a dialogue in which Socrates discussed with Gorgias the nature of rhetoric

Prescribed Sections: 452d–e, 459b–c

Read it here: LACTOR 12: *The Culture of Athens* (KCL, 1978) 399 and 400

PRESCRIBED SOURCE

Title: *Protagoras*

Author: Plato (*c.* 427–348)

Origin: Athenian

Genre: philosophical dialogue

Significance: Protagoras reflects on the nature of the sophists and defends his art

Prescribed sections: 316d–e

Read it here: LACTOR 12: *The Culture of Athens* (KCL, 1978) 209

DRAMA AND THE SOPHISTS

Aristophanes' *Clouds*

In 423 Aristophanes presented a comedy, *Clouds*, at the Great Dionysia which poked fun at the sophists (you can read more about Aristophanes and drama festivals on pp. 189–97). However, the version of the play which has survived is an amended one dating to a few years later. The play is a satire of the sophists and their behaviour. Crucially, Socrates is caricatured as a leading sophist. In *Apology* (18b–c, 19c **PS**) Plato presents Socrates as suggesting that the play led to some of the negative perceptions of his character and work. It is interesting that Socrates chose to focus on this play, since we know that he featured in a lost play by Ameipsias, *Connus*, which was also presented in 423. Moreover, there are other lost plays by comic playwrights in which Socrates is satirised, not least for his tendency to wear a single garment.

Clouds depicts a man, Strepsiades, whose grown-up son, Pheidippides, has become addicted to gambling on horse-racing. Strepsiades is therefore seriously in debt and decides to have his son trained in rhetoric so that he can argue his way out of the debts. The son is to be sent to the 'Phrontistērion', or 'Thinkery', a school headed by Socrates, to learn this form of argument. However, the young man refuses and his father goes instead. Here he meets Socrates, as well as the 'Clouds', the patron deities of the new learning. However, Strepsiades cannot learn anything and forces Pheidippides to go after all. In the final scene, Pheidippides' new learning enables his father to avoid two creditors (1214–1302 **PS**), but it also leads to the son arguing that children may beat their parents. At this point the Clouds reveal that they are really agents of the traditional gods, who punish arrogant men. Strepsiades is outraged that he has been tricked by the new learning and burns down the Thinkery.

Although the key figure in the play is Socrates, the Socrates presented seems more like an amalgam of a number of sophists, with their different methods and ideas all blended into one. For example, the real Socrates apparently never taught in a school,

---

PRESCRIBED SOURCE

Title: *Clouds*

Author: Aristophanes

Date: first presented in 423 at the Great Dionysia, revised *c.* 419

Genre: comedy

Significance: a comedy poking fun at Socrates and the ideas of the sophists

Prescribed Lines: 92–118, 365–381, 814–1302

Read it here: Aristophanes, *Lysistrata and Other Plays*, trans. Alan
    Sommerstein (Penguin, 2003)

never charged for his services, and did not teach science, grammar or rhetoric. Therefore, the image of Socrates in the *Clouds* can be taken to represent the sophists as a group phenomenon, rather than the individual figure of Socrates. We should remember, too, that Aristophanes was playing for laughs and dealing in stereotypes. He may not have been bitterly opposed to the real Socrates: in one dialogue of Plato, *Symposium*, he is depicted as attending the same dinner party as him.

Nonetheless, the play offers an insight into views about the sophists in Athens, not least their supposed teaching of an unscrupulous form of rhetoric. A centrepiece of the play is a contest (890–1104 **PS**) between two characters in the Thinkery, 'Right' and 'Wrong', who represent the old and the new ways of debating. 'Wrong' is shown to offer training in the art of skilled but deceptive argumentation:

> Let us say you've fallen in love with a married woman – had a bit of an affair – and then got caught in the act. As you are now, without arguing skills, you're **PS** done for. But if you come and learn from me, then you can do what you like and get away with it – indulge your desires, laugh and play, have no shame. And then suppose you do get caught with somebody's wife, you can say to him straight out: 'I've done nothing wrong. Just look at Zeus; isn't he always a slave to erotic desire? And do you expect a mere mortal like me to be stronger than a god?'
>
> Aristophanes, *Clouds*, 1076–82

Tragedy and the sophists

While the presence of the sophists as figures of fun in comedy is clear, their influence on tragedy is more subtle. Scholars of Greek tragedy have usually presented Euripides as the poet most influenced by contemporary philosophy, and his plays are full of the jargon used by the Sophists. He uses the word 'sophos' ('wise') frequently, and in some of his plays there is a keen interest shown in arguments which are clever, but morally questionable. In his *Orestes*, for example, Orestes is condemned to death because of the intervention of a clever speaker who will argue on behalf of anyone who pays him.

Parallels with the Sophists' thinking can be seen in a number of ways in *Hippolytus* **PS**, most notably in the character of the Nurse, who manipulates Phaedra into telling her secret against her better judgement. The trial scene (902–1101 **PS**) between Theseus and Hippolytus is filled with the tricks taught to aspiring public speakers, for example Hippolytus' appeal to sympathy because he is not a skilled public speaker (986 **PS**) and his use of the 'argument from probability' when he claims that it is not plausible that he would rape Phaedra (1009–1020 **PS**). Most infamously, when Hippolytus threatens to break his oath of silence, he claims (612 **PS**) that: 'It was my tongue that swore it. No oath binds my heart', in an attempt to justify doing something the Athenians would consider morally outrageous.

SOCRATES

Our portrait of Socrates is drawn primarily from Plato, but also from Xenophon, both of them his followers. They must first have met Socrates in their teens, and so fitted

Study questions
Read Aristophanes, *Clouds*, 92–118

1 What impression is given of the Thinkery?

Read Aristophanes, *Clouds*, 814–1302 **PS**

2 How might this section of the play reflect contemporary perceptions and prejudices about the sophists?

Study question
Read Euripides, *Hippolytus* 176–361 and 902–1101 **PS**

How might these passages reflect the influence of the sophists?

KEY INDIVIDUALS

Socrates

Dates: *c.* 470–399

An Athenian thinker who challenged people on the nature of truth and was eventually put to death for impiety and corrupting the young

Plato
Dates: 427–348

An Athenian follower of Socrates who wrote many brilliant works of philosophy after Socrates' death

FIGURE 3.5
Socrates was famously ugly, with a snub-nose and bulging eyes.

naturally into the type of young men that he was accused of corrupting. After Socrates' death, Plato devoted his life to philosophy, writing a number of 'dialogues' in which Socrates discusses ethical questions with other thinkers of the day. These dialogues are literary masterpieces, designed not only to illustrate Socrates' teachings, but also to engage their audience through their literary power. Xenophon also portrayed Socrates favourably in his own set of dialogues, *Memorabilia*, and saw his death as a great injustice (*Memorabilia* 1.2.62 **PS**) When we read their dialogues, therefore, we have to consider how idealised an image of Socrates is being presented.

Socrates was born *c.* 470. He apparently worked as a stonecutter and was at least moderately wealthy, since he could afford the armour to serve as a hoplite – he tells us that he fought at Potidaea in 432, at Delium in 424 and at Amphipolis in 422 (*Apology* 28e **PS**). He also fulfilled his civic duties as a citizen, serving as a member of the council in 407/6. During the last twenty years or so of his life, he seems to have wandered the streets of Athens, constantly engaging people in debate. As an old man, he claimed to be poor, and it is likely that during these decades he had lived on the charity of friends.

Socrates' philosophical method

Xenophon (*Memorabilia* 1.1.16 **PS**) specifically comments on the sorts of issues which interested Socrates, and these tie in with what else we know about him. His great area of interest was human ethics: how a person should live a good life.

He was famous for the method of enquiry he used. He would start by asking someone a question about an issue, and he would usually be given a fixed and certain answer in reply. He would then cross-question the person until he was able to show that the answer he had been given was based on a false premise. This method of argument is often known as the 'Socratic method' or 'dialectic' (the Greek word was **elenchus**, which can be translated as 'cross-examining'). Socrates famously compared this art to that of a midwife, his mother's profession. To him, the learning process was just as painful as giving birth. Moreover, Socrates did not believe that he could actually teach anything himself, just as a midwife did not herself give birth – he was simply able to help another person discover his own wisdom.

Socrates once compared his relationship to Athens as like that of a gadfly which stings a horse, since he was constantly challenging citizens to reflect on morality and justice. The people he was challenging, however, were often significant figures in Athens, who were publicly humiliated. As a result, he engendered strong feelings, both positive and negative.

elenchus the Greek word for 'cross-examining' used to describe Socrates' method of argument

Socrates and democracy

Xenophon and Plato both present Socrates arguing against democracy. He apparently believed that the democratic system relied on people who were not skilled enough to fulfil their roles, and the constant changeover of officials allowed no time for citizens to develop such expertise. Socrates also reportedly argued that most people were not intelligent or educated enough to vote for what was good for them. This meant that politicians were forced to follow the whims of the people rather than standing up for hard truths. In Plato's *Republic*, Socrates puts forward his alternative view of a well-run state: a few should be trained as 'philosopher-kings' to rule over the rest with wisdom and honesty.

Republic contains two analogies which illustrate Socrates' objections to democracy. In the analogy of the ship (6.488–489 **PS**) a ship-owner is compared to the democratic state. He is in charge, but is not himself capable of steering the ship since he is unimpressive physically and is limited in seamanship – seamanship here represents the knowledge required to run the state. Meanwhile, the crew of the ship behave appallingly, arguing with each other rather than thinking about what is best for the ship: their only interest is satisfying their own selfish desires. These men represent the demagogues of the city. They also dismiss the ship's navigator as a worthless stargazer, even though he is really the one who has the expertise to steer the ship well. Such a navigator represents the educated 'philosopher-king'.

In the analogy of the animal trainer (6.493 **PS**), Socrates focuses on the relationship between a speaker and his audience. He compares the sophists to an animal trainer who has to control a large beast, which represents the people. The trainer learns what the beast likes and doesn't like, and so how to placate it. Having learnt this, he can in turn teach others how to do it. What the trainer doesn't worry about, however, is whether or not the desires of the animal are a good thing or not. In fact, he simply calls what pleases the animal 'good' and what annoys it 'bad'. In the same way, some speakers in the assembly simply work out what the people want to hear rather than trying to suggest policies which are truly good for them.

PRESCRIBED SOURCE

Title: *Memorabilia*

Author: Xenophon (*c.* 430–354)

Date: *c.* 370–355

Genre: philosophical dialogue

Significance: Xenophon describes the topics Socrates used to discuss

Prescribed sections: 1.1.16

Read it here: LACTOR 12: *The Culture of Athens* (KCL, 1978) 26

PRESCRIBED SOURCE

Title: *Memorabilia*

Author: Xenophon (*c.* 430–354)

Date: *c.* 370–355

Genre: philosophical dialogue

Significance: Xenophon expresses his sense of injustice at Socrates' execution

Prescribed sections: 1.2.62

Read it here: LACTOR 12: *The Culture of Athens* (KCL, 1978) 173

PRESCRIBED SOURCE

Title: *Republic*

Author: Plato (427–348)

Origin: Athenian

Genre: philosophical dialogue

Significance: two analogies presented by Socrates to explain his criticisms of Athenian democracy

Prescribed sections: 6.488–489; 6.493

Read it here: Plato, *The Republic*, translated by Desmond Lee (Penguin 2007)

Study questions

Read Plato, *Apology* 20a–24b

1 What does this passage show us about Socrates' philosophical methods? Why is it significant that Apollo features so prominently?

Read Plato, *Apology* 31c–32e **PS**

2 What do we learn about Socrates' performance of civic duties here?

ACTIVITY

Read through Plato's *Apology* **PS**. Draw up a table outlining the structure of the speech, and the key points made at each stage. What evidence is there that Socrates intended to be found guilty and face execution?

Trial and execution

After Athens suffered its final defeat in the Peloponnesian War in 404, the city was run by a pro-Spartan oligarchy of thirty men. Their rule was so brutal that they are sometimes known as the Thirty Tyrants and democracy was restored after a year. Some of the young men who had been Socrates' closest followers had become figures of suspicion and hate in the shattered city: the treacherous Alcibiades was one, while Critias and Charmides had both been among the thirty tyrants. When Socrates was put on trial in 399, he may have been a scapegoat for the surviving members of the brutal oligarchy, who could not be prosecuted under the terms of a general amnesty. Plato (*Apology* 24b–c **PS**) states that there were two charges: not acknowledging the city's gods, and corrupting the young. Xenophon (*Memorabilia* 1.1.3 **PS**) argues that the charge of atheism was very unfair, since Socrates' search for truth was really no different from the practice of religious diviners who seek to find out the will of the gods.

Plato's *Apology* is a carefully crafted defence speech, in which he seems also to want to explain why Socrates was found guilty. Socrates is presented as rousing the jury to anger on occasions, while he also refuses to follow the normal patterns of behaviour expected on such occasions, such as bringing his children into court to make the jurors feel pity for him. He seems to act in such a way as to ensure that he is found guilty by simply arguing that he had only ever brought benefit to the city.

In a court of 500 jurors, he was found guilty by a majority of sixty. At the second stage of the trial, when the sentence was decided, Socrates was given the chance to argue for a punishment other than the death penalty which was being demanded by the prosecutors. If he had asked for exile, his request would probably have been granted, but he was unwilling to compromise his principles. Instead, he continued to argue that he had benefited the city, and so requested that he should be given free meals at the public expense for the rest of his life, just as an Olympic victor was (36b–37a **PS**). This was too much for the jury, who voted by a much larger margin for his execution.

PRESCRIBED SOURCE

Title: *Memorabilia*

Author: Xenophon (*c.* 430–354)

Date: *c.* 370–355

Genre: philosophical dialogue

Significance: Xenophon defends Socrates against the charge that he introduced new gods

Prescribed sections: 1.1.3

Read it here: LACTOR 12: *The Culture of Athens* (KCL, 1978) 258

Even then, Socrates could have escaped from jail in the days before his death. He refused to do so, so becoming a model of one who follows their conscience no matter the consequences. On the evening of his death, Plato describes him calmly drinking the poison hemlock, confident in what death holds for him.

TOPIC REVIEW

- Outline the nature of the source bias against the sophists at Athens.
- Assess what Aristophanes' *Clouds* can tell us about how the sophists were perceived in Athens.
- Analyse why so many Athenians found Socrates so troublesome.
- Discuss the strengths and weaknesses of Plato's *Apology* as a source for understanding why Socrates was tried and convicted.

Further Reading

Colaiaco, J.A., *Socrates Against Athens: Philosophy on Trial* (Abingdon: Routledge, 2001).

Dillon, J. and T.L. Gergel, *The Greek Sophists* (London: Penguin, 2003).

Gottlieb, A., *The Dream of Reason* (London: Penguin 2001), chapters 7, 9, 10, 11.

Guthrie, W.K.C., *The Sophists* (Cambridge: Cambridge University Press, 1971).

Hughes, Bettany, *The Hemlock Cup: Socrates, Athens and the Search for the Good Life* (London: Jonathan Cape, 2011).

Knox, Bernard, *The Hippolytus of Euripides* (New Haven: Yale Classical Studies, Vol. 8, 1952), pp. 3–31. Also published in ed. E. Segal, *Oxford Readings in Greek Tragedy* (Oxford: Oxford University Press 1983).

de Romilly, J., *The Great Sophists in Periclean Athens* (Oxford: Oxford University Press, 1992).

Samons, L.J. (ed.), *The Cambridge Companion to the Age of Pericles* (Cambridge: Cambridge Univerisity Press, 2007), chapter 9.

Wallace, R.W., 'The Sophists in Athens', in D. Boedeker and K.A. Raaflaub, *Democracy, Empire and the Arts in Fifth-Century Athens* (Cambridge MA: Harvard University Press, 1998).

Waterfield, Robin, *Why Socrates Died: Dispelling the Myths* (London: Faber and Faber, 2010).

PRACTICE QUESTIONS

Read Thucydides 3.38 **PS**.

1. How useful is this passage for our understanding of the influence of rhetoric on the Athenian assembly?

[12]

3.3 Art and Architecture and their Significance in the Culture of Athens

TOPIC OVERVIEW

- the significance of the Persian Wars in relation to the building programme, including the use of Delian League funds
- the main buildings of the building programme in the fifth century on the Acropolis and in the Agora in Athens
- developments outside Athens in Attica, such as Sounion and Brauron
- sculpture on the Acropolis and its interpretation

The prescribed sources for this topic are:

- Pausanias, *Description of Greece*, 1.24.5, 7 and 1.28.2
- Plutarch, *Pericles*, 12–14, 31

- Buildings on the Acropolis and in the Athenian Agora built as part of the Periclean Building Programme; the Odeon of Pericles
- Temple at Sounion

This topic will examine the art and architecture which was developed in Athens during the second half of the fifth century BC as part of an official state building programme. This development in art and architecture is closely related to the other themes in this component, since the ideas which were current in Athenian society had a direct effect on the buildings and their decoration. In studying this topic, therefore, it is important to keep in mind these links and to interpret the archaeological evidence in its historical context.

THE ATHENIAN BUILDING PROGRAMME

After the Persians' sackings of Athens in 480 and 479, the Athenians swore an oath not to rebuild the temples on the Acropolis. Instead, they buried the statues that had been knocked down, and let the burnt remains of temples remind them of how close they had come to total destruction. However, with the cessation of hostilities with the Persians

---

EXAM TIP

When analysing art and architecture, you should be asking yourself the same sort of questions as when you analyse a literary text: who commissioned the artwork? Was it set up in public or in private? Who had access to it? Why was it set up? What materials were used and what did it cost? Which characters or what event is it showing and why? How does it interact with its surroundings?

---

from about 449, circumstances had changed. Pericles now promoted a remarkably ambitious building programme for the city, which is described by Plutarch at *Pericles* 12–14 **PS**. Plutarch reports that this was planned and supervised by the brilliant Athenian sculptor Pheidias, who sculpted the remarkable gold and ivory statue of Athena for the Parthenon. Alongside him worked other architects, including Callicrates and Ictinus. The programme extended beyond the Acropolis to other sites both within Athens and throughout Attica.

Plutarch (*Pericles* 12 **PS**) reports that Pericles' ambitious proposal required the use of the tribute from Athens' allies in the Delian League. Athens could protect her allies, and any surplus in the funds should be spent on developing the city, or so Pericles' argument ran. This was met with opposition. Some viewed the use of the money given by the allies as an act of tyranny. They compared the beautifying of the city to the act of a vain woman giving herself excessive jewellery. Pericles, then, responded that he would pay for the developments himself. This proposal offended the democratic sensibilities of the citizen body, and they voted to pass the proposal.

However, the criticisms continued. Plutarch (*Pericles* 31 **PS**) records a claim that Pheidias, a close friend of Pericles, became the object of so much jealousy that he was prosecuted in about 437. He was accused of stealing gold which was meant for the Athena Parthenos statue, and of depicting himself and Pericles on the shield of the statue. This was regarded as an impious act. Plutarch records that Pheidias was put in prison and died there, but his account is contradicted by another historian who claims that he returned to Olympia to complete his great statue of Zeus there. The finds from Pheidias' workshop at Olympia suggest that he did indeed produce the Zeus after the Athena Parthenos.

In considering the building programme, it is worth noting two points by way of background. The first relates to the building materials: in this programme much of the construction work was undertaken in solid marble, which was remarkable given its cost. It is all the more striking when it is considered that the majority of the inhabitants of Attica would have lived in mud-brick huts, now washed away without trace. The second point is that while we see the buildings today as gleaming white marble, they would have been painted in bright colours such as red, blue and yellow.

A further point is made by Thucydides, who draws a comparison between the buildings of Athens and Sparta early in his work. He observes that if the Sparta of his day were to

KEY INDIVIDUAL

Pheidias
Dates: *c.* 485–*c.* 425
A famous Athenian sculptor who supervised Pericles' building programme

Study question
Read Plutarch, *Pericles* 12 **PS**

What does this source tell us about Pericles' intentions for the building programme, and the reaction of the Athenians?

be abandoned, and only its temples and the foundations of its buildings were to remain, future generations would have great difficulty in understanding the great power which the city held within the Greek world. He then goes on to say:

> If, on the other hand, the same thing were to happen to Athens, one would conjecture from what met the eye that the city had been twice as powerful as in fact it is.

Thucydides, *The History of the Peloponnesian War* 1.10

This is a significant message: not only does it act as a warning to us when studying Athens and Sparta, but it also shows how aware Thucydides was of the importance of these buildings in developing the reputation of Athens, both in his own day and for the years to come.

THE ACROPOLIS

PRESCRIBED SOURCE

Title: *Description of Greece*

Author: Pausanias

Dates: AD *c.* 110–*c.*180

Genre: geographical travel writing

Significance: a series of passages giving information about some monuments on the Acropolis

Prescribed Sections: 1.24.5,7; 1.28.2

Read it here: LACTOR 12: *The Culture of Athens* (KCL, 1978) 360 and 258

Many Greek cities have a central rock or hill which was originally a military stronghold, around which the residents lived, and onto which they could retreat in the event of an attack. The word 'acropolis' means 'the high point of the city' and comes from two Greek words: acr- (high) and polis (city). In fifth century Athens the Acropolis was the religious centre of the city. Four buildings deserve particular attention: the Parthenon, the Erechtheion, the temple of Athena Nike and the Propylaea.

These buildings were designed with a careful eye to their position on the rock, and to their relationship with each other. To appreciate the attention given to this overall plan, it is important to note that there were two distinct styles, or orders, of architecture in Greece at this time: the Doric and the Ionic. They are most easily distinguished by the capitals (tops) of their columns. Those of the Doric order are simple and circular, those of the Ionic order have curls known as volutes. The Propylaea was designed using the Doric order, as was the Parthenon, although it had some added features of the Ionic order. By contrast, the Erechtheion and the temple of Athena Nike were built in the Ionic order. The more elaborate, or 'feminine', Ionic style complements the sturdier, 'masculine' Doric style, creating an aesthetically pleasing and balanced whole. It is interesting to note that the two Doric order buildings were constructed first.

We get a relatively detailed account of the buildings of the Acropolis from the Greek travel writer Pausanias in his *Description of Greece* (1.22.4–1.28.3). He lived in the second century AD and wrote a detailed account of the monuments of Greece as he found them in his day.

The Temple of Athena Nike

As a visitor to the Acropolis proceeded up towards the mighty rock, the first building which was noticeable was a small temple on an outcrop of rock to the right of the Propylaea. This building, beautifully designed to fit the space, made excellent use of the elegance of the Ionic order. It was a small temple to Athena Nike, Athena as goddess of Victory, built during during the 420s.

Map of the buildings on the Acropolis and the Odeon of Pericles

Significance: a map showing the key buildings on the Acropolis, as well as the Odeon of Pericles

View it here: Figure 3.6

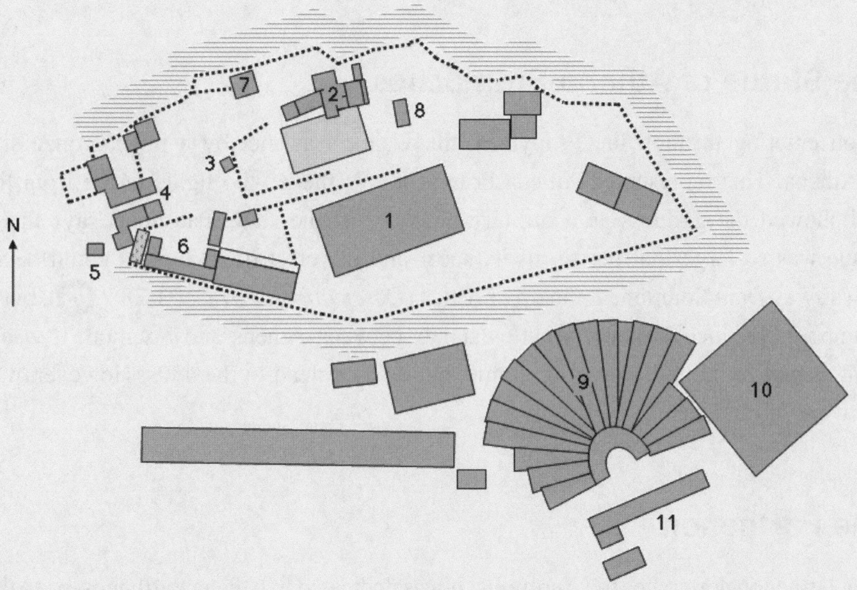

FIGURE 3.6
A plan of the main buildings on the Acropolis in the late fifth century.

1 Parthenon; 2 Erechtheion; 3 Statue of Athena Promachos; 4 Propylaea;
5 Temple of Athena Nike; 6 Sanctuary of Artemis Brauronia; 7 Arrēphorion;
8 Altar of Athena; 9 Theatre of Dionysus; 10 Odeon of Pericles; 11 Sanctuary of Dionysus

The temple was simple in design, with four Ionic columns on the west side, complemented by a further four on the east. There was a continuous **frieze**, or band of sculpture, all the way around the top of the building. Its east side shows a group of gods and goddesses, and the other three sides depict battle scenes: the north and south sides show the Greeks and Persians in combat, while the west side may show a battle against the Corinthians at Megara. Around the temple was a wall which had reliefs of the goddess Nike engaged in sacrifices. These include a famous image of Nike fastening (or unfastening) her sandal. Unlike other depictions of Victory, she did not have wings – perhaps to imply that Victory would never leave Athens.

> **frieze** a continuous strip of sculpted stone running around a temple which depicted a narrative of events

The Propylaea

The Propylaea formed the formal entrance to the Acropolis. In part, it served the function of offering a divide between the profane and the sacred. It posed considerable challenges

EXPLORE FURTHER

Read Pausanias'
description of the
Propylaea at *Description
of Greece* 1.22.4–7.

- How does Pausanias'
  description of the
  Propylaea help us to
  understand the nature
  of this building?
- Research the myths
  and characters named
  in Pausanias'
  description of the
  paintings in the
  Propylaea. What
  significance do you
  think these had for
  the Athenians?

for the architect, Mnesikles, as it was placed on the steep side of a rock. Nevertheless, it was largely completed within five years between 437 and 432, with the exception of some finishing touches which were probably left because of the outbreak of the war with Sparta. The building, though, was more than a mere gateway. It was designed to have five parts: a central hall, which formed the gateway, and then four wings, two off each side. It was made of marble, with a dark blue ceiling studded with golden stars. In the northwest wing there was a picture gallery.

The Statue of Athena Promachos

Upon entering through the Propylaea, the visitor was met by a huge bronze statue of Athena. This represented Athena Promachos, 'Athena who fights in the front line', and showed the goddess as a military defender of the state. Pausanias says that the statue was so large that the tip of its spear and the crest of its helmet could be seen miles away from Sounion, at the tip of Attica (*Description of Greece* 1.28.2 **PS**), but this is impossible since Mount Hymettos stands between Athens and Sounion. It was not built as part of the building programme, but dates instead to the 450s. However, it was the work of Pheidias.

The Parthenon

The Parthenon dominates the Acropolis. It was dedicated to Athena Parthenos, or 'Athena the maiden'. The building follows the pattern of a standard **peripteral** temple, which has a colonnade of columns surrounding an inner room or **naos** on all four sides. However, the architects of the Parthenon decided to make the temple more magnificent in its size. The finest Doric temple built until this time was the temple of Zeus at Olympia, which had thireen columns on each side and six columns at each end. The Parthenon was larger still, with eight by seventeen columns.

In addition to this, there is a wide range of design features which trick the human eye into thinking that the temple is lighter and more impressive than it might otherwise appear. These include careful placing of the columns and a slight curvature of the base and columns. Great care was also taken in the choice of materials, as noted by Plutarch (*Pericles* 12 **PS**). The Parthenon is constructed from solid marble, which came from Mount Pentelicus in Attica. Many temples of this time were built from limestone, and then coated with a layer of stucco – a thin layer of marble.

A key element of the Parthenon is its sculpture. In a Doric temple, there were two key spaces for sculpture. The first is the triangular space underneath the roof at either end of the temple, known as the **pediment**, and the second are the square spaces above the gaps between columns of the temple. These spaces are known as **metopes**. In many temples not all the metopes would be decorated, and the pedimental sculpture would be straightforward. In the case of the Parthenon, however, all the metopes were filled with sculptures depicting significant mythical themes, while each pediment portrayed an elaborate scene.

peripteral a style of Doric temple with columns around a central room

naos the central room in a temple

pediment the triangular space just below the roof at each end of a temple

metope a square space in the area above the columns in a Doric temple

The metopes

The metopes include a number of key themes. These are carefully laid out around the temple, so that as the visitor walks around, they are treated to a narrative of the different myths. The four sides depict:

- the sack of Troy
- the fight between the centaurs and the lapiths
- the attempt by the giants to take over Olympus
- the fight against the Amazons, a tribe of warrior women.

There has been much discussion about the significance of these themes, but in each case there is a common narrative: the attempt by an alien or uncivilised force (e.g. centaurs, who were half man, half horse) to interrupt the civilised world. This can be seen as analogous to the attempt by the Persians, who were regarded as barbarians, to take over the Greek world. The Athenians, from their point of view at least, led the defence of the Greek world, so this narrative harmonises with their own self-definition.

The pediments

The sculpture on the two pediments has not survived well. Although some parts of the sculpture remain, reconstruction of the two scenes is challenging. However, Pausanias gives us the outline of each design (*Description of Greece* 1.24.5):

> Everything on the pediment bears upon the birth of Athena; the other end is the quarrel of Poseidon with Athena over the country.
>
> Pausanias, *Description of Greece* 1.24.5 (LACTOR 12, 360)

The western pediment, seen as a visitor to the Acropolis passed through the Propylaea, depicted the contest between Poseidon and Athena for the land of Attica. In this myth, Poseidon had offered the Athenians a salt-water spring, whilst Athena had offered them an olive tree, and it was she who was successful. However, both deities were of great significance to the Athenians: Athena as their 'patron' goddess, and Poseidon as the god of the sea, on which the Athenians' empire was so dependent.

The western end was in fact the back of the temple, and the visitor had to make his way to the other end to enter under the eastern pediment. This depicted the unusual birth of Athena. Zeus, king of the gods, was told that the offspring of his relationship with Metis would be more intelligent than he. He therefore ate the pregnant goddess. Sometime later, he developed a severe headache. To ease his pain, the god of arts and crafts, Hephaestus, split open Zeus' head with an axe, and out sprang Athena, fully armed. As

Study questions

1 Research and describe in detail two metopes from the Parthenon.
2 Research the four myths depicted on the metopes of the Parthenon. Why do you think these myths were chosen?

Study question

Examine reconstructions of the Parthenon pediments. How does the art bring out important elements of each story for the Athenians?

FIGURE 3.7
A reconstruction of the western pediment of the Parthenon.

the goddess of wisdom she had to be fully formed and complete – hence this somewhat strange myth.

The frieze

The sculpture on the metopes and pediments was in line with expectations for a Doric temple, but the inner continuous frieze which the architects also included was a feature which might be expected in an Ionic temple. This is believed to depict the Panathenaic procession. Before examining this sculpture in detail, it is worth noting how difficult it would have been to see it. It was on the external wall of the inner building, high up and with minimal light. Today, when these works of art are seen in a museum, we are far closer to them than an ancient Athenian would have been.

The west side of the frieze shows horsemen preparing for the procession. Then around both the north and south sides are images depicting the procession with horsemen, chariots, old men, musicians, pitcher bearers and animal sacrifices. Then the procession culminates on the east side of the frieze with maidens, citizens and deities. This frieze gives a sense of the procession as a living event, at the heart of Athenian culture. There has been considerable debate about the meaning and significance of the figures depicted. In the first instance, it has been claimed that there are 192 horsemen: these men may represent those killed at Marathon in 490.

The statue of Athena Parthenos

In the naos of the Parthenon was a huge statue of Athena, some 12m tall, which was made from gold and ivory. These two materials – gold for the clothing, and ivory for the skin – were placed on a wooden frame. Pausanias (*Description of Greece* 1.24.5,7 **PS**) gives a description of the statue as he found it in his day.

The Erechtheion

On the north side of the Acropolis stood the Erechtheion. It was named after Erechtheus, a legendary king of Athens, but the main part of this temple was dedicated to Athena Polias, 'Athena the defender of the city'. Inside was a sacred olive-wood statue of Athena. Pausanias makes clear that this was the most revered image of the goddess in the whole of Attica. Indeed, Pausanias, who had a particular interest in religion, wrote a mere two sentences on the Parthenon, but gave more detail on its neighbouring temple. The Erechtheion also incorporated spaces for the worship of other deities, including Poseidon. Its southern porch has statues of six young women, known as the Caryatids, serving in place of columns. It remains unclear who these women are meant to represent.

The site of the Erechtheion was a particularly difficult one for the architects, and doubtless contributed to the innovative nature of the building. As Pausanias' description makes clear, there were numerous cults in this area of the Acropolis, so the significant spots (such as where Poseidon's trident hit the rock) had to be avoided. The ground was also very uneven, with the northern section having to rest on ground considerably lower

S & C A significant amount of the sculpture of the Parthenon is on display in the British Museum. Research the controversy about the 'Elgin Marbles', and the arguments about where they should belong today. Which set of arguments do you find more persuasive?

EXAM TIP

Make sure that you know the detail of the sculpture on the Parthenon, and why the images were significant for the Athenians.

EXPLORE FURTHER

Read Pausanias' description of the Erechtheion at *Description of Greece* 1.26.5–1.27. 2. What can we learn about the temple from this account?

METOPES

PEDIMENT

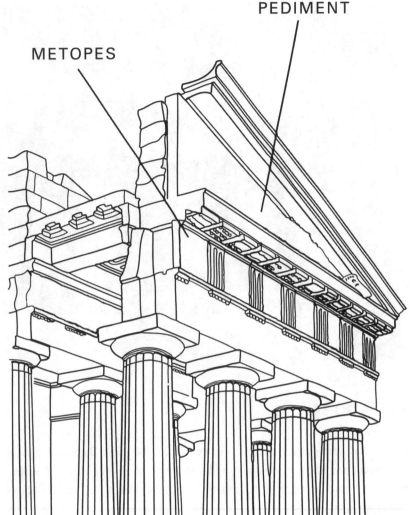

FIGURE 3.8
The main sculptural elements of a Greek temple.

than the south porch. Next to the Erechtheion was the olive tree which was said by Herodotus (*Histories* 8.54–5) to have sprouted to life so quickly after the destruction of the buildings on the Acropolis by Xerxes' men.

Work on the Erechtheion did not start until the late 420s, and it was almost certainly under construction during the Peloponnesian War. An inscription dated to 409/8 describes the incomplete state of the building at this point, and the decision to continue with its construction.

The Odeon of Pericles

Plutarch (*Pericles* 13 (PS)) reports that Pericles commissioned the construction of an Odeon, or roofed concert hall to the south of the Acropolis next to the Theatre of Dionysus (which dates to the sixth century). He claims that it was based on the design of the tent of the Persian king. This building has only been partially excavated, so the details of its use and plan have not yet been fully established. It was a square building, measuring about 60 metres down each side.

Study question
Consider the archaeological evidence from the Acropolis. What are its strengths and weaknesses as historical evidence? What makes it difficult or easy to interpret?

THE AGORA

Below the Acropolis, in the civic centre of the city, there were numerous other developments. Strictly speaking, the agora was the square in the centre of the city, bounded by stones marking its boundaries. In the fifth century, this was more or less an empty square, with the Panathenaic Way running across it, and up to the Acropolis. Around the edge of this square, however, were a number of significant buildings, including key buildings related to the democracy, as well as the stoa of Zeus Eleutherios and the temple of Hephaestus and Athena, known as the Hephaesteon, which overlooks the whole area. On the other side of this temple was the kerameikos which was an area where many potters worked. They of course took their inspiration from Hephaestus.

ATTICA

In the development of the polis of Athens, the wider needs of Attica were not neglected. One of the key religious centres of Attica to the west of Athens was Eleusis, where the mystery cult of Demeter was celebrated. Plutarch mentions the development of this sanctuary (*Pericles*, 13 **PS**), noting that three architects, Coroebus, Metagenes and Xenocles were involved in the work here. The developments at Eleusis were substantial, because the nature of the cult required sacrifices and rituals to be conducted indoors, so that only initiates – of whom there were many thousands – were involved. Just as in Athens, there was a connection with the events of the Persian Wars, as Herodotus

(*Histories* 9.65) refers to the destruction of the temple of Demeter at Eleusis during the Persian invasion.

Sounion is at the southernmost tip of Attica. Here a new temple was built for Poseidon over the ruins of an earlier incomplete temple which had been destroyed during the Persian invasions. Any ship approaching Piraeus from the east or south would be likely to pass this promontory and its striking temple, and to be reminded of the power of Poseidon. The temple was in a traditional peripteral Doric form and its frieze depicted scenes similar to those elsewhere in the city's new temples:

- the battle of the centaurs and the Lapiths
- the battle of the giants and the gods
- the labours of Theseus

Down the hill from this temple was one to Athena. This was in the Ionic order, with columns on two sides only. It too was built over an earlier temple which had been destroyed during the Persian invasions.

In Thorikos a marble stoa or colonnaded building was set up. This was of unusual design, with two separate U-shaped halves, executed to the highest standards of craftsmanship. This suggests that it may have been intended for a religious purpose, possibly as a temple to the goddess, Demeter.

At Brauron, on the east coast of Attica, there was a sanctuary to Artemis, which was of particular significance to the young women of Attica. There is a temple dating from the sixth century, and further developments occurred after the Persians attacked the site in 480. In the 420s, a stoa was started, but like so many buildings of this period, it was not completed. This building was designed to display the numerous votive offerings which were given to Artemis. The columns were placed more widely apart than was normal for the Doric order for ease of access. It is evident that there were dining rooms at the back of the building. Behind this area was another large room, the function of which remains unclear. The importance of the cult of Artemis at Brauron can be seen from the fact that it also had a sanctuary building on the Athenian Acropolis.

PRESCRIBED SOURCE

Temple of Sounion

Date: *c.* 440

Location: Cape Sounion

Order: Doric (6 × 13 columns)

Dedicated to: Poseidon

Significance: a temple to the god of the sea at the tip of Attica visible to ships on the busy sea lanes passing by.

View it here: Figure 3.10

FIGURE 3.10
The remains of the temple of Sounion today.

PS

Study question

Explain why the building developments around Attica were significant, and how they relate to developments within Athens.

At Rhamnous, in the north-east of Attica, a new temple to the goddess Nemesis was built in the Doric Order. It appears that work on this temple was interrupted by the Peloponnesian War, as the columns remain unfluted. The temple also included a statue of Nemesis by Pheidias or by his pupil Agorakritos. Pausanias (*Description of Greece* 1.33.2–3) states that the Persian invaders at Marathon in 490 had brought with them Parian marble to set up a victory monument, but that this marble was subsequently used by Pheidias to create the statue.

TOPIC REVIEW

- Name the key buildings built under the Periclean building programme, and state the function of each.
- Outline the sculpture on the Parthenon, and explain how it related to Athenian attitudes and values at the time.
- Outline the building work which took place outside Athens. Explain the significance of the buildings which you name.
- Consider any piece of sculpture from this period. Outline why it is challenging to interpret this as an historian.

Further Reading

Beard, M., *The Parthenon* (London: Profile Books, 2010).

Camp, J., *The Archaeology of Athens* (New Haven: Yale University Press, 2004).

Hurwit, J. *The Athenian Acropolis* (Cambridge: Cambridge University Press, 2000).

Jenkins, I. and I. Kerslake, *The Parthenon Sculptures in the British Museum* (London: British Museum, 2007).

Lapatin, K., *Art and Architecture* in L.J. Samons, *The Cambridge Companion to the Age of Pericles*, (Cambridge: Cambridge University Press, 2007).

Rhodes, R.F., *The Periclean Acropolis*, in M.M. Miles, *A Companion to Greek Architecture*, (Chichester: Wiley, 2016).

Rhodes, R.F., *Architecture and Meaning on the Athenian Acropolis* (Cambridge: Cambridge University Press, 1995).

Woodford, S., *The Parthenon* (Cambridge: Cambridge University Press, 1981).

PRACTICE QUESTIONS

Read the extract from Plutarch, *Pericles* 12 **PS**, and study a Parthenon metope of a centaur fighting with a Lapith.

1. How useful are these sources for our understanding of how the conflict with the Persians came to influence Athenian art and architecture? [12]

3.4 Drama and Dramatic Festivals and their Significance in the Culture of Athens

TOPIC OVERVIEW

- the function and nature of dramatic festivals in Athens, with particular reference to the City Dionysia and Lenaea
- tragedy and comedy as genres and their significance;
- interaction between comedy and contemporary events

The prescribed sources for this topic are:

- Aristophanes, *Thesmophoriazusae* 786–800, 830–842 (no. 120) *Wasps* 891–1008; *Knights* 147–395; *Clouds* 92–118, 365–381, 814–1302
- Euripides, *Hippolytus*
- Plutarch, *Pericles* 4, 13, 16, 30
- The Old Oligarch (Pseudo-Xenophon), *Constitution of the Athenians*, 2.18

- The Odeon of Pericles

This topic will examine the dramatic festivals at Athens, notably the City Dionysia and the Lenaea, and examine how they contributed to the cultural and political life of the city. It is important to view the dramatic festivals in the wider festival context of Athenian culture, which is described on pp. 202–3.

FESTIVALS OF DIONYSUS IN ATHENS

The context in which plays were performed in ancient Athens was quite different from our experience of the theatre today, since drama was performed only at religious festivals. These festivals were also intimately associated with the worship of Dionysus, the god of drama, transformation, wine and revelry. A further key element of a drama festival was an element of competition: a number of playwrights entered plays written for the occasion, and one of them was judged to be the winner.

However, the plays were just one aspect of such festivals, and they typically included other events such as processions, sacrifices and revelry in honour of Dionysus. The most

City Dionysia a drama festival in late March held in honour of Dionysus in Athens

Lenaea a drama festival held in Athens in late January at which comedy took precedence

Rural Dionysia a drama festival held in the rural demes of Attica in mid-winter

important dramatic festival was the **City Dionysia**, held in late March. In addition, there were two other important drama festivals in honour of the god. The **Lenaea** was held in late January, and competitions for comedy and tragedy were introduced to it in about 440 – comedy seems to have been most important. The fact that it was held so early in the year made it open only to Athenians, since the seas were too rough for a journey from further afield (by contrast, the City Dionysia made a point of welcoming outsiders). The **Rural Dionysia** was held in mid-winter. Unlike the other two, it was a local festival celebrated in the demes of Attica and the plays performed were probably revivals of those performed at the two main city festivals.

Although drama was only performed at festivals to Dionysus, it is unclear how exactly it related to the worship of the god. Out of all our surviving Greek drama, he appears as a character only in *Bacchae* and *Frogs*.

The City Dionysia

We know most about the organisation of the City Dionysia. During the days of the festival, public business ceased and the law courts were closed; in the later years of the fifth century, it ran for five days and was organised by the eponymous archōn. Preparations started during the summer of the previous year. Any tragic playwright wishing to compete presented a synopsis of four plays to the eponymous archōn (three tragedies and a satyr-play, a genre described on p. 194). By contrast, comic playwrights needed only to present the synopsis of a single play. We do not know how the archōn made his choice, but he selected three tragic playwrights and five comic playwrights to write their plays for the festival.

chorēgos the financial backer attached to a playwright to support the production of his plays

liturgy a tax on the super-rich requiring them to contribute to the functioning of Athens

Another of the archōn's duties was to select a **chorēgos** for each playwright. The chorēgos ('chorus-director') was the financial backer of a playwright's plays and his input was vital. He was drawn from the city's wealthy elite, who were required to fund various public services called liturgies; serving as a chorēgos was one such **liturgy**. Despite the expense, wealthy Athenians probably welcomed the opportunity to serve as a chorēgos: if they were associated with the success of such an important festival, it gave them status in the city (we know that Pericles himself financed Aeschylus' plays at the City Dionysia of 472). The chorēgos of a winning playwright could pay for a victory monument, which would be inscribed with his own name, together with those of the eponymous archōn, the main actors and the musicians.

proagōn An event which acted as a preview and introduction to the festival

A day or two before the festival began, the **proagōn** ('pre-contest') was held in the Odeon of Pericles **PS**. In this ceremony the plays were announced and each playwright delivered a short synopsis; he might also introduce his chorēgos, actors and musicians and have an actor read a short passage to give the audience a foretaste.

On the evening before the festival began, a wooden statue of Dionysus was brought into the city from a shrine just outside on the road to Eleutherae. This torchlight procession re-enacted Dionysus' arrival in Athens from the distant deme of Eleutherae. The statue was escorted to the theatre of Dionysus at the south-east foot of the Acropolis, where a sacrifice was made. Thereafter the statue remained in the theatre throughout the dramatic performances, a symbol of the god's presence at his festival.

FIGURE 3.11
A view down to the Roman-era remains of the theatre of Dionysus today.

Day	Event
A few days before	proagōn
The eve of the festival	torchlight procession
Day 1	procession dithyrambic contests kōmos
Day 2	opening ceremony 5 comedies
Day 3	3 tragedies, 1 satyr-play
Day 4	3 tragedies, 1 satyr-play
Day 5	3 tragedies, 1 satyr-play judging & prize giving
A few days later	the review

The likely outline of events at the City Dionysia in c. 430.

On the morning of day one the grand procession took place. It started outside the city and made its way to the agora, then on to the Temple of Dionysus, where it culminated in the sacrifice of a sacred bull together with many other animals. In the afternoon there were dithyrambic competitions in the theatre – the **dithyramb** was a choral dance in honour

dithyramb A choral dance sung in honour of Dionysus

of Dionysus, and each tribe entered choruses for this event. Each chorus had its own chorēgos and, again, victory could bring great prestige. Later that evening, a revel (known as a **kōmos**, described on p. 195) was held in the streets by the men of the city.

kōmos a loosely organised revel through the streets with song and dance in honour of Dionysus

Days two–five (the play days)

Although the programme of events changed over the years, in the latter part of the fifth century day two was the day when the comic playwrights presented their plays (it is possible that during the Peloponnesian War only three comic plays were presented, one on each of the other play days, so that the festival was a day shorter). On the following three days the tragic plays were presented: each day saw the three tragedies and satyr-play of one playwright. The action started early in the morning and continued into the afternoon.

Before the plays began on day two, there was a grand opening ceremony in the Theatre of Dionysus. The priest of Dionysus sacrificed a piglet on the altar in the acting area, and the ten generals poured libations to the twelve Olympian gods. Following this, three important presentations were made, each of which emphasised the civic nature of the festival:

- **Parade of tribute**. All the tribute from the allies was due at this time of year. The money was brought into the theatre and paraded for the audience to view.
- **Proclamation of honours**. A herald announced the names of those who had done outstanding service for the city, and awarded them a crown.
- **Parade of orphans**. The boys and youths whose fathers had died fighting for Athens paraded into the theatre. The state paid for their education as a mark of respect for their fathers' sacrifice. Those who had turned eighteen that year were awarded a suit of armour and declared independent citizens.

The spectators

Entry to the theatre cost two obols per day. As this was roughly a day's wage for an unskilled worker, the poor were probably excluded from the festival in its early years. However, at some point in the second half of the fifth century (or possibly later), the Athenian state established the **Theoric Fund**, which paid for the poorest citizens to attend the theatre if they could not afford the entrance fee. This ensured that the dramatic contests were open to the full range of citizens.

Theoric Fund a fund provided by the Athenian state to allow poorer citizens to attend the City Dionysia

At the City Dionysia the seats in the front rows were reserved for important officials: the members of the council, foreign and allied dignitaries, generals, other important magistrates and the priest of Dionysus. By the late fourth century, the seating area behind was divided by section to allow tribes to sit together. We do not know if spectators sat in similarly designated areas during the fifth century, but it is quite possible that they did. The issue of seating also raises the controversial topic of whether women made up part of the audience in the theatre – the sources are ambiguous, but if they did, it would not have been in large numbers.

The judging

At the end of day five, the judging took place. The system for this was randomised in order to avoid bribery. The judges voted on the winning tragic and comic playwright in a process which ran as follows:

- Before the festival began, the Athenian council drew up a list of names from the ten tribes of the city. The names from each tribe were sealed in an urn.
- On the first morning of the plays, the ten urns were placed in the theatre and the eponymous archōn drew out one name from each urn. These ten citizens swore an oath of impartiality and sat as judges for the competition.
- On the fifth day of the festival each judge wrote down his order of merit on a tablet. All ten tablets were placed in a single urn. The eponymous archōn drew out five of the ten tablets at random and the playwright with the most votes was declared the winner.

The review

A few days later, the Athenian assembly met in the theatre of Dionysus to review the festival, and any citizen could make a complaint if he felt that it had not been run well. If a complaint was upheld, then the eponymous archōn could be fined. However, if the assembly felt that the festival had been a success, it could vote to award the archōn a crown in recognition of his services.

TRAGEDY AS A GENRE

In the fifth century, the works of three great tragedians – Aeschylus, Sophocles and Euripides – were marked out as classics, so that their texts were preserved and have survived for us today. However, we know the names of as many as fifty tragic playwrights of the fifth century and some, such as Phrynichus, were clearly held in high regard.

Tragedy seems to have emerged in the second half of the sixth century from the dithyramb, the choral dance in honour of Dionysus. Throughout the fifth century, tragic plays continued to have songs sung by a chorus who remained separate from the main actors of the play. Indeed, music and dance was central to the performance, which was perhaps more like a combination of opera and ballet today. All the performers in a tragedy – the main ones and those in the chorus – wore masks. By convention, there were twelve or fifteen members of the tragic chorus, who acted at a level below the stage. On the stage, there could be no more than three main actors at any one time.

By the early fifth century, tragedy had come to focus on life's deepest questions, and in particular on the nature of suffering: in particular, why do people suffer and how can they bear their suffering heroically? Tragedy rarely gave easy answers to such questions. Indeed, many plays leave the intense pain of their protagonists unresolved – *Oedipus the King* is one famous example. In such cases, the audience was invited to suffer with the tragic hero. However, some tragedies do end on a happier note, with much of the pain resolved. For example, in Aeschylus' *Eumenides* a potential catastrophe is avoided, while in some of Euripides' escape tragedies the movement during the play is from chaos to a more settled situation. Yet in such plays the audience still watches a hero who has to engage with great suffering.

Tragic playwrights usually set their plays in the world of myth, although there were exceptions to this rule. A famous one was presented in 493, when Phrynichus presented *The Fall of Miletus* which depicted the destruction of Miletus by the Persians at the end of the Ionian Revolt in 494. Herodotus reports that the Athenian audience reacted with great distress to this play. Perhaps this encouraged playwrights to avoid depicting historical events since of our thirty-two surviving tragedies only one – Aeschylus' *Persians* – depicts a historical event (and *Persians* portrays the suffering of Persians rather than Greeks). All the other plays were set in the world of Greek mythology, meaning that the audience usually knew the outline of the plot in advance and the interest focused on how the playwright had chosen to interpret it.

Tragedy most commonly engaged with themes such as: relationships within the household, between the sexes, between mortals and immortals, between the individual and the polis; and on the conduct of the polis in its home and foreign affairs. The mythological setting did not prevent playwrights from making their plays relevant to contemporary society. For example, Aeschylus' *Eumenides* of 458 seeks to explain the origins of the Athenian legal system just after it had undergone the reforms of Ephialtes. Meanwhile, some of Euripides' plays, such as the *Trojan Women* and *Andromache*, posed powerful questions about the nature and ethics of war during the period of the Peloponnesian War.

A further aspect of the tragedian's repertoire was the **satyr-play**. This was a light-hearted parody of tragedy in which the actors wore the same type of costumes and masks as in tragedy. We only have one surviving satyr-play, *Cyclops* by Euripides, and so we are limited in our understanding of this form of ancient drama.

> **satyr-play** a play which parodied tragedy and was presented along with three tragedies by the same playwright

Euripides' *Hippolytus* and Tragedy

Hippolytus **PS** was first performed in 428, and was one of the few plays by Euripides to win first prize at the City Dionysia. He had already written an earlier play about Hippolytus, which was poorly received by the Athenian audience. It was very unusual for a tragic playwright to tell the same story twice, and scholars have suggested that Euripides was irritated by the play's failure, and so decided to rework the myth to make it more palatable.

In the lost version, Phaedra was apparently shameless and immoral, and made an attempt to seduce Hippolytus on-stage. The play was known as *Hippolytus Veiled*, after this scene, where Hippolytus veils his head in horror at Phaedra's brazenness. For a woman to seduce a man on-stage may have been too shocking for the Athenian audience. Conversely, in our surviving play (sometimes known as *Hippolytus the Garland Bearer*, after the scene where Hippolytus presents Artemis with a garland of flowers, 73–87 **PS**), Phaedra is conscious that her feelings are wrong, and she struggles nobly to suppress them. This attempt to rework a myth in order to get a better response shows us how important the competitive aspect of tragedy was. Euripides was not attempting to shock his audience 'for art's sake': rather, his aim was to win the competition.

This more nuanced portrayal of Phaedra creates a more morally ambiguous situation, where we sympathise with Phaedra because her intentions are good. Turning Phaedra into an unwilling victim of Aphrodite also raises questions of how far human beings are in control of their own destinies. Aphrodite explains her plan at the start of the play, and the action of the play depicts how it comes to pass. Yet on the human level, the characters believe they are making free choices: for example, Phaedra is persuaded to confide in her Nurse, the Nurse chooses to reveal the secret to Hippolytus, Phaedra decides to commit suicide rather than risk her reputation, and Theseus chooses to believe her suicide note rather than Hippolytus' claims to be innocent. Thus the play invited Athenians to think about the limitations of free will, and the nature of the gods.

COMEDY AS A GENRE

As with tragedy and satyr-plays, comedy seems to have emerged out of the worship of Dionysus. A key element in festivals of Dionysus was the kōmos, during which men came out into the streets of the city, drinking wine, singing and dancing in honour of the god. It is generally agreed that comedy emerged from the songs and dances of the kōmos: in Greek, *kōmōidia*, from which we derive 'comedy', literally meant 'the song of the kōmos'. Furthermore, the icon of the human phallus was a central symbol of the kōmos: during their song and dance, revellers held aloft leather phalluses as a way of giving thanks to Dionysus. The god was commonly associated with the life force, so that the phallus was a symbol of his power and ability to bring new life. The phallus remained a prominent symbol in Greek comedies, where it was worn as part of the costume.

Our detailed knowledge of fifth century comedy really only concerns one playwright, Aristophanes, who lived between *c.* 450 and 386. His are the only plays which have survived, although we do have references to other comic playwrights, as well as fragments from their plays. For example, Cratinus was active between *c.* 454 and 423 and we know the titles of twenty-four of his plays. Eupolis, a friend of Aristophanes, is often also thought of as his main rival. He was writing between 429 and 411 and we know of the titles of fifteen of his plays; he was very successful, winning three times at the City Dionysia and four times at the Lenaea.

Although comedy had the same distinction between leading actors and chorus as tragedy, there were important differences between the two genres when it came to acting: it is likely that comedy allowed a fourth leading actor to appear on stage, while a comic chorus consisted of twenty-four members rather than the twelve or fifteen of tragedy; moreover, in some plays a chorus was divided into two semi-choruses of twelve, each of which supported a different side of the argument in the play.

Perhaps the most noticeable difference between the two genres was their respective costumes and masks. While those of tragedy were dignified and sombre, those of comedy were designed to make the actors look ridiculous and build up the element of farce. A comic actor wore a short tunic, a cloak reaching just below the waist, and tights. The whole costume was thickly padded, which enabled him to fall and roll around, since

Study questions

1 Why do you think that tragedy was so popular as an art form in Athens?
2 Are there forms of art similar to Athenian tragedy today?

KEY INDIVIDUAL

Aristophanes
Date: *c.* 450–386

Athenian comic playwright

Known as the father of comedy, Aristophanes wrote forty plays, eleven of which have survived

FIGURE 3.12
This scene from a comedy illustrates the typical costumes worn by comic actors.

comedy often contained physical humour and slapstick. The oversized leather phallus provided a further element of comedy.

Another key difference was that comic actors sometimes broke the dramatic illusion by acknowledging the presence of the spectators and at times even addressing them directly. Indeed, at one point in the play (or more than one), the chorus-leader stepped forward to deliver an address to the audience in the words of the playwright. This was a feature unique to comedy, and was called the **parabasis** ('stepping aside'). The topic of the parabasis did not need to relate to the plot of the play; instead, it dealt either with the playwright's career or more commonly with current affairs. For example *Thesmophoriazusae* 786–800 **PS** and 830–842 **PS** are both drawn from the play's parabasis, which focuses on the status and treatment of women in Athens.

> **parabasis** a section of a comedy in which the chorus addresses the audience directly, often about contemporary issues, speaking in the voice of the playwright

Comedy and contemporary events

The parabasis was just one way in which comic playwrights could reflect on contemporary events, a key element of comedy. Indeed, Aristophanes' plays centred on public life at

Athens and made fun of contemporary politics and public figures. They could therefore influence the politics of the day, a point reflected by both the Old Oligarch (2.18 **PS**) and Plutarch (*Pericles* 4, 13, 16, 30 **PS**).

The theme of the war with Sparta is never far from the surface of his plays. In *Acharnians*, first presented in 425, the lead character Dicaeopolis makes his own private peace with the Spartans after failing to convince the Athenian assembly to do the same. We have seen that *Knights* satirised Cleon as a demagogue who manipulates the citizen-body of Athens. Perhaps the most famous 'war play' is *Lysistrata*, in which the heroine, an Athenian woman, gathers a group of women from various Greek cities who swear to hold a sex-strike until their husbands agree to stop the war. While this play no doubt raised many laughs, it had a poignant political backdrop: it was written in 411 just after Athens and its allies had lost a huge number of young men in the ill-fated expedition to Sicily – and so the idea of women surviving without men must have been painfully close to reality.

Both *Knights* and *Wasps* are examples of plays which focus on the workings of the democratic system. Another example is *Birds*, presented in 414, in which the main characters are so fed up of political life at Athens that they head off to found their own ideal city in the sky. It was not just politics which was mocked, but other areas of public life too, as in *Clouds*. Aristophanes even enjoyed parodying the theatre itself, and especially tragic playwrights. Euripides was a particular target: he is made fun of in five plays that we know of, and appears as a character in three, including *Thesmophoriazusae*.

Study question

Why do you think that tragedy tended to deal with myth and comedy with contemporary events?

ACTIVITY

In class, act out your prescribed sources from Aristophanes' plays: *Wasps* 891–1008 **PS**; *Knights* 147–395 **PS**; *Clouds* lines 92–118, 365–381, 814–1302 **PS**; *Thesmophoriazusae* 786–800, 830–842 **PS**. How does each source create humour out of contemporary events and public figures?

TOPIC REVIEW

- Explain the differences between tragedy and comedy. Use examples from each type of play to support your answer.
- Outline the events of the City Dionysia.
- Outline the plot of Euripides' *Hippolytus*.
- Discuss how drama festivals were both politically and religiously significant.

Further Reading

Cartledge, P., *Aristophanes and His Theatre of the Absurd* (London: Bloomsbury 1990).

Csapo, Eric and William J. Slater, *The Context of Ancient Drama* (Ann Arbor, MI: University of Michigan Press, 1995).

Goldhill, S., *Reading Greek Tragedy* (Cambridge: Cambridge University Press, 1986).

MacDowell, Douglas M., *Aristophanes and Athens: An Introduction to the Plays* (Oxford: Oxford University Press, 1995).

Mills, Sophie, *Euripides: Hippolytus* (London: Bloomsbury 2002).

Sommerstein, Alan, *Greek Drama and Dramatists* (London: Routledge, 2002).

Storey, Ian C. and Arlene Allan, *A Guide to Ancient Greek Drama* (Chichester: John Wiley and Sons, 2014).
Swift, Laura, *Greek Tragedy* (London: Bloomsbury 2016).
Wiles, D. *Greek Theatre Performance*: *An Introduction* (Cambridge: Cambridge University Press, 2000).
Winkler, J.J., and F. Zeitlin, *Nothing to do with Dionysos?*: *Athenian Drama in its Social Context* (Princeton: Princeton University Press, 1992).

PRACTICE QUESTIONS

1. 'The City Dionysia was more important to Athenians as a political event than a religious event.' To what extent do you agree with this statement? Explain your answer with reference to the sources.

[36]

3.5 Religion and its Significance in the Culture of Athens

TOPIC OVERVIEW

- contemporary attitudes to religion in Athenian society
- nature and significance of religious festivals in the Athenian calendar
- the Panathenaia and its presentation on the Acropolis
- changing ideas about the relationship between men and the divine
- sophists and their views on Athenian religion
- the role and significance of Athena and Poseidon in Athenian religion

The prescribed sources for this topic are:

- Aristophanes, *Clouds*, 365–381; 814–839
- Euripides, *Hippolytus*
- Isocrates 5.117 (Lactor 12, no. 222)
- Plato, *Apology*, 17a–24c, 26b–28a
- Plutarch, *Pericles* 4–6, 13, 16, 32; *Alcibiades* 19, 20.2–4
- The Old Oligarch (Pseudo-Xenophon), *Constitution of the Athenians*, 2.9, 3.1–2
- Thucydides, *The History of the Peloponnesian War*, 2.34–2.46
- Xenophon, *Memorabilia*, 1.1.3 (Lactor 12, no. 258)

- Buildings on the Acropolis and in the Athenian Agora built as part of the Periclean building programme
- The Temple at Sounion

This topic will examine the role and influence that religion had in the culture and society of Athens. It will reflect on the approach of Athenians towards their gods, most notably through festivals such as the Panathenaia. It will also explore how the new thinking of men such as the sophists challenged traditional views of the gods. Finally, it will review the ways in which Athena and Poseidon were of particular importance to the Athenians.

When approaching this topic, it is important to be aware that we have already seen much evidence of the role of religion in the lives of Athenians, and that it infused every aspect of Athenian life.

RELIGION AND THE ATHENIANS

> **polytheism** the worship of many gods
>
> **Olympians** the twelve major gods of Greek religion, who were believed to live on Mount Olympus

The Athenians worshipped the same gods that all other Greeks did. Greek religion was **polytheistic**, in other words it had many gods (in Greek, poly: many, theos: god), and the most important gods were the twelve **Olympians**, who were believed to live on Mount Olympus in northern Greece. However, there were hundreds of others besides, some particular to just one village or region. An advantage of this system was that there were gods for every area of life, as each god had different responsibilities. Therefore, an Athenian could pray to Demeter for a good harvest, to Zeus for rain, to Ares or Athena for help in war, to Poseidon for a safe sea voyage, and to Dionysus for success in a drama competition. It was believed that the gods could be kept on side through appropriate sacrifice and worship.

> **anthropomorphic** giving non-humans the appearance of human beings

Another feature of Greek religion was that the gods were **anthropomorphic**. In other words, they were represented in human form (in Greek, anthrōpos: human being, morphē: shape). There were countless statues of the gods, all of them represented with human bodies. Furthermore, the gods were 'human' in another way too: they had the imperfections of human beings, and could be cruel or kind, helpful or vindictive, while all had their favourites. As we have seen on p. 168, some Greek thinkers were troubled by the presentation of their gods with moral flaws: Plato wanted to ban from his ideal city all poets who portrayed the gods with human weaknesses.

> **chthonic** relating to worship of those gods who were associated with the earth or the Underworld

There was another set of gods who were quite different from the Olympians in nature. These were the **chthonic** gods, who were associated with the earth (in Greek, chthōn meant 'earth'). These gods were generally linked to the Underworld; their most common symbol was the snake, which was believed to be born of the earth. Although some chthonic gods are associated with dark and destructive forces, others are linked with fertility and abundance, since the earth provides food and vegetation. Hades, the god of the Underworld, was the most powerful chthonic god. Other chthonic deities include the Furies, female spirits of vengeance with snakes for hair. The souls of the dead were also worshipped as chthonic beings.

Chthonic worship was different from Olympian worship. Olympians were worshipped in a spirit of rejoicing, but chthonic worship was much more fearful. Isocrates, an Athenian orator, describes the difference as follows:

> In the case of the gods too, those who bring us good are called Olympians, whereas those who control disasters and punishments have less pleasant names. The former have altars and temples dedicated to them by individuals and by cities; the latter are not honoured by prayer or sacrifice – we simply take steps to avert them.
>
> Isocrates, 5.117 (LACTOR 12, 222)

Isocrates is not strictly correct that chthonic deities were not worshipped with sacrifices in their own sanctuaries, as these did exist. However, such sanctuaries would not normally contain temples. Moreover, since chthonic worship was focused on the earth, the priest usually sacrificed an animal over a pit instead of an altar. The animal would then be burnt entirely and no part of it would be eaten, in great contrast to Olympian sacrifice.

The Athenian attitude to religion

The Athenians took their religion very seriously. This showed itself in a number of ways, not least in art and architecture and in the organisation of a large number of festivals throughout the year. Activities which today would not be associated with religion, such as sport and drama, were central to the celebration of the gods. Moreover, religion was tied up with the functioning of the state: for example, a sacrifice was made before every meeting of the assembly, while at the heart of the agora was the Altar of the Twelve gods, dedicated to the Olympians.

Nevertheless, the influence of the sophists also led to a questioning of the role and existence of the gods in Athens, and of the relationship between men and the divine. When Anaxagoras moved there in about 460, he was the first of these thinkers to bring new ideas to this traditionally conservative and pious city. He had a great influence, not least on Pericles, as Plutarch recounts (*Pericles* 4–6, 16 **PS**). Anaxagoras was particularly interested in astronomy, and apparently claimed that the sun was not a god, but a red-hot stone, while the moon was a mass of earth (Plato, *Apology*, 26d **PS**). He also held that there was a key principle of 'nous', or intelligent mind, which created the world as we know it from a primordial mixture.

Protagoras was another sophist who challenged the traditional view of the gods. He is said to have read a treatise on the gods in Euripides' home, which included the following statement of agnosticism:

> Concerning the gods I am unable to know whether they exist or not, nor can I know what they look like; there are many obstacles to knowledge: the obscurity of the subject and the shortness of human life.

DK80 B4

There is evidence for a wide variety of views about the gods amongst intellectuals in Athens. One might contrast, for example, the two great historians, Herodotus and Thucydides. Herodotus takes religion very seriously. In his *Histories*, he actively includes references to the divine, recalling, for example, how the long-distance runner Pheidippides, on his route from Athens to Sparta, saw the god Pan, who asked him why the Athenians paid him so little attention. The Athenians believed the runner's story, and built a temple to Pan under the Acropolis, and held a festival in his honour.

By contrast, Thucydides avoids almost all mention of religion when he writes a generation or so later. In Pericles' funeral oration (2.34–46 **PS**), there is no mention of religion, while in his account of the plague which struck Athens early in the Peloponnesian War, his description of its causes and development are entirely scientific. One might contrast this with the opening of Sophocles' tragedy *Oedipus the King*, probably first presented in the 420s, where the plague in Thebes is believed to have been sent by Apollo, and the Thebans have to consult his oracle at Delphi to understand how to appease the god.

Thucydides also notes critically how the Athenian commander Nicias failed to take action in Sicily because of an eclipse of the moon. He was, according to Thucydides, too given to divination. However, it is clear that such superstitious thinking was not

PRESCRIBED SOURCE

Isocrates

Author: Isocrates, a wealthy Athenian orator

Date: 436–338 BC

Genre: rhetoric

Significance: Isocrates describes how Athenians worship Olympian and chthonic deities

Prescribed Section: 5.117

Read it here: LACTOR 12: *The Culture of Athens* (KCL, 1978) 222

ACTIVITY

Research how the Athenians worshipped each of the Olympian gods through festivals and sacrifice and draw up a table to illustrate this.

EXPLORE FURTHER

Read the following passages: Herodotus, *Histories* 6.105; Thucydides 2,47–55; 6.28; 7.5; Plutarch, *Nicias*, 23–24. What do they suggest about differing Athenian attitudes to religion?

Study questions
Read Euripides' *Hippolytus* **PS**, 1–57 and 1286–end

1 What do these sections of the play suggest about beliefs about the gods in Athenian society?

Read Aristophanes, *Clouds*, 365–381 **PS** and 814–839 **PS**

2 What do these lines suggest about the changing attitudes to religion in Athens? How might the ending of the play affect our interpretation of these lines?

Read Plato, *Apology* 17a–24c **PS**

3 What does this passage tell us about Socrates' religious beliefs?

uncommon in Athenian society. The attacks on Anaxagoras (Plutarch, *Pericles* 32 **PS**) and the charges placed against Alcibiades (Plutarch, *Alcibiades* 19, 20.2–4 **PS**) and Socrates (Plato, *Apology*, 26b–28a **PS**, Xenophon, *Memorabilia* 1.1.3 **PS**) all demonstrate the power which religious matters held in the state and how seriously the Athenians took them.

As we have seen, religious issues are also central to drama. In *Clouds* sceptical questions about the gods are raised directly through the character of Socrates, who suggests that Zeus no longer exists and that rain and thunder come about through processes of nature, rather than by the will of Zeus (365–381 **PS**). At one point, Strepsiades is converted to believe in new gods such as the Clouds (814–839 **PS**). Nevertheless, by the end of the play the character who started by being so enthusiastic about the new ways of seeing the world has very different views, such that he burns down the Thinkery.

Euripides' *Hippolytus* **PS** also raises questions about the nature of the gods. Hippolytus has been a devotee of Artemis all his life, refusing to have any involvement with Aphrodite. Aphrodite outlines her plan for revenge in the prologue (1–57 **PS**). In the end, Artemis watches as her favourite dies, although she does effect a reconciliation between Hippolytus and his father (1283–1461 **PS**). Despite Artemis' love for Hippolytus, she is bound by the rule that deities do not interfere with each other's areas of authority. Each god is entitled to protect his or her honour, and however much you are beloved by one god, it will not help you if you offend another.

This is a traditional feature of Greek polytheism (it is found, for example, in Homer), but it is problematic in that the gods pursue their personal interests, and mortals end up suffering disproportionately to their crimes. Hippolytus' rejection of Aphrodite is dangerously arrogant (a human is in no position to decide which god deserves to be worshipped), but in other ways he is a good man who suffers a horrible fate, and on a human level it is hard to feel that he deserved what happened to him. Euripides thus encourages his audience to reflect upon the cruelty of the traditional view of the gods, and the difficulty of navigating a system where divine wills are in competition with each other.

This period, therefore, is an interesting one: on the one hand there was the committed practice of traditional religion with gods and heroes worshipped, and on the other hand there was a questioning of whether such practices had any meaning. Nonetheless, archaeological remains suggest that religion held a powerful influence. For example, we have seen that the temples constructed as part of the building programme were of the highest quality. If belief in the gods was weak, it is unlikely that the Athenians would have agreed to such expenditure in this form.

RELIGIOUS FESTIVALS IN THE ATHENIAN CALENDAR

As Pericles reflects in his funeral speech (Thucydides 2.38 **PS**), festivals offered the Athenians an opportunity for rest and respite from the challenges of daily life. In a world without weekends this was important, and festivals occurred regularly throughout the year. The Old Oligarch (3.1–2 **PS**) even observed, no doubt with some exaggeration, that there were so many festivals in Athens that it was difficult to get business transacted.

The table below lists Athenian festivals according to twelve-month lunar calendar. All such festivals were dedicated to one (or more than one) deity and, as we have seen with the City Dionysia, such festivals often included a wide range of activities. The Old Oligarch (2.9 **PS**) also makes an important point that the state of Athens put on public festivals so that those citizens who were too poor to pay for their own sacrificial victims can have an opportunity to worship the gods fully.

Athenian Month	Equivalent Months	Festivals
Hecatombaion	July/August	Kronia, Synoikia, Panathenaia
Metageitnion	August/September	Metageitnia, Heracleia at Cynosarges
Boedromion	September/October	Genesia, Artemis Agrotera, Boedromia, Eleusinian Mysteries
Pyanepsion	October/November	Proerosia, Pyanepsia, Theseia, Stenia, Thesmophoria, Chelceia, Apaturia
Maikakterion	November/December	Maimacteria, Pompaea
Poseideon	December/January	Poseidea, Haloa, Rural Dionysia
Gamelion	January/February	Lenaea, Gamelia
Anthesterion	February/March	Anthesteria, Diasia
Elaphebolion	March/April	Elaphebolia, Asclepieia Proagon, City Dionysia, Pandia
Munichion	April/May	Festival of Eros, Procession to Delphinion, Munichia, Olympieia
Thargelion	May/June	Thargelia, Bendidia, Plynteria, Callynteria
Skirophorion	June/July	Skira, Dipoieia, Diisoteria

S & C Research some of the festivals in the list. Which gods were worshipped at them? What events were held during them?

THE PANATHENAIA

The grandest festival of the Athenian year was the **Panathenaia**, which celebrated Athena's birthday in late July or early August. Panathenaia meant 'all-Athenian', and the festival was a chance for all Athenians to come together and worship Athena in her role as the founder and protector of their city. At the heart of the festival was a grand procession to the Acropolis, where many animals were sacrificed and a newly woven robe was presented to the statue of Athena Polias in the Erechtheion. Every four years, the Panathenaia was held on an even grander scale, and known as the **Great Panathenaia**.

Panathenaia a grand civic Athenian festival held every year in honour of Athena

Great Panathenaia a larger version of the Panathenaia held every four years and spread over a number of days

This was spread over a number of days and included a wider range of activities, including athletic, choral, poetic and naval competitions.

Musical competitions

Plutarch (*Pericles* 13 **PS**) tells us that Pericles introduced musical competitions to the Panathenaia, and that they were held in the Odeon. In fact, there had long been musical competitions as well as competitions for men who recited passages of Homer's *Iliad* and *Odyssey* (such men were known as **rhapsodes)**, and so Pericles may have revived them after they had ceased at some point after 480. There were four categories of musical competition:

- singers accompanying the **lyre**
- lyre-players
- singers accompanying the **aulos**
- aulos-players after these competitions

The lyre and the aulos were the two most common Greek musical instruments. The former was a small harp, while the latter was a reed instrument with a double pipe, similar to an oboe. Victors could win an enormous amount of money.

> **rhapsode** a professional reciter of epic poetry

> **lyre** a small harp
>
> **aulos** a reed instrument with a double pipe, similar to an oboe

Sporting events

The Great Panathenaia also saw sporting contests. All the events contested at the great athletic games of ancient Greece, such as the Olympics, were held. These included:

- **Running events**. The most famous of these was the 200 metre sprint, known as the **stadion**.
- **Combat events**. There were three of these: boxing, wrestling and **pankration**, a combination of the two which was really a fight with few rules.
- **The Pentathlon**. This had five events: discus, long jump, javelin, stadion and wrestling.
- **Equestrian events**. These consisted of both horse races and chariot races. There was one equestrian event distinctive to the Panathenaia. This was called the **apobatēs**, and it involved charioteers dismounting from their chariots during the race.

> **stadion** the most important running event, a 200 metre sprint
>
> **pankration** a combat event which was a combination of boxing and wrestling
>
> **pentathlon** a competition consisting of five events: discus, long jump, javelin, stadion and wrestling
>
> **apobatēs** an equestrian event which involved charioteers dismounting from their chariots during the race

Competitors in all events were divided into three classes: boys, beardless youths, and men. Some events were open to all Greeks, not just Athenians.

A victorious athlete at the Panathenaia won a large number of amphorae (jars) full of olive oil; each amphora could typically hold about thirty-eight litres. Many Panathenaic amphorae are well preserved today; on one side of was always an image of Athena with the inscription 'from the games at Athens'; on the other was painted the event in which the victor had competed. A fourth-century inscription gives details of the sporting prizes: the most important event was the chariot race, in which the winning charioteer won 140 amphorae of olive oil.

Tribal contests

The most distinctively Athenian element to the festival's competitions were the tribal contests, four events contested by teams drawn from the city's ten tribes:

- **Euandria**. A competition in 'manly excellence'
- **Boat Race**. A regatta at Piraeus
- **Pyrrhic Dance**. A war dance performed to the aulos.
- **The Torch Race**. A relay race from outside the walls of Athens to the altar beside the Parthenon

Day	Event
1	Rhapsodic and Musical Contests
2	Boys' and Youths' Athletics
3	Men's Athletics
4	Equestrian Events
5	Tribal Contests
6	Procession, Sacrifice
7	apobatēs and boat race
8	Prize-giving

The events of the Great Panathenaia

The Procession

The procession to the Acropolis was the centrepiece of the whole festival. As we have seen, it was probably represented on the Parthenon Frieze, which gives an idea of what was involved. It began at sunrise at the **Dipylon Gate**, one of the main gates of the city (see Figure 3.4 on page 158). It proceeded along a wide street, the **Panathenaic Way**, which led through the agora to the foot of the Acropolis. Young girls who served Athena carried a specially woven robe, the **peplos**, which was to be dedicated to the statue of Athena Polias. They were known as the **Arrēphoroi**. They were also responsible for grinding flour for sacrificial cakes at many other Athenian public sacrifices and lived for a year in a special building on the Acropolis, the Arrēphorion (see Figure 3.6 on p. 181), under the supervision of the priestess of Athena Polias.

Priestesses and other women followed behind, carrying gifts for the goddess. There were many sacrificial animals behind them, since each of Athens' allies had to provide a cow for sacrifice. Behind the animals came wealthy metics dressed in purple cloaks, musicians, old men carrying olive branches, charioteers alongside chariots, soldiers and cavalrymen, as well as victors in the games. The final, longest section of the procession was made up of ordinary Athenians who were organised by deme. Once the procession arrived at the Acropolis, preparations were made for the great sacrifice to Athena. At least a hundred animals were slaughtered. After some of the meat had been offered to the goddess, the rest was taken to the kerameikos district and shared out amongst the people.

Dipylon Gate one of the main entry gates into Athens

Panathenaic Way the wide street leading from the Dipylon Gate to the Acropolis

peplos the newly woven robe dedicated to Athena Polias at the Panathenaia

Arrēphoroi girls aged between seven and eleven who served the cult of Athena Polias on the Acropolis

FIGURE 3.13
A view of the Panathenaic Way looking towards the Acropolis today.

The peplos

One of the key contributions made by women to the festival was the weaving of the peplos, the design of which showed Athena's victory over one of the Giants, Enkelados, in the battle of Gods and Giants. In Euripides' *Hecabe*, the Trojan women lament:

> Perhaps I shall come to live in Athena's city,
> And there on the saffron robe of Pallas [Athena]
> Weaving bright threads in a flowery pattern,
> Yoke the horses to her glorious chariot;
> Or depict the race of raging Titans
> Quelled by Zeus, son of Kronos,
> With the flame of his lighting.

Euripides, *Hecabe,* 465–474

The offering to Athena, and the opportunity to take part in the festival, gave women opportunities to be part of the wider community. The weaving of the peplos was of considerable ritual significance for the Athenians. It stood for the weaving of a first woollen garment, as instructed by Athena. Moreover, the scene depicting the defeat of Enkelados showed the Olympian deities asserting their supremacy over the forces of disorder.

Study questions

1 Compare the Panathenaia with a modern national or regional festival: what are the main similarities and differences?
2 In how many different ways was Athena honoured during the Panathenaia?

FIGURE 3.14
A scene from the Parthenon frieze in which a child holds up the peplos for an adult, perhaps a magistrate.

THE ROLE AND SIGNIFICANCE OF ATHENA AND POSEIDON IN ATHENIAN RELIGION

At the heart of Athenian culture in the fifth century were two key considerations: an enthusiasm for intelligence, both military and intellectual, and a naval empire. These two ideas are reflected in the two deities which were of particular importance to the Athenians: Athena and Poseidon. We have read much about these two deities, and how they appear in Athenian literature and art. Use the study question to the right to review the evidence, and to consider how the worship of these two deities shows itself in numerous areas of Athenian life.

Study question
What can each of the following tell us about the role and significance of Athena and/or Poseidon in Athenian religion:
- The Erechtheion
- The Temple of Athena Nike
- The Parthenon frieze and pedimental sculpture
- The Temple at Sounion
- Euripides, *Hippolytus*, 790–end **PS**
- The Panathenaia

TOPIC REVIEW

- Outline the ways in which religion was significant in the daily lives of Athenians, and give a source for each.
- Evaluate how the events of the City Dionysia and the Panathenaia compare, and whether one has a more religious flavour to it than the other.
- Assess how much evidence there is for a change in attitudes towards the gods by Athenians during the fifth century.
- Explain why Athena and Poseidon were particularly significant for Athenians, and how this is reflected in the historical record.

Further Reading

Boedeker, D., 'Athenian Religion in the Age of Pericles', in J.J. Samons., *The Cambridge Companion to the Age of Pericles* (Cambridge: Cambridge University Press, 2007).

Dowden, Ken, 'Olympian Gods, Olympian Pantheon' in D. Ogden, *A Companion to Greek Religion* (Malden: Wiley-Blackwell, 2007).

Hornblower, S., 'The Religious Dimension to the Peloponnesian War, or, What Thucydides Does Not Tell Us', *HSCP,* Vol. 94 (1992), pp. 169–97.

Lefkowitz, M., *Greek Gods, Human Lives* (New Haven: Yale University Press, 2003), chapters 5 and 6.

Mikalson, Jon, *Ancient Greek Religion* (Malden: Wiley-Blackwell, 2009).

Neils, J., *Goddess and the Polis* (Princeton: Princeton University Press, 1993).

Parker, R., *On Greek Religion* (Ithaca: Cornell University Press, 2011).

Parker, R., *Polytheism and Society at Athens* (Oxford: Oxford University Press, 2007).

Sourvinou-Inwood, C., *Tragedy and Athenian Religion* (Lanham MD: Lexington Books, 2003).

PRACTICE QUESTIONS

Read Pausanias *Description of Greece* 1.24.5,7 **PS** and look at images of:

- the temple of Sounion
- the centre of the west pediment of the Parthenon

1. How useful are these sources for our understanding of the role and importance of the worship of Athena and Poseidon to Athenians of the late fifth century? [12]

DEPTH STUDY 3
The Rise of Macedon, 359–323 BC

Introduction to the Rise of Macedon, 359–323 BC

This Depth Study focuses on the interplay of political, military, social, economic, cultural and religious factors that contributed to the rapid rise to pre-eminence of Macedonia from *c.* 359 BC. The initial focus on Philip helps to contextualise the campaigns of Alexander, his son and heir. Learners will gain insight into the factors and beliefs that motivated two of the most renowned men in ancient history.

The topics in this depth study are all interrelated, and learners are encouraged to see the connections between them in order to deepen their understanding of the period.

EXAM OVERVIEW   **H407/13 SECTION B**

Your examination for Macedon, in Section B of your paper, will require you to show knowledge and understanding of the material you have studied. This component is worth 48 marks – 12 based on AO1 skills, 12 on AO2, and 24 on AO3.

In this section, you will answer two questions:

- a 12-mark stimulus question focusing on an issue relating to a historical event or situation, where you will need to assess the source's utility;
- one of two essay questions, each worth 36 marks. The questions will require you to use, analyse, and evaluate source material to address issues in the question. The essays will target one or more of the themes listed.

4.1 The Growth in Macedonian Power and the Role of Philip in that Process

TOPIC OVERVIEW

- Philip's opportunism and diplomacy
- military reorganisation, practices, technology and advantages
- Philip's court and patronage
- the expansion of Macedon
- organising and securing an expanding Macedonia
- Philip's marriages
- the Peace of Philocrates and a potential common peace
- Philip's influence on Greek institutions
- the expeditions into Thrace and Greece
- the significance of the sieges at Perinthus and Byzantium, including the roles of Athens and Persia
- the Battle of Chaeronea, including its causes and aftermath
- the creation of the League of Corinth
- election as hegemon

The prescribed sources for this topic are:

- Demosthenes, *Speeches*, 2.6–8; 2.15–20; 5.20–25; 8.5–8, 8.11–15; 9.7–12; 9.32–35; 19.39–41
- Diodorus Siculus, *Library of History*, Book 16: 1–4, 7.3, 8, 34.3–5, 35, 38.1–2, 52.1–3, 53–55, 58.1–3, 59–60, 71, 72.1, 74–77.1–2, 84–86, 88–89, and 91–92
- Justin, *Epitome*, 8.1–6 and 9.4–5

Everyone has heard of Alexander the Great, but his father, Philip II of Macedon, deserves just as much attention. Not only did he change the course of Greek history he made all that Alexander achieved possible. Born in 382, Philip came to the throne of Macedon at the age of twenty-three. During his kingship from 359 until his assassination in 336, Philip set about restoring Macedon to its former might and wealth and transformed its military capability. He expanded its power so that might take on the **Achaemenid** Empire. He subdued the Greek city-states, which never regained their independence again. The result was that Philip created a superpower, the most formidable state this part of the world had ever seen.

> **Achaemenid** the royal dynasty of Persia

THE SOURCES

Before we study the evidence, we need to consider the nature of the sources and their reliability.

Diodorus Siculus

You have already encountered Diodorus in the Greek Period Study. You will recall that he was a historian, known for writing the monumental *Library of* History between 60 and 30 BC. Only parts of this larger work are extant, although the sections covering the rise of Macedon survive intact. Little is known about his life but he was alive during the rise of Rome under Octavian/Augustus. It seems fitting that Diodorus was writing about the rise of another power, Macedon, albeit many years earlier. His comments about the purpose of the historian in book 16.1 **PS** are helpful in terms of appreciating his own approach to history. As already mentioned, a fundamental aim was to illustrate moral lessons from history. Given Diodorus was writing in the first century BC, his account is to be regarded very much as a secondary source.

Demosthenes

Further details about Philip's reign can be found in the speeches of Athenian statesman and orator Demosthenes. Philip was a central figure in many of his works. The advantage of Demosthenes is that he was writing his speeches at the time of the events. Demosthenes lived *c*. 384–322. The disadvantage is that Demosthenes' writing is particularly one-sided against Philip. Demosthenes' counterpart in Athens, an orator called Aeschines, referred to Demosthenes as a 'Philip-hater'. Demosthenes devoted his most productive years to opposing Macedon's expansion. He idealised his city of Athens and strove to restore Athens' supremacy and he urged his fellow citizens to stop Philip. Since his speeches were never intended to be historical material, they must be treated with some circumspection.

> **KEY INDIVIDUAL**
>
> **Aeschines**
> **Dates:** 389–314
>
> an Athenian orator, statesman, contemporary and opponent of Demosthenes

Justin

Justin was a Roman historian, writing in Latin, who lived under the Roman Empire, probably around the second century AD. Almost nothing is known about Justin's life beyond work which survives. He was the author of an **epitome** of Trogus's *Philippic Histories*, an older work which was compiled during the reign of Augustus. Justin's preface explains that he aimed to collect the most important and interesting passages of that work. The main theme of Trogus's work which is now lost was the rise and history of the Macedonian Empire. Justin permitted himself considerable licence to embellish events, and there is therefore some scepticism about how much reliance can be placed on this author.

> **epitome** an abbreviation or summary of a piece of work

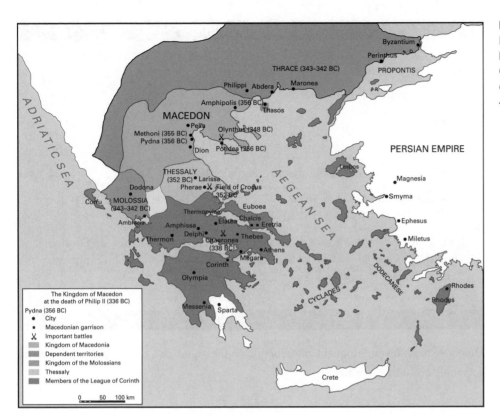

FIGURE 4.1
Map showing the political boundaries of Macedon, Greece and Persia on the death of Philip II in 336 BC.

FIGURE 4.2
Map showing Macedon and her near neighbours between 431 and 336.

PRESCRIBED SOURCE

Title: *Library of History*

Author: Diodorus Siculus

Date: first century AD

Genre: history

Significance: Diodorus is our main source for Philip

Prescribed sections: Book 16: 1–4, 7.3, 8, 22.3, 34.3–5, 35, 38.1–2, 52.1–3, 53–55, 58.1–3, 59–60, 71–72.1, 74–77.1–2, 84–89, and 91–92

Read it here: *Diodorus Siculus: Library of History*, Vols VII (trans. C. L. Sherman) and VIII (trans. C. B. Wells) (Loeb Classical Library 389 and 422; Cambridge MA: Harvard University Press, 1952 and 1963)

Diodorus provides an eloquent introduction to the significance of Philip and what he accomplished during his life.

PHILIP'S OPPORTUNISM AND DIPLOMACY

Many of Philip's skills were acquired during his youth. He had been held as a **hostage** in Thebes which was then the leading city of Greece. While a captive there, Philip received a philosophical, military and diplomatic education in the house of Pammenes, a renowned Theban general. He also spent time observing Epaminondas, another great Theban general and friend of Pammenes. This valuable training is outlined by Diodorus.

When Philip came to the throne in 359, the Macedonians were in some difficulties. They had fought a costly war with the Illyrians. Macedon was also under considerable threat from the neighbouring Paeonians and the Thracians. Look at Figure 4.2 to appreciate the proximity of these territories to Macedon. Athens too was openly hostile. Athens planned to depose Philip and put Argaeus on the throne instead. The Athenians dispatched 3,000 Athenians hoplites to Methone (Figure 4.1) for they were keen to recover Amphipolis (Figure 4.1) in Thrace. Philip turned all these problems into opportunities.

After Aegaeus' failed attempt to take Aegae and on his retreat to Methone, he was murdered. He may have been captured and executed for treason, or he may have been killed by Philip in the fighting that ensued between Macedonians and Athenians (sometimes called 'the Battle of Methone') where many Athenian troops and mercenaries were also slaughtered.

At that time, Philip relied on diplomacy to confront the challenge posed by Athens. He immediately released the Athenian prisoners he had taken during the Battle of Methone. He also withdrew from Amphipolis and declared it autonomous. Having sent ambassadors to Athens, Philip then persuaded the assembly to make peace on the grounds

hostage a captive held for money and/or political leverage. The practice of taking high-profile figures captive was relatively common in the ancient world. According to Diodorus, Philip was initially taken by the Illyrians and then sent to Thebes

KEY INDIVIDUAL

Argaeus
Dates: fourth century

A pretender to the Macedonian crown. With the assistance of the Illyrians, he had already ruled in Macedon for about a year in 393. In 359, he persuaded the Athenians to support his claim to the Macedonian throne in place of Philip.

KEY PLACES

Athens: city in central Greece and the capital of an empire. Athens had enormous power and influence in Greece and key interests in the north Aegean and Chersonese

Amphipolis: an important city in Thrace with a commanding position, controlling the river Strymon and the road from Macedon to Thrace (see the Period Study). The Athenians had founded Amphipolis but in the 420s it fell to the Spartans. Since its loss, Athens had longed to get it back and much of Athenian policy in relation to Philip was based on this aim

Aegae: ancient capital city of Macedon

MODERN PARALLEL

Compare Philip and Hitler (in the 1930s) in terms of this mix of diplomacy and opportunism.

Study question

Read Diodorus, 16.3–4.

How is Philip presented here?

KEY INDIVIDUAL

Theopompus
Dates: *c.* 380–*c.* 315
A Greek historian and rhetorician

KEY EVENT

Social War: 357–355 between Athens and the allied city states of Chios, Rhodes, Cos and Byzantium. These city states had been provoked by Athens' increasingly dominating stance during its Second Athenian Empire. It is referred to in Diodorus, 16.7.3.

KEY PLACE

Pydna: a key port on the Themaic Gulf and a strategic place for exporting timber

Study question

Read Diodorus 16.7.3.

What does Diodorus write here to suggest that that Social War was a difficult one for Athens?

he had forfeited any claim to Amphipolis. Philip, moreover, decided to make peace with the Paeonians and the Thracians through use of gifts and generous promises.

However, behind the diplomacy was a rather more aggressive agenda. During the break from hostilities with Athens, and upon hearing the king of the Paeonians had died, Philip seized the moment to attack the Paeonians. In addition, he led an expedition into Illyrian territory and defeated them. As a result, Philip secured Illyrian withdrawal from all Macedonian cities. This dazzling mix of diplomacy, military skill and opportunism is set out in Diodorus, 16.3–4 **PS**. Such actions were certainly boosting the confidence of Philip's Macedonians.

At this point in his narrative, Diodorus refers to another much older historian called Theopompus of Chios who wrote a history of Philip. It is likely that Diodorus relied on his history. It would be interesting if he did since Theopompus was writing his history of Philip during the fourth century BC, so much closer to the actual events. Theopompus even spent some time at the court of Philip. Although he disliked Philip for his immorality, Theopompus, considered him the greatest man of his time. Diodorus may well have been influenced by such an agenda.

Further displays of opportunism on the part of Philip can be witnessed two years later in 357. It was then that Athens became heavily involved in the Social War which lasted three years. Philip chose this moment to lay siege to Amphipolis, which he had not long before promised would be left autonomous, and he successfully conquered it.

In the same year as Amphipolis, Philip also took Pydna, which had previously been controlled by Athens (Figure 4.1). He then made an alliance with Olynthus (Figure 4.1). This was a large and strategically placed city which anyone hoping to gain supremacy in the area would want to control. This alliance again brought Philip into an immediate rivalry with Athens. Philip involved himself in much subtle diplomacy at this point. He agreed with the Olynthians to conquer Potidaea (Figure 4.2), a place where the Athenians actually had a garrison, and to give it to Olynthus. At the same time, he treated the Athenian garrison in Potidaea well and sent it safely back to Athens.

Diodorus Siculus paints a relatively positive picture of Philip's opportunism and diplomacy. However, there is another version of Philip's actions during this time. Another

Study questions PS
Read Diodorus, 16.8 on Amphipolis, Pydna and Olynthus.

How might the events in 16.8.1–5 assist with the increase of Macedon's power?

S & C
Investigate the role of public speaking in classical Greece and some of the rhetorical devices employed by ancient orators.

Study questions PS
Read Demosthenes, 2.6–7.

1 What can this source tell us about Philip's actions?
2 How does his narrative compare with Diodorus' account?
3 What are the strengths and limitations of each in terms of reliability?

PRESCRIBED SOURCE

Title: *Speeches*

Author: Demosthenes

Date: 384–322

Genre: oratory

Significance: a source produced at the time of Philip

Prescribed sections: 2.6–8; 2.15–20; 5.20–25; 8.5–8, 8.11–15; 9.7–12; 9.32–35; 19.39–41

Read it here: *Demosthenes: Orations*, Vols I (trans. J. H. Vince) and II (trans. C. A. Vince and J. H. Vince) (Loeb Classical Library 238 and 155; Cambridge MA: Harvard University Press, 1930 and 1926)

---

very useful collection of sources for the rise of Macedon are the texts of Demosthenes. Demosthenes's evidence comprises oratory a very different genre to history. His speeches were designed to persuade and convince in the most immediate way and in the strongest possible terms. He dedicated much of his life to a campaign to try to curb the (as he saw it) dangerous and amoral ambitions of Philip.

MILITARY REORGANISATION, PRACTICES, TECHNOLOGY AND ADVANTAGES

As soon as Philip came to the throne in 359 he instigated a programme of military reforms. Diodorus attests to Philip's swift action on this front:

> . . . and having improved the organization of his forces and equipped the men suitably with weapons of war, he held constant maneoeuvres of the men under arms and competitive drills.

Diodorus, *Library of History* 16.3

Philip re-trained the army, which was already battle-hardened, and gradually accumulated a supply of ready money to pay for more troops. He also benefited from the innovations started by his predecessor Alexander II (see Figure 4.3) and built on them, including the reform of the infantry. In particular, this involved the introduction of the Macedonian phalanx, a tightly compact corps with overlapping shields, which Diodorus describes in Book 16.3. The phalanx was far more flexible than the older infantry. Philip made it deeper and he also equipped them with light-weight armour and a **sarissa**. He also reinforced the **hypaspists**, a corps of elite shield-carrying shock-troops. Many of these ideas Philip may have witnessed being experimented with by Epaminondas in Thebes.

sarissa a pike, longer even than a spear, that had to be wielded with both hands

hypaspists shield bearers and an elite infantry force

Philip also developed siege equipment which he would use later in his military career in places like Amphipolis and Perinthus (see below). During the siege in Perinthus in 340, the Macedonians used a tower that was thirty meters high and an artillery of catapults with groups of engineers to offer expertise. Philip created or reorganised other units. There were light-armed spearmen and Cretan archers and Agrianes, very light troops, often used in the mountains. The result was Greece's first professional army: large, well-trained, heavily armed, fast, and practically invincible.

PHILIP'S COURT AND PATRONAGE

The long-standing system of government Philip inherited when he acceded to the throne was an autocratic monarchy (the Argead dynasty – see Figure 4.3). Macedon had been a monarchy since the beginnings of its history, one that was very much modelled on Homeric kingship. Herodotus provides a list of Macedonian kings stretching back to mythical times.

Modern scholars think that Philip copied several Persian practices in his court. Like the Persian king, Philip ensured that he had the money to buy whatever he needed. It is thought, he also established a new layer of aristocracy loyal to him. For example, the

KEY PEOPLE

Agrianes

A subject tribe of the Paeonians, expert in the javelin. They often fought alongside the hypaspists

KEY INDIVIDUAL

Herodotus
Dates: *c.* 484–*c.* 425

Greek author who wrote the *Histories* (see the Period Study).

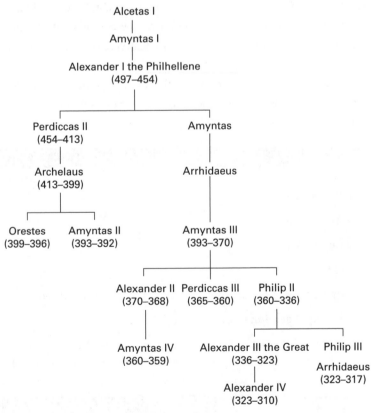

FIGURE 4.3
The Argead dynasty.

companions in Greek 'hetairoi'. A court inner-circle of elites, not unlike the Prussian *Junker* class

sons of the noblemen were given an education at court. He also distributed land and military offices and built up a new inner–circle called the '**companions**'. We witnessed a glimpse of Philip's approach in Diodorus' account about the siege of Methone:

> Philip then razed the city and distributed its territory among the Macedonians.
>
> Diodorus, *Library of History* 16.34.5 **PS**

Diodorus is broadly favourable in his depiction of Philip. However, we do have a very different interpretation of Philip's court presented to us by Demosthenes. In *Speeches* 2.19 Demosthenes wrote the following:

> All the rest about his court, he said, are robbers and toadies, men capable of getting drunk and performing such dances as I hesitate to name to you here. This report is obviously true, for the men who were unanimously expelled from Athens, as being of far looser morals than the average mountebank – I mean Callias the hangman and fellows of that stamp, low comedians, men who compose ribald songs to raise a laugh against their boon companions – these are the men he [Philip] welcomes and loves to have about him. **PS**
>
> Demosthenes, *Speeches* 2.19

Philip also extended patronage at court to non-Macedonians. Diodorus describes how Philip gave sanctuary to two men who had important dealings in Persia. One was Artabazus, a Persian satrap who had rebelled against the Persian king (then Artaxerxes III). The other was the Greek Memnon who had served as a mercenary soldier in Persia and had agreed to lead Artabazus' army in the revolt. When in 354 Artabazus and Memnon were unable to make headway against Artaxerxes, they fled to Macedonia. Philip welcomed them and invited them to stay as long as they liked.

There exists another author who charts the activities of Philip, namely, Justin. His accounts of Philip are almost uniformly negative. For example, Justin comments on how Philip used his court to lure and manipulate men for his own political purposes. He describes one such episode involving the nurturing of Olympias' brother Alexander with the prime aim of subsequently sending him to Epirus in order to replace the then king of Epirus, Arrybas, Olympias' uncle.

Study questions **PS**
Read Demosthenes, 2.15–20.

1 What is suggested about Philip and his court?
2 What aspects of his narrative might cause you to question whether we can place full reliance on the information provided by Demosthenes?

Study question
Read Diodorus, 16.52.1–3.

Why do you suppose Philip was so willing to provide a safe haven to these men at his court?

Study questions
Read Justin, *Epitome*, 8.6.

1 How does Justin depict Philip in this passage?
2 How credible do you find it as evidence?

PRESCRIBED SOURCE

Title: *Epitome*

Author: Justin

Date: *c.* second century AD

Genre: history

Significance: it constitutes one of a few sources for Philip

Prescribed sections: 8.1–6; 9.4–5

Read it here: *Marcus Junianus Justinus: Epitome of the Philippic History of Pompeius Trogus*, trans. J. S. Watson (London: Henry G. Bohm, 1853)

THE EXPANSION OF MACEDON

Once Philip had secured his reign and country's immediate borders, he could turn to the business of expanding his territory and influence. We have already seen how Philip's military skills and expansionist vision of Macedonian greatness brought him early success. In the north, Philip had taken control of Amphipolis, Pydna, Potidea and Crenides (see below). There was another victory again in the north with the siege of Methone (not to be confused with the Battle of Methone discussed earlier). Philip started besieging Methone, the last Athenian possession in that part of the north, sometime between 355 and 353. The siege lasted for about a year and Philip was to lose an eye during the siege when he was hit by an arrow.

Philip would surely have been pleased that the siege ended when it did, for by then he was keen to turn his attentions to Greece. At that point, Thessaly and Thebes (Figure 4.2) were involved in a war with Phocis, the Third Sacred War. This messy conflict had started some years earlier in 356. It started because the Phocians had refused to pay a fine imposed on them by the **Amphictyonic League** on account of the Phocian's illegal cultivation of sacred land.

The Phocians could not afford to pay the fine imposed on them and so advocated a pre-emptive policy of seizing the site of Delphi itself. Under the general Philomelus they also plundered the shrine to cover the costs of war. Onomarchos, Philomelus' brother, then succeeded him. This was too much for the members of the Amphyctionic League who declared a 'Sacred War' on the Phocians.

It appears that Philip may have used the distraction of the Sacred War to increase his own power in northern Greece. Justin, in his typically sardonic style, makes reference to the earliest stage of this Sacred War.

There were several stages of this war, but we encounter it again in your prescribed sources in around 354. Philip had received a summons to help Thessaly resolve a long-standing internal struggle and defeat one of its feudal states, Pherae, which had allied itself with the Phocians. Pherae had requested assistance from the Phocians, and Onomarchos dispatched Phallyos with 7,000 men. Philip got involved and repelled this force before it could join up with the Pheraeans. This period is alluded to by Justin in his *Epitome*.

What resulted was a much more robust response from the Phocians. Onomarchos brought his whole force into Thessaly to attack Philip. It is possible that Onomarchos hoped to conquer Thessaly in the process. The exact details of the campaign that followed are unclear, but Onomarchos inflicted two defeats on Philip, and there were heavy Macedonian losses. After these defeats, Philip retreated to Macedon for the winter in order to take some time to boost the morale of his men. Diodorus outlines all these events. He also describes how Philip then returned to Thessaly and re-mustered a large force (16.35).

What followed has been called the Battle of Crocus Field. This was a very bloody battle that took place on a large plain by the sea. The Macedonians and Thessalians were victorious, many Phocians were killed and, according to Diodorus, Onomarchus was hanged (although according to Diodorus elsewhere (16.16.1), Onomarchos was cut to pieces in battle and crucified).

Study question
Read Diodorus, 16.34.3–5.

What does Diodorus emphasise in his account of the siege of Methone?

KEY EVENT

Third Sacred War
Dates: 356–346

Conflict between the forces of the Delphic Amphictyonic League, principally represented by Thebes (and latterly by Philip II of Macedon) and the Phocians. Although the Phocians suffered several major defeats, they were able to continue the war for many years.

Amphictyonic League a pan-Hellenic, religious organisation which governed the most sacred site in Ancient Greece, the Temple of Apollo at Delphi. Thessaly had at one time been the dominant force in this League, but more recently Thebes had supremacy

---

Study questions
Read Justin, *Epitome*, 8.1–2.

1 What does Justin suggest about the state of Greece at the time of Philip?
2 What, according to Justin, were the causes and nature of the war?

Study questions
Read Justin, 8.4–5.

1 How does he present the Greek city-states relationship with Macedon?
2 How accurate do you think his version of accounts is here?

---

archōn a ruler

Study question
Read Diodorus, 16.35.

Why do you think Philip considered the Phocians to be 'temple robbers'?

Study questions
Read Diodorus, 16.8.6–7.

1 What difference did the money from the mines make?
2 Why do you think Philip changed the name of 'Crenides' to 'Philippi'?

Study question
Read Diodorus, 16.53–54.

What does Diodorus indicate about the precise purposes of Philip's expansionism at this point?

Study questions
Read Diodorus 16.38.1–2

1 What is interesting about the way Diodorus describes what Philip did at Pherae?
2 Why do you think the Athenians were so keen to stop Philip at Thermopylae?

This battle was of immense significance. It earned Philip considerable prestige, and it was probably in the aftermath of his victory that the Thessalians appointed Philip **archōn** of Thessaly. It gave Philip control over all the revenues of the Thessaly, and furthermore made Philip leader of the united Thessalian army.

An interesting move then came with Philip's subsequent march south in 352 to the pass of Thermopylae (Figure 4.1), the gateway to central Greece. He was intending to follow up his victory over the Phocians by invading Phocis itself. However, the Athenians swiftly dispatched a force to Thermopylae and occupied the pass.

ORGANISING AND SECURING AN EXPANDING MACEDONIA

To support his expansionist projects, Philip needed to ensure he had necessary funds. As a result, he often targeted towns which were rich in natural resources, such as mines. One example of this was earlier in 356 when Philip took charge of Crenides and established a powerful garrison there to control its mines.

By 349, Philip was involved in a full expansionist policy that would see the reduction of the Chalchidic peninsula. A number of towns had already fallen to him in that region but Philip then directed his attentions to its dominant city, Olynthus (Figure 4.1). In 357, Olynthus had been in alliance with Philip (see his policy concerning Potidaea earlier), but subsequently, concerned by the growth of his power, it had allied itself to Athens. Philip besieged Olynthus in 348. Unsurprisingly, this caused great upset in Athens and the Athenians were deeply concerned about the consequences. Athens sent military assistance but it arrived too late. Since the city was betrayed from within, the siege was short and Olynthus fell quickly to Philip. Diodorus provides an account of Philip's attack on Olynthus.

When Olynthus was being threatened by Philip it had sent three embassies to Athens. These occasioned Demosthenes' three 'Olynthiac orations'. It was these speeches that finally persuaded Athens to send help to Olynthus (albeit too late). An extract from Demosthenes' second Olynthiac speech is one of your prescribed sources. It was quoted briefly earlier, but you should now read it in full. Another depiction of Philip at Olynthus is provided by Justin.

For Philip, securing his political influence in Greece was as important as acquiring territory. Ongoing hostilities with the Phocians brought Philip down into Greece once again in 346/5. Phocis had effectively divided the allegiances of various city-states

Study questions
Read Demosthenes, 2.6–8.

1 What is Demosthenes' view of Philip?
2 How does this passage compare with Diodorus' account of Olynthus?

Study question
Read Justin, 8.3.

How does Justin present Philip's actions just prior to Olynthus during the siege?

Study question
Read Diodorus 16.59.

What aspects of Diodorus' references to Philip might be significant here?

throughout Greece. Phocis was supported by Athens and Sparta. On the other hand, the Thessalians and the Thebans opposed it. The Thebans requested Philip's assistance against the Phocians once again. Diodorus provides an account of how Philip with his army passed through Thermopylae. He then describes how Philip completely intimidated the Phocians and their mercenaries under the Phocian general, Phalaecus, and how Philip finally brought the Sacred War to a conclusion. This was a direct catalyst for the Peace of Philcocrates. The ultimate result of all this was that Philip became a major player in the Amphictyonic Council.

KEY INDIVIDUAL

Phalaecus
Dates: fourth century BC

Son of Onomarchus, a Phocian general

PHILIP'S MARRIAGES

It is thought that Philip entered into seven marriages during his lifetime. It is almost certain that except for his final marriage, every woman in his life served a political aim. His wives are listed here in order of marriage, although the marriage status of some (especially the two Thessalians) is questioned. The order as set out here is also contested.

1. Audata, the daughter or granddaughter of the Illyrian king Bardyllis
2. Phila of Elimeia
3. Nicesipolis of Pherae
4. Olympias of Epirus, mother of Alexander the Great
5. Philinna of Larissa, mother of Arrhidaeus later called Philip III of Macedon
6. Meda of Odessos, daughter of the king of Thrace
7. Cleopatra (Eurydice), niece of general Attalus of Macedonia

ACTIVITY

Read Diodorus 16.72.1 and Justin, *Epitome*, 8.6. Compare the way these two authors describe the same event.

Although Philip had married Audata, daughter (or granddaughter) of the Illyrian king, this did not prevent him from marching against the Illyrians in 358 and crushing them in battle.

One of the most significant marriages was Philip's to Olympias. She would provide Philip with his son and ultimate heir, Alexander, in 356. Olympias was the daughter of the king of the Molossians, a tribal state of Epirus that was located between the Greeks, Macedonians, and Illyrians. The marriage usefully helped secure Macedon's western border. It also proved useful for propelling a new king, Olympias' brother, into Epirus some years later. Two of your sources discuss this.

THE PEACE OF PHILOCRATES AND A POTENTIAL COMMON PEACE

After Olynthus and many towns on that peninsula fell to Philip, and once Athens realised that Themopylae and some of its key mainland allies, including Halos, could no longer be defended, they decided to negotiate a peace treaty with Philip. The situation was so bleak that even Demosthenes favoured the compromise. In 346, an Athenian delegation of ten men, including Demosthenes, Aeschines and Philocrates, was sent to Pella to negotiate terms. The negotiations were protracted and continued even when the delegation returned to Athens. During a second subsequent delegation to Macedon, Philip was away and it took a frustrating amount of time to get the Macedonian leader to sign up to the final agreement.

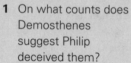

Study questions
Read Demosthenes, 19.39–41.

1 On what counts does Demosthenes suggest Philip deceived them?
2 How might the disagreements in Athens have played to Philip's advantage?

Finally, Philip ratified the 'Peace of Philocrates'. It did little more than reinforce the status quo, for example, Philip's claim to Amphipolis. The peace, moreover, was a decidedly fragile one, with Philip on the face of it trying to maintain the peace and Athens trying to undermine it. Many questioned the sincerity of Philip's assurances that he made to Athens.

Even the architects of the peace treaty themselves were divided about what the agreement meant. Aeschines was optimistic about the agreement and had hoped that the it would, in essence, represent an alliance. Demosthenes, although he deeply distrusted Philip, supported the peace but only because he understood the terribly vulnerable position Athens was currently in. Almost as soon as it was made, Demosthenes repented of it. Over the next few years, Demosthenes became leader of the 'hawks' in Athens, and at every opportunity he sought to call into question the peace. Athenian politics was riven by in-fighting as Demosthenes accused his fellow envoy, Aeschines, of 'selling-out' to Philip. A long judicial conflict ensued between these two men, both of them making speeches against each other. In 343 Demosthenes wrote and delivered his speech *On the False Embassy* 19.39–41 **PS**. Demosthenes accused Aeschines of being bribed by Philip and misleading the Athenian people.

PHILIP'S INFLUENCE ON GREEK INSTITUTIONS

After Philip successfully subdued Phocis and brought the Sacred War to a close, and around the time that the Peace of Philocrates was being negotiated, he gained considerable influence in an important Greek institution, the Amphictyonic Council of the Amphictyonic League. This Council exerted its power through a voting system and Macedon was now awarded the votes that Phocis had formerly exercised. The Council made other decrees, too, concerning the sanctuary of Delphi which Philip helped formulate. Yet more significantly, Philip was accepted as a Greek by being appointed to organise the Pythian games at Delphi. Diodorus' account contains details of these.

The Athenians were not present at the meeting that voted for Philip's election into the Council. Many Athenians opposed Philip's election, in such a way that the Peace of Philocrates was almost completely suppressed. Yet Athens finally legitimised Philip's entrance into the Council. Again, Demosthenes followed a pragmatic approach and he was among those who recommended affirmation of Philip's election to the Amphyctionic Council in his speech *On the Peace*.

Philip had an important impact on the Greek institution of athletic festivals. He was acutely sensitive to the value of high-profile contests of athleticism and displays of sporting prowess. He himself participated in Olympic games. In the year of Alexander's birth, Plutarch (*Life of Alexander*, chapter 3) reports that Philip also received news that he had secured a victory in the horse race at the Olympic games. After settling the Sacred War in 346, Philip presided over the Pythian games. He also established the Philipeion, the first temple structure at Olympia and the site of the Olympic games, to be named after a mortal benefactor. Philip was assassinated whilst celebrating his daughter's marriage with another Olympic festival.

PHILIP'S EXPEDITIONS INTO THRACE

In 343/2 Philip turned his military activities toward Thrace. This was partly to stop incursions being made by the king of Thrace, Cersobleptes, into neighbouring territories on the Chersonese (Figure 4.4). The war in Thrace lasted for about three years, and was one of Philip's most difficult campaigns. The details in the ancient sources are few – Diodorus, 16.71 **PS** provides one account – but we learn that Philip eventually overcame the Thracians in battle. A tax was levied on the Thracians, and Philip founded several strong cities in the region as a way to prevent further trouble in the future. Considering the difficult terrain and severe winter conditions, some modern scholars classify this Thracian campaign as one of Philip's major achievements.

It is in the context both of the Peace of Philocrates and Philip's expedition into Thrace that we should read Demosthenes' speeches *On the Chersonese* and his *Third Philippic*. When the Macedonian army approached the Chersonese on their Thracian expedition, the Athenians became very anxious. This disquiet was articulated particularly by Demosthenes, who now used it as an opportunity to renew his hostile stance against

---

ACTIVITY **PS**

Read Diodorus 16.60.

- Make a list of all the decrees that were passed.

Study question

How did Philip's involvement in this Council improve his and Macedon's position?

Study questions

Read Demosthenes, **PS** 5.20–25 delivered in support of Philip's election into the Amphictyonic Council.

1 What does Demosthenes emphasise about Philip in these extracts?
2 How does what Demosthenes write here compare with Diodorus, 16.60?

FIGURE 4.4

Map showing the area between Macedon and the Chersonese.

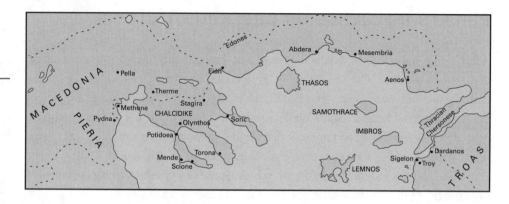

Study questions

Read Demosthenes, 8.5–8 and 11–15.

1 How does Demosthenes view Philip's invasion of Thrace?
2 What does he warn of?
3 How reliable a source is this speech?

Read Demosthenes 9.7–12 and 9.32–35.

4 How does Demosthenes interpret Philip's treatment of their peace treaty?
5 What arguments does he use to persuade the Athenians to stop Philip?

Philip. At Demosthenes' bidding, an Athenian general, Diopeithes, was sent to the Chersonese where he ravaged the maritime district of Thrace. This incensed Philip who sent a letter of censure to Athens which demanded the immediate withdrawal of the Athenian troops from Cardia which was occupied by the Macedonian army.

THE SIGNIFICANCE OF THE SIEGES AT PERINTHUS AND BYZANTIUM, INCLUDING THE ROLES OF ATHENS AND PERSIA

Study question

Read Diodorus 16.74.

How does Diodorus portray Philip's siege?

Philip's aggression did not stop there. In 341/340 Philip started to besiege Perinthus and Byzantium (Figure 4.1). These were coastal towns near the Black Sea, opposite to and just north of the borders of the Persian Empire. Such sites were strategically important because of the control they afforded over the sea passages from the Mediterranean to the Black Sea and from Europe to Asia. Sources suggest that Perinthus was loyal to Athens. Diodorus describes the siege of Perinthus in some detail.

Just at this point, the unthinkable happened: the king of Persia, Artaxerxes III, ordered direct Persian intervention in the west, something that had not happened since the reign of Xerxes in the fifth century BC. Artaxerxes ordered help and mercenaries to be sent to Perinthus. Byzantium, a nearby town also sent reinforcements. The siege was thus prolonged, with many casualties on both sides.

Study questions

Read Diodorus 16.75.

1 Why did the Persian king become involved in this siege?
2 How does Diodorus characterise (a) Philip and the Macedonians and (b) their opponents?

Read Diodorus 16.76.

3 What made this siege a particularly challenging one for Philip?
4 What does Diodorus say about how Philip dealt with Byzantium?

Study question

Which authors does Diodorus mention at the end book 16.76?

EXPLORE FURTHER

Find out about these authors from your answer to this Study Question and whether they in turn might have provided accurate and reliable evidence (or not).

We should always consider the reliability of our ancient sources. An author like Diodorus was not composing a contemporary account, but working like a historian from his own older sources. He mentions some at the end of his account of this siege.

As Diodorus describes in **PS** 16.77.1–2, Philip's siege on Perinthus did not go his way. The Athenians, who imported food from this Black Sea area, could not allow Philip to obtain a stronghold in Perinthus or Byzantium. Thus, in 340, Athens declared that Philip had broken the peace treaty and they declared war. Philip was forced to withdraw.

THE BATTLE OF CHAERONEA, INCLUDING ITS CAUSES AND AFTERMATH

Philip was a remarkable figure who had the ability to benefit even from his defeats. While he accepted the loss of Perinthus, he saw it as the price he had to pay for something better: a reassertion of his authority in southern Greece. In 339, Philip entered Elateia in Phocis, ready to embark on a fourth sacred war: he had been invited by the Amphictyons to conduct the fourth sacred war against Amphissa in Phocis. Diodorus describes the alarm this caused at Athens since they almost certainly regarded Phocis as a key post in southern Greece.

Demosthenes persuaded Thebes into an alliance with Athens. This, then, set the scene for the final confrontation between Athens and Thebes against Philip. Diodorus, having outlined this cause of the battle of Chaeronea, proceeds to give an account of it. The Athenians were clearly devastated by this defeat at Chaeronea. Diodorus (16.88 **PS**) gives some sense of this and its wider significance. He describes Lycurgus' prosecution

ACTIVITY **PS**

Read Diodorus 16.85–86 on the Battle of Chaeronea of 338.

● Summarise the course of the battle in your own words.

Study questions

1 How does **PS** Diodorus chracterise (a) the Athenians, (b) the Boeotians and (c) Philip?
2 What did Philip do once he had secured victory?
3 How accurate an account does this seem?

Study questions

Read Diodorus 16.84 on Philip's occupation of Elateia.

1 How does Diodorus portray Philip?
2 What does Diodorus say about Demosthenes?
3 Does this agree with the speeches of Demosthenes you have read?

Study questions

1 Read Diodorus 16.88 on the aftermath of Chaeronea. How does Diodorus present the defeat at Chaeronea?
2 How helpful is this account for understanding the rise of Macedon?

Study questions
Justin, *Epitome*,
9.5.

1 How does Justin describe the formation of the League?
2 What military arrangements does he suggest were now put in place?

of an Athenian general (Lysicles) who fought at the battle of Chaeronea. It comprises a scathing indictment of Lysicles' dereliction of duty and the shame he has brought on the country.

Justin, on the other hand, provides a rather more pessimistic account of the end of the battle of Chaeronea.

Study questions
Read Justin 9.4 on Chaeronea.

1 How does Justin depict Philip's actions at the end of the battle?
2 How does this compare to Diodorus' coverage of the end of the battle?

THE CREATION OF THE LEAGUE OF CORINTH

The League of Corinth (also referred to as the Hellenic League) was a federation of Greek states created by Philip in 338/7 during the immediate aftermath of the Battle of Chaeronea. It was the first time in history that most of the Greek states, with the exception of Sparta, managed to become part of a single political entity. The League maintained an army levied from member states in approximate proportion to their size. Many think it was a means to facilitate Philip's use of military forces in his war against Persia.

Diodorus can usefully supplement Justin's description.

Study questions
Read Diodorus, 16.89.

1 To what extent does this agree with Justin's version?
2 How much reliance do you think we can place on their information?

ELECTION AS HEGEMON

hegemon a leader

The League of Corinth was governed by a **hegemon**. We should not underestimate the astuteness and further diplomacy of Philip in securing this post. Diodorus makes reference to it in 16.89 **PS**. He also elaborates on Philip's celebrations as hegemon and his plans for Persia in book 16.91–2 **PS**.

Study questions
Read this Diodorus, 16.91–2.

1 How did Philip view his new role as hegemon of Greece?
2 How does Diodorus depict the events of this time?

DEBATE

Was the emergence of a strong leader inevitable at this point in the history of Greece?

EXPLORE FURTHER

Look at the following website for more information on the League of Corinth and its terms: http://www.livius.org/sources/content/justin-epitome/the-corinthian-league/

Study question
Read Diodorus, 16.91–92.

How reliable do you think Diodorus' account is here?

Philip's star was, it seems, in the ascendant. But in 336 everything changed: the hegemon was assassinated. The circumstances of Philip's murder are strange and complicated. They also raise very interesting questions about the motivations (overt and covert) behind Philip's murder. It took place at Aegae. A key source for Philip's assassination is Diodorus who sets the scene: Philip was in a buoyant and convivial mood.

ACTIVITY

Assemble a time-line of the events of Philip's reign.

EXPLORE FURTHER

Investigate the assassination of Philip in more detail by reading Diodorus, book 16.93–94, Arrian, book 2.14 (where it is suggested Darius arranged for the assassination of Philip) and Justin, book 9.7.

TOPIC REVIEW

- List the main factors for the rise of Macedon after Philip came to the throne.
- Explain the main obstacles to his progress.
- Discuss Philip's actions during this rise to power.
- Outline the main responses of other Greek powers to the rise of Macedon.
- Explain how the prescribed authors colour our view of Philip's achievements.

Further Reading

Anson, E.M., 'Introduction of the SARISSA', *Ancient Society* 40 (2010), pp. 51–68

Buckler, J., *Philip II and The Sacred War* (Leiden, New York, Copenhagen and Köln: Brill, 1989).

Buckler, J., and Hans Beck, *Central Greece and the Politics of Power in the Fourth Century BC* (Cambridge: Cambridge University Press, 2008).

Carney, E., *Women and Monarchy in Macedonia* (Norman: University of Oklahoma Press, 2000), pp. 60–2.

Lane Fox, R. (ed.), *Brill's Companion to Ancient Macedon* (Leiden and Boston: Brill, 2011).

Mitchell, L. *Greeks Bearing Gifts. The Public Use of Private Relationships in the Greek World, 425–323* (Cambridge: Cambridge University Press, 2002), pp.145–66.

Roisman, J. and I. Worthington (eds.), *A Companion to Ancient Macedonia* (Oxford: Wiley-Blackwell, 2010).

Ryder, T.T.B., 'Demosthenes and Philip II' in I. Worthington (ed.), *Demosthenes, Statesman and Orator* (London: Routledge, 2000), pp. 45–89.

Tronson, A., 'Satyrus the Peripatetic and the Marriages of Philip II', *JHS* 104 (1984), pp. 116–26.

Worthington, I. *Philip II of Macedonia* (New Haven: Yale University Press, 2008).

PRACTICE QUESTIONS

1. 'Philip of Macedon transformed Macedon into a super power in Greece'. How far do you agree with this view?

You must use and analyse ancient source you have studied as well as your own knowledge to support your answer. How far do the ancient sources support this? [36]

4.2 The Major Events of Alexander's Career and their Significance

TOPIC OVERVIEW	

- Alexander's reassertion of control over Greece
- appointment as hegemon
- his actions at Troy and Gordium
- victories at the Granicus, Halicarnassus, Issus, Gaugamela
- the nature and role of his foundation cities
- occupations of Babylon and Persepolis
- the pursuits of Darius and Bessus
- conspiracies against Alexander
- the treatment of the Branchidae
- the murder of Cleitus and opposition of Callisthenes
- marriage to Roxane
- the Indus valley campaign
- mutiny at the Hyphasis, and conflict with the Mallians
- the crossing of the Gedrosian Desert
- return from the east and the purges
- the marriages in Susa
- the mutiny at Opis
- the Exiles' Decree
- the death of Hephaestion
- return to Babylon and death

The prescribed sources for this topic are:

- Plutarch, *Life of Alexander* 1, 9, 11, 14, 15, 16, 18, 47, 48, 49, 50, 51, 52, 53, 54, 55, 59, 60, 61 and 62
- Arrian, *The Campaigns of Alexander* 1.7–8, 1.11–12, 1.13, 1.16, 1.20–23, 2.6–7, 2.14, 3.8.7–10, 3.13–15, 3.16, 3.18–21, 3.28.8–30.5, 4.8–12, 4.13–14, 4.19, 5.25–29, 6.8–11.2, 6.27, 6.29.9–30, 7.4, 7.8–11, 7.14, 7.22–23, 7.25–26
- Curtius Rufus, *History of Alexander* 5.6.1–8, 5.7.1–11, 7.5.28–35
- The Alexander sarcophagus, showing Alexander at the battle of Issus
- Silver tetradrachm minted by Ptolemy I showing Alexander with elephant scalp headdress
- Silver tetradrachm minted by Lysimachus showing Alexander with horns, Zeus Ammon and Athena

Alexander's successes were to a great degree made possible by Philip's achievements in Macedon and Greece. Alexander built on his father's legacy and pursued the invasion of Persia his father had started. Yet Alexander's ambitions took him further even than the outermost borders of the vast Persian Empire. Years of war, conquest and exploration took him as far as India. Here Alexander sensed he was getting close to the outer edges of the world and would have continued had his men not refused to go further. The sources detailed below draw attention to what Alexander accomplished from his accession to the Macedonian throne at the age of twenty until his death at the age of thirty-two. They also point to the scale of military, diplomatic and personal challenges these entailed.

THE SOURCES

Arrian

Arrian (*c.* 86/89–*c.* after 146/160 AD) was a Greek historian and philosopher living under the Roman Empire. It is thought that he held senior offices in the Roman imperial hierarchy and had considerable military experience. It is possible that Arrian had taken part in the Roman war against the Parthians, which would have entailed visiting that part of the world, including sites such as Gaugamela. His *Campaigns of Alexander*, written in Greek, is considered the most accurate and reliable source on the campaigns of Alexander. He placed more reliance than other writers on contemporary authors like Ptolemy and Aristobulus.

Plutarch

Plutarch (*c.* AD 46–AD 120), as outlined in the Period Study, was a Greek biographer, known primarily for his *Parallel Lives*, including his *Life of Alexander*. Plutarch was born in Chaeronea (the site Philip's last major battle for supremacy in Greece). He was also a Roman citizen. For many years, Plutarch served as a priest at the temple of Apollo at Delphi. Plutarch's *Life of Alexander* was written as a parallel to that of Julius Caesar. His biography is anecdotal in style and modern scholars tend to find Plutarch less historical than Arrian. This is in part because the sources he relied upon are deemed less trustworthy than those used by Arrian. For example, Plutarch used Cleitarchus who himself incorporated stories told by soldiers who sometimes exaggerated or did not fully understand what was happening. However, Plutarch does sometimes depend on Aristobulus.

Both Arrian and Plutarch were writing with specific agendas in mind which may have shaped their accounts.

Title: *The Campaigns of Alexander*

Author: Arrian

Date: *c.* AD 86/89 to after *c.* 146/160

Genre: history

Significance: Arrian is considered to be one of the most reliable sources on Alexander and his campaigns.

Prescribed sections 1.7–8, 1.10–1.13, 1.16, 1.20–1.23, 1.29
2.6–7, 2.12, 2.14–15
3.8.7–10, 3.13–16, 3.18–21, 3.28.8–3.30.5
4.7–4.14, 4.18–19
5.25–29
6.8–6.11.2, 6.12–13, 6.27, 6.29.9–30
7.4, 7.6, 7.8–12, 7.14, 7.22–23, 7.25–26

Read it here: *Arrian: The Campaigns of Alexander*, trans. A. de Sélincourt; revised by J. R. Hamilton (Harmondsworth: Penguin, 1971)

Title: *Life of Alexander*

Author: Plutarch

Date: AD 46–120

Genre: biography

Significance: Plutarch is one of very few sources on Alexander to have survived.

Prescribed sections: 1, 7–16, 18, 23, 27–28, 45, 47–55, 59–62

Read it here: *Plutarch: Greek Lives: A Selection of Nine Greek Lives*, trans. R. Waterfield; introduction and notes by P. A. Stadter (Oxford: Oxford University Press, 1998)

Curtius Rufus

Quintus Curtius Rufus was a Roman historian and senator, probably of the first century AD. His only surviving work is the *History of Alexander the Great*, written in Latin. Much of this is now missing. Little is known of him. His historical account contains some errors; it is thought Curtius Rufus was using Cleitarchus as a main source (though may also have used Aristobulus and Ptolemy too). Curtius Rufus' narrative tends to focus on Alexander's psychological development from a talented young conqueror to a paranoid despot. In adopting this approach, it may be that he had been influenced by his own experience of living under the Roman emperors.

ALEXANDER'S REASSERTION OF CONTROL OVER GREECE

The assassination of Philip in 336 meant Alexander inherited the throne of Macedon. Philip had also subdued most of Greece, but Alexander's inheritance of Philip's position as Greek hegemon was less assured. News of Philip's death had roused many states into revolt, including Thebes, Athens, Thessaly, and the Thracian tribes north of Macedon (Figure 4.1 and 4.2). Philip had become leader of the League of Corinth only in 338/7 and there was no guarantee that the cities of Greece, many of which deeply resented Macedon's power, would cooperate with Philip's new successor. Plutarch captures something of the potential difficulties Alexander faced in 336.

Study questions PS
Read Plutarch, 11 and Arrian, 1.7–8.

1 How do their descriptions of the Battle of Thebes compare?
2 What does each author say about the approach of Alexander to possible peace terms and subsequent military action against them?

Sacred Band the elite fighting corps of Thebes. Pairs of lovers fought side by side

S & C
Read Plutarch, 9 on Chaeronea in 338.
How might that experience have influenced his actions at the later Battle of Thebes?

A dangerous thorn in the side of Macedon was the city-state of Thebes. They had for many years courted Philip's favour but ultimately opposed his incursions into Greece. Philip had finally defeated them at the battle of Chaeronea in 338. They had also been forced to become a member of the League of Corinth. Alexander had been present at this battle and helped crush the Thebans, including their elite fighting force, the **Sacred Band**.

When Alexander was involved in quashing rebellions to the north of Macedon, Thebes decided to rebel. Given the prestige of Thebes, Alexander was concerned that this might trigger a wave of rebellions across Greece. His response was swift and severe, resulting in the Battle of Thebes in 335. Both Plutarch and Arrian offer accounts of this battle.

ALEXANDER'S APPOINTMENT AS HEGEMON

Alexander gradually came to be recognised as hegemon of Greece. This happened in stages. At Thermopylae, he was confirmed as hegemon of the Hellenes. Then at Corinth his appeals to hold the position of hegemon of the Corinthian (or Hellenic) League were also successful. Like Philip, he was also appointed as commander of a campaign against Persia.

Plutarch describes (14 **PS**) this appointment in Corinth, where great numbers tried to gain an audience with him. He also tells a famous anecdote about Diogenes, a philosopher of Corinth, who showed himself completely oblivious to Alexander's appointment. It reflects the respect Alexander had for an outspoken man who exhibited no fear.

FIGURE 4.5
Sixteenth-century image of Diogenes and Alexander held in the Musée des Beaux-Arts de Lyon.

S & C
Explore the different versions of this episode in Arrian, 7.2.1, Cicero, *Tusculanae Disputationes* 5.32.92 and Diogenes Laërtius 6.32, 38, 60, and 68. Consider how they affect your reading of Plutarch.

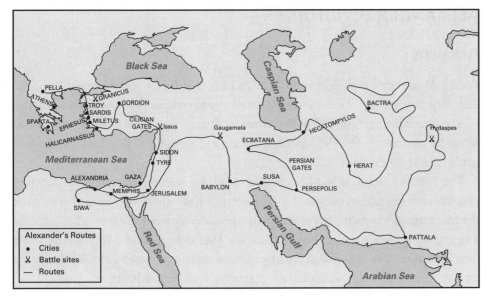

FIGURE 4.6
Map showing the route of Alexander's expedition and the battles in Persia and beyond.

ALEXANDER'S ACTIONS AT TROY AND GORDIUM

In 334, Alexander launched a pan-hellenic expedition into Persia (Figure 4.6). One of the first places Alexander insisted on visiting was Troy. Troy was the ancient site of Trojan Wars that had, as told by Homer, been fought between Greeks and Trojans as far back as the thirteenth century BC. The sources point to the profound importance of the Trojan Wars to Alexander who may have felt that his Persian expedition marked a new reincarnation of them. It also appears that Alexander identified strongly with Achilles, one of the most formidable warriors on the Greek side. Alexander also believed that he was related to Achilles: his mother's line claimed royal descent from Achilles' son, Neoptolemus.

It is significant that Alexander opted to call in at Troy and perform certain symbolic acts of worship and commemoration. Plutarch and Arrian make reference to these. Even in the time of both authors, Homer's writings and the myth of Troy still had common currency. It is clear too that Arrian, at least, thought he had a duty to celebrate Alexander's achievements in that way Homer had memorialised those of Achilles.

When Alexander had been Asia for about a year, he arrived at the town of Gordium. Here was the legendary 'Gordian knot', a knot on a chariot which no one had for years been able to untie. The legend was that whoever undid it was destined to become the absolute ruler of Asia. Plutarch describes Alexander's response to this challenge. He also suggests that were different versions.

Study questions
Read Plutarch, 18. **PS**

1 How does Plutarch depict Alexander?
2 Why might this story have in fact been fabricated in the days and years after Alexander's trip to Gordium?

KEY INDIVIDUAL

Homer
Dates: unknown, *c.* 700 BC

Epic poet who wrote the *Iliad*, a semi-mythical account of the Trojan Wars

Study question
Read Plutarch, 15.4–5 and Arrian, 1.12. **PS**

What do these actions reveal about the way Alexander viewed his mission to Persia?

EXPLORE FURTHER

● Compare Plutarch's account of the Gordian knot with Arrian's in 2.3.
● Does this comparison offer help when it comes to assessing the reliability of these accounts?

ALEXANDER'S VICTORIES

Granicus

During Alexander's campaign in Asia, he and his men fought many battles. Some are described as 'decisive' insofar as they allowed him to conquer Asia with total authority.

The Persians had advanced to the Granicus River (Figure 4.6), which they hoped would be an obstacle for Alexander and his army. The battle of Granicus was the first battle against the Persians.

The Battle of Granicus had been long-awaited, yet still, the Persians were not fully prepared, nor was Darius present at it. The Persians had initially been able to drive back the Macedonian vanguard, but confronting Alexander's main force was more difficult. The aim of the Persians had been to defeat the Macedonian cavalry first, which would then leave them free to surround the Macedonian phalanx. However, already during the cavalry fight, the infantry lines clashed, shattering such Persian hopes.

It was during the initial cavalry surge when Alexander almost lost his life. Cleitus, one of his companions saved him just in time. This illustrates how indebted Alexander became to his loyal companions in military encounters.

In the Battle of Granicus, the Persian army was destroyed. The last to resist were the Greek mercenaries and they were probably massacred. Ultimately, the Battle of Granicus proved that Alexander and his army had enough strength and ability to unsettle the Persian Empire in a major way. The casualties on each side suggest that this was a clear victory for Alexander. Plutarch gives some sense of its military importance:

> . . . It was presumably going to be necessary to fight at the gateway to Asia, so to speak, for the right to enter the Persian Empire.
>
> Plutarch, *Alexander* 16

Halicarnassus

The siege of Halicarnassus (Figure 4.6) took place not long after Granicus in 334. Alexander, though it is thought he continued to have a Macedonian naval presence at the Hellespont, had just disbanded the Greek fleet. As a result, he found himself being constantly threatened by the Persian navy and felt the need to put a final stop to their naval challenges. That year the Persian fleet, under the command of Memnon, sailed to Halicarnassus to establish a new defence. Alexander had sent spies to meet with possible traitors inside the city of Halicarnassus who had promised to open the gates and allow Alexander to enter. However, this plan came to nothing. A small battle resulted, and Alexander's army managed to break through the city walls. Memnon, however, responded with more robust force, and Alexander's army pulled back. It is likely that Alexander would have been defeated here had his infantry not managed to break through the city walls, surprising the Persian forces.

According to the ancient sources, Alexander, having realised how important naval strength was, had reconstituted a fleet by the following spring.

Study question
Read Plutarch, 16 and Arrian, 1.13.

What are the main similarities and differences in these authors' respective versions?

EXPLORE FURTHER

There is another version of this moment when Alexander almost lost his life at Granicus in Diodorus, 17.20 which you should read.

Study question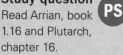
Read Arrian, book 1.16 and Plutarch, chapter 16.

How reliable do you think the figures they provide for each side are? Do you think they might have been exaggerated?

KEY INDIVIDUAL

Memnon
Dates: 380–333
Commander of the Greek mercenaries in the service of the Persian king Darius

Study questions
Read Arrian, 1.20–23.

1 What were main military tactics employed in this siege?
2 From what Arrian says, how major a threat did the siege of Halicarnassus appear to pose Alexander?

EXPLORE FURTHER

For details about Alexander's navy, see Curtius Rufus, 3.1.19–20 and 4.1.36 and 4.5.14–22.

Issus

The following year, in 333, Alexander and his army fought the Battle of Issus. This was the second great battle of Alexander's campaign, but the first battle at which he confronted the Persian king, Darius III (Figure 4.6). It was an immensely significant encounter, not least because if victorious Alexander could claim to have conquered the king of Persia.

Darius' plan was ambitious (Arrian, 2.6–7 **PS**). It was to muster a very large force to defeat the army of Alexander on the plains of northern Syria, and, following his victory, cut off Alexander's line of retreat. However, it did not turn out this way since, prior to the battle itself, Darius decided to switch battle-fields.

Concerning the Battle of Issus we have an alternative piece of evidence to the written sources. This is the Alexander **sarcophagus**. One long side of it is believed to depict Alexander in his role as an expert cavalry soldier at the Battle of Issus. He is shown mounted on a horse, wearing a lion skin on his head and preparing to throw a spear. This carving appears to be glorifying Alexander, the Macedonians and their cavalry expertise. This sarcophagus was discovered in the late nineteenth century but originates from the fourth century BC. Interestingly, it was possibly commissioned by a Persian noble, Mazaeus.

EXPLORE FURTHER

For more details on the battle itself see: http://www.livius.org/articles/battle/issus/

sarcophagus a tomb; literally, the word means 'flesh-eating'

PRESCRIBED SOURCE

The Alexander sarcophagus, showing Alexander at the battle of Issus

Date: fourth century BC

Significance: commissioned and made close in time to Alexander

Original location: Sidon in Lebanon

Current location: Istanbul Museum

View it here: Fig 4.7

FIGURE 4.7
The Alexander sarcophagus, showing Alexander at the battle of Issus, held in the Istanbul Archaeology Museum.

In Arrian (2.14 PS) we are told about a letter that Darius wrote to Alexander following the Battle of Issus. Darius offered some sort of alliance rather than more conflict. Alexander in response made it clear that it was Darius who had begun the quarrel and that he was now rightful King of Persia. If true, this was an interesting index of the complete victory Alexander considered that he had now achieved.

Gaugamela

In the Battle of Gaugamela in 331 Alexander again clashed with the king of Persia and his forces. Darius did not make the same mistake twice and he made sure that it took place on a flat, open plain. Arrian is a key source for the build-up to the battle and the course of the battle itself. During his account (Arrian 3.9 PS), he outlines a speech made by Alexander just prior to going into battle in which he exhorted them all to play their part.

As Arrian describes it (3.13–15 PS), after a day of fighting Alexander's army emerged in control of the field. The battle was hard-fought but ultimately represented another victory for Alexander. Sources report that in the end Darius panicked, turned around and in this way put the mass of the Persian army to flight. Alexander's victory essentially marked the collapse of the Persian Empire.

THE NATURE AND ROLE OF ALEXANDER'S FOUNDATION CITIES

During Alexander's campaign he founded many cities across the territory that he conquered. He named many after himself. These Greek cities would have helped to unify and keep secure the Eastern Empire he was gradually acquiring. In addition, of course, they surely reflected a form of self-aggrandisement on Alexander's part. Plutarch states that Alexander founded no fewer than seventy such cities in total, though this is almost certainly exaggerated. The actual number is probably closer to twenty, and a good number of these were founded by his successors. Often, they began as military settlements or to commemorate a military triumph. Perhaps the most famous of these cities is Alexandria in Egypt (and is now Egypt's second largest city). This was founded by Alexander in 331.

Plutarch, one of your prescribed sources, writes the following about two other cities that Alexander founded.

OCCUPATIONS OF BABYLON AND PERSEPOLIS

Following the Battle of Gaugamela, Alexander successfully advanced to Babylon (Figure 4.6). Arrian (3.16 PS) observed that Alexander's arrival at Babylon was a cautious one. Alexander accordingly approached the city in battle-order. However, the people of the city in fact welcomed him fulsomely with offers to give him the city's well-endowed treasury.

Alexander's next destination was an obvious one for anyone set on conquering Persia. He made for the Eastern capital of the Persian Empire, Persepolis. However, before he could reach this key military target, he had to get through a difficult pass called the Persian Gates. This involved another battle, the battle in 330 against Ariobarzanes, a satrap Darius had left in charge of Persepolis.

As the Macedonians approached the narrow pass, the Persians, who had occupied it, attacked the Macedonians who were forced to move back. Alexander was in an impossible situation, but as luck would have it, a local guide then offered his services. This may have happened, but the anecdote looks suspiciously like Herodotus's story of Ephialtes, a traitor, who showed the Persian king Xerxes a road to break the Spartan defence of Thermopylae in 480. Whatever the case, Alexander's men set out at night and used another valley. In this way, Alexander came upon the Persian rear. At dawn, the Alexander's troops attacked Ariobarzanes' camp. Many Persians were slaughtered.

The Battle of the Persian Gate was a significant encounter. As a result of this victory, Alexander was free to march to the jewel of the Persian empire. Curtius Rufus provides a detailed account of Alexander's arrival at the beautiful and sumptuous city of Persepolis, and his view of the capital city.

A particularly notorious act in the history of Alexander's occupation of Persepolis was the burning of the palace. The palace was a show piece of luxury and refinement. There are slightly different accounts of this in our ancient sources, though most agree that it happened and that Alexander later regretted his actions. The reasons for the arson vary: Curtius Rufus blames the whole episode emphatically on alcohol and a woman (Thais) whereas Arrian makes no mention of a woman or drunkenness. It may be that the action represented a symbolic act of revenge on the Persians. The Greek forces were sent home immediately after the burning of Persepolis. It is most likely that the burning of the palace of Persepolis constituted a way to fulfil the obligations Alexander had as leader of the allied forces.

PRESCRIBED SOURCE

Title: *The History of Alexander*

Author: Curtius Rufus

Date: *c.* first century AD

Genre: history

Significance: he constitutes another source for Alexander.

Prescribed sections: 5.6.1–8, 5.7.1–11, 7.5.28–35

Read it here: *Quintus Curtius Rufus: The History of Alexander*, trans. J. Yardley; introduction and notes by W. Heckel (Harmondsworth: Penguin, 1984)

Study questions
Read Arrian, 3.16.

1 What is significant about Alexander's actions in Babylon?
2 What does Arrian convey about (a) Alexander's expectations and (b) the attitude of the Babylonians?

Study questions
Read Arrian, 3.18.

1 How does Arrian portray the course and outcome of this battle?
2 Which elements of his narrative would you want to have more evidence for?

ACTIVITY
Read Arrian, 3.18 and 6.30 and Curtius Rufus, 5.7.1–11. Compare in detail how two authors describe the burning of the palace.

Study question
How reliable do you think the ancient sources when they refer to Alexander's later remorse for this deed?

Study questions
Read Curtius Rufus, 5.6.1–8 and Arrian, 3.18.

1 How did Alexander and his men conduct themselves on first arriving in Persepolis?
2 What information in these accounts do you think seems more reliable and what seems less credible?

THE PURSUITS OF DARIUS AND BESSUS

It seems that Alexander was obsessed with his foe, the king of Persia, Darius. Alexander had been desperate to kill him in battle, both at Issus and then Gaugamela. Each time, Alexander had been denied his scalp. After Gaugamela, Darius fled. Arrian is a useful source for Alexander's pursuit of Darius:

> Without delay, Alexander's march began. Its objective was Darius . . . So rapid was the march that many of the men, unable to stand the pace, dropped out, and a number of horses were worked to death; but Alexander pressed on regardless of loss . . .

Arrian, *The Campaigns of Alexander* 3.20

Study questions
Read Arrian, 3.20–21.

1 How does Arrian portray (a) Alexander and (b) Bessus?
2 Why was this episode such an important one in Alexander's conquest of Persia?

When Darius reached Bactria (Figure 4.6), Bessus launched a coup against Darius. Bessus had fought side by side with Darius at Gaugamela and travelled with him during his flight. Now, however, Bessus deposed Darius and arrested him. It is not quite clear what motivated Bessus to act in this way; he may have intended to surrender Darius to the Macedonians. However, when Alexander ordered his forces to continue to pursue the Persians, according to sources, Bessus' co-conspirators in panic stabbed Darius and left him dying in a cart. He was found by a Macedonian soldier. When Alexander discovered the news of Darius' murder, he was furious – Darius was meant to be his. He then angrily hunted down Bessus.

In 329, Alexander, as recounted by Arrian (PS 3.28.8–30.5) eventually tracked down Bessus with the aid in particular of one of his most valued generals, Ptolemy. After Bessus' fortified compound was stormed, he was finally captured.

Study questions
Read Arrian, 3.15–16 and 3.19–21.

1 What do these passages indicate about Alexander's attitude to the 'chase'?
2 What was Darius' route and what were his intentions and policies as he fled?
3 What do you think were the effects of the defections from Darius?

THE CONSPIRACIES AGAINST ALEXANDER

As the campaign in Asia went on, Alexander grew increasingly suspicious of some of those closest to him. It is very difficult to know what the reality of the situation was, but the fact is Alexander took the threats seriously and dealt with them firmly.

Plutarch and Arrian outline several of the conspiracies that were apparently being hatched. One of these occurred in 330. According to Plutarch, it involved Philotas, one of Alexander's most able companions. Plutarch, who thrives on personal portraits, refers to Philotas' arrogant behaviour over a sustained period. He then refers to a 'trap being set' for Philotas who was openly criticising Alexander. When Philotas failed to take appropriate action when another plot against Alexander's life was uncovered, suspicions were further aroused. Alexander's companions tortured him, had him killed and also murdered Philotas' father, Parmenio.

Another plot was alleged to have been concocted two or three years later in 328/7, this time involving Hermolaus and, by association, Callisthenes. By all accounts, Hermolaus had been out hunting with Alexander. At the point when Alexander was about to charge at a boar, he was interrupted by Hermolaus, whom Alexander then had whipped by way of punishment. Hermolaus, insulted by such treatment, determined to kill Alexander with the help of others. Hermolaus' plans were uncovered and Arrian recounts some of the charges he laid against Alexander at his trial. Both Plutarch and Arrian suggest that Callisthenes may have been implicated in the conspiracy of Hermolaus.

These accounts can be considered alongside another alleged plot which was brought to Alexander's attention by his mother Olympias some years later. Her accusations centred on Antipater. On this occasion, according to Arrian, Alexander took no action.

> ### Study questions
> Read Plutarch, 48–49, Arrian, 4.13–14, Plutarch, 55 and Arrian, 7.12.
>
> 1 How is Alexander portrayed in each of these accounts?
> 2 How do his actions reflect his state of mind?
> 3 Which sources does each cite?
> 4 What is the problem, from a historical perspective, with plots and hearsay?

THE TREATMENT OF THE BRANCHIDAE

During Alexander's pursuit of Bessus, he arrived at a small town inhabited by a group of people called the Branchidae. These were men and women whose ancestors had originally come from Miletus, a Greek city-state located on the west coast of modern day Turkey. The story went that when Xerxes had invaded Greece, the Milesians had been compelled to destroy a temple called the Didymeon. After this sacrilegious act, they left Miletus and emigrated to the East and settled in a new home there. Alexander consulted the Milesians in his own army about how to treat the Branchidae.

Study questions
Read Curtius Rufus, 7.5.28–35.

1 How does this account reflect Alexander's character?
2 What does it tell us about Curtius Rufus' own concerns as a writer of history?

Study questions
Read Arrian, 4.8–9 and Plutarch, 50–51.

1 What are the points of correspondence and difference between these passages?
2 Do these authors offer their own views of this episode, and if so, why?

ACTIVITY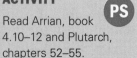

Read Arrian, book 4.10–12 and Plutarch, chapters 52–55.
   Compare and contrast the main details of these accounts.

Study question
What might the Roman view of such flattery have been?

EXPLORE FURTHER

Research what happened to the son Roxane and Alexander had after Alexander's death.

proskynesis/ obeisance deferential respect or obeisance, such as blowing a kiss in worship

Study question
Read Plutarch, 47 and Arrian, 4.19.

How do they portray (a) Alexander, (b) Roxane and (c) the nature of their relationship?

THE MURDER OF CLEITUS AND OPPOSITION OF CALLISTHENES

As the years progressed on the Asian campaign, relations between Alexander and his inner circle became increasingly strained. Two such episodes are discussed here.

Murder of Cleitus

Cleitus was one of Alexander's closest friends and most trusted officers. He had saved Alexander's life in the Battle of Granicus. However, with so many of Alexander's intimate relationships with his companions, this one also turned very sour. Accounts suggest that Cleitus, who had been upset by Alexander's own conduct, provoked Alexander by openly challenging him. An argument ensued, which ended in Alexander killing Cleitus. Sources suggest that Alexander deeply repented of his actions immediately afterwards. Two of your prescribed authors provide detailed accounts of this most shocking and tragic event.

The episode of Cleitus' killing is a highly dramatic one and fits well with Plutarch's lively and sensational biographical style. His narration of it allows him to draw out forcefully the characterisation of both men: Cleitus he portrays as being of harsh temper and willful; and Alexander as prone to bouts of anger and unable to cope with criticism. Interestingly, Plutarch also casts the whole event as a sudden event that was triggered by too much alcohol. He does not suggest at all that Alexander might have intended before that night to kill Cleitus. It is also important that we question the entire episode as he tells it. The inclusion of so much direct speech seems extraordinary.

In his account, Arrian provides his own moral judgements: he seems to suggest that the blame for the episode lies more with Cleitus than Alexander. Cleitus, he claims, had been the one who had really provoked Alexander and had not allowed himself to be taken away by his friends. Arrian also expressed disapproval about the quantities of alcohol Alexander had drunk. Arrian also blamed one of Alexander's philosophers, Anaxarchus, for planting the idea that all actions taken by king were inherently just.

Both Arrian and Plutarch then proceed to describe the opposition voiced by Callisthenes against Alexander. His main point of contention centred on Alexander's use of **proskynesis** and the flatterers Alexander had begun to surround himself by. As with the Cleitus story, both authors provide very vivid accounts and record the actual dialogues between Callisthenes and Alexander. It appears that these arguments eventually cost Callithenes his life.

ALEXANDER'S MARRIAGE TO ROXANE

Roxane was the daughter of a Bactrian nobleman named Oxyartes, who served Bessus. After Bessus was captured, Oxyartes and his family continued to resist the Greeks. However, they were eventually defeated by Alexander. Apparently, Alexander then fell in love with Roxane and married her in 327. He also appointed Oxyartes as the governor of Punjab and promoted a brother of Roxane into his elite cavalry. This might all sound unremarkable – he was just treating his new family with respect. However, it was not at all an insignificant union. Roxane was a non-Macedonian/Greek woman and her family had been the very people Alexander and his men had been so recently fighting against. To many Greeks, Roxane and her family were barbarians. However, as far as Alexander was concerned, such a union could help buttress relations with the peoples he had just conquered.

After Alexander's death, Roxane bore him a son. This would be of considerable significance at a time when it was being decided who would be his successors.

THE INDUS VALLEY CAMPAIGN

After leaving the outer reaches of the Persian empire, Alexander instigated in 326 a new stage of the campaign, the exploration and conquest of India. We may well ask ourselves why Alexander insisted on going so far. Some sources suggest that Alexander was determined to reach the outer limits of the known world and the rivers that encircled it; as far as the Greeks were concerned, this ended in India. It may also be that strategically, since he was now both king of Macedon and Persia, he needed to establish the frontiers of that empire. There is no point having an empire with borders if you do not understand the threats there are on the other side; Arrian wrote that as long as there remained any hostility in that territory, there could be no end to the war (5.24). Perhaps Alexander simply had an insatiable appetite for what was new and exciting, and never intended that the campaign should stop.

It appears from the sources that Alexander during this part of his campaign fought in ways that incurred disapproval. This may have been in part because the Indians were ferocious fighters. Plutarch recounts one episode in which Alexander ambushed a number of Indian mercenaries on the road in a way that completely transgressed the usual rules of combat.

Alexander would involve his forces in some difficult and costly battles at this stage of the campaign. This included the Battle of Hydaspes River against Porus in 326. Although Alexander was ultimately victorious, this battle was one of the hardest battles he ever fought. It involved Alexander's army crossing the swollen and dangerous river Hydaspes before the battle had even begun. Some ancient sources report that it was during this battle that Porus' son wounded Alexander and killed his beloved horse, **Bucephalas** (though others report that the horse died of old age). This was a particularly punishing battle on account of the war elephants that were used by Porus. Plutarch, claiming that he is relying on Alexander's own letters, offers glimpses of what Alexander put his men through in the battle.

Another piece of evidence that provides some insight into the significance of Alexander's Indian campaign is a silver coin that was minted by Ptolemy after Alexander's death, one of Alexander's companions and successors. It is referred to as a silver tetradrachm. It depicts Alexander wearing an elephant headdress and is clearly meant to

---

S & C

In this topic, you have read about Thais, a woman who supposedly persuaded Alexander to burn the palace, and about Roxane. Consider the way women are referred to by the sources.

Study questions

Read Plutarch, 59.

1 How does Plutarch portray Alexander's actions here?

2 What does this passage indicate about Plutarch's priorities in assembling his biography of Alexander?

KEY INDIVIDUAL

Porus (or Poros)
Dates: d. 321–315

A ferocious Indian King who fought Alexander at the battle of Hydaspes

---

Buchephalus or Bucephalas name of Alexander's horse. The name in Greek literally means 'ox' (bous) and 'head' (kephalē)

Study question
Read Plutarch, 60.

How reliable an account of this military encounter do you think Plutarch offers here?

commemorate his conquests in India. This coin dates to somewhere between 305–282 and therefore belongs to the period just after the death of Alexander.

PRESCRIBED SOURCE

Silver tetradrachm of Alexander

Date: *c.* 30–282

Minted: by Ptolemy

Significance: a source close in time to Alexander

Current Location: an example can be found in the British Museum (1987,0649.508)

View it here: Figure 4.8

FIGURE 4.8
Silver tetradrachm minted by Ptolemy I showing Alexander with elephant scalp headdress.

Study questions

Look at the coin in Figure 4.8.

1 Why do you suppose it was minted?
2 What can it tell us about Alexander's Indus valley campaign?
3 Are there limitations with this as historical evidence?

S & C

The modern scholar Carney (see further reading on p. 247) disputes that the term 'mutiny' is the correct one to use, preferring 'sedition'. To what extent do you agree with this?

THE MUTINY AT THE HYPHASIS, AND CONFLICT WITH THE MALLIANS

The mutiny at Hyphasis

The bitter fighting during the Indian campaign made Alexander's men reluctant to continue with the conquest of India. His men must have been exhausted by years of war and desperately homesick. In the summer of 326, Alexander's men refused to join their king in his attempt to reach the Ganges Valley. To go there would have involved facing another vast Indian enemy with thousands of fighting elephants. At the river Hyphasis, his men mutinied. Alexander tried to persuade them to go on. However, an officer named Coenus spoke on behalf of the soldiers and his appeal won the day. Alexander, upon seeing the unwillingness of his men, agreed to turn back.

The conflict with the Mallians

Alexander conducted a campaign against the Mallians of the eastern Punjab from the winter of 326 to spring 325. Alexander was on his way back to Persia but remained keen to define the eastern limits of his power. Alexander launched a swift offensive against the Mallians. Alexander was seriously injured during the course of the campaign, almost losing his life. His conduct during the siege was noteworthy; he had always been a general who led his troops from the front, but in this campaign he took this to new limits:

> The men with ladders were not quick enough to satisfy Alexander; in his impatience, he snatched one from the fellow who carried it and with his own hands reared it up against the fortress wall; then crouched under his shield, up he went.
>
> Arrian, *The Campaigns of Alexander* 6.9

Study questions
Read Arrian, 5.25–29.

1 How reliable do you think Arrian's account of these speeches is?

Read Plutarch, 62.

2 How does Plutarch's account of the mutiny compare with Arrian's?

Study questions
Read Arrian, book 6.8–11.2.

1 What were the siege tactics used here?

2 How does Arrian portray Alexander?

At the end of your prescribed reading on the Malians (6.11.2), Arrian makes a bold claim. He refers to many mendacious rumours that have sprung up concerning this episode (which he proceeds to rehearse), stressing that these falsehoods can only be dispelled by his own history. Evidently Arrian himself valued accuracy and regarded his own work as a more faithful version; this is important when considering the issue of reliability.

MODERN PARALLEL

Can we compare Alexander's action against the Mallians to kamikaze pilots in the Second World War?

THE CROSSING OF THE GEDROSIAN DESERT

After the conflict with the Mallians, Alexander set in motion the long journey back to Persia. He now divided his army into three parts. One third would return by sea with Nearchus, and another third through Arachosia with Craterus. The route Alexander chose for his third involved travelling through the Gedrosian Desert, a feat that was unthinkable, even for locals. Arrian (book 6.27) refers to the preparations for this and how Alexander distributed draught-animals and camels. Crossing the desert was a gruelling ordeal and many died from hunger and thirst. The baking heat was unbearable, and then the monsoon arrived causing huge landslides, causing many to drown.

ACTIVITY

Read Arrian 6.27.
Alexander's decision to take so many through the desert back to Persia is an interesting one that has intrigued scholars. Write down what his reasons might have been for doing this.

KEY INDIVIDUALS

Nearchus
Dates: *c.* 360–300

One of Alexander's naval officers. An account of Nearchus' voyage from the Indus river to the Persian Gulf following the Indian campaign is given in Arrian's *Indica*

Craterus
Dates: *c.* 370–321

A Macedonian general under Alexander and one of Alexander's successors

EXPLORE FURTHER

Though not a prescribed source, Arrian describes Alexander's journey through the Gedrosian Desert in 6.23–26. It is a fascinating account of suffering and endurance.

THE RETURN FROM THE EAST AND THE PURGES

Upon his return to Persia, a priority for Alexander was a trip to the tomb of Cyrus. However, when he arrived there, he found the tomb had been raided. He launched an investigation into what he considered to be an outrage and threatened to punish the culprits.

KEY INDIVIDUAL

Cyrus
Dates: *c.* 600 or 576–530

Persian king, commonly known as Cyrus the Great

Study question

Read Arrian, 6.29.9.

PS

Why do you think Alexander was so concerned about the tomb of a former Persian king?

Study question

Read Arrian 7.4.

PS

Arrian was writing during the Roman Empire – what do you think the Roman attitude would have been to Alexander's actions here?

Upon arriving back to Persia, Alexander discovered that many of the Persian satraps, Macedonian and Greek generals and administrators he had put in charge while he was away in India had committed irregularities. Many of them, according to Arrian (book 7.4 **PS**), thought that he would never return. Alexander decided to make an example of any local governors he suspected of committing even the slightest crime. Arrian also suggests that these purges were bound up with Alexander's neurotic and capricious state of mind at this stage.

THE MARRIAGES IN SUSA

When Alexander was back in Persia, he travelled to Susa (Figure 4.6) in 324. Alexander now arranged a mass marriage ceremony at which many of his leading comrades married local Persian women. Alexander himself also married two distinguished Persian women. Although arranged marriages were common practice at this time (and even when Arrian was writing), given its scale, it was an extraordinary event. Arrian sets out in detail the identity of the brides Alexander allocated to himself and his companions. Alexander himself married Barsine, the eldest of Darius' daughters. He gave another daughter of Darius to Hephaestion and other noble Persian women to some eighty comrades in all. Arrian also observes that the marriages were celebrated according to Persian custom and that Alexander himself gave a dowry to each couple. And as for all the Macedonians who had already married Asian women (some 10,000), Alexander offered them all wedding gifts.

What was Alexander's purpose behind this? With Hephaestion at least, it seems that he wanted to bring them closer through their respective marriages. Arrian does not condemn Alexander for this action; in fact, he expressly mentions that it was done in the spirit of comradeship. Alexander was certainly generous in the gifts he distributed. An important aim was surely diplomatic – a way to unite Greek and Asian elites. Equally, it might just illustrate how attractive Alexander found the Persian culture and its people.

THE MUTINY AT OPIS

orientalism the gradual process of adopting Eastern customs

We have already seen how unhappy many of Alexander's men had become towards the latter stages of the campaign. In August 324, just after the mass marriages at Susa, Alexander's soldiers raised objections once again: they were apparently distressed by their king's **orientalism**. They also felt, when Alexander attempted to discharge many of them at Opis (see Key Topic 5), that he undervalued them. Arrian provides an account. A considerable portion of it pertains to Alexander's reaction to this act of protest and the speech he made to his Macedonians.

The mutiny was in the end happily resolved. In an attempt to craft a lasting harmony between his Macedonian and Persian subjects, Alexander took an oath of unity before 9,000 Persian and Greek troops at Opis.

Study questions
Read Arrian, 7.8–11.

1 What impression of Alexander does Arrian create here?
2 Much of this section takes the form of a speech. What was the role of oratory when Arrian was writing?

THE EXILES' DECREE

It was at Opis in 324 that Alexander announced his intention to disband the mercenary armies that his generals had acquired while he was away in the East. This is often referred to as 'the Exiles' Decree'. The full Decree was read aloud at the Olympic games later that year and applied to all Greek exiles. A key objective of the Decree was to reinstate in their native cities veteran mercenaries who had served with Alexander. Antipater was ordered to use force against any city that refused to receive its exiles back.

There had never been a measure like this before. It is likely that this Decree was a facet of Alexander's broader programme of liberation of Greece, one that his expedition to Persia in many ways represented. He probably also wanted to help ensure that he built a strong support base in Greece, especially as he now intended to embark on a new journey to Arabia. However, modern scholars consider that Alexander must have known the destabilising effects on Greek cities this would have, for it would often entail exiles, who had often been exiled for political reasons, being allowed to return to their hometowns. They also surmise that Alexander was completely overstepping his authority as hegemon of the League of Corinth in passing this Decree, insofar as he was riding roughshod over the autonomy of different city-states.

THE DEATH OF HEPHAESTION

Hephaestion was a life-long friend of Alexander. The two were almost the same age and had probably been educated together by Aristotle. They may also have been lovers at some point. This seems to be the presumption in Arrian's description (book 1.11). Although more inexperienced than many of Alexander's companions, Hephaestion fought in the battles – he was wounded at the battle of Gaugamela (Arrian, book 3.15). Hephaestion was almost certainly Alexander's favourite of all his companions. But when Hephaestion died suddenly in 324 in Ecbatana, Alexander was overwhelmed with grief and resolved to keep his friend's memory alive forever.

RETURN TO BABYLON AND DEATH

Return to Babylon

Alexander had first entered Babylon in 331. He retuned some eight years later in 323. It would be the scene of the final chapter of his life. This period of Alexander's life was dominated by various signs and portents which seemed to predict Alexander's imminent death.

EXPLORE FURTHER
Read Diodorus, 18.8 on the Exiles' Decree.

Study questions
Read Arrian, 7.14 and 7.23.

1 What are the differences between the accounts of Alexander's reactions upon Hephaestion's death?
2 What do the stories Arrian describes indicate about Alexander's character?

S & C Read an English translation of book 18 of Homer's *Iliad* which describes Achilles' grief upon the death of his beloved friend Patroclus. Compare this with Alexander's response to Hephaestion's death.

Study question
Read Arrian, book 7.22–23.

How did Alexander react to these events?

ACTIVITY

Assemble a time-line of the main events in Alexander's life.

Alexander's Death

Arrian offers quite detailed accounts of the last days of Alexander's life. These are based on what are believed to be first-hand reports of his daily activities recorded in the royal diaries or journals.

Alexander was just thirty-two when he died. This seems very young, but the account Arrian provides is plausible enough. Hephaestion had died young just the year before. The general state of Alexander's health cannot have been very good after the serious injury he sustained fighting the Mallians and the amount of alcohol some sources suggest he was drinking. We cannot know exactly what the circumstances of Alexander's death were. But, perhaps inevitably, after his death, stories started to circulate which pointed to foul-play rather than natural causes. It is true that Alexander had made many enemies, particularly towards the end of his life, but the majority of ancient sources are clear that he was not murdered.

After his death, a cult of Alexander was quickly established and he was effectively **deified**.

There is a piece of material evidence that can perhaps help us understand the nature of this **posthumous** cult. It comprises another tetradrachm. It shows on the left side an image of Alexander who has been deified with the ram's horns of Zeus-Ammon and wearing the royal crown. The right side depicts the goddess Athena seated and holding Nike, a goddess of victory. The coin was minted by one of Alexander's companions, Lysimachus (and his name appears on the right-hand side) shortly after Alexander's death. It almost certainly reflects the way in which Alexander's successors were pleased that he had a special relationship with the gods, especially **Zeus-Ammon**.

deification the process of turning someone into a god through worship of that person as though they were divine

posthumous after death

Zeus-Ammon the Egyptian version of Zeus

Study questions
Read Arrian, book 7.25–26.

1 What was the reaction of his men as his health deteriorated?
2 How reliable does Arrian seem in his account of Alexander's death?

Study question PS
Study the coin in Figure 4.9.

1 What can this coin tell us about Alexander and those who knew him?

PRESCRIBED SOURCE

Silver tetradrachm of Alexander

Date: just after 323 BC

Minted: by Lysimachus

Significance: a source close in time to Alexander

Current Location: an example can be found in the British Museum (1919,0820.1)

View it here: Fig 4.9

FIGURE 4.9 PS
Silver tetradrachm minted by Lysimachus showing Alexander with horns, Zeus Ammon and Athena.

- Review the factors that were responsible for Alexander's achievements.
- Discuss the ways Alexander's own personality instrumental in his success.
- Assess how successful he was militarily.
- In terms of governance of a new Persian empire and the one back home, explain how Alexander coped
- Discuss how Alexander dealt with adversity.
- Outline what Alexander achieved from the age of twenty until his death.

Further Reading

Anson, E.M., 'Alexander at the Beas' in P. Wheatley and E. Baynham (eds), *East and West in the World Empire of Alexander. Essays in Honour of Brian Bosworth* (Oxford: Oxford Univeristy Press, 2015), pp. 65–74.

Bowden, H., *Alexander the Great, A Very Short Introduction* (Oxford: Oxford University Press, 2014).

Cartledge, P., *Alexander the Great: The Hunt for a New Past* (London: Pan, 2004).

Carney, E., 'Macedonians and Mutiny: Discipline and Indiscipline in the Army of Philip and Alexander', *CPh* 91.1 (1996), pp. 19–44.

Heckel, W., 'Alexander's Conquest of Asia', in W. Heckel and L. Tritle (eds), *Alexander the Great: A New History* (Oxford and Chichester: Wiley-Blackwell, 2011), pp. 26–52.

Howe, T. and S Müller, 'Mission Accomplished: Alexander at the Hyphasis' *AHB* 26 (2012), pp. 21–38.

Lane-Fox, R., *Alexander the Great* (London: Penguin, 1973).

Matarese, C., 'Proskynesis and the Gesture of the Kiss at Alexander's Court: The Creation of a new Élite', *Palamedes* 8 (2013), pp. 75–85.

Read Arrian, 3.15.4–5 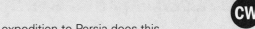.

1. How useful an insight into Alexander's priorities during his expedition to Persia does this afford? [12]

4.3 Change and Continuity in the Aims of Philip and Alexander

TOPIC OVERVIEW

- Alexander and Philip's aims during their careers, including
  - personal
  - political
  - military
  - economic
  - exploratory
  - and cultural considerations

The prescribed sources for this topic are:

- Arrian, *The Campaigns of Alexander* 1.7–8, 1.10, 1.23, 2.7, 2.14–15, 3.10, 3.16, 3.18, 5.25–26, and 7.9–10
- Plutarch, *Life of Alexander* 7–11 and 47
- Diodorus Siculus, *Library of History* 16.1, 16.8, 16.22.3, 16.53–54, 16.60, 16.75, 16.84, 16.86
- Demosthenes, *Speeches* 2.6–8 and 15–20
- Curtius Rufus, *History of Alexander* 5.6.1–7
- Justin, *Epitome* 8.3 and 9.5
- A gold coin of Philip
- The Poros Medallion

Study questions
Read Arrian, 7.9–10.

1 What can you infer about the aims of (a) Philip and (b) Alexander during the course of their careers?
2 How far can we rely on Arrian here for evidence of these aims?

We cannot ever know for sure what the aims of the figures of the past were. We can only judge them by their actions and what the ancient sources tell us. Philip and Alexander were father and son, and both were kings of Macedon. It therefore seems likely that many of Philip's aims were also Alexander's, especially concerning the kingdom of Macedon and its relationship with the rest of Greece. Alexander certainly viewed himself as the natural successor to all Philip accomplished. Yet, there were also fundamental differences. Some of these emerged while Alexander was still at the court of Philip. More importantly, their careers were different. One aim, only in its infancy during Philip's reign, which Alexander brought to full fruition was the expedition to Persia. Not only that, Alexander conquered Persia and even regions beyond it. We must therefore expect variation in their original aims. We should also be prepared for the fact that their respective aims changed during their lifetimes.

A fascinating passage in Arrian seems to distill the entire sweep of Philip and Alexander's achievements. It can be found in a speech attributed to Alexander at Opis when he feared that his army was going to revolt again.

PHILIP AND ALEXANDER'S AIMS DURING THEIR CAREERS

Personal aims

It is clear that Philip had high aspirations both for himself, his family and the kingdom of Macedon. Alexander also shared his self-belief and self-promotion. A revealing episode that reflects the personal aims of both men can be found in Plutarch.

A very cynical view of Philip's aims is set out in Demosthenes' tracts against Philip. One example (below) highlights the extent to which self-glorification was the overriding goal of Philip. We should, of course, be cautious about accepting such definitive statements since Demosthenes had his own specific agenda. Also evident in this passage is a clear antipathy for Macedon and a sense of Athenian superiority.

> For indeed Philip by all that might be deemed to constitute his greatness, by his wars and his campaigns, has only reduced his country below its natural level of insecurity. You must not imagine, men of Athens, that his subjects share his tastes. No: glory is his sole object and ambition . . .
>
> Demosthenes, *Speeches* 2.15

Alexander in many ways wanted to be like his father and there are in your prescribed sources a number of examples which point to a deep personal emulation of Philip by Alexander. But he had other role models too. These include Aristotle, his tutor, Achilles, the hero of Homer's epic the *Iliad*, the god Heracles and even certain Persian kings like Cyrus. However, in addition to wanting to be like them, we sometimes get the impression that Alexander wanted to outstrip each of these role models.

Political aims

When Philip came to the throne, Macedon faced considerable threats and challenges. Diodorus' introduction to his history of Philip's reign provides a rich seam of information about Philip's political aims on becoming king. For example, Diodorus (16.1 **PS**)

Study questions
Read Plutarch, 10. **PS**

1 What does this chapter reveal about the broader aims of (a) Philip and (b) Alexander?
2 Do you sense that the aims of each are working in the same direction here?

Study questions
Read Demosthenes, 2.6–8 and 2.15–20. **PS**

1 What are other aims Demosthenes attributes to Philip?
2 In each case, what are the specific limitations of Demosthenes' account as evidence?

ACTIVITY

Read through your prescribed sources and compile a list of examples which illustrate the particular and changing personal aims of Alexander.

Study question **PS**
Read Diodorus, 16.1–4.

How does Diodorus' view compare with Demosthenes' Second Olynthiac (above 2.6–8 and 2.15–20)? Are there any other of your prescribed sources which indicate that Philip was aiming to gain a Macedonian supremacy over the whole of Greece, and if so, what seems to be the slant of the source?

ACTIVITY

You should re-read the Prescribed Sources about Alexander's pursuit of Darius to reinforce your appreciation of this aim of Alexander.

KEY INDIVIDUAL

Ada of Caria
Dates: *c.* 377–326

A member of the House of Hecatomnus and ruler of Caria, first as Persian satrap and later as Queen under Alexander

Study question
Read Arrian, book 1.23. **PS**

Can you identify other prescribed sources which illustrate the similar political aims regarding Alexander's newly acquired empire?

ACTIVITY

You should try to find examples of this approach of divide and rule for both Alexander and Philip.

ACTIVITY

There are other possible examples of this in the sources that you should consider. One of these was the Exiles' Decree (see Key Topic 2).

describes how during his twenty-four years as king, Philip built a great kingdom from the most insignificant beginnings and transformed it from 'slave' to 'mistress'. Diodorus also alludes to the scale of Philip's expansionist aims. He also indicates that as Philip's grip on the political situation became more secure, his aims seemed to become increasingly more ambitious. It appears that Philip desired to have absolute sovereignty over the whole of Greece. Diodorus later suggests as much when he is narrating the build-up to the battle of Chaeronea:

> In this year, Philip the king, having won most of the Greeks over to friendship with him, was ambitious to gain the uncontested leadership of Greece by terrifying the Athenians into submission.

Diodorus, *Library of History* 16.84

Whilst these aims outlined by Diodorus seem plausible enough, we should bear in mind that Diodorus is also an apologist for Philip and packages all these aims in a positive emphasis on the 'valour' of Philip.

When Alexander inherited the throne from Philip in 336, he gained the strong kingdom that his father had established. There were some initial risks that parts of Greece that were hostile to Macedon would take advantage of a new, young king, and cause problems. However, as Key Topic 2 illustrates, Alexander dealt with these threats expeditiously. He seems to have shared his father's aims about keeping Macedon strong and autonomous.

Much of the focus in an evaluation of Alexander's political aims rightly has to be his Asian expedition. It is clear that Alexander had some precise political aims upon reaching Persia. One of these was the ousting of the Persian king Darius.

Alexander's conquest of the Persian Empire was remarkably swift. As an outsider, he had to manage the administration and governance of an empire which was vast as it was unfamiliar. A number of sources provide some clues as to Alexander's political aims as regards the maintenance of this empire. One example is Arrian. In his narrative of affairs just after the siege of Halicarnassus, he refers to Ada (1.23 **PS**), a Carian noble woman, whose rightful claim to the throne had been overturned by her brother, and how Alexander restored her to her throne and placed her in charge of the whole of Caria. This was a shrewd move since she had already demonstrated her support for him (she adopted him as her son) and so Alexander was ensuring he had loyalty in that region.

An interesting dimension of Alexander's aim to secure this part of the Persian Empire was the way he capitalised on episodes of Persian in-fighting. This policy of divide and rule, or taking advantage of others' conflicts was an interesting one. It is also one that on display in Philip's rise to ascendancy in Greece.

Alexander's promotion of Ada to the governorship of Caria might reveal another rather more subtle political aim that underlay many of Alexander's actions. This was the desire to right a wrong. Ada had been wrongly denied her position, and Alexander may well have been motivated by this when he restored her to her seat of power.

Military aims

Philip's military aims changed through his life. A primary aim upon becoming king was the reorganisation of his military forces. This included not just the fresh training and re-equipment of his troops but the use of innovative military tactics, some of which he acquired from the Greeks themselves.

In terms of military encounters, Philip started with defensive wars against those threatening Macedon's borders. Once he had secured his kingdom, Philip soon progressed to more offensive campaigns in strategic locations. The later campaigns were designed to provide long-term security to Macedon, expand territory and gain influence and booty.

One aspect of Philip's military aims was to take actions that seemed to designed to provoke the city-state of Athens in particular. He seemed keen to erode Athens' influence at every possible opportunity. As Diodorus writes concerning Philip's alliance with Olynthus in 358/357:

> Since the Olynthians inhabited an important city and because of its huge population and great influence in war, their city was an object of contention for those who sought to extend their supremacy. For this reason, the Athenians and Philip were rivals against one another for the alliance with the Olynthians.

Diodorus, *Library of History* 16.8

Philip's military ambitions knew few bounds. He soon turned his attention to subjugating cities in central Greece. These military aims culminated in the battle of Chaeronea in 338. Diodorus' account of this battle is interesting because we see both Philip and Alexander fighting side by side. The account (Diodorus, 16.86 **PS**) conveys well how both men were pursuing the same military aims but for slightly different reasons, though, of course, we must of course raise questions about the certainty with which Diodorus imputes such motivations.

Upon or just before becoming hegemon of Greece that Philip conceived of his expedition to Persia. Various sources provide information about Philip's military aims on this front.

As suggested above, many of Philip's military aims were initially shared by Alexander. Both, for example, found the need to put the neighbours of Macedon in their place. When Alexander was just sixteen he was appointed regent of Macedon by his father. While Philip was away on campaign, we read in Plutarch (chapter 9 **PS**) how Alexander quashed a rebellion of a nearby tribe, the Maedi. He acted quickly, capturing their main settlement, expelling the natives, placing it under military and civilian custody and renaming the place 'Alexandropolis'. However, Plutarch also suggests that Alexander seemed yet more ambitious than Philip. According to Plutarch 11 **PS**, Alexander, upon his father's death, contrary to the advice he received from Macedonians, was not simply content to win back the immediate neighbours who were revolting but preferred to act decisively against regions in the far north and also against Thebes in the south. Alexander's aims as regards Thebes at this time are also set out in Arrian 1.7–8 **PS** though these are presented in a rather more measured and defensive way.

Philip, while he was a hostage in Thebes, was heavily influenced by the Battle of Leuctra in 371. Many of the military innovations of Philip and Alexander are traced to this battle.

- Read Diodorus, 15.53–56 on the battle of Leuctra in 371 in which Boeotians, led by the Thebans fought the Spartans.

Study question **PS**

Read Diodorus, 16.22.3 on Philip's defeat of the Thracians', Paeonians' and Illyrians' joint forces in 356.

What does this extract tell us about Philip's immediate military aims?

ACTIVITY

Re-read the prescribed sources for Philip.

- What evidence is there that Philip wanted to subdue Athens?
- Why do you think Athens was of particular importance to Philip?

S & C

As regards the timing of Philip's decision to launch an invasion of Persia, see Speusippus' letter to Philip and Demosthenes 10.31–34.

Study questions
Read Diodorus,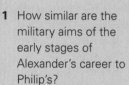
16.1.5–6 and
16.60.4–5 and Justin, 9.5.

1 What do these passages suggest were Philip's aims in Persia?
2 How do they differ and how are they similar in their presentation of Philip?

Study questions
Read Plutarch, 9 and 11 and Arrian, 1.7–8.

1 How similar are the military aims of the early stages of Alexander's career to Philip's?
2 How far do you think the aims outlined in these passages are credible?

Study questions
Read Arrian, 2.14.

1 What does Arrian write about the military aims of Alexander in this passage?
2 Might his Roman perspective have affected Arrian's account?

ACTIVITY

Re-read your prescribed sources on the Indus Valley campaign for evidence of Alexander's military aims at this point in the expedition.

> . . . he [Alexander] was in a hurry to proceed with his Asian campaign . . .
>
> Arrian, *The Campaigns of Alexander* 1.10

Like Philip, a key military aim of Alexander's was to embark on a military expedition to Asia.

There were many underlying reasons for this. An important reason was to finish what his father had begun: before his death, had been elected by the Greeks as leader of an invasion against Persia and when he died, Parmenio and Attalus, two of Philip's most senior generals, were already in Asia. It also became increasingly clear, as his campaign progressed, that there were other military pretexts for this, including revenge for previous Persian interference with Greece.

As we saw earlier, Alexander was determined to conquer Darius, the king of Persia. This was undoubtedly because he wanted to conquer the Persian empire. In this respect, his aims appear to have diverged from Philip's. Alexander defined himself as a military leader and he was also adamant that he should conquer Persia properly and completely.

Alexander's campaign in Asia extended beyond the conquest of the Persian Empire. There were a number of reasons for that explored in this topic, but one was a military aim, namely the securing of borders and frontiers. For instance, in Alexander's famous speech at Hyphasis when his men mutinied, he mounted an argument about the border territories they now controlled (Arrian, 5.25–26 **PS**).

Study questions
Re-read Arrian, 3.10 on the exchange between Alexander and Parmenio before the battle of Gaugamela and 2.7 on Alexander's speech before the battle of Issus.

1 What do these passages suggest about Alexander's military aims?
2 Can you locate in any of your other prescribed sources evidence for similar military aims concerning the conquest of Persia?

Economic

To fund their military activities, neither Philip nor Alexander could ignore the imperative to raise money quickly. As Plutarch would write in another of his biographical sketches (that of Aemilius Paulus): '[Philip and Alexander] mastered the world through their belief that empire was to be bought with money, not money with empire. Many of their military encounters seem to have been financially motivated. We have already read about the use of gold in Philip's campaigns and also his appropriation of mines. Diodorus elaborates on this in 16.8 **PS**, referring to how Philip seized Crenides only to transform the output of the mines and thereby amass a fortune. You might also consider what Diodorus (16.53 **PS**) writes about Philip and how, after plundering Olynthus, he enslaved inhabitants, selling both men, property and booty. This was so that Philip might procure large sums for prosecuting the war and intimidate the other cities that were opposed to him. In Diodorus 16.75 **PS**, there is also a reference to the wealth of the city of Perinthus that Philip was then besieging and the hopes of profit that success might bring.

Alexander was driven on by similar economic ambitions. However, the opportunities for plunder in Persia were of an entirely different order. Arrian (2.15 **PS**) describes how, following the Battle of Issus, he issued instructions for the treasure and money Darius had attempted to smuggled out be taken back to Damascus for safekeeping. We read in Arrian, 3.16 **PS**, for example, about the capture by Alexander of the Persian city of Susa where the treasure which Alexander took upon entering the city amounted to 50,000 talents of silver (a huge amount!) in addition to other valuables formerly in possession of the king. Also at Alexander's disposal were all the treasures which Xerxes had brought from Greece. The same abundance of plunder was to be had by Alexander at Persepolis too (Arrian, 3.18 **PS**).

Both Philip and Alexander were generous with the plunder gained in military campaigns. It appears that for both men, a vital aim was to keep their troops happy and loyal through the promise of handsome financial rewards.

Coins have survived until today which contain images of Philip and Alexander. These may have been minted by each leader when they were alive. While one aim may have been economic, the production of such coins certainly also involved a high degree of self-promotion and propaganda (see also Diodorus, 16.8 **PS**). The two coins are shown in Figures 4.10 and 4.11.

The coin in Figure 4.10 was almost certainly minted by Philip in Pella *c.* 340, though it might date to immediately after his death. A name in Greek capital letters was written at the bottom of the reverse (the lower image in Fig 4.10), though it is barely visible (ΦΙΛΙΠ[ΠΟΥ] or PHILIP[POU]). The obverse shows the garlanded head of Apollo. The reverse depicts a chariot and a charioteer in a race. He is holding goad in his right hand and reins in his left below. The rider may well be Philip himself who we know participated in and enjoyed victory at the Olympic games.

Study question
Read Arrian, 3.16 and 3.18 on Alexander's seizure of treasure in Susa and Persepolis and Curtius Rufus, 5.6.1–7 on Persepolis.

How do Arrian's descriptions of Alexander's economic aims compare to what Curtius Rusus writes in 5.6.1–7?

PRESCRIBED SOURCE

A gold coin of Philip

Date: *c.* 340 BC

Mint: Pella

Significance: a source that dates to the time of Philip

Current Location: an example can be found in the British Museum (1911,0208.2)

View it here: Figure 4.10

Study question **PS**
Read Diodorus, 16.8, 16.53–54 and 16.75.

How do these sources compare with what Justin, 8.3 **PS** writes?

ACTIVITY

Identify in your prescribed sources examples of when and how Philip's and Alexander's conquests enabled them to enrich their troops.

FIGURE 4.10
A gold coin of Philip.

FIGURE 4.11
Porus Medallion held at the British Museum.

Study questions
Study the coins in Figs 4.10 and 4.11.

1 If these coins were minted during Philip and Alexander's respective lifetimes, what can these coins tell us about them?
2 What are the (a) strengths and (b) limitations of these coins as historical evidence?

The Porus Medallion (Figure 4.11) was discovered in modern Afghanistan in the late nineteenth century AD. The obverse (top in Fig 4.11) shows a cavalryman, probably a Macedonian, with a helmet and characteristic sarissa, charging at an elephant with two warriors mounted on its back. The reverse shows another figure, this time standing and being crowned by a winged Victory. This figure is carrying what could either be a sarissa or a royal sceptre in his left hand, and in his right hand he holds the thunderbolt of Zeus. The coin almost certainly alludes to the Macedonian victory at the Hydaspes and it is likely that the figure is intended to be Alexander himself. On the obverse, the standing figure mounted on the elephant and brandishing a spear has been identified as Porus because of the figure's height. Porus is described in almost all ancient sources as extremely tall. The dating of the coin is difficult. However, experts consider that the coin was minted in Babylon at the very end of Alexander's lifetime or shortly after his death in 323.

Exploratory

Aims of exploration apply in the main to Alexander. When Alexander and his men arrived at the furthest reaches of the Persian Empire and then ventured into the Indus Valley, they were entering into a world completely unknown to the Greeks. The sense of adventure and exhilaration that Alexander clearly felt at this point in the expedition is powerfully conveyed in the sources. A good example of this is Alexander's speech at the mutiny of Hyphasis.

Study questions
Read Arrian, 5.25–26.

1 What does Arrian's account suggest about Alexander's exploratory aims?
2 How do you think the Roman readers (those living in the Roman Empire) of Arrian would respond to this?

Cultural considerations

Philip, in addition, to military ambitions, appears to have been driven on by cultural considerations. In many of the Greek sources, Macedon is depicted as somewhat of a cultural desert. Some scholars think this reputation may have been exaggerated by the sources and that under predecessors of Philip, there was a thriving culture at the Macedonian court. For instance, we know that Euripides, an Athenian playwright spent time in the court of Archelaus. Whatever the case, Philip seemed enthusiastic about cultivating or continuing to maintain a high level of culture in Macedon. It is interesting to read, for example, about the education Philip secured for his own son, Alexander, and also for the offspring of other Macedonian nobles.

Such cultural aims appear to be been internalised by Alexander who, according to our ancient sources, never forgot his education and insisted on reading Greek literary texts throughout his expedition to the east.

It would be easy to claim that Alexander's Asian expedition was an act of colonialism by a leader keen to 'Hellenise' or even civilise the foreign lands they conquered, particularly through the foundation of Greek cities in Persia. However, Alexander's cultural aims do not appear to have been so straightforward. Our sources point instead to a desire on Alexander's part to create a fusion of cultures, to enjoy the best of the east and the west had to offer. Alexander, as we saw in Arrian, book 1.23 **PS**, had no problem being considered the adoptive son of Ada, the ruler of Caria. We might also recall how Alexander in 324 arranged a series of weddings between Greek men and Persian wives.

More examples of Alexander's adoption of Eastern values are set out in Key Topic 4. Indeed, modern scholars believe that Philip too admired certain Persian ways and had tried to incorporate some of them into his court at Macedon. It might be possible to argue that both Philip and Alexander genuinely admired the Persian culture and wanted it to enrich Macedonian and Greek life. At the same time, there were for Alexander, a number of pressing practical reasons to establish a harmonious fusion of cultures, namely to keep the empire he had conquered intact.

> **Study question**
> Read Plutarch, 7–8 on Philip's **PS** appointment of Aristotle as tutor.
>
> What does Plutarch's account here indicate about Philip's cultural aims?

> **Study questions**
> Read Plutarch, 47. **PS**
>
> 1 What does Plutarch suggest about Alexander's cultural aims in this chapter?
> 2 How trustworthy is this as a source?

TOPIC REVIEW

- Compare the aims of Philip and Alexander.
- Explain how Alexander's aims changed and why.
- Discuss the ambitions that seemed most important to both of them.
- Review how the different authors who write about Philip and Alexander present their aspirations in similar or different ways.
- Consider the extent we can learn from the sources what the aims of each of these men were.

Further Reading

Buckler, J., 'Philip II's Designs on Greece' in R.W. Wallace and E.M. Harris (eds), *Transitions to Empire: Essays in Greco-Roman History, 360–146* BC, *in honor of E. Badian* (Norman and London: University of Oklahoma Press, 1996), pp. 77–97.

Buckler, J., *Philip II and the Sacred War* (Leiden, New York, Copenhagen and Köln: Brill, 1989).

Cohen, A., 'Alexander and Achilles-Macedonians and Mycenaeans' in J.B. Carter and S.P. Morris (eds), *The Ages of Homer: A Tribute to Emily Townsend Vermeule* (Austin: University of Texas Press, 1995), pp. 483–505.

Dmitriev, S., 'Alexander's Exiles Decree' *Klio* 86 (2004), pp. 348–81.

Nagle, D.B., 'The Cultural Context of Alexander's Speech at Opis', *TAPA* 126 (1996), pp.151–72.

Natoli, A.F., *The Letter of Speusippus to Philip II* (Stuttgart: Franz Steiner Verlag, 2014).

Worthington, I., 'From East to West. Alexander and the Exiles Decree' in P. Wheatley and E. Baynham (eds), *East and West in the World Empire of Alexander. Essays in Honour of Brian Bosworth* (Oxford: Oxford University Press, 2015), pp. 93–106.

PRACTICE QUESTIONS

'Alexander and Philip shared many of the same aims'.

1. How far do you agree with this view? You must use and analyse the ancient sources you have studied, as well as your own knowledge to support your answer. [36]

4.4 The Character and Beliefs of Philip and Alexander

TOPIC OVERVIEW

- Analysis of Philip's character in connection with the major events of his career, including
  - his treatment of those he defeated
  - attitude to diplomacy
  - attitude to the gods
  - role as a figurehead and prosecution of warfare

- Analysis of Alexander's character, including
  - as a military leader
  - his treatment of his companions and those he defeated
  - adoption of Persian dress and customs
  - his beliefs towards his own divinity
  - his attitude towards the gods as well as mythological and historical precedents

The prescribed sources for this topic are:

- Diodorus Siculus, *Library of History* 16.3–4, 16.4, 16.8, 16.34, 16.55, 16.58, 16.74, 16.84, 16.85, 16.86, 16.87, 16.92
- Demosthenes, *Speches* 8.11, 19.41
- Justin, *Epitome* 8.2–3, 8.5 and 9.4
- Plutarch, *Life of Alexander* 16, 23, 27–28, 45, 47 and 59
- Arrian, *The Campaigns of Alexander* 1.11–12, 1.13, 1.16, 1.20–23, 1.29, 2.7, 2.12, 3.10, 3.14–16, 4.7–8, 4.10–12, 4.18, 6.8–10, 6.13, 7.6 and 7.22
- Gold coin of Philip

It is very difficult to ever really know the true character of someone alive today, let alone of someone who lived such a long time ago. However, it is possible to make inferences about both Philip and Alexander from the sources available to us. Both men had extraordinary lives, full of action, excitement and danger and their personalities do emerge. This topic will review different aspects of their thought, including religion and friendship. It will also survey the behaviour of each man in extreme situations such as war. We should be mindful, too, that there are many cultural and societal considerations peculiar to their times which also have to be factored into any meaningful assessment of their characters.

ANALYSIS OF PHILIP'S CHARACTER IN CONNECTION WITH THE MAJOR EVENTS OF HIS CAREER

Philip's treatment of those he defeated

Philip of Macedon was more or less constantly at war during his entire period of kingship. This naturally entailed considerable stamina and a toughness of spirit. He could be ruthless and, when it came to his enemies, unforgiving. However, he also it seems had a humane side and could exercise magnanimity and leniency when he wanted.

We might compare the aftermaths of three episodes in Philip's military career: the sieges of Amphipolis, Methone and Chaeronea. Diodorus deals with each, describing Philip's actions in a business-like fashion, and highlighting the pragmatism of Philip more than anything else. He describes (16.8.2 **PS**) how Philip unleashed all the military power at his disposal against Amphipolis, but that afterwards he exiled only those who remained disaffected; the rest were treated considerately. After the siege of Methone (16.34.3–5 **PS**), Philip was brutal, forcing each citizen to leave the city with only one garment each. This siege, however, had lasted a year and, as Diodorus tells us, Philip had lost an eye during it. After Chaeronea (16.87 **PS**), Philip agreed to release all Athenian prisoners without ransom, and sent envoys to secure peace terms with Athens and Thebes.

These accounts may be set alongside Justin's accounts of how Philip treated those he had defeated in that battle. Justin places considerable focus on Philip's own malevolent feelings about his victory and the vanquished foe.

Philip's attitude to diplomacy

In conjunction with this sub-section, you should re-read the section on diplomacy and opportunism in Key Topic 1.

Diplomacy seems to have been a vital tool for Philip in establishing his hegemony in Greece. Diodorus writes about the extent to which Philip had won the friendship of many Greek cities (book 16.84 **PS**) to shore up his power. He was very generous with his gifts as king. Diplomacy, however, does not appear to have been end in itself, and if it failed to work, Philip would have no hesitation about going to war. Philip was highly unusual in the extent to which he combined diplomacy with military force. We can read about initial diplomatic efforts which in the end failed and resulted in war.

By some, Philip's actions were understood not as diplomatic but as completely underhand. According to Demosthenes, for example, Philip's diplomacy was part of a calculated strategy to lull other's suspicions. In an extract from his speech *On the False Embassy* (19.41 **PS**) Demosthenes stresses that the terms of the Peace of Philocrates were secured in bad faith. He comments that Philip promised the Athenians benefits, but once the treaty was signed, none were forthcoming. He additionally accuses Philip of taking advantage of loopholes wherever possible.

Study questions

Read Diodorus, 16.8.2, 16.34.3–5 and 16.87 and Justin 8.3 and 9.4.

1 Do these accounts seem credible to you?
2 How do the accounts of Justin compare with what Diodorus writes?

Study question

Read Diodorus, 16.4.4 and 16.85.3–4.

What can these extracts tell us about Philip's (a) character and (b) attitude to diplomacy?

Study questions

Read Demosthenes, 19.41.

1 From a historical perspective, what are the merits and drawbacks of this speech?
2 Can you find any other examples of such a view in other speeches of Demosthenes or in other sources?

Philip's attitude to the gods

When considering ancient attitudes to the gods, we must try to escape a more modern understanding of religion and our own assumptions. Religion was central to conquest and the serious business of running an empire. Public worship of the gods was important because every commander and every ruler at the time practised it. The act of sacrifice was also widely relied upon in order to keep the gods on side. Philip and Alexander shared the contemporary views of their time, namely that gods existed, they were powerful and had to be respected. Likewise, religious detail was for the authors we are reading neither extraneous nor insignificant. Many were living among Romans who endorsed polytheism and considered that the worship of gods and their signs was vital.

Philip evidently had a deep respect for the gods. The process of winning their support and keeping them on side was important to him. Diodorus (16.55.1 and 16.86.6 **PS**) describes how Philip, after his victory at Olynthus and Chaeronea respectively, offered magnificent sacrifices to the gods.

Philip, according to some ancient sources, appears to have taken seriously the religious wrongs committed by others, and was keen to punish them. You may recall from Key Topic 1 how Philip became involved in the Sacred Wars which had started in part because of the capture of the sacred sanctuary of Delphi by the Phocians. Diodorus (16.58.3 **PS**) points out how keen Philip was not to seem indifferent to the pillaging of an oracle. However, other sources are more cynical about the degree to which Philip was just manipulating others' devotion to the gods. We read the following in Justin (8.2 **PS**), for example, that Philip portrayed himself as the avenger of sacrilege, adding the whole affair brought him great personal glory. In their way, both sources suggest that Philip was more concerned about appearances than anything else. We do well, however, to bear in mind that outward ritual was in many ways more important than inward devotion in ancient Greek religion. More significant perhaps is Justin's open contempt for Philip.

Depending on how you read the sources, it is possible to assert that Philip was not just a strict observer of religious protocol but essentially thought of himself as a god. We might be able to infer this from Diodorus (16.92 **PS**) and the gold coin of Philip **PS**). However, before assessing him in such terms, it is worth bearing in mind that in ancient Macedon, subjects would give to a monarch the kind of honours they gave to a god, willingly, because he was so powerful, and generally beneficent. Those writing under the Roman system would also understand the notion of deification of an emperor.

Philip's role as a figurehead and prosecution of warfare

Some of the ancient sources present Philip, like his son Alexander, as a singularly brilliant military general. They characterise him as brave and strong, in no way an 'arm-chair' general but rather always leading by example, at the front line of battle. This certainly comes across in Diodorus' descriptions of Philip's heroic conflict against the Illyrians (Diodorus, 16.4 **PS**). As a general observation, the author Diodorus tends to present Philip's qualities as a leader in a sympathetic light. For instance, he highlights Philip's positive and generous treatment of his soldiery. In 16.3 and 16.86.6 **PS**, Diodorus

ACTIVITY

Consider what the contemporary readers of Diodorus would think about Philip's religious observations following a military victory.

Study question **PS**

Read Diodorus, 16.92 and review the gold coin of Philip.

Can we infer anything from these about how Philip viewed his own status?

ACTIVITY

Re-read your Diodorus Siculus sources on Philip and identify any other leadership traits that he highlights.

Study question PS

Read Diodorus, 16.3, 16.8 and 16.74.

What does the information Diodorus gives here about Philip's military innovations tell us about Philip's character as a leader in warfare?

Study questions PS

Read Demosthenes, 8.11 and Justin, 8.5.

1 How do these compare with Diodorus' portrayal?
2 What makes these source reliable or problematic?

Study questions PS

Read Plutarch 16 and Arrian 1.16.1–3, 1.20–23, 3.14–15 and 6.8–10 on Alexander's performance in the battles of Granicus and Gaugamela, in the siege of Halicarnassus and in the conflict with the Mallians.

1 What do these sources tell us about Alexander's character as a military leader?
2 How might Arrian's experience with the Roman military have influenced his accounts?

describes how Philip gave morale-boosting speeches to his men in Macedon, and how after the battle of Chaeronea, he publicly acknowledged men who had distinguished themselves on the battle-field.

Diodorus also refers to Philip's modernisation of his armed forces. He outlines that Philip was responsible for many military innovations to a degree unparalleled before and developed siege tactics. These initiatives, to the extent we can place reliance on them, can reveal much about Philip's personality as a leader.

In his capacity as general, Philip achieved much in a short time. By 354/353, in just five years from his accession, Philip had unified Macedon and turned it into the dominant power of the region. He had completely reduced Athenian influence in the region. By 338 he was the recognised supreme authority in the whole of Greece and had started to work on protecting Greek areas that were under threat of Persian aggression. It may be that we have to take Diodorus's descriptions of Philip's qualities seriously in order to explain such speed of conquest and success. However, Demosthenes, Philip's arch-enemy, and another later author, Justin, also had their own views on Philip's form of leadership.

ANALYSIS OF ALEXANDER'S CHARACTER

Alexander as a military leader

There are many points of correspondence between Alexander and his father Philip in their approaches to military leadership. Many of these traits exhibited by Alexander were arguably inherited from his father. The many positive accounts of Alexander's leadership, must always be questioned and not simply accepted as straightforward accounts. We should bear in mind that the issue of morality underpins the agendas of particularly Plutarch but also Arrian to some extent.

Alexander's capacity for decision-making is an important theme in the sources. A general can and should be prepared to take difficult decisions and be seen to be decisive. However, he must always remain reliant to a certain extent on advice from senior colleagues. The degree to which a general is willing to receive recommendations and act on them, or otherwise, can tell us much about that general's character. According to Arrian (1.13 and Plutarch 16 PS) Alexander made the decision to cross the river Granicus at night in spite of Parmenio's advice to the contrary. Again, just before the battle of Gaugamela, Alexander (Arrian, 3.10 PS) rejected Parmenio's recommendation to launch a night-attack. The authors tend to use such moments to present the brilliance of Alexander, but we should bear in mind such unilateral decision-making can be a demonstration of less attractive attributes such as impetuosity. In our sources, of course, we do at least have an example of Alexander actually listening to Parmenio, also just before Gaugamela (3.10 PS).

Another leadership quality evident in the sources is Alexander's strategic instinct. Arrian offers one such example during a description of Alexander's journey to Gordium (PS Arrian, 1.29). Alexander comes across the town of Celaenae in Phrygia which was well-fortified by nature and was also garrisoned by Carian troops and Greek mercenaries.

Arrian writes that Alexander agreed to a request by the town's garrison which had offered to surrender provided that no reinforcements arrived on a certain day. Arrian then explains the sensible rationale for this decision on the grounds: a siege would have been too difficult here. Arrian makes similar observations about Alexander's nous when it comes to military organisation. In Arrian's account just after Gaugamela, he writes:

> He [Alexander] was joined by Amyntas, son of Andromenes, with the fresh troops for Macedonia, both horse and foot, the former he attached to the Companion cavalry and distributed the latter according to nationality among the various infantry units. He also – this was an innovation – formed two companies in each cavalry squadron and put them under the command of such officers of the Companions who had distinguished themselves.

> Arrian, *The Campaigns of Alexander* 3.16

Alexander is depicted as a fearless, stoical and caring leader. Arrian, for example (2.12.1 **PS**) refers to Alexander's visits, in the immediate aftermath of the battle of Issus, to the wounded even though he had sustained a serious wound in his own thigh. Plutarch (45 **PS**) too, when writing about the expedition in Parthia, comments on the wounds Alexander had sustained and the way in which he chased an army of Scythians for a long way despite suffering from dysentery.

On the other hand, the sources are not uniformly glowing. It is possible to locate in the ancient authors some rather less positive aspects of Alexander's leadership. Arrian (4.18.4–7 **PS**), for instance, describes how it was pure anger on account of the insults of local tribesmen that drove Alexander to scale the Rock of Sogdiana. Additionally, after the conflict with the Mallians, Arrian (6.13.4–5 **PS**) describes how Alexander was angry with those who had rebuked him for taking unnecessary risks with his life. Arrian, with a typical authorial interjection, adds that even Alexander himself realised that he had been rash and taken foolish risks when fighting the Mallians. Plutarch (59 **PS**) is likewise rather disparaging when he describes how Alexander ambushed some Indians he had already entered into a truce with, and also hanged many philosophers.

ACTIVITY

Identify in your sources other examples which illustrate the type of military commander Alexander was. You should also consider the limitations of such accounts when it some to the issue of reliability.

Alexander's treatment of his companions and those he defeated

There are many episodes in the ancient sources you have read which provide details about Alexander's treatment of his companions. He was a general who was greatly admired by his men not least because he respected them and treated them well; with some he forged very intimate relations. At the same time, the ancient sources sometimes present Alexander as a general who took his companions for granted, disregarded their collective wishes, and even treated them in a way that almost put them on the same level as the enemy.

Like his father, Alexander's approach to those he defeated was mixed. He could be very ruthless, but he could also exercise great clemency. This is not to suggest that Alexander did not know his own mind. It appears there was a logic to all his actions. Plutarch (11 **PS**) describes Alexander's severe treatment of the Thebans after he defeated

ACTIVITY

Make a list of six episodes described in your sources:

(a) three that illustrate how well Alexander treated his companions; and

(b) three that demonstrate a less positive approach to his companions.

them: he captured, plundered and razed the city to the ground. Plutarch explains that this was because Alexander wanted it to serve as a deterrent to further insurrection and as a show of support for his allies the Phocians and Plataeans. Arrian (1.23 PS) also presents us with a leader who, after the siege of Halicarnassus, ordered anyone helping to set fire to that city to be summarily killed. On the other hand, Arrian (1.16.6 PS) also informs us that Alexander even buried dead Persian commanders and Greek mercenaries after the battle of Granicus.

Alexander's adoption of Persian dress and customs

Once he had established himself as ruler of the Persian empire, Alexander adopted Persian dress and customs. Alexander's apparent preference for these aspects of Asian etiquette is sometimes given as an example of his increased 'orientalism', which essentially meant an abandonment of his Greek ways for Asian ones. The Persian custom most frequently commented on in regard to Alexander was proskynesis. Similar to this and, as some sources mention, were acts of extreme flattery or prostration taking place in the court of Alexander.

When reading about the adoption by Alexander of Persian customs in the sources, we must be careful to understand how authors like Arrian and Plutarch may have been projecting their own value-systems onto their accounts. For many of Alexander's contemporaries, such customs would not have seemed very surprising. The Macedonian court certainly used some similar rituals. Alexander had taken over a great empire and he had to find ways of governing it, and it is not surprising that this included adopting the practices of the previous rulers, including their formal dress and court practices. But this was difficult for writers like Plutarch and Arrian to understand.

This sort of behaviour by Alexander would, according to the sources, eventually bring Alexander into serious conflict with many of his closest friends, especially Cleitus and Callisthenes. However, there were some companions, particularly Hephaestion and Peucastas, who seemed more willing to follow Alexander's lead in this cultural assimilation.

Alexander's beliefs towards his own divinity

According to our sources, Alexander from a young age was led to believe in his divine ancestry. In particular, he felt a close affinity with Zeus-Ammon. This belief of Alexander's seemed only to grow as his journey to the East progressed. In 332, Alexander visited Siwah, an oasis in the Egyptian desert, where he consulted the oracle of Ammon. The journey was long, far from Persia, and, though there were strategic reasons for visiting Egypt, it was a highly risky trip. Plutarch (27 PS) highlights the highly numinous aspects of journey. He suggests that Alexander received divine help (in the form of birds) in crossing the desert. Nobody knows exactly what Alexander asked and what the god replied, although Plutarch provides some theories. He indicates that the prophet implied the god was Alexander's father and alludes (27–28 PS) to other details which reflected Alexander's aspirations to be regarded as the son of a god. Plutarch also offers his own view on the matter, writing that Alexander used the belief in his own divinity to dominate others.

'For my part,' he [Callisthenes] said, 'I hold Alexander fit for any mark of honour that a man may earn; but do not forget that there is a difference between honouring a man and worshipping a god.

Arrian, *The Campaigns of Alexander* 4.11

Just as Alexander's adoption of Persian customs caused some upset among his men, so too did his ideas about his own divinity.

Alexander's attitude towards the gods as well as mythological and historical precedents

Alexander appears to have a deep respect for the great exploits of the past, especially the mythological past which had such cultural currency at the time. Alexander was an avid reader of the epic poems of Homer. He also seems to have prized above all other qualities the Homeric ideals of glory and honour. The ancient sources reflect this, for example, Arrian (1.11–12 **PS**).

Alexander, like his father Philip, also took seriously the existence of the gods and his relationship with them. Sacrifices were important.

It was in Babylon that Alexander came into contact with the Chaldaeans; in all matters of religious ceremonial he took their advice, offering sacrifice to **Bel** in particular, according to their instructions.

Arrian, *The Campaigns of Alexander* 3.16.5

Alexander involved himself regularly in **divination**. Divination was a standard practice of the age because there was so much that humans could not establish for themselves. Every commander and every ruler at the time relied on it to know what the gods wanted and what the gods would tell them. However, towards the end of his life, it does seem that Alexander became increasingly oppressed by divine omens towards the end of his life.

In addition to the myths of the distant past, Alexander, it seems, also had an interest in more recent history and a keen sense of his place in it. You might consider Alexander's frequent recollections of the previous Persian invasion of Greece and how he viewed himself as exacting revenge for this.

Just before the battle of Issus Alexander made a speech to his troops in which he recalled another Greek encounter with the Persians (Arrian, 2.2.7–9 **PS**). He reminded them of the Greek general Xenophon and his force of **Ten Thousand** who found themselves stranded in Persia after an attempted coup by Cyrus the Younger whom they were assisting failed. Xenophon had helped lead these Greek mercenaries to safety towards the Black Sea.

Bel a foreign god, a Babylonian deity.

divination the practice of seeking knowledge of the future or the unknown by supernatural means

Ten Thousand a large army of Greek mercenaries

KEY INDIVIDUALS

Xenophon
Dates: 430–354
A Greek general and historian. He accompanied the Ten Thousand. He recorded the feat in his work, *Anabasis*

Cyrus the Younger
Dates: d. 401 BC
A Persian prince and general who tried to seize the throne of Persia from his brother, Artaxerxes II

TOPIC REVIEW

- Outline the essential character traits of Philip.
- Outline the essential character traits of Alexander.
- Discuss the beliefs of each concerning the gods.
- Both Philip and Alexander enjoyed many military victories. Review the ways in which they behaved in such circumstances.
- Assess how our sources may have distorted the character descriptions of Philip and Alexander.

Further Reading

Bloedow, E., 'Egypt in Alexander's Scheme of Things', *Quaderni Urbinati di Cultura Classica* 77.2 (2004), pp. 75–99.
Ryder, T.T.B., 'The Diplomatic Skills of Philip II', in I. Worthington (ed.), *Ventures into Greek History* (Oxford: Clarendon, 1994), pp. 228–57
Worthington, I., *Philip II of Macedonia* (New Haven: Yale University Press, 2008), pp. 228–33

PRACTICE QUESTIONS

Read Plutarch, *Life of Alexander*, chapter 45.1–2 PS.

1. How useful is this passage for informing us of Alexander's relationship with Persian culture?

[12]

4.5 The Relationships between the Monarchs and Others, including the Army and Greek and Conquered States

This topic is about the nature of the relationships Philip and Alexander forged between different sets of people over the years. Such relationships can shed valuable light on the characters of these men. They can also tell us something about cultural variations and social norms across the ancient world. In their respective careers both Philip and Alexander encountered a myriad of different situations which needed responding to and coping with. Philip and Alexander were both Macedonian leaders rather than Greek. Macedon was geographically close to Greece, but as their paths became increasingly intertwined with the Greek city states, so they needed to negotiate that relationship with commensurate care. Both men too were leaders of military forces and this topic will focus too on the type of relationship Philip and Alexander had with their armies. Alexander spent most of his adult life in Persia and so a further important aspect considered in this topic with be Alexander's relations with the Persians.

Study question PS
Read Diodorus, 16.1 and 16.58 and Justin, 8.4.

When it comes to assessing Philip's treatment of the Greeks, what are the strengths and limitations as history of each author?

Study questions PS
Read Arrian, 1.7–8 and 1.10 and Plutarch, 12 and 13 on the battle of Thebes and its aftermath.

1 Is there anything in these sources to suggest how the Greek city states felt about Macedon generally?
2 How did Alexander behave towards Thebes and other city states and how did they view him?
3 How does Alexander's relationship with Thebes compare to Philip's?

THE RELATIONSHIP BETWEEN ALEXANDER AND PHILIP AND THE VARIOUS GREEK STATES AND OTHER PEOPLES AT DIFFERENT TIMES

The nature of Philip and Alexander's relationships with the various Greek city states and other peoples is a complex issue. The ancient sources do not paint a straightforward picture. It also appears that both Philip and Alexander could often be inconsistent in their approaches.

Philip's relationship with the city states of Greece was a fraught one, especially given his increasing supremacy over them. However, even his rise to power over them can be understood in very different ways. Depending on the sources you read (and the way you read them), the Macedonian Philip may be presented as guardian or oppressor of the Greek states. Diodorus (16.1 PS), for example, refers to Philip's 'liberation' of Greek city states. Conversely, he also in (16.58 PS) describes the enjoyment Philip seemed to derive from the obsequious requests for help he received from the Boeotians. Justin, offers an even starker assessment of Philip's aloof and contemptuous manner when it came to his treatment of Greek city-states.

We can infer much about Philip's relationship with the Greek city states from later accounts of Alexander's attempts to reassert control over Greece after his father died. At the same time, these accounts provide insights into Alexander's own relationship with the Greek states at the start of his career. We can also consider how the respective relationships of Philip and Alexander with the Greek states differed or were similar.

Both Alexander and Philip had a particularly erratic relationship with Athens. Athens had been a leading power (culturally, militarily and financially) in Greece in the previous century. It appears that Alexander and Philip felt a combination of deep admiration and fierce rivalry with Athens. Certainly, when Philip first took the throne, Athens may well have had the edge militarily over Macedon. You will also recall the prolonged sparring between Philip and Athens during his rise to power (see Key Topic 1). There are a number of accounts in the ancient sources about the relationship between Philip and Alexander and Athens.

Diodorus (16.8 **PS**) alludes both to the deference Philip held Athens in, on account of the importance and repute of that city, yet at the same time actively worked against their strategic interests in places like Olynthus. Demosthenes, an Athenian himself, and deeply hostile towards Philip, offers a much bleaker analysis of Philip's approach (for example, in 9.7–12 and 9.32–35 **PS**) where he refers to the 'brutality' of Philip towards Athens.

A similar spectrum of possible interpretations emerges when it comes to Alexander and Athens. After the battle of Granicus, Arrian and Plutarch (1.16 and 16 **PS**) inform us that Alexander sent to Athens 300 Persian shields, together with inscription, as an offering to Athena, the patron goddess of Athens. He did something similar upon arriving at Susa (Arrian, 3.16 **PS**), sending treasure back to Athens, like the bronze statues of Harmodius and Aristogeiton, that Xerxes had once taken. Plutarch also imagines Alexander making direct reference to 'men of Athens' during his battle against Poros (60 **PS**). On the other hand, Arrian also conveys well the ambivalent attitude felt by Alexander towards Athens in 1.29 **PS** where Alexander is presented as refusing to release Athenian prisoners of war taken at Granicus.

In Arrian (2.15 **PS**) we read of the Greek envoys who were captured after Issus. These men had initially been fighting for Darius. These envoys represented certain city-states in Greece – Thebes, Sparta and Athens – and it is interesting to read how Alexander treated each of them. We are told that he immediately discharged those from Thebes as he felt that state had suffered enough. The one from Athens he treated with honour, as Arrian puts it 'out of affection'. However, the Spartan he kept under arrest on account of the bitterness he harboured towards that city-state. The passage is suggestive of the way that personal feeling affected his treatment of different Greek city-states.

The significant number of Greek mercenaries fighting on behalf of the Persians suggests that many Greeks viewed Macedon as worse than the Persians. It might also be the case that Persia paid them more. However, we must also consider the changing attitudes of Greek city-states to Alexander as the campaign progressed. Arrian offers an interesting insight at the end of Alexander's career:

> Successive delegations from Greece also presented themselves and the delegates, wearing ceremonial wreaths, solemnly approached Alexander and placed golden chaplets on his head, as if their coming were a ritual in honour of a god. **PS**
>
> Arrian, *The Campaigns of Alexander* 7.23

THE TREATMENT BY PHILIP AND ALEXANDER OF GREEKS IN DIFFERENT CONTEXTS

The treatment by Philip of the Greeks varied, in part, according to his own immediate aims at any given time.

Our impression of Philip's treatment of the Greeks is naturally going to be dependent on the standpoint of the author describing it. Demosthenes and Justin, for example, present us with quite a different picture to Diodorus. However, even some of Demosthenes' works present us with differing views about Philip in Athens.

Study question
Read Diodorus, 16.8, **PS** Demosthenes, 9.7–12 and 32–35, Arrian, 1.16, 1.29 and 3.16 and Plutarch, 16 and 60.

What might be some of the limitations of these sources when it comes to considering the relationship of Philip and Alexander with Athens?

ACTIVITIES

- Review your prescribed sources on Philip of Macedon and compile a list of episodes in which he (a) appears to assist or support Greeks and (b) where he treats them in a destructive or hostile way.
- Add to your list the precise contexts for each of these episodes.

Study questions

1 Locate at least one example from (a) Diodorus, (b) Demosthenes and (c) Justin on Philip's treatment of the Greeks.
2 Comment on how the attitude or historical agenda of each author might have affected the presentation of the episode being described.

Alexander's treatment of the Greeks similarly varied. Some passages point to the deep respect he felt for the Greeks. When encountering these, it might be worth keeping in mind the awe in which many Romans held Greek culture at the time of writers like Arrian and Diodorus. Other passages allude to the harsh treatment he meted out against Greeks. This is particularly the case in respect of Alexander's treatment of Greek mercenaries fighting for the Persians: see, for example, his ruthless butchery of mercenaries at the battle of Granicus (**PS** Arrian, 1.16 and Plutarch, 16). It is very likely that Alexander bitterly resented what he understood to be a fundamental act of disloyalty (Arrian, 1.29 **PS**).

ACTIVITIES

- Review your prescribed sources on Alexander.
- Identify three episodes which contain information on Alexander's dealings with Greeks. Comment on the type of treatment Alexander exhibits in each of them and the factors we need to take into account when considering the reliability of these episodes.

ALEXANDER'S RELATIONSHIP WITH HIS ARMY AND COMPANIONS

MODERN PARALLEL

Can we compare the reverence and love the troops have for Alexander to the way worshippers treat a saint, for example, or a religious leader?

ACTIVITIES

Read Arrian, 5.25–29 on the mutiny at Hyphasis and 7.8–12 at Opis.

- Compile a list of points Alexander makes in each of his speeches which convey the way he perceived the nature of the relationship he had with his army.
- Comment on how the reactions of his men in each of these episodes reflects their attitudes to him.

The evidence points very strongly to the close relationship Alexander had with his men. His rapport with them and their admiration for him may well help to explain the many victories, often against high odds, the Macedonians enjoyed during their years in Asia. There are a number of sources available that reflect the deep bonds that existed between Alexander and his army.

After the battle of Granicus, Arrian describes Alexander's attentive visits to the wounded (**PS** 1.16) and Plutarch alludes to the Alexander's plan to honour the dead by commissioning sculptures of them (60 **PS**). Similar gestures of respect for his men are reflected in Arrian's narrative in the immediate aftermath of the battle of Issus (2.12 **PS**). These feelings of respect it seems were reciprocated and, during the conflict with the Mallians, Arrian describes the loyalty leading companions exhibited for Alexander (6.10 **PS**) when they joined him in the fray. He also described in detail the deep distress that affected Alexander's men when they thought he had been killed there (6.12 **PS**). As Arrian describes, his men appeared at a complete loss when they thought they were suddenly without Alexander, and writing:

> And every difficulty seemed hopelessly insoluble without Alexander to get them through

Arrian, *The Campaigns of Alexander* 6.12

When his men realised that Alexander was in fact alive, many burst into tears through sheer relief (6.13 **PS**) and flocked around him, desperate to touch him. Later we read, again in Arrian, about love that was stirred in Alexander's troops when they knew he was dying (7.26 **PS**). The eye-contact Arrian refers to all points to a strong and trusting relationship between Alexander and his men.

Alexander's companions were in theory the men closest to him and on the most intimate terms with him. In one source we read the following:

> Although he [Alexander] set out with such meagre and restricted resources, he did not board his ship until he had discovered how things stood with his Companions and had given one of them a farm, another a village, and another income from some hamlet or harbor. After he had used up and distributed almost all his royal properties, Perdiccas asked, 'But what are you leaving for yourself, my lord?' 'My hopes', he replied. 'Alright,' said Perdiccas, 'then that's what we'll have too, after all, we're joining you on this expedition'. Then he refused to accept the property that had been assigned him, and some other friends of Alexander's followed his example.
>
> Plutarch, *Alexander* 15

As the Asian expedition progress, relations between Alexander and individual companions both strengthened and deteriorated for various reasons.

THE CHANGING STATUS OF THE GREEK AND MACEDONIAN CONTINGENTS IN ALEXANDER'S ARMY

Alexander began his Persian expedition in his capacity as leader of the Greeks. Technically it was a pan-hellenic campaign. Many Greek forces accompanied him east and fought side-by-side with him in battle. Alexander's army was comprised of: Macedonians (cavalry and infantry), Greek allies from (a) Thessaly, (b) from the League of Corinth (cavalry, infantry, and fleet) and (c) contingents from subject peoples, such as Paeonians, Thracians, Illyrians, and finally mercenaries.

Despite the fact that on the face of it this was a pan-hellenic expedition, at several points in the campaign, it seems as though the expedition was essentially a Macedonian one. At particular points, for example, at Ecbatana and then at the Oxus river, Greek contingents were dismissed (Arrian, 3.19 and 3.29 **PS**). It may that at this stage, Alexander considered that the main conquest had been achieved.

At Opis in 324, according to Arrian, Macedonian veterans and those unfit were discharged and escorted back to Macedon by Craterus.

ALEXANDER'S RELATIONSHIP WITH PERSIANS

Alexander's relationship with the Persians cannot be easily categorised. He could be ruthless when facing them in battle. Moreover, if he sensed that they had not acted honourably towards him or the Greeks, he could be very severe. Yet, although Alexander was to all intents and purposes a foreign invader of Persia, he was not always overtly hostile in his approach towards the Persians. He often treated the Persians with great respect, sometimes showing more concern for them than the Macedonians and Greeks. He surely knew that in such a vast region he needed to win their support. But evidence also suggests he felt protective of the Persians: in Arrian 6.27 **PS**, we read that Alexander 'permitted no subjects under his say to be wronged by their rulers'. As the years wore on, he acted as though he were the legitimate successor of the Persian Empire which was his to govern rather than simply to plunder.

Darius' family

Alexander viewed Darius, the king of Persia, as a personal foe, but evidence suggests that he treated Darius's family in a kindly manner. Arrian (2.12 **PS**) outlines two accounts of Alexander's behaviour. One story went that Alexander, upon hearing about the distress of Darius' mother, wife and children who thought he had been killed in the Battle of Issus, reassured them that Darius still lived and told them he would treat them as royals. The other version had Alexander and Hephaestion entering the tent of Darius' family. When the mother of Darius confused Hephaestion and Alexander, Alexander gently laughed it off, stating the Hephaestion was also Alexander. It is likely the first version is more reliable since Arrian attributes it to Aristobulus and Ptolemy. It is interesting, though, that Arrian also provides his own moral commentary, and expressly praises the compassion of Alexander.

In Arrian's description of the letter exchange between Darius and Alexander (2.14 **PS**) we read that upon Darius' request for the release his wife, mother and children, Alexander indicated that provided Darius approached him humbly enough, he would certainly release his family. This letter seems to suggest that Alexander harboured no ill-will against Darius' kith and kin per se.

The people of Persepolis

When Alexander and his men arrived in Persepolis, the sources suggest that Alexander gave his men free range to loot the city and kill its people at will. The great palace was also burnt to the ground.

Study questions
Read Curtius Rufus, 5.6.1–8 and 5.7.1–11 and Arrian, 3.18.

1 Identify details which reflect Alexander's approach to the people of Persepolis.
2 To what extent can we reconcile Alexander's approach here with the generosity he extended towards the Persians at other times?
3 Might the times in which these authors were writing have affected their view of history?

Persian courtiers

Alexander increasingly surrounded himself with Persians at court in addition to his Macedonians. When Alexander was considering the introduction of the act of obeisance, many of the Persian courtiers complied with this Persian custom. One way to read his actions was that Alexander was hoping to create a greater measure of equality between Persians on the one hand and Macedonian and Greek nobles on the other.

ACTIVITIES

Review your prescribed sources on Alexander.

- Identify three examples which make reference to Alexander's interactions with Persian courtiers.
- Comment on how this reflects his relationship with them.
- What might a Roman audience reading these accounts have thought of the idea of foreigners being part of an inner circle?

> **Epigonoi** the group of young Persians Alexander trained up and referred to as his 'inheritors'

The Epigonoi

In 324 some 30,000 youths arrived in Susa (Arrian, 7.6 **PS**). These Alexander rather intriguingly called his '**Epigonoi**' which means something like 'descendants' or 'heirs' in Greek. These were Persian youths trained in Macedonian military tactics. Alexander had ordered the formation of this unit as early as 330 and it seems likely that the Epigonoi were intended to be Alexander's new army to replace or at least heavily supplement his Macedonian phalanx. Alexander had already been adding foreign troops in unprecedented numbers into his companions' units (Arrian, 7.6 **PS**). Peucestas was also supporting Alexander's policy in this regard and had, for example, marshalled 20,000 Persian troops (Arrian, 7.23). There seems little reason for doubting this happened. What is interesting is Arrian's repeated references to the Macedonian disquiet about this (7.6 and 7.8 **PS**).

> **EXPLORE FURTHER**
>
> - Read Diodorus, 17.108.2 and Plutarch, *Life of Alexander*, 71.1.
> - What additional information do these sources provide about the Epigonoi?

The satraps appointed to manage the Empire

A single ruler could not maintain control of the entire Persian Empire. Various Persian kings therefore would set in place satraps as local governors in key locations. As

> **S & C** Research the Roman view of the East at the time Arrian was writing.

EXPLORE FURTHER

Read:

- Arrian, 3.25.1–2, 5–7, 28.2–3
- Diodorus Siculus, 17.78.1–4, 83.4–6 and
- Curtius Rufus, 6.6.13, 20–32, 7.3.2, 4.34–38

Study question

Re-read Arrian, 7.4 on the mass marriages at Susa in 324.

What can you infer about Alexander's relationship with the Persians from this passage?

KEY INDIVIDUAL

Taxiles

Dates: fourth century

A prince or king who reigned over the tract between the Indus and the Hydaspes rivers in the Punjab

Study questions

Read Plutarch, 59–60.

1 What qualities does Alexander appear to admire in these leaders?
2 What are some of the drawbacks with these sources?

Alexander swept through Persia, he recognised the importance of these leaders and often harnessed their local influence and administrative experience (Arrian, 6.29 PS). Satraps (and the sons of satraps) were incorporated into Alexander's Macedonian forces as part of the initiatives outlined above Arrian, 7.6 PS). They were also useful figures in Alexander's divide and rule policy. In Arrian 3.21 PS, Alexander appointed a Persian called Oxydates to the governorship of Media. Arrian writes that Oxydates had previously been arrested by Darius, 'a circumstance which induced Alexander to trust him'.

Alexander's relationships with the Persian satraps was not always constructive. He was compelled to rely on them to some extent, but as the expedition progressed, he grew increasingly uncertain about the loyalty of some of them to him and/or doubtful about their competence. We also read how Alexander often took draconian action against them. Arrian (3.29 PS) describes how just before crossing the river Oxus, Arrian sent Stasanor, one of his companions, to arrest and take the place of Arsames, satrap of the Areians, because he had heard that this satrap appeared to be unsupportive. Later, when Alexander arrived at the Gedrosian capital (Arrian 6.27 PS), he removed Apollophanes from his satrapy when he heard that this satrap had disobeyed his orders. Alexander also made an example of some of his own generals who he had left in charge of forces in Media (namely Cleander, Sitacles and Heracon) as a direct way of, as Arrian puts it, 'putting fear into any other satraps or governors'. These three generals had been accused by the natives of plundering temples and treating the local inhabitants roughly. Arrian also describes (7.4 PS) the execution of the governors of Susa, Abulites and his son Oxathres, for misfeasance.

Similar issues arose with local governors once Alexander got even further East.

In relation to the marriages at Susa

It is difficult to know whether the mass marriages at Susa were a publicity stunt, the product of politics or motivated by genuine idealism on Alexander's part. Maybe it was a combination of all three. Whatever the case, it is clear that these were conducted according to Persian custom.

ALEXANDER'S RELATIONSHIP WITH THE LEADERS OF THE INDUS VALLEY

Alexander encountered a number of leaders (for example, Taxiles and Porus) when his campaign reached the Indus Valley. To conquer the territory there, Alexander would need to defeat them in battle. Despite this, Alexander, according to the sources, held these leaders in high esteem. Plutarch (59 PS) describes a cordial dialogue between Taxiles and Alexander and how he also presented this Indian leader with a gift of 1,000 talents of money as a means to disarm the hostility of the natives. Plutarch also (60 PS), after giving a potted description of the formidable warrior Porus and his very well-trained elephant, includes another verbal exchange between him and Alexander. A short extract conveys well the apparent respect in which Alexander held Porus:

Porus was taken prisoner, and when Alexander asked him how he should treat him, he replied, 'As a king should'. Alexander went on to ask him if he had anything else to add, but he said, '"As a king should" covers everything'. So Alexander not only let him rule over his former kingdom with the title of satrap, but also gave him extra territory . . .

(PS)

Plutarch, *Life of Alexander* 60

Plutarch then makes reference to the vast territory he subsequently allocated to Porus. Similar behaviour is also mentioned by Arrian who, in **(PS)** 5.29, refers to the land he awarded Porus.

THE PORTRAYAL OF GREEKS, MACEDONIANS AND PERSIANS IN THE SOURCES

When we address the nature of how the Greeks, Macedonians and Persians are depicted in the ancient sources, we must be mindful of the fact that all of the extant literary sources are Greek or Roman, not Macedonian or Persian. This should immediately put the modern reader on the alert for possible bias and prejudice. It is also worth remembering that the ancients indulged in stereotypes just as much as we do now. The Greek view of foreignness was often delineated through the notion of 'the other' or 'the barbarian', that is the opposite of all the qualities they claimed for themselves. The view we get of the Persians was entirely refracted through non-Persian sources.

The charge of Persian flattery was a common one in the Greek sources. For example, the reason given for Darius's poor decisions prior to the battle of Issus was his weakness for flattery (for example, Arrian, 2.6).

The ancient sources are considerably more favourable when it comes to the depiction of the Greeks. Greek virtues are often referred to in direct opposition to Persian vices. A frequent refrain is the freedom and autonomy that the Greeks cherished compared to the slavery that the Persians submitted to.

When it comes to a consideration of the Macedonians, although it is correct to distinguish them from the Greeks, you should be aware that there is a modern scholarly debate about whether Macedonians are wholly separate to Greeks or a different sub-set of Greeks (see Engels and Hatzopoulos in the Further Reading). Alexander and Philip were Macedonian, but at times assumed the Greek identity and embraced many Greek outlooks and customs. The Macedonian royal line claimed descent from

Study questions
Read Arrian, 2.7, **(PS)** Alexander's speech at Issus and Plutarch, 18.4–5 on Darius's dream.

1 How do these sources depict the Persians?
2 What are the main problems involved with taking these sources at face value?

MODERN PARALLEL

Consider the ways in which we stereotype about people nowadays.

ACTIVITY

Review your sources on Alexander and identify passages which seem to convey this Persian trait of flattery and comment in each case on why we must be careful to challenge this characterisation of the Persians

Study questions
Re-read your sources on Philip and Alexander.

1 What can you infer from these sources about the depiction of the Macedonians (as opposed to the Persians and Greek)?
2 What aspects of these passages might prompt you to question their reliability?

Study questions
Re-read your sources on Alexander and Philip.

1 What can you infer from these sources about the depiction of the Greeks (as opposed to the Persians and Macedonians?)
2 What aspects of these passages might prompt you to question their reliability?

Greeks of Argos, but it seems the Greek were always reluctant to accept them as Greek. According to Herodotus (*Histories*, 5.22), for example, Alexander I had to 'prove' to the officials at Olympia that he was 'Greek' in order to compete in the Olympic games.

TOPIC REVIEW

- Consider how did (a) Philip's and (b) Alexander's relationship with the Greeks changed or developed over time.
- Discuss the nature of Alexander's relationship with his army.
- How would you characterise Alexander's approach to the Persians and their culture?
- Review whether this stayed the same or whether it changed
- Explain how is the issue of identity is dealt with in your sources.

Further Reading

Anson, E.M, 'Alexander at the Beas', in P. Wheatley and E. Baynham (eds), *East and West in the World Empire of Alexander. Essays in Honour of Brian Bosworth* (Oxford: Oxford University Press, 2015), pp. 65–74.: Bloomsbury, 2013), pp. 153–9.

Borza, E., 'Fire from Heaven: Alexander at Persepolis', *CPh* 67 (1972), pp. 233–45. Reprinted in *Makedonika* (1995), pp. 217–38.

Bosworth, A.B., 'Alexander and the Iranians', *JHS* 100 (1980), pp. 1–21.

Brosius, M., *Women in Achaemenid Persia* (Oxford: Clarendon Press, 1996).

Carney, E., 'Alexander and Persian Women', *AJPh* 117.4 (1996), pp. 563–83.

Carney, E. 'Macedonians and Mutiny: Discipline and Indiscipline in the Army of Philip and Alexander', *CPh* 91.1 (1996), pp. 19–44.

Engels, J., 'Macedonians and Greeks', in J. Roisman and I. Worthington (eds), *A Companion to Ancient Macedonia* (Oxford: Blackwell, 2010), pp. 81–98

Hatzopoulos, M., 'Macedonians and Other Greeks' in R. Lane Fox, ed., *Brill's Companion to Ancient Macedon* (Leiden and Boston: Brill, 2011), pp. 51–78.

Heckel, W., *The Conquests of Alexander the Great* (Cambridge: Cambridge University Press, 2008).

Howe, T. and S Müller, 'Mission Accomplished: Alexander at the Hyphasis', *AHB* 26 (2012), pp. 21–38.

Olbrycht, M.J., 'Macedonia and Persia', in J. Roisman and I. Worthington (eds), *A Companion to Ancient Macedonia* (Oxford: Blackwell, 2010), pp. 342–69.

Poddighe, E., 'Alexander and the Greeks: The Corinthian League' in W. Heckel and L. Tritle (eds), *Alexander the Great: A New History* (Oxford and Chichester: Wiley-Blackwell, 2009), pp. 99–120.

Roisman, J. (ed.), *Brill's Companion to Alexander the Great* (Leiden and Boston: Brill, 2003).

Sancisi-Weerdenburg, H., 'Alexander and Persepolis' in J. Carlsen, B. Due, O.S. Due, and B. Poulsen (eds), *Alexander the Great: Reality and Myth* (Rome; L'Erma di Bretschneider, 1993), pp. 177–88.

van der Spek, R. J. 'Darius III, Alexander the Great, and Babylonian Scholarship', *Achaemenid History* 13 (2003), pp. 289–346.

PRACTICE QUESTIONS

Read Justin, *Epitome*, 8.4 **PS**.

1. How useful is this passage for our understanding of Philip's relationship with the rest of Greece? [12]

What to Expect in the AS Level Exam for the Greek Period Study

This chapter aims to show you the types of questions you are likely to get in the written examination. It offers some advice on how to answer the questions and will help you avoid common errors.

Your Greek history examination paper is worth 60 marks and 50% of the AS Level. It will ask you questions about the Greek Period Study: *Relations between Greek States and between Greek and non-Greek states, 492–404 BC*. The whole examination will last for 1 hour and 30 minutes.

STRUCTURE

There are two sections in the exam, **Section A** and **Section B**. You should answer all the questions in Section A and **one** question in Section B.

Section A

There are two questions:

- **Question 1** is worth 10 marks. It will ask you to demonstrate what you know about an issue relating to one of the content points within one of the five timespans. It therefore has a clear and restricted focus.
- **Question 2** is worth 20 marks. It is a source-based mini-essay question. You will be given prescribed sources on the paper, and asked a question relating to them.

Section B

There is a choice of two questions.

- **Questions 3** and **4** are both essay questions, each worth 30 marks. You are required to answer only **one** of them. These will be much broader based questions, in which you will be able to use, analyse and evaluate the ancient source material that you have studied in order to answer the issues addressed in the question.

ASSESSMENT OBJECTIVES

There are three Assessment Objectives in the Ancient History AS Level. These are detailed in the table below.

Assessment Objective	Learners are expected to:
AO1	Demonstrate knowledge and understanding of the key features and characteristics of the historical periods studied.
AO2	Analyse and evaluate historical events and historical periods to arrive at substantiated judgements.
AO3	Use, analyse and evaluate ancient sources within their historical context to make judgements and draw conclusions about: • historical events and historical periods studied • how the portrayal of events by ancient writers/sources relates to the historical contexts in which they were written/produced.

The weighting that these Assessment Objectives are given in the three question types for the exam is as follows:

Question number	Question type	AO1 marks	AO2 marks	AO3 marks	Total marks
1	Issue	5	5	–	10
2	Source-based mini-essay	5	–	15	20
3 or 4	Essay	5	10	15	30

Each question type is marked according to a distinct marking grid which can be viewed in the specimen papers on the OCR website.

SAMPLE QUESTIONS

This section will examine how to prepare for the question types, and what to expect from them.

Section A: Question 1

As mentioned, this question will focus on one particular area of the specification. An example of such a question might be:

Question: How determined were the Greek states to resist the invasion of Darius in 490?

[10]

There is plenty of material to discuss here. It is likely that you would suggest that the vast majority of states did not seek to resist the invasion. You would want to use details contained in Herodotus 6.48–9 to explain that most of the mainland states and all the island states, including Aegina, gave earth and water to Darius' heralds in 491. You could mention that the Spartans and Athenians reject the offers of the Persian heralds to show that these two states at least were determined to stand firm (as mentioned in Herodotus 7.133). Your focus could then turn to the events of the invasion, thinking about the Persian treatment of Naxos, Delos and Eretria, and the responses of the Greeks in these states. The Battle of Marathon itself involves just the Athenians and Plataeans. The Spartans arrive too late for the action, something you may wish to reflect on. We hear of no other Greek state which comes to support.

All in all, therefore, this question requires you to show a good knowledge of the relevant issue, and to draw together this knowledge into a logical set of conclusions.

Section A: Question 2

You will be given one or more than one passage from your prescribed sources, and beneath them will be a question for you to answer relating to them. For example:

The Athenians took over the leadership in this way, as the allies wanted because they hated Pausanias. They made an assessment of which allied cities should provide money for the war against the Persians and which were to provide ships. They did this because a pretext for the alliance was to take revenge for their losses by devastating the Persian King's territory.

Thucydides 1.91.1

After this they made war on the Naxians, who had revolted, and besieged and subdued them. This was the first allied city deprived of its freedom contrary to the Greek custom, but subsequently the same thing happened to each of the others as occasion arose. The causes of revolts were various, but the main ones were their failure to pay tribute or provide ships.

Thucydides 1.98–9

The Chalcideans are to swear an oath on the following terms: 'I will not revolt from the people of Athens by any means or device whatsoever, neither in word nor in deed, nor will I obey anyone who does revolt, and if anyone revolts I will denounce him to the Athenians, and I will pay to the Athenians whatever tribute I persuade them to agree, and I will be the best and fairest ally I am able to be and will help and defend the Athenian people, in the event of anyone wronging the Athenian people, and I will obey the Athenian people.'

The Chalkis Decree

Question: On the basis of these passages, and other sources you have studied, to what extent did the Athenians intend to turn the Delian League into an empire from which they would benefit the most?

When answering this question, you must, of course, focus primarily on the three passages given, quoting from them where necessary. From the first passage, you might highlight the fact that the allies willingly chose the Athenians to lead them, while also thinking about the meaning of the word 'pretext'. You should also of course give the date of this event, 477, and perhaps say more about the choice of Delos as a venue which was welcome to all Greeks. The second passage is then a contrast. It dates to about 470 and shows Athens becoming much harsher for the first time. You might focus on the fact that Thucydides says that all the cities of the League were eventually deprived of their freedom. The final passage is of course from a very different source. You could discuss the uncompromising terms which the Khalkidians are forced to swear by, and the use of words such as 'obey' and 'denounce'.

You must, of course, focus on the question throughout. It asks about the intention of the Athenians, and this is hard to know. You might aim to demonstrate that the Athenians did indeed turn the League into an Empire, perhaps focusing on the building of the Long Walls for defence, and the relocating of the Delian League treasury to the Athenian Acropolis followed by the building programme of the 440s and 430s. From this evidence, and the evidence of Athenian foreign policy in the 480s and early 470s, you can draw a conclusion as to the ultimate intention of the Athenians.

It is important to reflect on the reliability of the sources in these passages. The Chalkis Decree **PS** would seem to be a very reliable source, given that it is written at the time for the people of Chalkis and Athens. Thucydides is generally reliable, but his account of the years between 478 and 431 is relatively short and there are some confusions in it. This means that he does not focus in any detail on the intentions of Athens or any other Greek city during this period. You may therefore conclude that it is relatively hard to know the extent of Athenian intention during the period.

Remember too that the question asks you to introduce other sources which you have studied. You might well want to introduce other examples from the Pentecontaetia, such as Thucydides' observation at 1.97 **PS** that at first the allies were independent and shared a common assembly with the Athenians. This could be followed up with his further observation at 1.99 **PS** that Athenian rule grew to be oppressive. You may also wish to mention the revolt of Thasos in 465 and the Athenian treatment of the islanders (1.101 **PS**). Outside of Thucydides, you could cite Diodorus 11.50 **PS** about the debate in Sparta in the 470s as to the danger provided by the Athenians, or Diodorus 12.38.2 **PS** about the moving of the Delian League Treasury to Athens. As with the sources above, make sure that you reflect on the reliability of any sources you introduce.

Section B: the essay question

Your first task with this question is to decide whether to answer Question 3 or Question 4. Remember that you should answer **only one question**. Read each question carefully. It may be that you are immediately clear which one you would prefer to answer. If so, still check that you have read the question carefully. It is essential that you answer the question given to you on the paper, not a similar question which you have answered before, or a similar question you would prefer to be on the paper!

Once you have made your decision, try to highlight key words or phrases and focus on them. Let us look at an example:

Question: 'It was Athens' relationship with Corinth, rather than with any other state, which posed the greatest danger to peace in the Greek world during this period.' To what extent do the sources support this view?

You must use and analyse the ancient sources you have studied as well as your own knowledge to support your answer. [30]

Let's focus on the key words and phrases here. Clearly, the focus of the essay is 'Athens' relationship with Corinth', and you are asked to compare this with Athens' relations with other states. Remember that 'any other state' could mean a non-Greek state as well as a Greek state. The phrase 'the Greek world' invites you to think of the Greeks living around the Aegean but also further afield, such as the Greek states in Cyprus or in Sicily. The phrase 'the greatest danger' allows for the fact that there may have been a number of dangers, and it does not mean the 'only danger'. And 'during this period' allows you to draw on the entire period of 492–404 BC. Finally, remember that the phrase 'to what extent' means that you are not being asked simply if you agree or not, but about the level to which you agree. You might think that the argument has merit in some ways, but not in others.

In answering this question, you will need to show good knowledge of the relevant sources, and of their strengths and weaknesses, which can lead you to substantiated judgements. You will of course need to know details of Athens' relationship with Corinth, and how it worsens after *c.* 460 with the defection of Megara from the Peloponnesian League. You will want to bring in the conflicts between Athens and Corinth during the 430s, particularly regarding relations with Corcyra, Epidamnus and Potidaea. However, you will also want to think about Athens' relationships with other states: for example, Sparta, Persia, and the states of the Delian League. You will need to weigh up which relationship posed the greatest danger to peace in the Greek world.

Remember, too, that you will need to think about the reliability of the sources in this period. For example, it is likely that in his account of the Corinthians' efforts at Salamis in 480, Herodotus (8.94 **PS**) reflects anti-Corinthian bias in the Athenian sources he was speaking to in the 430s or so. Moreover, it is hard to know about the First Peloponnesian War with much certainty since Thucydides' account of it in the Pentecontaetia is so brief. However, Thucydides may be thought to be a good source for the events of the 430s, which he himself lived through at Athens. By contrast, you may reflect that Thucydides' relative silence on relations between the Greeks and the Persians makes it hard to know how dangerous a threat to peace the Persians posed during the years 479–411.

Above all, plan your answer carefully. Make sure you include a range of evidence and of analysis. Finally, keep your answer focused to the question asked, and aim to refer back to the key words in the question during your answer.

What to Expect in the A Level Exam

This chapter aims to show you the types of questions you are likely to get in the written examination. It offers some advice on how to answer the questions and will help you avoid common errors.

Your Greek history examination paper will have two sections. **Section A**, worth 50 marks, will ask you questions about the Greek Period Study: *Relations between Greek states and between Greek and non-Greek states, 492–404 BC*. **Section B**, worth 48 marks, will ask you questions about your chosen depth study.

The whole examination will last for 2 hours and 30 minutes, and you are advised to divide your time roughly equally between the two sections.

ASSESSMENT OBJECTIVES

There are four Assessment Objectives in the Ancient History A Level. These are detailed in the table below.

Assessment Objective	Learners are expected to:
AO1	Demonstrate knowledge and understanding of the key features and characteristics of the historical periods studied.
AO2	Analyse and evaluate historical events and historical periods to arrive at substantiated judgements.
AO3	Use, analyse and evaluate ancient sources within their historical context to make judgements and reach conclusions about: • historical events and historical periods studied • how the portrayal of events by ancient writers/sources relates to the historical contexts in which they were written/produced.
AO4	Analyse and evaluate, in context, modern historians' interpretations of the historical events and topics studied.

SECTION A

Structure

Section A has two question types, as follows:

- **Essay Question** worth 30 marks (Question 1 or 2). You will be given a choice of two essays. You should answer **only one**. You will need to use, analyse and evaluate the ancient source material you have studied in the period study to answer the issues addressed in the question.
- **Interpretations Question** worth 20 marks (Question 3). You will be given an unseen extract from an academic historian, writing from the start of the eighteenth century onwards, related to one of your three prescribed historical debates. You will be asked to analyse and evaluate the extract in the context of the historical debate. You may include the views of other historians, and you should draw on your own knowledge and understanding of the historical event under debate: you will be given credit for knowledge of ancient source material, but only if it is presented in a way which is relevant to the question about the extract.

The weighting of Assessment Objectives for the two question types in Section A is as follows:

Question number	Question type	AO1 marks	AO2 marks	AO3 marks	AO4 marks	Total marks
1 or **2**	Essay	5	10	15	–	30
3	Interpretations	5	–	–	15	20

Each question type is marked according to a distinct marking grid which can be viewed in the specimen paper on the OCR website.

Sample questions

Let us examine how to prepare for the question types in Section A, and what to expect from them.

The Essay Question

Your first task with this question is to decide whether to answer Question 1 or Question 2. Remember that you should answer **only one question**. Read each question carefully. It may be that you are immediately clear which one you would prefer to answer. If so, still check that you have read the question carefully. It is essential that you answer the question given to you on the paper, not a similar question which you have answered before, or a similar question you would prefer to be on the paper!

Once you have made your decision, try to highlight key words or phrases and focus on them. Let us look at an example:

> 'It was Athens' relationship with Corinth, rather than with any other state, which posed the greatest danger to peace in the Greek world during this period.' To what extent do the sources support this view?

You must use and analyse the ancient sources you have studied as well as your own knowledge to support your answer. [30]

Let's focus on the key words and phrases here. Clearly, the focus of the essay is 'Athens' relationship with Corinth', and you are asked to compare this with Athens' relations with other states. Remember that 'any other state' could mean a non-Greek state as well as a Greek state. The phrase 'the Greek world' invites you to think of the Greeks living around the Aegean but also further afield, such as the Greek states in Cyprus or in Sicily. The phrase 'the greatest danger' allows for the fact that there may have been a number of dangers, and it does not mean the 'only danger'. And 'during this period' allows you to draw on the entire period of 492–404 BC. Finally, remember that the phrase 'to what extent' means that you are not being asked simply if you agree or not, but about the level to which you agree. You might think that the argument has merit in some ways, but not in others.

In answering this question, you will need to show good knowledge of the relevant sources, and of their strengths and weaknesses, which can lead you to substantiated judgements. You will of course need to know details of Athens' relationship with Corinth, and how it worsens after *c*. 460 with the defection of Megara from the Peloponnesian League. You will want to bring in the conflicts between Athens and Corinth during the 430s, particularly regarding relations with Corcyra, Epidamnus and Potidaea. However, you will also want to think about Athens' relationships with other states: for example, Sparta, Persia and the states of the Delian League. You will need to weigh up which relationship posed the greatest danger to peace in the Greek world.

Remember, too, that you will need to think about the reliability of the sources in this period. For example, it is likely that in his account of the Corinthians' efforts at Salamis in 480, Herodotus (8.94 **PS**) reflects anti-Corinthian bias in the Athenian sources he was speaking to in the 430s or so. Moreover, it is hard to know about the First Peloponnesian War with much certainty since Thucydides' account of it in the Pentecontaetia is so brief. However, Thucydides may be thought to be a good source for the events of the 430s, which he himself lived through at Athens. By contrast, you may reflect that Thucydides' relative silence on relations between the Greeks and the Persians makes it hard to know how dangerous a threat to peace the Persians posed during the years 479–411.

Above all, plan your answer carefully. Make sure you include a range of evidence and of analysis. Finally, keep your answer focused to the question asked, and aim to refer back to the key words in the question during your answer.

The Interpretations Question

The interpretations question will be based on one of the three prescribed historical debates relating to this period study. The three prescribed historical debates are:

- the reasons for the victory over the Persians in 480–479 BC
- the causes of the Peloponnesian War in 431 BC
- the reasons for Athenian failure in the Peloponnesian War.

In the exam, you will be given an extract from an academic historian which will relate to one of these three debates. You will then be asked a question relating to the extract. An example of such extract and question relating to the first debate above might be as follows:

> What is most striking is that the Persian leaders were unable or unwilling to conceive of tactics that would closely unite the cavalry and infantry, other than spur-of-the-moment engagements that were not really coordinated. It appears that the cavalry was never able to disrupt the compact mass of Greek infantry . . . The Persians' favourite tactic was to set up a sort of wall consisting of their shields rammed into the ground; with this protection, they let fly arrows and spears at the intimidated attacker. But as Pausanias reminds us, the Greeks had had the experience of Marathon, 'where they were, as far as we know, the first to advance toward the enemy at a run'. As soon as the Greek hoplites carried off this manoeuvre, the rampart of shields was quickly breached. Forced to unstring their bows, the Persian infantrymen no longer measured up, as at Plataea and Mycale . . . Herodotus stresses the Persians' courage, but he clearly shows at the same time that the moment the rampart of shields was downed, they had nothing but their courage with which to oppose the well-oiled machine of the phalanx.
>
> Pierre Briant, *From Cyrus to Alexander* (Eisenbraums 2002), pages 337–8

Question: How convincing do you find Briant's interpretation that Persian tactical weakness in land battles was a key cause of the Greek victory in the Persian wars?   [20]

Note that of the 20 marks for this question, 5 are available for AO1, and 15 for AO4. This means that your answer should engage carefully with what Briant has said in this passage. There might be a temptation to answer this question very generally, without referring to the detail of what Briant has said. So you should aim to read through the extract carefully more than once, and perhaps highlight key points or phrases. Such phrases from the extract above might be:

- 'what is most striking'
- 'the Persian leaders were unable **or** unwilling to conceive of tactics that would closely unite the cavalry and infantry'
- 'the Greeks had had the experience of Marathon'
- 'Forced to unstring their bows, the Persian infantrymen no longer measured up'
- 'the well-oiled machine of the phalanx'

There are other phrases which you could also pick out, but those given above open up a range of possibilities for your answer. For example:

- You can reflect on the extent to which you agree that the clash in fighting styles of infantrymen of each side was a significant factor in the outcome of the war.
- You might think about whether the inability of the Persian leadership to unite the cavalry and infantry is the most striking factor in influencing the outcome of the war.
- The phrase 'unable or unwilling' indicates that Briant feels that we are limited in our knowledge of the Persian strategy. If so, this may limit our ability to make a clear judgement about the question.
- The references to Marathon, Plataea and Mycale invite you to comment on what you know about those battles, especially strategy and tactics. You may well also want to introduce the other key land battle, Thermopylae.

It will also be important for you to draw on your wider knowledge and to introduce other areas of the debate about the reasons for the Greek victory over the Persians in 480–479. It will also be impressive if you can introduce the views of other academic historians here. For example, some would suggest that Salamis was the key battle, and that it was here that the Persians made their greatest tactical blunder. Cawkwell has argued that Xerxes' greatest strategic mistake was to join battle at Salamis when he had no need to do so. You may wish to set this view against the views of Briant put forward above regarding the Persian leadership on land. You might also wish to talk about whether it was the lack of Persian supplies which ultimately cost them victory, or whether it was simply an inability or lack of will to continue to commit so many troops to this region on the edge of the Persian Empire.

In all that you do, however, you must keep your answer focused on the arguments put forward by Briant above, whether you are agreeing with them or challenging them. Remember too that the question asks you 'to what extent'. You do not have to entirely agree or disagree (although you may wish to do so), instead you can think about how much you agree. This gives you plenty of flexibility to examine different perspectives on the debate.

You are not required to know details about the about the historical methods and approach the academic historian used, nor how his or her interpretation may have been affected by the time in which he or she was writing. However, you will be given credit for this approach to evaluation if you do it in a way which is relevant to the question.

SECTION B – DEPTH STUDY (SPARTA)

Structure

Section B has two question types, as follows:

- **Source Utility Question** worth 12 marks (Question 4). You will be asked to read between one and four of your prescribed sources. You will then be asked a question focusing on how useful this source or set of sources are for telling us about a certain historical event or situation.

- **Essay Question** worth 36 marks (Question 5 or 6). This is similar in format to the essay question for the period study (but note that it is worth six more marks). You will be given a choice of two essays. You should answer **only one**. You will need to use, analyse and evaluate the ancient source material you have studied in the depth study to answer the issues addressed in the question.

The weighting of Assessment Objectives for the two question types in Section B is as follows:

Question number	Question type	AO1 marks	AO2 marks	AO3 marks	AO4 marks	Total marks
4	Source utility	6	–	6	–	12
5 or 6	Essay	6	12	18	–	36

As in Section A, each question type is marked according to a distinct marking grid which can be viewed in the specimen papers on the OCR website.

Sample questions

Let us examine how to prepare for the question types in Section B, and what to expect from them.

The Source Utility Question

An example of a source utility question might ask you to read the passages below and answer the question relating to them:

Just before the battle could begin, the Corinthian contingent, reflecting that they were acting wrongfully, changed their minds and withdrew. Then Demaratus son of Ariston, one of the two Spartan kings and joint commander of the expedition, though he had no previous disagreement with Cleomenes, followed suit. This divergence in a matter of policy gave rise to a new policy in Sparta; previously both kings had gone out with the army, but this was now made illegal, and it was further provided that, as one had to remain in the capital, one of the Tyndaridae as well should stay behind – both of whom had hitherto accompanied the army as auxiliaries.

Herodotus, *Histories* 5.75

The prerogatives of the Spartan kings are these: two priesthoods, Zeus Lacedaemon and Zeus Uranius, and the power of declaring war on whom they please. In this, no Spartan may attempt to oppose their decision, under pain of sacrilege. On service, the kings go first and return last; they have a bodyguard of a hundred picked men, and are allowed for their own use as many cattle as they wish. To them personally are allotted the skins and joints of all animals offered for sacrifice.

Herodotus, *Histories* 6.56

Question: How useful are these passages for our understanding of the role that Spartan kings played on military campaigns? [12]

You will want to ensure that you comment on each passage in your answer. You might wish to point out that the first passage can be located in about 504 BC, when the Spartans were trying to lead the Peloponnesians in overturning the newly formed democratic government in Athens and restoring Isagoras. The withdrawal of both the Corinthians and Demaratus was a key moment in the development of the Peloponnesian League, since after this its bi-cameral format seems to have been established. It is therefore likely that this story was well known among the people that Herodotus was speaking to. It would also be worth pointing out that in future campaigns the Spartans never seem to have sent out two kings. Indeed, in some campaigns, the Spartan forces were not even commanded by one of the kings.

The second passage comes at the beginning of a more general survey by Herodotus of the privileges of the two Spartan kings. It would be worth focusing here on how reliable the historian might be in his research. You would want to point out that he was researching in the third quarter of the fifth century, and relied largely on oral history. Although we know that the Spartans tended not to welcome non-Spartans into their state, Herodotus tells us at 3.55 that he himself visited a Spartan citizen, Archias, in Sparta, and so he could have accessed reliable information about Spartan society (Archias is in fact one of only four sources named by Herodotus). Nonetheless, some of the information given in the second passage is contradicted elsewhere in your prescribed sources, since we know that it was the Spartan assembly which voted to go to war (e.g. in 432 BC, Thucydides 1.87 **PS**). You may conclude therefore that Herodotus is referring to a ceremonial process whereby the kings formally declared war, or that the process may have changed over time (although, as mentioned above, Herodotus was gathering his information in time around 432 BC).

A further point you may wish to make is the role that religion played for Spartans on campaign, especially in relation to the kings. The statues of the Tyndaridae – which carried great religious importance – are linked to the two kings in the first passage; in the second passage, the two priesthoods are mentioned in the same line as the right of the kings to declare war. The kings are also given huge offerings of sacrificial victims on campaign, suggesting the importance the Spartan army conferred on them. This in turn suggests that a king played a vital role on campaign both as a military commander and as a symbol of the presence of Sparta's gods.

Remember that this section is only worth 12 marks, a quarter of the marks for Section B. You should only spend about 15 minutes on it therefore.

The Essay Question
As mentioned, this question is very similar in format to the essay question in Section A. However, it is worth 36 marks (as opposed to 30 marks in Section A), and so you are expected to spend more time on it and to go into more detail. The assessment objectives are divided in the same ratio as in the Section A essay question. The techniques required to answer this question are the same as in Section A, and you should of course draw as

much as possible on the prescribed sources you have studied in your depth study to back up your arguments. Be aware that this question constitutes three quarters of the marks in Section B, and you should therefore aim to spend about 55–60 minutes on it.

SECTION B – DEPTH STUDY (ATHENS)

Structure

Section B has two question types, as follows:

- **Source Utility Question** worth 12 marks (Question 4). You will be asked to read between one and four of your prescribed sources. You will then be asked a question focusing on how useful this source or set of sources are for telling us about a certain historical event or situation.
- **Essay Question** worth 36 marks (Question 5 or 6). This is similar in format to the essay question for the period study (but note that it is worth six more marks). You will be given a choice of two essays. You should answer **only one**. You will need to use, analyse and evaluate the ancient source material you have studied in the depth study to answer the issues addressed in the question.

The weighting of Assessment Objectives for the two question types in Section B is as follows:

Question number	Question type	AO1 marks	AO2 marks	AO3 marks	AO4 marks	Total marks
4	Source utility	6	–	6	–	12
5 or 6	Essay	6	12	18	–	36

As in Section A, each question type is marked according to a distinct marking grid which can be viewed in the specimen papers on the OCR website.

Sample questions

Let us examine how to prepare for the question types in Section B, and what to expect from them.

The Source Utility Question

An example of a source utility question might ask you to read the passage below and answer the question relating to it:

Socrates: Yes, you know, these are the only real divinities; all the rest is bunkum.
Strepsiades: What on earth do you mean? You don't think Olympian Zeus is a god?
Socrates: Zeus? Who's Zeus? What rubbish you talk! There *is* no Zeus!

Strepsiades: What do you mean? Who makes the rain then? That's the first thing I
    want to know.
Socrates [*indicating the Chorus*]: *They* do, of course, and I'll prove it to you very
    clearly. Have you ever seen it raining when the sky was blue? Surely Zeus, if it
    was him, would be able to send rain even when the Clouds were out of town!
Strepsiades: You've certainly got a good point there – though I really did think before
    that rain was just Zeus pissing through a sieve. But tell me too, who makes the
    thunder that sends shivers up my spine?
Socrates: *They* do too, when they roll about.
Strepsiades: You'll stop at nothing. How do you mean?
Socrates: When they are suspended in the sky, filled with a large quantity of water,
    they are necessarily compelled to move while full of rain, collide with each other,
    and owing to their weight they burst open with a crash.
Strepsiades: Ah, but who compels them to move? *That's* got to be Zeus!
Socrates: No, it's a celestial vortex.

Aristophanes, *Clouds* 365–380

Question: How useful is this passage for our understanding for the change in
attitude of Athenians towards the gods during the second half of the fifth century? [12]

You will want to reflect on the context in which this play was produced in 423 at the City
Dionysia. The audience of thousands would largely have comprised Athenian citizens,
and so Aristophanes clearly felt that he could get away with representing such views –
albeit in a comedy mocking the sophists – in front of such a large group of Athenian
citizens. However, it might be argued the other way that the comedy aimed to discredit
Socrates and the new learning, since Plato reports in *Apology* (18b–c, 19c **PS**) that
Socrates himself argued that the presentation of him in the play had contributed to
hostility against him. It is also pertinent to comment that the City Dionysia was a religious
festival worshipping Dionysus, so it is particularly interesting that Aristophanes is
prepared to represent these views at such an occasion.

   You should of course also refer to the text itself. It is clear that the ideas of scientific
rationalism can be seen here, through the reference to the idea that it is the clouds rather
than the god which cause rain and thunder (ideas which have of course long been
accepted in the modern world). This indicates that the spirit of scientific rationalism was
challenging conventional views about the gods.

   You could comment on how some of the language seems to make fun of the gods, for
example the idea that rain is caused by Zeus 'pissing through a sieve'. It is perhaps
surprising to see the king of the gods' referred to in terms of his bodily functions.
Socrates' statements that 'all the rest is bunkum' and 'there *is* no Zeus' are also very
dismissive, which suggest that Socrates himself is quite certain of his intellectual
position. However, when evaluating this as evidence for the change of Athenian beliefs
about the gods, you will need to decide how much this is simply Aristophanes making
fun through caricature, and to what extent satire can ever give us an insight into the views
being satirised.

The Essay Question

As mentioned, this question is very similar in format to the essay question in Section A. However, it is worth 36 marks (as opposed to 30 marks in Section A), and so you are expected to spend more time on it and to go into more detail. The assessment objectives are divided in the same ratio as in the Section A essay question. The techniques required to answer this question are the same as in Section A, and you should of course draw as much as possible on the prescribed sources you have studied in your depth study to back up your arguments. Be aware that this question constitutes three quarters of the marks in Section B, and you should therefore aim to spend about 55–60 minutes on it.

SECTION B – DEPTH STUDY (THE RISE OF MACEDON)

Structure

Section B has two question types, as follows:

- **Source Utility Question** worth 12 marks (Question 4). You will be asked to read between one and four of your prescribed sources. You will then be asked a question focusing on how useful this source or set of sources are for telling us about a certain historical event or situation.
- **Essay Question** worth 36 marks (Question 5 or 6). This is similar in format to the essay question for the period study (but note that it is worth six more marks). You will be given a choice of two essays. You should answer **only one**. You will need to use, analyse and evaluate the ancient source material you have studied in the depth study to answer the issues addressed in the question.

The weighting of Assessment Objectives for the two question types in Section B is as follows:

Question number	Question type	AO1 marks	AO2 marks	AO3 marks	AO4 marks	Total marks
4	Source utility	6	–	6	–	12
5 or 6	Essay	6	12	18	–	36

As in Section A, each question type is marked according to a distinct marking grid which can be viewed in the specimen papers on the OCR website.

Sample questions

Let us examine how to prepare for the question types in Section B, and what to expect from them.

The Source Utility Question

An example of a source utility question might ask you to read the passage below and answer the question relating to it:

> Are you not aware that if Heracles, my ancestor, had gone no further than Tiryns or Argos – or even than the Peloponnese or Thebes – he could never have won the glory which changed him from man into god, actual or apparent? Even Dionysus, who is god indeed, in a sense beyond what is applicable to Heracles, faced not a few laborious tasks; yet we have done more: we have passed beyond Nysa and we have taken the rock of Aornos which Heracles himself could not take. Come, then; add the rest of Asia to what you already possess – a small addition to the great sum of your conquests. What great or noble work could we ourselves have achieved had we thought it enough, living at ease in Macedon, merely to guard our homes, accepting no burden beyond checking the encroachment of the Thracians on our borders, or the Illyrians and Triballians, or perhaps such Greeks as might prove a menace to our comfort? I could not have blamed you for being the first to lose heart if I, your commander, had not shared in your exhausting marches and your perilous campaigns; it would have been natural enough if you had done all the work merely for others to reap the reward. But it is not so. You and I, gentlemen, have shared the labour and shared the danger, and the rewards are for us all. The conquered territory belongs to you . . .'

PS

> Arrian, *The Campaigns of Alexander*, book 5.26

Question: How useful is this passage for understanding the role Alexander's character and beliefs played in the course of his campaigns in the East? [12]

You will first want to mention the context of this passage, namely, Alexander's speech in 326 to his troops at Hyphasis in India following their show of reluctance for proceeding further. This passage therefore captures a sense of Alexander's character and beliefs at an advanced stage of his Eastern expedition, when the Persian Empire itself had by now been conquered.

With reference to the text itself, you should highlight certain aspects of Alexander's speech and consider the degree to which, in the broader content of Alexander's campaigns, they help us make sense of what he achieved. You could begin by identifying Alexander's overt references to two divinities: Heracles and Dionysus and their glorious achievements. Arrian's narrative here suggests that Alexander measured himself by the standards of the gods, particularly Heracles to whom, evidence suggests, he believed himself to be related, and whom he quite explicitly described transforming from man to god. He appears too to have used the gods as a means to spur himself on, declaring 'we have done much more'. Such beliefs may have been at work at other points during Alexander's campaign, for example, the siege of the rock of Aornos earlier that year. Secondly, the rather disparaging references (words like 'merely' and 'no burden beyond' . . .) to the small-scale problems his men would have had to face back home in Macedon are interesting and suggestive of a figure with huge ambitions. Such insights into Alexander's character might help us appreciate how Alexander within ten years managed to not only cross the Persian Empire but also reach the Hindu Kush, and also the fact he never returned to Macedon. They might even hint at a sense of superiority over his father Philip. Another aspect to mention is Alexander's own notions of his role as leader. The speech appears to acknowledge a deep rapport between the leader and his men here based on fellowship in arms and sense of equality. This was certainly in evidence in many of the major battle descriptions, such as at Granicus and Gaugamela, and also much later in the campaign, for example, against the Mallians when Alexander was first up the wall. His generosity towards and care for his men are also reflected in descriptions of various distributions of spoils for example, after the plunder of Persepolis. Of course, the strength of Alexander's beliefs and character had limits, and in fact he was unable to persuade his men to go any further. He could not go without them. Shortly after this speech, Alexander's army made the long return to Persia.

Students will also need to evaluate the status of the source itself. This extract belongs to a larger body of work by a historian, Arrian, whose account was composed several centuries (in the second century AD) after the events he describes. Arrian, as he himself declares, was relying more generally on older (contemporary) sources, such as Aristobulus and Ptolemy, though he does not mention these sources for this passage of direct speech Arrian here ascribes to Alexander. The speech represents a powerful piece of rhetoric and the sort of passage that would have entertained later Roman audiences, schooled in Greek, for whom Arrian was writing. For this reason, while the content appears plausible enough, we must question the extent to which this has been written in order to fit the story rather than being the story itself.

Remember that this section is only worth 12 marks, a quarter of the marks for Section B. You should only spend about 15 minutes on it therefore.

The Essay Question

As mentioned, this question is very similar in format to the essay question in Section A. However, it is worth 36 marks (as opposed to 30 marks in Section A), and so you are expected to spend more time on it and to go into more detail. The assessment objectives are divided in the same ratio as in the Section A essay question. The techniques required to answer this question are the same as in Section A, and you should of course draw as much as possible on the prescribed sources you have studied in your depth study to back up your arguments. Be aware that this question constitutes three quarters of the marks in Section B, and you should therefore aim to spend about 55–60 minutes on it.

GLOSSARY

Component-specific glossaries can be found on the companion website.

Achaemenid the royal dynasty of Persia

Agiad one of the two dynasties of kings in Sparta

agōgē a traditional term for the Spartan education and training system for boys and young men, although not used by any source in the classical period

agora the civic centre and main market-place of Athens

Amphictyonic League a pan-hellenic, religious organisation which governed the most sacred site in Ancient Greece, the Temple of Apollo at Delphi. Thessaly had at one time been the dominant force in this League, but more recently Thebes had supremacy

anthropomorphic giving non-humans the appearance of human beings

Arrēphoroi girls aged between seven and eleven who served the cult of Athena Polias on the Acropolis

apobatēs an equestrian event which involved charioteers dismounting from their chariots during the race

archōn a magistrate responsible for a key area of Athenian government each year

Attica the large region which formed the entire polis of Athens

aulos a reed instrument with a double pipe, similar to an oboe

Bel a foreign god, a Babylonian deity

boulē (council) an advisory body which prepared business for the assembly and oversaw the day to day running of the city

bouleutērion the council-house in the agora

Brasidians helots armed as hoplites whom the general Brasidas had taken with him to Thrace in 424 BC; they were freed in 421 BC (Thucydides, 5.34.1)

Buchephalus or **Bucephalas** the name of Alexander's horse. The name in Greek literally means 'ox' (bous) and 'head' (cephalus)

chorēgos the financial backer attached to a playwright to support the production of his plays.

chthonic relating to worship of those gods who were associated with the earth or the Underworld

colony A city founded by settlers from another city. Many colonies retained close links with their 'mother city'.

companions in Greek 'hetairoi'. A court inner-circle of elites, not unlike the Prussian *Junker* class

Corinthian Complaint the speech reported by Thucydides which was made by Corinthian representatives at Sparta in 432 urging war against Athens.

Council of the Areopagus the council of ex-archōns

deification the process of turning someone into a god through worship of that person as though they were divine

Delian League the modern name for the naval alliance established by the Athenians and their allies in 477

demagogue a politician who encourages and exploits the support of the common man through populist language and measures

deme a village or district of the town of Athens which formed a single political unit

democracy all the citizens have the right to vote on political decisions

dēmos the ancient Greek word to describe the people in a state

dikast a citizen who was both judge and juror in the Athenian court system

dikē a lawsuit filed by a citizen who claimed to be the victim of an offence committed by another

Dipylon Gate one of the main entry gates into Athens

dithyramb a choral dance sung in honour of Dionysus

divination the practice of seeking knowledge of the future or the unknown by supernatural means

dokimasia the scrutiny test given to a citizen before he could serve as a magistrate

earth and water the symbolic tokens offered to the Persians by foreign states submitting to their rule

ecclēsia (assembly) a formal meeting of the people open to any citizen

eirēn (pl. eirenes) a young man in charge of troops of younger boys and able to punish them, aged at least twenty

elenchus the Greek word for 'cross-examining' used to describe Socrates' method of argument

enōmotarchēs (pl. enōmotarchai) commander of an enōmotia

enōmotia (pl. enōmotiai) the equivalent of a platoon in the Spartan army

ephor one of the Five Spartan magistrates elected annually

Epigonoi the group of young Persians Alexander trained up and referred to as his 'inheritors'

epistatēs the president of the Council and the chairman of the Assembly. He was drawn from the prytaneis and served for one day only.

epistoleus the second-in-command to the nauarchos

epiteichismos the action of building a fort on the territory of the enemy. Successfully employed by the Athenians at Pylos and by the Spartans at Decelea

epitome an abbreviation or summary of a piece of work

eponymous ephor the ephor by whose name the Spartans identified the year

Eurypontid one of the two dynasties of kings in Sparta

euthunai the report in which a magistrate gave an account of his year in office

First Stēlē the huge pillar on which the first fifteen Tribute Quota Lists were inscribed

frieze A continuous strip of sculpted stone running around a temple which depicted a narrative of events

gerousia the Spartan Council of 28 Elders plus the two kings

graphē a lawsuit filed against a citizen claiming that an offence had been committed against a third party

Great Dionysia a drama festival in late March held in honour of Dionysus in Athens

Great Panathenaia a larger version of the Panathenaia held every four years and spread over a number of days

Greek rationalism a modern term used to describe the movement in the sixth and fifth century Greek world which sought to find scientific explanations, based on reason, for the way the world worked

gymnopaidia a festival of dancing for teams of men who competed against each other

hegemon, hegemony the Greek terms for leader and leadership, particularly in a political or military sense

Hellenic League modern term for the alliance of Greek states who resisted the Persian invasion of 480–79

helots the enslaved populations of Lakonia and Messenia

hippagretai the three men appointed to choose the Three Hundred hippeis, each picking 100

hippeis the elite unit of the Spartan army, sometimes also called after their number: Three Hundred. The word means cavalrymen literally, so this may have been their original function. They were chosen from young men aged between twenty and twenty-nine and acted as the kings' bodyguard

hippeis the second class of Athenian citizens

hoplite a heavily armoured infantry man, armed with breastplate, shield, helmet and spear. Hoplites fought in a phalanx – a dense formation of fighting men

hostage a captive held for money and/or political leverage. The practice of hostage-taking was relatively common in the ancient world. According to Diodorus, Philip was a hostage of the Illyrians and sent to Thebes

hypaspists these are shield bearers and an elite infantry force

kerameikos the potters' district in Athens, near the agora, where many ostraka have been found

kōmos A loosely organised revel through the streets with song and dance in honour of Dionysus

krypteia the secret institution in which a select group of young Spartans were sent out equipped only with daggers; one of their roles was to kill potentially troublesome helots

Lakedaimonioi used by Thucydides to refer to any Spartan force, whatever its composition

Lakonia the area of the south-eastern Peloponnese controlled by Sparta

Lenaea a drama festival held in Athens in late January at which comedy took precedence

liturgy A tax on the super-rich requiring them to contribute to the functioning of Athens

lochagos (pl. lochagoi) commander of a lochos

lochos (pl. lochoi) the groups or regiments of the Spartan army

Long Walls defensive walls which joined Athens to Piraeus and Phaleron

lyre a small harp

medise the act of a Greek state submitting to the Persians

Messenia the south-western Peloponnese, conquered by the Spartans in the Archaic Period

metic a non-Athenian resident of Athens. Metics had no political rights, but were given some legal rights. They had to have an Athenian sponsor and pay a monthly tax

metope A square space in the area above the columns in a Doric temple

mora (pl. morai) a division of the Spartan army

mothax (pl. mothakes) a Spartan brought up not in his father's household

naos The central room in a Doric Temple

nauarchos a Spartan naval commander

neodamōdeis helots who had been set free because of good service

oliganthrōpia the shortage of, and decline in, manpower in Sparta

oligarchy rule of a state by a minority of its citizens

Olympians the twelve major gods of Greek religion, who were believed to live on Mount Olympus

orientalism the gradual process of adopting Eastern customs

ostracism an annual vote to banish one prominent citizen for a period of ten years

ostrakon a piece of broken pottery on which a citizen wrote the name of the person he wanted to see ostracised

paidonomos the official in charge of the agōgē

Panathenaia a grand civic Athenian festival held every year in honour of Athena

Panathenaic Way the wide street leading from the Dipylon Gate to the Acropolis

pankration a combat event which was a combination of boxing and wrestling

parabasis a section of a comedy in which the chorus addresses the audience directly, often about contemporary issues, speaking in the voice of the playwright

pediment the triangular space just below the roof at each end of a temple

Peloponnesian League modern term for the alliance of Peloponnesian states led by Sparta which had existed in its fullest form since *c.* 504

pentakosiomedimnoi the wealthiest class of Athenian citizens

pentathlon a competition consisting of five events: discus, long jump, javelin, stadion and wrestling

Pentecontaetia modern term given to Thucydides' account of the events between 479 and 431 in Book 1 of his history

pentēkontēr (pl. pentēkonterai) commander of a pentēkostus

pentēkostus (pl. pentēkostues) a company of men in the Spartan army

peplos the newly woven robe dedicated to Athena Polias at the Panathenaia

perioikos (pl. perioikoi) literally 'dwellers-around', free inhabitants of settlements around Lakonia and Messenia

peripteral A style of Doric temple with columns around a central room

Pnyx the location of the Athenian assembly

polemarchos a Spartan officer

polis a Greek word often translated as 'city-state', referring to a city and all the land it controlled as one political entity.

polytheism the worship of many gods

posthumous after death

principal assembly the main assembly of each prytany

proagōn an event which acted as a preview and introduction to the festival

probouleusis the power to debate matters first and to form proposals which were then put to the assembly

proskynesis/obeisance deferential respect or obeisance, such as blowing a kiss in worship

prytaneis the fifty councillors of the tribe serving a prytany

prytany one of ten administrative periods within the Athenian year, each lasting thirty-five or thirty-six days

quorum the minimum number of voters needed to make a decision valid

rhapsode a professional reciter of epic poetry

rhetoric the ability to speak persuasively in public

Rural Dionysia a drama festival held in the rural demes of Attica in mid-winter

Sacred Band the elite fighting corps of Thebes. Pairs of lovers fought side by side

sarcophagus a tomb

sarissa a pike, longer even than a spear, that had to be wielded with both hands

satrap a Persian provincial governor

satyr-play a play which parodied tragedy and was presented along with three tragedies by the same playwright

Skiritai perioikoi from northern Lakonia

sortition the principle of selection by lot

Spartiate adult male Spartan citizen (they are sometimes also called 'Equals', or 'homoioi' in books)

stadion the most important running event, a 200-metre sprint

stratēgos (general) one of the ten Athenian generals who commanded troops in times of war

syssition (pl. syssitia) Spartan dining-mess, consisting of about fifteen Spartiates

Ten Thousand a large army of Greek mercenaries

Theoric Fund a fund provided by the Athenian state to allow poorer citizens to attend the Great Dionysia

Thesmophoria an all-women festival in honour of Demeter and Persephone in which the women of Athens camped out near the pnyx for three days.

thētes the fourth and lowest class of Athenian citizens

tholos the building in the agora in which the prytaneis were housed

Three Hundred the elite unit of the Spartan army, otherwise known as the hippeis

tribe a group of citizens who were placed together for administrative purposes

Tribute Quota Lists annual lists inscribed on stone giving 1/60 of the contributions of allied cities into the Delian League. Each 1/60 was offered as a dedication to Athena

tyranny a sole ruler takes power and rules unconstitutionally

zeugitai the third class of Athenian citizens

Zeus-Ammon the Egyptian version of Zeus

SOURCES OF ILLUSTRATIONS

SOURCES OF QUOTATIONS

Period Study: Relations between Greek States and between Greek and Non-Greek States

6 'My business is . . .' Herodotus, *Histories*, Prologue, trans. Aubrey de Sélincourt, *Herodotus: The Histories* (London: Penguin 1996); **7** 'At any rate, . . .' Herodotus, *Histories* 6.44, trans. de Sélincourt; **8** 'To Athens and . . .' Herodotus, *Histories* 7.133 trans. de Sélincourt; **9** 'I reward the . . .' DNb, LACTOR 16, 103, trans. I. M. Brosius, LACTOR 16: *The Persian Empire from Cyrus II to Artaxerxes* (London: KCL, 2000); **10** 'If we refuse . . .' Herodotus, *Histories* 6.109, trans. de Sélincourt; **10** 'The Athenians . . . were . . .' Herodotus, *Histories* 6.112, trans. de Sélincourt; **12** 'Xerxes the king . . .' XPa, LACTOR 16, 63, trans. I. M. Brosius; **12** 'At this point . . .' Herodotus, *Histories* 6.112, trans. de Sélincourt; **17** 'There are many . . .' Herodotus, *Histories* 8.144, trans. de Sélincourt; **20** 'In immediate military . . .' Paul Cartledge, *Thermopylae: The Battle That Changed the World*, p.166 (London: Pan Books, 2007); **25** '. . . the Spartans showed . . .' Thucydides, *The History of the Peloponnesian War* 1.92, trans. Rex Warner, *Thucydides: History of the Peloponnesian War* (London: Penguin 1972); **27** '. . . to compensate themselves . . .' Thucydides, *The History of the Peloponnesian War* 1.96, trans. Warner; **28** 'This was the first . . .' Thucydides, *The History of the Peloponnesian War* 1.98, trans. Warner; **29** 'It was chiefly . . .' Thucydides, *The History of the Peloponnesian War* 1.103, trans. Warner; **32** 'The Chalcidians are . . .' ML 52 (SEG 42.10), LACTOR 1, 78, trans. R. G. Osborne, LACTOR 1: *The Athenian Empire* (4th edn; London: KCL, 2000); **35** 'And with regard . . .' Thucydides, *The History of the Peloponnesian War* 1.22, trans. Warner; **38** 'As to the reasons . . .' Thucydides, *The History of the Peloponnesian War* 1.23, trans. Warner; **40** 'In particular the delegates . . .' Thucydides, *The History of the Peloponnesian War* 1.67, trans Warner; **40** 'But the chief . . .' Thucydides, *The History of the Peloponnesian War* 1.139, trans. Warner; **40** 'It is not . . .' Plutarch, *Pericles* 31, trans. OCR; **43** 'When one is . . .' Thucydides, *The History of the Peloponnesian War* 1.69, trans. Warner; **45** 'The Megarians, being . . .' T. Buckley, *Aspects of Greek History 750–323 BC*, p. 323 (2nd edn; Abingdon: Routledge, 2010); **52** 'This event caused . . .' Thucydides, *The History of the Peloponnesian War* 4.40, trans. Warner; **52** 'Brasidas . . . was a . . .' Thucydides, *The History of the Peloponnesian War* 4.81, trans. Warner; **52** 'The Spartans were . . .' Thucydides, *The History of the Peloponnesian War* 4.80, trans. Warner; **53** 'The Athenians also . . .' Thucydides, *The History of the Peloponnesian War* 4.108, trans. Warner; **54** 'Cleon and Brasidas . . .' Thucydides, *The History of the Peloponnesian War* 5.16, trans. Warner; **56** 'People were ready . . .' Plutarch, *Nicias* 9, trans. Ian Scott-Kilvert, *Plutarch: The Rise and Fall of Athens and Nine Greek Lives* (London: Penguin, 1960); **62** 'As for democracy, . . .' Thucydides, *The History of the*

Peloponnesian War, 6.89, trans. Warner; **70** 'Deprived of Alcibiades' . . .' S. Hornblower, *The Greek World 479–323 BC* (Abingdon: Routledge, 2011), p. 189.

Depth Study 1: The Politics and Society of Sparta

All quotations are from LACTOR 21: *Sparta,* ed. M. G. L. Cooley (London: KCL, 2017) unless otherwise specified. LACTOR references are given in brackets.

78 'There is a general . . .' Plutarch, *Lycurgus* 1.1 (F2); **78** 'Well, having considered . . .' Xenophon, *Constitution of the Spartans* 1.1–2, trans. C. Cottam; **79** 'So when they . . .' Xenophon, *Constitution of the Spartans* 3.4 (D77); **79** 'Lykourgos set in . . .' Pausanias, *Description of Greece* 3.14.8–10 (D81); **80** 'He made it . . .' Xenophon, *Constitution of the Spartans* 2.9 (D74); **80** '. . . when we think . . .' Plutarch, *Lycurgus* 18.1 (D80); **81** 'the so-called . . .' Plutarch, *Agesilaos* 1.2 (E82); **81** '. . . so that the . . .' Plutarch, *Lycurgus* 22.3 (D93); **81** 'Lakonian : Here, kind . . .' Aristophanes *Lysistrata* 1241–1246 (G7); **81** 'Lichas used to . . .' Xenophon, *Memorabilia* 1.2.61 (C76); **82** 'Reading and writing . . .' Plutarch, *Lycurgus* 16.6 (D76); **83–84** '[3] The ephors start . . .' Xenophon, *Constitution of the Spartans* 4.3–4 and 6 (D79, D50); **83** 'For when Paidaretus . . .' Plutarch, *Lycurgus* 25.4, trans. C. Cottam; **83** 'In these states . . .' Plato, *Protagoras* 342d (D72); **84** 'So we may . . .' Aristophanes, *Lysistrata* 1304–1310 (G7); **85** 'As far as . . .' Xenophon, *Constitution of the Spartans* 1.4 (D68); **85** 'He had no . . .' Plutarch, *Lycurgus* 14.2 (D70); **86** 'Sometimes they in . . .' Plutarch, *Lycurgus* 14.3 (D70); **86** 'Those burying the . . .' Plutarch, *Lycurgus* 27.2 (B35b); **86** 'Another admirable feature . . .' Xenophon, *Constitution of the Spartans* 9.1 (D96); **87** 'good for firing-up . . .' Plutarch, *Cleomenes* 2.3, trans. C. Cottam; **88** 'At Sparta it . . .' *Sophists at Dinner*, 432d and f (D60); **89** '. . . the endurance . . .' Plato, *Laws* 633b (C74, C85, D42); **91** 'Agesilaus . . . ordered . . .' Plutarch, *Agesilaus* 26.5, trans. C. Cottam; **92** 'He (Lycurgus) did . . .' Plutarch, *Lycurgus* 24, trans. C. Cottam; **92** 'each mess member . . .' Plutarch, *Lycurgus* 12.2 (D63); **93** '. . . specified tracts of . . .' Xenophon, *Constitution of the Spartans* 15.3 (D9); **93** '. . . but they were . . .' Thucydides, *The History of the Peloponnesian War* 1.101.2 (D38); **93** 'After the Peloponnesians . . .' Thucydides, *The History of the Peloponnesian War* 4. 8.1 (E87); **95** 'On this occasion . . .' Thucydides, *The History of the Peloponnesian War* 5.67.1 (E101); **95** 'The helots farmed . . .' Plutarch, *Lycurgus* 24.3, trans. C. Cottam; **95** 'Each man's allocation . . .' Plutarch, *Lycurgus* 8.4 (D57); **96** 'In addition there . . .' Plato, *Laws* 633c (C74, C85, D42); **96** 'For the Lakedaimonians . . .' Strabo, *Geography* 8.5.4 (D35, H3); **97** 'Ten thousand Lakedaimonians . . .' Herodotus, *Histories* 9.28.1 (E84); **97** 'By the time . . .' Thucydides, *The History of the Peloponnesian War* 5.64.2 (E99); **97** 'They also welcomed . . .' Thucydides, *The History of the Peloponnesian War* 4.80.2 (E68); **97** 'On this occasion . . .' Thucydides, *The History of the Peloponnesian War* 4.80, 5 (E68); **98** 'they impose on . . .' Myron of Priene, *Messenian History*, FGrH 106 F2, quoted in Athenaios (14.74), (D41); **99** 'Like mules distressed . . .' Tyrtaeus frg 6, in Pausanias 4.14.5 (A6); **100** '. . . just as the helots . . .' Aristotle, *Politics* 1269a.38–1269b.12 with omission (D27); **100** 'When Phaion was . . .' Diodorus, *History of Library* 11.63.1 (E63); **100** 'The helots and . . .' Diodorus, *History of Library* 11.63.4 (E63); **101**

'And if the . . .' Thucydides, *The History of the Peloponnesian War* 5.23 (B18); **102** 'In addition the . . .' Aristotle, *Politics* 1269b (D69); **103** 'There has been . . .' J. Ducat, *Spartan Education* (Swansea: The Classical Press of Wales, 2006), p. 124; **103** 'world turned upside down', P. Cartledge, *The Spartans: An Epic History* (London: Pan Books, 2002), p. 157; **104** 'It seems that . . .' Aristotle, *Politics* 1269b (D69); **104** 'Aristotle is wrong . . .' Plutarch, *Life of Lycurgus* 14.1 (D70); **109** 'When a (Spartan) king . . .' Aristotle, *Politics* 1285a, trans. C. Cottam; **109** 'The fourth of . . .' Aristotle, *Politics* 1285b, trans. C. Cottam; **109** '. . . and there is . . .'Thucydides, *The History of the Peloponnesian War* 2.39, trans. C. Cottam; **110** '. . . In the same . . .' Diodorus, *History of Library* 11.50.1–2 (E28); **111** 'But when they . . .' Thucydides, *The History of the Peloponnesian War* 5.63.2–4 (E98); **111** 'He did all . . .' Thucydides, *The History of the Peloponnesian War* 8.5 (E41, E150); **113** 'Aristotle most certainly . . .' Plutarch, *Lycurgus* 28.4 (D44); **115** 'The Spartans sent . . .' Thucydides, *The History of the Peloponnesian War* 2.85, trans. C. Cottam; **119** 'This is because . . .' Aristotle, *Politics* 1271a 39–40 (D98); **119** 'For four hundred years . . .' Thucydides, *The History of the Peloponnesian War* 1.18 (F4); **123** 'When this battle . . .' Thucydides, *The History of the Peloponnesian War* 5.75.1 (E104); **124** 'Thus equipped, he . . .' Xenophon, *Constitution of the Spartans* 11.4 (D88); **125** '. . . and he was . . .'Thucydides, *The History of the Peloponnesian War* 4.84, trans. C. Cottam; **126** '. . . Our navy? We . . .' Thucydides, *The History of the Peloponnesian War* 1.80.4 (E29); **127** 'And so they . . .' Thucydides, *The History of the Peloponnesian War* 6.93, trans. C. Cottam; **129** 'Greeks made a . . .' Plutarch, *Lycurgus* 30.5 (D82); **132** 'For example, if . . .' Thucydides, *The History of the Peloponnesian War* 1.10 (G2); **132** 'Someone enquired how . . .' Plutarch, *Sayings of the Spartans* 215d = *Agis* 5 (F32); **133** '. . . if the Spartans . . .' Thucydides, *The History of the Peloponnesian War* 1.144.2, trans. C. Cottam; **133** '. . . The Spartans . . .'Thucydides, *The History of the Peloponnesian War* 1.118, trans. C. Cottam; **135** '. . . There was written . . .' (Cambridge University Press, 1989), No. 27; **135** 'They then recalled . . .' Thucydides, *The History of the Peloponnesian War* 1.87.4 (E31); **135** 'Even so, the . . .' Thucydides, *The History of the Peloponnesian War* 1.119.1 (E142); **136** 'the Lakedaimonians no . . .' Thucydides, *The History of the Peloponnesian War* 1.95.7 (E25); **138** '*Tell the Lakedaemonians, . . .*' Herodotus, *Histories* 7.228.2 (B4); **138** 'They do whatever . . .' Herodotus, *Histories* 7.104.5, trans. C. Cottam; **139** 'On this spot . . .' Herodotus, *Histories* 7.225.3 (F19,F20); **139** 'While we, led . . .'Aristophanes, *Lysistrata* 1254–1259 (G7); **139** 'This was for . . .' Thucydides, *The History of the Peloponnesian War* 4.40.1 (E95); **140** 'The Spartans first . . .' Thucydides, *The History of the Peloponnesian War* 1.6.4 (D52).

Depth Study 2: The Politics and Culture of Athens

155 'Each voter took . . .' Plutarch, *Life of Aristeides* 7.4–5, trans. Ian Scott-Kilvert, *Plutarch: The Rise and Fall of Athens and Nine Greek Lives* (London: Penguin, 1960); **161** 'So, in what . . .'Thucydides, *The History of the Peloponnesian War* 2.65, trans. Rex Warner, *Thucydides: History of the Peloponnesian War* (London: Penguin 1972); **162** 'Mix all the . . .' Aristophanes, *Knights* 214–216, trans. David Barrett and Alan H.

Sommerstein, *Aristophanes: The Birds and Other Plays* (London: Penguin, 2003); **168** 'Homer and Hesiod . . .' DK21 B11, trans. M. R. Wright, Appendix A in Giannis Stamatellos, *Introduction to Presocratics: A Thematic Approach to Early Greek Philosophy with Key Readings* (Chichester: Wiley-Blackwell, 2012); **169** 'Speech is a . . .' Gorgias, *Encomium of Helen*, 8, trans. John Dillon and Tania Gergel, *The Greek Sophists* (London: Penguin, 2003); **171** '*Socrates*: So the ignorant . . .' Plato, *Gorgias* 459b–c (LACTOR 12, 400), trans J. P. Sabben-Clare and M. S. Warman, *LACTOR 12: The Culture of Athens* (2nd edn; London: KCL, 1991); **173** 'Let us say . . .' Aristophanes, *Clouds*, 1076–82, trans. Alan H. Sommerstein, *Aristophanes: Lysistrata and Other Plays* (London: Penguin, 2003); **180** 'If, on the . . .' Thucydides, *The History of the Peloponnesian War* 1.10, trans. Warner; **183** 'Everything on the . . .' Pausanias, *Description of Greece* 1.24.5 (LACTOR 12, 360), trans J. P. Sabben-Clare & M.S. Warman; **200** 'In the case . . .' Isocrates, 5.117 (LACTOR 12, 222), trans J. P. Sabben-Clare and M. S. Warman; **201** 'Concerning the gods . . .' DK80 B4, trans. J. Renshaw; **201** 'Perhaps I shall . . .' Euripides, *Hecabe,* 465–474, trans. Philip Vellacott, *Medea and other plays* (Harmondsworth: Penguin, 1963).

Depth Study 3: The Rise of Macedon

216 '. . . and having improved . . .' Diodorus, *Library of History* 16.3, trans. Charles L. Sherman, *Diodorus Siculus: Library of History*, Vol. VII (Cambridge MA: Harvard University Press, 1952); **218** 'Philip then razed . . .' Diodorus, *Library of History* 16.34.5, trans. Sherman; **218** 'All the rest . . .' Demosthenes, *Speeches* 2.19, trans J. H. Vince, *Demosthenes: Orations*, Vol. I (Cambridge MA: Harvard University Press, 1930); **234** '. . . It was presumably . . .' Plutarch, *Life of Alexander* 16, trans. Robin Waterfield, *Plutarch: Greek Lives: A Selection of Nine Greek Lives* (Oxford: Oxford University Press, 1998); **238** 'Without delay, Alexander's . . .' Arrian, *The Campaigns of Alexander* 3.20, trans. Aubrey de Sélincourt, *Arrian: The Campaigns of Alexander* (Harmondsworth: Penguin, 1971); **242** 'The men with ladders . . .' Arrian, *The Campaigns of Alexander* 6.9, trans. de Sélincourt; **249** 'For indeed Philip . . .' Demosthenes, *Speeches* 2.15, trans. Vince; **250** 'In this year, . . .' Diodorus, *Library of History* 16.84, trans. C. B. Wells, *Diodorus Siculus: Library of History*, Vol. VIII (Cambridge MA: Harvard University Press, 1963); **251** 'Since the Olynthians . . .' Diodorus, *Library of History* 16.8, trans. Sherman; **252** '. . . he [Alexander] was . . .' Arrian, *The Campaigns of Alexander* 1.10, trans. de Sélincourt; **261** 'He [Alexander] was . . .' Arrian, *The Campaigns of Alexander* 3.16, trans. de Sélincourt; **263** "For my part,' . . .' Arrian, *The Campaigns of Alexander* 4.11, trans. de Sélincourt; **263** 'It was in Babylon . . .' Arrian, *The Campaigns of Alexander* 3.16.5, trans. de Sélincourt; **267** 'Successive delegations from . . .' Arrian, *The Campaigns of Alexander* 7.23, trans. de Sélincourt; **268** 'And every difficulty . . .' Arrian, *The Campaigns of Alexander* 6.12, trans. de Sélincourt; **269** 'Although he [Alexander] . . .' Plutarch, *Life of Alexander* 15, trans. Waterfield; **273** 'Porus was taken . . .' Plutarch, *Life of Alexander* 60, trans. Waterfield.

What to Expect in the AS Level Exam for the Greek Period Study

278 'The Athenians took . . .' Thucydides 1.91.1, trans. Rex Warner, *Thucydides: History of the Peloponnesian War* (London: Penguin 1972); **278** 'After this they . . .' Thucydides 1.98–9, trans. Warner; **278** 'The Chalcidians are . . .' The Chalkis Decree (ML 52 (SEG 42.10), LACTOR 1, 78), trans. R. G. Osborne, *LACTOR 1: The Athenian Empire* (4th edn; London: KCL, 2000).

What to Expect in the A Level Exam

284 'What is most . . .' Pierre Briant, *From Cyrus to Alexander* (Warsaw IN: Eisenbraums, 2002), pp. 337–338; **286** 'Just before the . . .' Herodotus, *Histories* 5.75, trans. Aubrey de Sélincourt, *Herodotus: The Histories* (London: Penguin 1996); **286** 'The prerogatives of . . .' Herodotus, *Histories* 6.56; **288–289** 'Socrates: Yes, you . . .' Aristophanes, *Clouds* 365–380, trans. Alan H. Sommerstein, *Aristophanes: Lysistrata and Other Plays* (London: Penguin, 2003); **291** 'Are you not . . .' Arrian, *The Campaigns of Alexander* 5.26, trans. Aubrey de Sélincourt, *Arrian: The Campaigns of Alexander* (Harmondsworth: Penguin, 1971).

INDEX

In this index figures and illustrations are indicated in italics

A

Abydos, naval battle 66
Achaemenid Empire 211, 293
Acharnians (Aristophanes) 40–1, 42, 64, 197
acropolis 180–6
Ada of Caria 250
Aegean Greek world 432 BC 38–9
Aegean Greek world 5c. *8*
Aegina 7, 29, 42
Aegospotami 118, 127
Aelian 122
Aeschines 212
Aeschylus 193, 194
Agesilaus (Plutarch) 81, 91, 109
Agesilaus 91–2
Agiad 107, 112
Agis 60, 64
Agis II 107, 110–11, 117
agōgē 79–83, 86–8, 293
agora 152, *153*, 186, 201, 293
Alcibiades 60, 61–2, 64–5, 66, 67, 107, 111, 116–18, 127, 162, 176
Alcibiades, Laws, Protagoras (Plato) 85, 140
Alcidas (Alkidas) 115
Alcman 85
Alexander sarcophagus 235
Alexander the Great 229–46
    adoption of Persian dress and customs 262
    change and continuity in the aims of Philip and Alexander 248–55
    character and beliefs of 260–3
    companions of 234, 261, 269
    conflict with the Mallians 242
    conspiracies against 239
    crossing of the Gedrosian Desert 243
    death of 246
    death of Hephaestion 245
    divinity of 262–3
    Exiles' Decree 245
    expedition and battles *233*
    foundation cities 236
    Greek and Macedonian contingents in his army 269–70
    as hegemon of Greece 232
    Indus Valley campaign 241–2, 272–3
    and invasion of Greece 480–479 17
    marriages of 240–1, 244

mass marriages in Susa 244, 272
    murder of Cleitus/opposition of Callisthenes 240
    mutiny at Hyphasis 242
    mutiny at Opis 244
    occupation of Babylon and Persepolis 236–7
    and the Persians 270–2
    pursuits of Darius and Bessus 238
    reassertion of control over Greece 231–2
    relations with his army and companions 268–9
    return to Babylon 245
    return to Persia and purges 243–4
    treatment of companions/those he defeated 261–2
    treatment of the Branchidae 239
    at Troy and Gordium 233
    victories of 234–6
Ambracian Gulf 42
Amphictyonic League 219, 223, 293
Amphipolis 53, 55, 56, 60, 64, 116, 214–15
Anaxagoras 168, 201
Andocides 65
Andromache (Euripides) 194
Antipater 239, 245
Apology (Plato) 156–7, 176
Archidamian War 431–420 BC 46–56
Archidamus II 43, 52, 64, 107, 110, 112, 126, 136
architecture, Athens 178–88
archōns *25*, 149, 151, 190, 220, 293
Argaeus 214
Arginusae (Arginusai) 118, 127
Argos
    and the 30 Year Peace 35
    and Athens 29
    and Corinth 135
    and Sparta 55, 56, 59–60, 61, 91, 111, 116, 133, 134, 136, 137
Aristeides 26, 27
Aristobulus 230
aristocracy 55, 149, 161, 217–18
Aristophanes, as a source 77, 82, 157, 161–2, 165, 195
Aristotle 32, 76, 99, 102, 103–4, 150–1, 171
army, of Sparta 122–4 (*see also* military)

Arrēphoroi 205, 293
Arrian 230
art and architecture, Athens 178–88
Artaxerxes III 224
Artemis, cult of at Brauron 187
Artemis Orthia, temple of 79–80
Artemisium, battle of 14, 15
Aspasia 40, 163
assembly, the
    Athens 149, 154
    Sparta 114
Athena 206, 207
Athena Nike, temple of 180–1
Athena Polias 184, 203, 205
Athena Promachos, statue of 182, 184
Athenian Constitution (Aristotle) 150–1
Athens (*see also* Greece)
    Archidamian War 46–56
    art and architecture 178–88
    and Athena and Poseidon 207
    battle of Chaeronea 225–6
    building programme of 178–80
    citizenship/non-citizenship 147–9, 151, 162–5
    and Corcyra 38–9
    and Corinth 29, 38–9, 40, 42, 43, 62
    and Darius I 7–8
    and the Delian League 28
    democracy 66, 146, 149–59
    drama and dramatic festivals 189–97
    festivals of Dionysus 189–93
    imperialism of 43, 48, 137
    influence of new thinking/ideas on society 167–77
    as leader of an Empire/treatment of allies 159–61
    leadership in 5th c. 161–2
    legal system 149, 156–7
    map of 5th c. *158*
    navy of. *See* navies
    oligarchy, tyranny and democracy 146–7, 149
    oppression of 28
    ostracism 29, 154–6, 294
    Panathenaia 203–6, 294
    Pericles funeral oration 158–9, 202
    and Philip and Alexander 266–7
    Pisistratids 8, 11
    plague of Athens 48, 49, 151, 201
    and Potidaea 40

religion, politics and culture of
144–65, 177–87, 189–93,
199–207
Sicilian expedition 415–413 BC 61–3,
127
sophists 168–73, 201
and Sparta 28–9, 34–7, 38, 54–5, 63–6,
137
state of 147–9
and Thebes 225
Attica 47–8, 49–53, 148, 186–8, 293

B

Babylon, occupation of 236
Bel 263, 293
Bessus 238
bias, in sources 37, 55, 147, 170, 273,
280, 283
Birds (Aristophanes) 197
Boeotia 17, 29, 32, 53, 60
boulē (council) 150, 152, 293
Brasidas 52–3, 55, 76, 97, 107, 115–16,
125
Brasidians 122, 123–4, 293
Buchephalus (Bucephalas) 241, 293
building programme, of Athens 178–80
Byzantium, siege of 224–5

C

Callicratidas (Kallikratidas) 118, 127
Callisthenes 239, 240, 262
Campaigns of Alexander (Arrian) 230,
231, 238, 242, 261, 263, 267
Chaeronea, battle of 225–6
Chalcidice peninsula *54*, 125
Chalkis Decree 32
Chios 64, 65
chorēgos 190, 293
chthonic gods 200, 293
Cimon (Kimon) 26, 27, 28, 30, 137
citizenship/non-citizenship, Athens 147–9,
151, 162–5
City Dionysia 190–3
Cleitarchus 230
Cleitus 234, 240, 262
Cleombrotus (Kleombrotos) 137
Cleomenes (Kleomenes) 109
Cleon (Kleon) 51, 52, 54–5, 116, 125,
160, 161–2
Cleonymos Decree 49–50
Cleophon 66, 68
Clouds (Aristophanes) 172–3, 197, 202
coins *see under* gold coin of Philip, Porus
Medallion, tetradrachm
comedy, as a genre 195–7
companions 218, 234, 269, 293
complaints attested/barely attested/
unattested 38–42, 39–40
Constitution of the Athenians (The Old
Oligarch) 146–7
Constitution of the Spartans
(Xenophon)78, 79, 82–3, 86, 93,
112, 113, 124, 133, 140, 141, 142

Corcyra 38
Corinth
and Athens 29, 38–9, 40, 42, 43, 62
and Corcyra 38
and the revolt of Samos 37
and Sparta 135
Corinthian Complaint 43, 293
Corinthian War 37
Council of the Areopagus 149, 150, 151,
293
council, the (boulē) 150, 152, 293
Crocus Field, battle of 219
cultural aims, of Philip and Alexander
255
culture, and Athens 144, 178–88
Curtius Rufus 231, 237
Cynossema, naval battle 66
Cyrus 67, 68, 118, 119, 126, 127, 243
Cyrus the Younger 263–4

D

Darius I 6–9, 10–11
Darius II 64, 67
Darius III 235–6, 238
Decelea 63–4, 111
Delian League 26–9, 30, 293
Delos 10, 27
demagogues 49, 293
Demaratus 14, 109, 112, 122, 139
democracy
and Alcibiades 62
Athens 66, 146, 149–59
and Pericles 161
and Socrates 175
term 293
Demosthenes 50, 51, 53, 63, 129, 212,
216, 222, 223–4
Description of Greece (Pausanias) 79, 80,
180, 183
dikasts 156–7, 293
dikē 156, 293
Diodorus Siculus 22–3, 66, 67, 101, 212,
214
Dionysus, festivals of in Athens 189–93
diplomacy, of Philip II of Macedon
214–15, 226, 258
Dipylon Gate 205, 293
dithyramb 191, 193, 293
divination 263, 293
dokimasia 154, 293
drama and dramatic festivals 172–3,
189–97

E

earth and water 7, 293
ecclēsia (assembly) 149, 293
eirenes 82, 293
Elis 59–60, 133, 135, 137
Encomium of Helen (Gorgias) 169
enōmotiai 123, 124, 293
Ephialtes, reforms of 150, 151
ephors 40, 60, 106, 107, 113, 114, 115,
119, 293

Epidamnus-Corcyra, complaint attested
38–9
Epigonoi 271, 293
epistatēs 152, 294
Epistoleus 127
epiteichismos 50, 55, 60, 294
Epitome (Justin) 218
eponymous archōns 149, 190
eponymous ephors 107, 115, 294
Erechtheion 164, 180, 184–5, *186*
Eretria 7, 10, 66
Euboea 32, 34, 64, 66
Eumenides (Aeschylus) 194
Euripides 164, 173, 193, 194–5
Eurybiades 15
Eurymedon, battle of 27
Eurypontid 107, 294
euthunai 154, 294
exams
exam overview – assessment for the
Period Study option 3
exam overview – Athens Section B
144
exam overview – Depth Studies
options 72
exam overview – Macedon Section B
210
what to expect – AS level Greek
Period Study 276–80
what to expect – A level Greek Period
Study 281–92
Exiles' Decree 245

F

festivals
of Dionysus 189–93
drama and dramatic 172–3, 189–97
religious 201, 202–3
First Stēlē 30, 294
foundation cities 236
friezes 181, 184, *206*, 294

G

Gate of All Lands 11–12
Gaugamela, battle of 236
Geography (Strabo) 96
gerousia 106, 109, 112, 113, 119, 294
gods (*see also* names of individual gods;
religion)
and Alexander the Great 263
in Greek religion 200, 293
and Philip II of Macedon 259
gold coin of Philip 253, *253*, 259
Gordian knot 233
Gordium 233
Gorgias 169
Gorgias (Plato) 170–1
Governance of the Spartans (Kritias) 88
Granicus, battle of 234, 267
graphē 156, 294
Great Dionysia 172, 294
Great Panathenaia 203, 294
Greece (*see also* Athens)

ancient 5
in conflict 479–446 BC 21–32
consequences of the Persian wars 24–9
Dorians 90
First Peloponnesian War 29–32
peace and conflict 446–431 34–43
Peloponnese and southern Greece 25
Peloponnesian war 431 BC 38–43 (see also Peloponnesian War 431 BC)
Persian invasion of 480–479 11–18
revolt of Samos 37
Greek city states, and Philip and Alexander 266–7
Greek rationalism 36, 294
Greeks, portrayal of in the sources 273
Gylippus 62, 63, 117, 127–9
Gymnopaedia (Gymnopaidia) 81

H
Halicarnassus, siege of 234
Harpokration 31
Hecabe (Euripides) 206
hegemon, League of Corinth 226–7, 245
hegemon of Greece, Alexander the Great as 232
Helen of Troy 169
Hellenic League 12–13, 14, 18, 294 (see also League of Corinth)
Hellenica (Xenophon) 66, 78, 113, 115, 117, 118, 124, 126, 127, 136
helots 50, 52, 90, 91, 92, 95–101, 135, 294
revolt of the helots 100–1, 124–5, 137
Hephaestion 244, 245, 262
Hermolaus 239
Herodotus 5–6, 88, 109, 217
Hetoemaridas (Hetoemeridas) 107, 113
Hippagretai (hippagretae) 82, 294
hippeis 83, 149, 294
Hippias 8, 149
Hippias Major (Plato) 170
Hippias of Elis 168
Hippocrates 53, 168
Hippolytus (Euripides) 164, 165, 173, 194, 202
Histories (Herodotus) 5–6, 11, 17, 88, 97, 111, 114, 122, 136, 138, 139, 140
Histories (Phylarchos) 118
History of Alexander the Great (Curtius Rufus) 231, 237
History of My Times (Xenophon) see Hellenica
History of the Peloponnesian War (Thucydides) 25, 28, 29, 35–6, 38, 40, 43, 51, 52, 53, 55, 62, 84, 93, 95, 97, 101, 109, 110, 111, 112, 114, 115, 116, 117, 119, 122, 123, 124, 125, 126, 127, 128, 129, 130, 132, 133, 135, 137, 139, 140, 142, 159–60
Homer 233, 263
hoplites 18, 46, 47, 62, 97, 150, 294
Hydaspes River, battle of 241
Hyphasis, mutiny at 242

I
imperialism, of Athens 43, 48, 137
Indus Valley campaign 241–2, 272–3
Ionian Revolt 7, 8
Ionian War 413–404 BC 64–6
Isocrates 200, 201
Issus, battle of 235–6

J
Justin 212, 218

K
kerameikos 158, 186, 294
Knights (Aristophanes) 161–2, 197
kōmos 195, 294
Kritias 87–8
Krypteia (Crypteia) 83, 96, 99

L
Lakedaimonoi (Lacedaemonii) 95
Laconia (Lakonia) 90, 94, 95, 294
Lamachus 61, 62
Laws, The (Plato) 119
League of Corinth 226, 245 (see also Hellenic League)
Lenaea 41, 190, 294
Leonidas 112
Leotychidas 18, 112, 136
Lesbos 49, 64, 160
Leuktra, battle of 124
Library of History (Diodorus) 100, 101, 110, 112, 113, 114, 124, 133, 136, 214, 216, 250, 251
Life of Alcibiades (Plutarch) 162
Life of Alexander (Plutarch) 230, 273
Life of Aristeides (Plutarch) 23, 50, 155
Life of Aristides 110
Life of Cimon (Plutarch) 28, 31
Life of Lycurgus (Lykourgos) (Plutarch) 81, 83, 86, 95, 109, 112, 113, 114, 120, 129, 140, 141
Life of Lysander (Plutarch) 117, 118, 129, 141
Life of Nicias (Plutarch) 156
Life of Pericles (Plutarch) 23, 152, 156
liturgy 190, 294
Lives of Agesilaus, Aristeides, Lycurgus, Lysander (Plutarch) 77
lochoi 122, 123, 294
Long Walls 25–6, 29, 294
Lycurgus 76, 83, 87, 93, 102, 103, 109, 140, 225–6
Lysander 67, 68, 77, 108, 117, 118–19, 126, 127
Lysistrata (Aristophanes) 77, 81, 82, 84, 132, 139, 197

M
Macedon – the rise of 359–323 BC
Alexander the Great 229–46
change and continuity in the aims of Philip and Alexander 248–55
character and beliefs of Philip and Alexander 257–63
and the Chersonese 224
expansion of 219–21
growth of power and role of Philip 211–27
and her near neighbours 431–336 BC 213
political boundaries of Macedon, Greece and Persia 336 BC 213
relationships between the monarchs and others 265–74
Macedonian phalanx 216
Macedonians, portrayal of in the sources 273–4
magistrates, Athens 153–4 (see also archōns)
Mallians 242–3
Mantinea
battle of 60–1, 97, 111, 116, 122, 123, 125, 136
and Corinth 135
and Sparta 116, 137
Marathon, battle of 10–11
Mardonius 7, 11, 15–16, 17
marriages
of Alexander the Great 240–1, 244
mass marriages in Susa 244, 272
of Philip II of Macedon 221–2
Spartan 103
medise 7, 294
Megara 29, 32, 34, 40–2
Megarian decree 40, 41–2
Memnon 218, 234
Memorabilia (Xenophon) 81, 154, 170, 174, 175, 176
Messenia 91, 94, 95, 294
Messenian History (Myron of Priene) 98
Methone 214, 219
metics 41, 149, 151, 162–3, 294
metopes 182–3, 185, 294
Miletus 7, 37, 65
military, Spartan 121–9, 216–17, 251–2, 259–61
Mindarus (Mindaros) 66, 127
Miscellaneous History (Aelian) 122
morai 124, 294
Moralia (Plutarch) 77
mothakes 118, 127, 294
Mycale, battle of 18
Myron of Priene 98
mythology, and Alexander the Great 263
Mytilene Debate 160–1
Mytilene revolt 49, 160

N
naos 182, 294
Naqs-e Rustam 8–9
nauarchos 118, 119, 126, 127, 294
navies
of Alexander the Great 234
Athenian 12, 30, 35, 47, 48, 49, 61, 66, 67, 150

Corcyra 38
Corinthian 42, 48, 49
and the Delian League 26–7, 31–2
Greek 12, 15–17, 18
Peloponnesian 67
Phoenician 65–6
Samian 37
Spartan 126–9
Naxos 7, 10, 28
Nearchus 243
Nemesis, temple to 188
neodamōdeis 52, 97, 122, 123–4, 294
Nicias (Nikias) 51, 52, 54, 61, 62–3,
    127–9, 161, 162, 201
    peace of 55–6, 59–60, 111, 116
Notium (Notion) 117, 118, 127

O

Odeon of Pericles 185, 190
Oedipus the King (Sophocles) 193
Old Oligarch 146–7, 157, 159
oliganthrōpia 88, 100, 140, 294
oligarchy 66, 146, 149, 294
Olympians 200, 294
Olympias 221, 239
Olynthus 215, 220, 251
On the False Embassy (Demosthenes)
    222, 258
On the Peace (Demosthenes) 223
Opis, mutiny at 244
Orestes (Euripides) 173
orientalism 244, 262, 294
ostracism 29, 154–6, 294
Oxyrhynchus Historian 67

P

paidonomos 82, 294
Panathenaia 203–6, 294
Panathenaic amphorae 204
Panathenaic Way 205, *206*, 295
Parmenio 239, 260
Parthenon 180, 182–4
Parthenon frieze 184, *206*
Pausanias (author) 18, 26, 79, 80, 180
Pausanias (Spartan regent) 107, 109–110,
    112, 136
Pausanias (son of King Pleistoanax) 112
Peace (Aristophanes) 53
Peace of Callias 31
peace of Epilycus 64
Peace of Nicias 55–6, 59–60
Peace of Philocrates 221, 222, 258
pediments 182, 183–4, *185*, 295
Pella 222
Peloponnese, map of *134*
Peloponnese regional boundaries *94*
Peloponnesian League 13, 24–6, 37, 91,
    133–6, 295
Peloponnesian War 431 BC
    battle of Mantinea 60–1, 97, 111, 116,
        123, 125, 136
    end of and its aftermath 419–404 BC
        59–68

events leading up to/causes of 38–43
Ionian War 413–404 BC 64–6
occupation of Decelea 63–4, 111
outbreak of war 43
and Pericles 42, 43
Persia's impact on the war 66–8
Sicilian expedition 415–413 BC 61–3,
    127
Peloponnesian War, First 29–32
pentakosiomedimnoi 149, 295
pentēkostues 123, 124, 295
Pentecontaetia 22, 24, 31, 37, 295
peplos 205, 206, *207*, 295
Pericles
    and the Archidamian War 47–8
    building programme of 179
    and democracy 161
    emergence of 30
    and Euboea 32, 34
    funeral oration of 158–9, 202
    and the Megarian decree 40, 42
    and ostracism 156
    and Peloponnesian War 42, 43
    reforms of 150, 151
Perinthus, siege of 217, 224–5
perioikoi 90, 93–5, 122, 123, 295
peripteral temples 182, 295
Persepolis 237, 270
Persia
    influence on the Peloponnesian War
        66–8
    and Sparta 67
Persian Empire 492–479
    battle of Artemisium 14, 15
    battle of Mycale 18
    battle of Plataea 17–18, 48, 122, 139
    battle of Salamis 15–17
    battle of Thermopylae 14–15, 138–9
    challenge of 4–18
    Darius I's policy towards the Greeks
        6–9
    invasion of Greece 11–18
    Persian Empire in c. 500 *5*
Persian Gate, battle of 237
Persians (Aeschylus) 194
Persians, portrayal of in the sources 273
Peucastas (Peucestas) 262, 271
Phalaecus 221
Pharnabazus 64, 66, 67
Pheidias 40, 179, 182, 188
Philip II of Macedon
    assassination of 223, 227
    battle of Chaeronea 225–6
    change and continuity in the aims of
        Philip and Alexander 248–55
    character and beliefs of 258–60
    court and patronage of 217–18
    election as hegemon 226–7
    expansion of Macedon 219–20
    expeditions into Thrace 223–4
    and the growth in power of Macedon
        211–27
    influence on Greek institutions 223

League of Corinth 226
    marriages of 221–2
    and the military 216–17
    opportunism and diplomacy of 214–16,
        226, 258
    organising and securing Macedonia
        220–1
    Peace of Philocrates 222
    political boundaries of Macedon,
        Greece and Persia 336 BC *213*
Philocrates 222
Philotas 239
Phocians 17–18, 219
Phocis 219, 220–1, 225
Phormio 49, 115
Phrynichus 193, 194
Phylarchos 117
Piraeus 24–5
Pisistratids 8, 11
plague of Athens 48, 49, 151, 201
Plataea, battle of 17–18, 48, 122, 139
Plato 83, 85, 157, 170–1, 173–4, 175, 176–7
Pleistarchus 112
Pleistoanax 32, 34, 52, 55, 112, 137
Plutarch 22, 23–4, 76–77, 152, 156, 162,
    230
Pnyx 154, *155*, 164, 295
polemarchos 124, 295
polis of Athens 148
Politics (Aristotle) 32, 102, 109, 114, 119,
    141
politics
    and comedy drama 196–7
    and Philip and Alexander 249–50
    of Sparta 74–88, 106–19, 121–9
polytheism 200, 202, 295
Poroi ('Revenues') (Xenophon) 163
Porus 241, 254, 272–3
Porus Medallion 254, *254*
Poseidon 187, 207
Potidaea 39–40, 49, 215
principal assembly 154, 295
proagōn 190, 295
probouleusis 113, 295
Prodicus of Ceos 168
Propylaea 180, 181–2
proskynesis 240, 262, 295
Protagoras (Plato) 83
Protagoras 168, 201
prytaneis 152, 154, 295
prytany system 152, 295
Ptolemy 230
Pydna 215
Pylos 50–2, 60, 115, 125, 126

Q

quorum 154, 295

R

religion (*see also* gods)
    and the culture of Athens 199–207
    and Philip II of Macedon 259
Republic (Plato) 175

rhapsodes 204, 295
rhetoric 154, 169–71, 295
Rhetoric (Aristotle) 171
Rural Dionysia 190, 295

S

Sacred Band 232, 295
Sacred Wars 259
Salamis, battle of 15–17
Samos 37, 66
sarissas 216, 295
satraps 7, 37, 64, 244, 271–2, 295
satyr-play 194, 295
Sayings of Spartan Women (Plutarch) 114, 139
Sayings of the Spartans (Plutarch) 132
Scione 54, 56, 116
Serpent Column 13
Sestos, siege of 24
Sicilian expedition 415–413 BC 61–3, 116, 127
siege warfare 124
sieges
    Byzantium 224–5
    Halicarnassus 234
    Methone 219
    Olynthus 220
    Perinthus 217, 224–5
    Sestos 24
Skiritai (Sciritae) 95, 97, 122, 123, 295
slaves 95, 148–9, 163–4
social structure, of Sparta 90–104
Social War 357–355 BC 215
society, of Sparta 74–88, 121–9
Socrates 157, 167, 170, 172–3, 173–7
Socratic method 174
sophists 168–73, 201
Sophocles 193
sortition 152, 295
sources
    bias in 37, 55, 147, 170, 273, 280, 283
    and portrayal of Greeks, Macedonians, Persians 273–4
    and Sparta 131–3
Sparta
    Archidamian War 46–56
    and Argos 55, 56, 59–60, 61, 91, 134, 136, 137
    and Athens 28–9, 34–7, 38, 54–5, 63–6, 137
    and the battle of Plataea 17–18
    and Darius I 7–8
    education and values in 75–88
    education of boys 79–83
    education of girls 83–6
    invasions of Attica 49–53
    kings of 109–12, 136
    lack of leadership and recovery 136–8
    military of 121–9, 216–17, 251–2, 259–61
    navy of 126–9
    need for land 91
    occupation of Decelea 63–4, 111
    other states views of 131–40
    and the Peloponnesian League 24–6, 133–6
    and the Peloponnesian War 43
    and Persia 67
    politics of 74–88, 106–19, 121–9
    and the revolt of Samos 37
    site of *108*
    social structure of 90–104
    society of 74–88
    Spartan mirage and events at Thermopylae 138–40
    wealth in 140
    women 102–104
Spartan Constitution (School of Aristotle) 76, 99
Spartiates 11, 91–3, 96, 97, 100, 122–3, 137, 140, 295
Speeches (Demosthenes) 216, 218, 249
Sphacteria (Sphakteria) 50–2, 125, 126, 139
Sthenelaidas 43, 107, 110, 114
Strabo 96
stratēgos (general) 150, 295
Susa, mass marriages 244, 272
Syracuse 61, 62–3, 116, 127, 128–9
syssitia 92, 103, 295

T

Tanagra, battle of 29, 137
Taxiles 272
Tegea 60, 91, 133, 134–5, 137
temple of Artemis Orthia 79–80
temple of Athena Nike 180–1
temple of Demeter at Eleusis 186–7
Temple of Dionysus 191
temple of Sounion 187
Ten Thousand 263, 295
tetradrachm 241, 242, *242*, 246, *246*
Thasos 7, 28, 137
thētes 149, 295
theatre of Dionysus 190–1
Thebes 10, 17, 48, 225, 232
Themistocles 12, 15, 24–5, 136
Theopompus (historian) 31, 215
Theopompus (Spartan king) 113
Theoric Fund 192, 295
Thermopylae, battle of 14–15, 138–9
Thesmophoria 164, 295
Thesmophoriazusae (Aristophanes) 165, 197
Thespians 15
Thessaly 11, 14, 18, 29
Third Sacred War 219, 221
30 Year Peace 35, 38–9, 40, 137
tholos 152, 295
Thoudippos Decree 49–50, 56
Thrace 52–3, 115–116, 125, 223–4
Three Hundred 83, 295
Thucydides 22–3, 35–6, 37, 77, 79, 114
Thucydides (son of Melesias) 156
Tissaphernes 64, 65, 66
Tombstone of Eualkes 123
Torone 54, 55
tragedy 173, 193–5
Treaty of Boeotius 67
tribes 150, 193, 205, 295
Tribute Quota Lists 30, 32, 50, 295
tribute 50, 56, 64, 95, 159, 160, 179
triremes 48, *62* (*see also* navies)
Trojan Women (Euripides) 194
Troy 233
tyranny 146, 295
Tyrtaeus 87, 91

U

Universal History (Diodorus Siculus) 22, 23

W

Wasps (Aristophanes) 50, 157, 197
women
    Athenian 149, 164–5
    education of girls/Sparta 83–6
    Spartan 102–4, 132

X

Xenophon 66–7, 75–6, 78, 154, 163, 170, 175, 176, 263–4
Xerxes I 486–465 11, 16

Z

zeugitai 149, 151, 295
Zeus-Ammon 246, 295